IDEAL FORMS
IN THE AGE OF
RONSARD

UNA'S LECTURES

Una's Lectures, delivered annually on the Berkeley campus, memorialize Una Smith, who received her B.S. in History from Berkeley in 1911 and her M.A. in 1913. They express her esteem for the humanities in enlarging the scope of the individual mind. When appropriate, books deriving from the Una's Lectureship are published by the University of California Press:

THE RESOURCES OF KIND: GENRE-THEORY IN THE RENAISSANCE
by Rosalie L. Colie, 1973

FROM THE POETRY OF SUMER: CREATION, GLORIFICATION, ADORATION
by Samuel Noah Kramer, 1979

THE MAKING OF ELIZABETHAN FOREIGN POLICY, 1558–1603
by R. B. Wernham, 1980

THREE CHRISTIAN CAPITALS: TOPOGRAPHY AND POLITICS
by Richard Krautheimer, 1982

IDEAL FORMS IN THE AGE OF RONSARD
by Margaret M. McGowan, 1985

IDEAL FORMS IN THE AGE OF RONSARD

Margaret M. McGowan

UNIVERSITY OF CALIFORNIA PRESS
Berkeley • Los Angeles • London

UNIVERSITY OF CALIFORNIA PRESS
Berkeley and Los Angeles, California

UNIVERSITY OF CALIFORNIA PRESS, LTD.
London, England

© 1985 by
THE REGENTS OF THE UNIVERSITY OF CALIFORNIA

Library of Congress Cataloging in Publication Data

McGowan, Margaret M.
 Ideal forms in the age of Ronsard.

 (Una's lectures; 5)
 Bibliography: p.
 Includes index.
 1. Ronsard, Pierre de, 1524–1585—Style.
 2. French literature—16th century—History and
criticism. 3. Praise. I. Title. II. Series.
PQ1678.M33 1985   841'.3   82-23839
ISBN 0-520-04864-4

Printed in the United States of America

1 2 3 4 5 6 7 8 9

La parolle, Ronsard, est la seule magie,
L'ame par la parolle est conduicte et régie
Elle esmeut le couraige, esmeut les passions,
Esmeut les volontez et les affections.

La Promesse, 1564

Words, Ronsard, are the only real magic; through
words, the soul is directed and controlled; they
rouse up the heart, stimulate the passions, and
stir both the will and feelings.

Contents

List of Illustrations ix
Note on Texts xi

Introduction I

I • THE PERFECT PRINCE 9

II • ART AND POETRY PARALLELS IN
SIXTEENTH · CENTURY FRANCE 51

III • ICONIC FORMS 89

IV • TRIUMPHAL FORMS 121

V • LA BELLE FORME 159

VI • DANCING FORMS 209

Conclusion 243

Notes 251
Bibliography 313
Index 333

Illustrations

1. *Imperium,* in J. Dorat's *Paenes* (1569)   *pg. 16*
2. Agnolo del Moro, Engraved Portrait of Henri II   *pg. 18*
3. Henri II at the Centre of the Zodiac (1555)   *pg. 21*
4. E. Delaune, design for coin 1556, Mars and Minerva Celebrate Henri II's Device   *pg. 25*
5. E. Delaune, design for coin 1556, Henri II Rids the World of Vice   *pg. 25*
6. J. Duvet, Majesty   *pg. 26*
7. J. Duvet, Henri II as Royal French Monarch   *pg. 27*
8. N. da Modena, Allegorical Portrait of François I   *pg. 28*
9. F. Clouet, drawing for Equestrian Portrait of Henri II   *pg. 29*
10. F. Primaticcio, Apollo and the Muses   *pg. 32*
11. The French Court as Olympus, ceiling fresco at the Château de Tanlay   *pg. 34*
12. The French Court as Olympus, ceiling fresco at the Château de Tanlay   *pg. 34*
13. N. Beatrizet, Henri II, the Warrior King   *pg. 43*
14. The Ballroom of Henri II, Fontainebleau   *pg. 45*
15. The Power of Magestas (1571)   *pg. 67*
16. Mercury and Argus from Ovid's *Metamorphoses* (1557)   *pg. 69*
17. Triumph of Venus, from *L'Amour de Cupido et de Psiché* (1586)   *pg. 70*
18. Diana Pleads with Jupiter, tapestry after E. Delaune's design (ca. 1552)   *pg. 71*
19. A. Caron, Royal Feats and Triumphs, for *L'Histoire de la royne d'Arthemise* (1562)   *pg. 73*
20. G. Pilon, Henri II's Funeral Urn   *pg. 77*
21. G. B. Rosso, Mars and Venus   *pg. 84*
22. The Education of Achilles, Galerie François Ier, Fontainebleau   *pg. 85*
23. P. Redon, Charles IX's Gold and Enamelled Shield   *pg. 91*
24. Ecole de Fontainebleau, Ornamental Cup Design   *pg. 96*
25. M. A. Raimondi, Neptune Calming the Storm   *pg. 99*

26. A. Caron, The Siege of Metz (1552)   *pg. 103*
27. N. della Casa, Henri II, Aged 28   *pg. 106*
28. E. Delaune, Hand Mirror Depicting the Death of Julia (1561)   *pg. 108*
29. Henri II's Parade Armour (1556–59), designed by E. Delaune   *pg. 109*
30. Henri II's Shield (now at Windsor castle)   *pg. 110*
31. Henri II's Shield (Louvre), made from designs by E. Delaune   *pg. 111*
32. The Triumph of Henri II, Rouen, 1550   *pg. 120*
33. N. Jallier, Battle of Greeks and Trojans (ca. 1552)   *pg. 125*
34. N. Jallier, Duel of Achilles and Hector (ca. 1552)   *pg. 125*
35. A. Caron, the Trophy Carriers   *pg. 127*
36. Henri II's Cup   *pg. 138*
37. François I Paralleled with Caesar (ca. 1519)   *pg. 140*
38. The Triumph of Religion, Rouen (1550)   *pg. 146*
39. The Triumph of Fame, Rouen (1550)   *pg. 146*
40. A. Caron, the Triumph of Winter   *pg. 150*
41. The Trophy Carriers (manuscript illumination), Rouen (1550)   *pg. 152*
42. The Trophy Carriers (woodcut), Rouen (1550)   *pg. 153*
43. C. de la Haye, Catherine de' Medici   *pg. 162*
44. Ronsard and Cassandra   *pg. 167*
45. F. Clouet, Mary, Queen of Scots, in Mourning   *pg. 178*
46. L. Limosin, the Rape of Europa   *pg. 181*
47. J. Cousin, *Eva Prima Pandora*   *pg. 182*
48. Maître de Flore, *Triumph of Flora*   *pg. 183*
49. J. Goujon, Nymphs from the Fontaine des Innocents   *pg. 183*
50. G. B. Rosso, Leda and the Swan   *pg. 187*
51. E. Delaune, Design for an Ornate Ewer   *pg. 189*
52. P. Woeriot, Design for a Sword Hilt   *pg. 190*
53. F. Clouet, Diana Bathing   *pg. 195*
54. Venus Going to the Baths, Galerie François Ier, Fontainebleau   *pg. 195*
55. J. Mignon, Venus Going to the Baths   *pg. 196*
56. The Birth of Venus, stucco at the base of a fresco in the Galerie François Ier, Fontainebleau   *pg. 199*
57. Ecole de Fontainebleau, Lady at Her Toilet   *pg. 200*
58. L. Limosin, Venus and Cupid   *pg. 202*
59. Maître de Flore, Allegorical Painting   *pg. 205*
60. J. de Bellange, Costume of a Shepherdess   *pg. 208*
61. F. Clouet, Marguerite de Valois   *pg. 211*
62. Sixteenth-Century Saltcellar (French or Italian)   *pg. 216*
63. J. Goujon, Nymphs from the Fontaine des Innocents   *pg. 217*
64. F. Primaticcio, Thalestis and Alexander   *pg. 218*
65. Ball at the Court of Henri III   *pg. 221*
66. Portrait of Diana (ca. 1580)   *pg. 225*
67. *Ballet des Polonais*, 1573   *pg. 228*
68. Dancing Dryads, Galerie François Ier, Fontainebleau   *pg. 239*
69. P. Millan, *Dancing Dryads*   *pg. 239*

Note on Texts

For ease of consultation, references to Ronsard's *Oeuvres complètes* are given both to the Pléiade edition (ed. G. Cohen, 1965, 2 vols) and to the Société des Textes Français Modernes (ed. Paul Laumonier, 1914–75, 20 vols, completed by Isidore Silver and Raymond Lebègue). Quotations from *Les Amours* are taken from the critical edition of H. Weber and C. Weber (Classiques Garnier, 1963) and from the Laumonier edition. These editions are referred to as Pléiade (P), Laumonier (L), and Garnier (G), respectively.

Introduction

THIS IS A BOOK about praise and celebration. When I was invited to give the Una Lectures in the Humanities at Berkeley in the spring of 1980, I welcomed the opportunity to attempt an explanation of the singular pre-occupation in the Renaissance with forms of praise. It rapidly became clear to me that to do this adequately, I had to establish the social and intellectual context in which such forms might be viewed and to see them not as empty gestures relevant only to outdated political systems but as forms eagerly seized upon by poets and artists who recognised in them a positive challenge to their creative powers. This book is an expanded version of the reflections that began with those lectures.

Nowadays, we tend to despise and distrust praise; we are unsympathetic to the *forms*, particularly written ones, in which it is found. As scholars, we study rhetoric: but as readers, we remain suspicious of it. We are often impatient with long poems that require patience and leisure; and, if we are attracted by so-called scientific approaches to criticism and to textual deconstruction, short structures prove infinitely more convenient. The very word *panegyric* arouses the immediate antagonism of reader or listener. Yet, in the Renaissance, praise was the dominant mode in public life, in literature, and in art. In poetry, praise privileged certain forms. These multiplied in many European courts in the sixteenth century, when odes, encomia, epitaphs, epithalamia, hymns, and orations came forth in abundance. I have chosen to concentrate attention on France since there the phenomenon of praise, with all its kaleidoscopic richness, was truly unified. Social and political needs encouraged the production of varied forms of praise; rhetorical training ensured that writers could exploit modes appropriate to the person and the occasion; Petrarch's example of the benefits that could be derived from idealising techniques exerted considerable influence; and, finally, powerful aesthetic arguments abroad encouraged textual proliferation.[1]

If we are to grasp the fundamental importance of praise in this period and appreciate the aesthetic advantages and disadvantages it brought, then the phenomenon must be considered in this wider arena where praise is seen to have its own rituals and its own decorum and where, as a consequence, it produced a style of writing that even Montaigne admired for its decorative extravagance, its 'riches descriptions'.

My purpose is to attempt to bring alive for twentieth-century readers the cultural atmosphere in which these modes of praise were created and extolled so that, despite our democratic prejudices, we might begin to understand some of the complex reasons that praise so dominated artistic expression in Renaissance Europe. It is an interesting fact that we respond more immediately to art works from the past than to its written edifices. We admire Renaissance paintings and sculptures, detaching them easily from their context; thus isolated, they impose no worries of conscience and they do not inhibit our aesthetic judgement with notions of use, patronage, and the like. Works of applied art, however, already begin to raise such problems: arms and armour, the delicate achievements of engravers and goldsmiths, jewelry and tableware, for instance, cannot easily be wrested from their functions, and the complications of use, social status, and context begin to appear. Yet, for such works, these difficulties do not seem to embody any moral, intellectual, or political dimensions. Precisely these dimensions inevitably attend upon words. In the following pages, I shall try to recall the moral, social, intellectual, and political preoccupations relevant to the time so that a poem, for example, may be viewed as nearly as possible as it was first seen by its contemporaries. I stress *as nearly as possible* in the knowledge that our information is partial and that what we have has been contaminated by its transmission over time.

When one considers sixteenth-century poetry in France, at least two divergent conceptions of style seem to emerge. It was perhaps Guillaume Des Autelz who drew attention most sharply to the distinctions that separated the almost homely approach to poetry written in the vernacular in the first four decades of the sixteenth century, and the magnificence and decorative quality that characterized French poetry from the mid-century on. He contrasts the simplicity and conversational tone of Clément Marot's verse, for instance, with the inventive and imaginative sweep and the lofty style of Ronsard.

Marot donq est facile, humble, imitant quasi la coutume de parler, et qui semble facile à tous d'estre suyvi. . . . En luy, ie voy une admirable douceur et naïve grace, que les Grecs appellent Charité. . . . il n'ha encores trouvé son pareil: mais d'un autre à mouvoir les affections, d'un autre en imaginations et apprehensions ingenieuses, inventions divines, propres et poétiques descriptions, haultesse de style, gravité de sentences, magnificence de mots innovez et translatez, et en toutes sortes de diverse et variable érudition.[2]

Marot's style, then, is easy-flowing and lowly, almost as if it were modelled on speech, which seems easy for anyone to follow. . . . I see in him a marvellous sweetness and that natural elegance which the Greeks call Grace. . . . In these respects no one has yet equalled him. It requires quite another, however, to move the passions with ingenious thoughts and ideas, with divine inventions, appropriate poetic descriptions, and with a loftiness of style marked by deep reflexions, by magnificence in newly coined or borrowed words, and, in all things, by wide and varied learning.

In this comparison, written in 1551, Des Autelz, while clearly recognising the difference between the two poets, seems to approve equally of both. Before the end of the century, however, no one any longer doubts the superiority of Ronsard, whose ornate style is not only recognised as 'doulx et sublime' (sweet and sublime), but also—conditioned as it is by a profound knowledge of Greek and Latin writers and of Italian and Spanish poets—held up for emulation. Blaise de Vigenère, who advocated this imitation, was himself an impressive scholar, an enthusiastic amateur of art, and a tireless proponent of the 'style orné' (ornate style). He saw his publication in 1578 of *Les Images des deux Philostrates grecs* as providing a fund of images and fables for poets and artists and as tracing out themes and phrases useful for anyone attempting to write in French: 'pour atteindre à une heureuse perfection d'un riche, orné, propre et élaboré langage' (to attain that happy perfection of a rich, ornate style with an appropriate and elaborate vocabulary), as he put it.[3] With such a programme, it is not surprising that, twenty years later, Vigenère still sees Marot as a lowly figure 'n'ayant eu que le naturel' (only having a natural talent). Set beside Ronsard, he is comparable with an ambitious courtier who will never be noticed without someone making a special effort on his behalf to make him known to the great at court:

> à maniere d'un Courtisan qui desire de s'advancer, lequel s'il n'est assisté de quelque suport qui l'introduise aupres Grands, et luy donne entree, ne se peult pas poulsser si tost qu'un autre lequel bien que moindre assez en merite, seroit favorisé de ceux qui y ont desia quelque autorité et crédit.[4]

> just like an overly ambitious courtier, who, if he has no introduction to take him into the presence of the great, makes slow progress compared with another who is less able but who is favoured by those who already enjoy some authority and credit.

Only at court will poets such as Marot learn how to speak properly, Vigenère implies, and he is expressing a view which is crucial for the study of the literature of praise, but which in the sixteenth century was not shared by everyone.

On the one side, a formidable phalanx of poets made similar claims, and we may take Joachim Du Bellay as their spokesman. Writing on the need for erudition in his preface to the reader in *L'Olive*, he commented:

> Les gentilz espris, mesmes ceulx qui suyvent la court, seule escolle ou voluntiers on apprent à bien et proprement parler, devroient [en] vouloir pour l'enrichissement de notre langue.[5]

> Noble minds, even those who follow the court—the only school where one learns painlessly to speak well and properly—should be eager for [erudition] that it might enrich our language.

On the other side, there were writers such as Estienne Pasquier, who were less dependent on the court or who, like Henri Estienne, were frankly critical of it; they forcefully opposed the idea that superiority of expression and correctness of style belonged only, or even principally, to the court. Pasquier wrote in these round terms to his friend Claude de Kerquefinen:

> Si vous disiez que c'est là [at court] où il faut aller pour apprendre à bien faire ses besongnes, je le vous allouerois franchement: mais pour apprendre à parler le vray français je le vous nie tout à plat.[6]

> Were you to say that one had to go there to learn how to succeed, I'd agree with you straightaway: but to go there in order to learn to speak true French, I cannot allow under any circumstances.

Pasquier maintained this opinion in all his letters, where he coupled successful writing with frank expression, and he argued that the influence of the court had deleterious effects, even upon Ronsard.

> Quand nostre Ronsard escrivit ses premieres *Amours* sous le nom de sa Cassandre, si j'en suis creu, il se rendit inimitable, car il n'avoit autre object que *de se contenter soy-mesmes*. Mais lors que sous les noms de Marie et Heleine, il se proposa de complaire *aux Courtisans*, il me semble que je ne ly plus Ronsard, le lisant.[7]

> When our Ronsard wrote his first love poems to his Cassandra, believe me, he was inimitable since he had appointed himself *the sole task of his own pleasure*. However, since he has begun to write poems to Marie and Hélène in order to please *the court*, I no longer feel I'm reading Ronsard when I read his work.

Modern studies of Ronsard's love poetry have largely undermined this charge and revealed the extent of Pasquier's prejudices. Less explored, however, is the question of Vigenère's justification in acknowledging Ronsard's superior power through the courtly comparison, and how far contemporaries would have agreed that a poet's success as a writer was closely associated with prevailing court habits and taste.

In this study of ideal forms in the French Renaissance, Ronsard is my principal witness. There are many reasons that might justify such a choice: his popularity, which ensured that his poems quickly found their way into personal libraries;[8] the sheer quantity and variety of his poetry, which mark him out as a representative figure; or the influence he wielded on other poetry making, which has never been challenged. Furthermore, in his own time, he was recognised as a lofty spirit comparable with Homer, chosen to reveal the marvels of God, of nature, and of man, and thus a poet centrally concerned with the problem of praise. My main reason for limiting my enquiry to one major poet, however, is that by doing so I hope to demonstrate more specifically the aesthetic consequences of the necessity of praise; to embed Ronsard's work in its precise social and intellectual context; and to avoid both the dangers of heterogeneity and overgeneralised thematic parallels.

Vigenère's comments immediately refer us to the French court: and even a cursory glance at a collection of Ronsard's poems, with their explicit dedications to important members of the social hierarchy, suggests that the court played a significant role in his artistic consciousness. Recently, the significance was discussed in Daniel Ménager's thesis, a compelling display of Ronsard's role as 'poète du roi'.[9] By analysing three principal themes—'le Roi, la Cité, et la Religion'—he shows how the poet tried, through his heroic vision of poetry and through conspicuous celebration, to retrieve man's fallen state; and, in the process, he turns Ronsard's vast poetic enterprise into a magnificent, unified whole that the poet himself, in successive rewritings and incessant reorderings, had failed to achieve.

My own explorations extend in rather different directions, although Ronsard's poems provide a focus. They are seen, however, within the context of a court whose tastes and general character encouraged a spirit of competition between artists and poets. Such one-upmanship and the frequent convergence of poetic and artistic ideas and practice emerge as important and positive factors in sixteenth-century art and writing. In addition, the demands of knowledgeable patrons had other specific aesthetic effects: their art of connoisseurship included not merely the acquisition and display of riches and possessions but also the encouragement and appreciation of intricate and sophisticated stylistic practices. Under the Valois, the French court had become a centre of chic and excellence; and, since *chic* implies a certain distancing from the natural, we are constantly confronted by works that mingle the artificial and the real. Artists and poets were very much aware of the aesthetic consequences of such social interest and of its determining effect, and they frequently struggled with them both in their theoretical writing and in their artistic practice. Their preoccupation constitutes a major theme in this study.

My stress on sixteenth-century cultural setting naturally requires some discussion of classical influences. These, as one might expect, had a crucial role. I am concerned here less with the kind of linguistic and thematic impact studied by Dorothy Coleman[10] than with those poetic and artistic classical traditions that affected particular modes or produced specific features such as the narrative inset or the triumphal arch. Renaissance artists and poets appropriated structures from the past, and these gave a kind of preordained stamp of achievement to their own practice. They enthusiastically accepted the superiority of such forms, and they viewed their own ability to reproduce them as implicit acknowledgement of their own creative power. Moreover, they recognised that such appropriation had other significant advantages since the particular forms they borrowed fitted the heroic image they were trying to project as well as matching the exalted ideas they had of themselves.

Throughout this work, I have adopted a nonchronological approach: partly because the dating of works of art is still so uncertain but largely because my interest has centred on Ronsard's response to individual forms. On the whole, his concern with them is not restricted to identifiable periods in his career; and although it is possible to say that in the early to middle 1550s he especially favoured heroic forms, until his death he amended earlier ideas in each new edition of his work.

The book falls into three parts: the first two chapters provide the general background against which four major ideal forms are studied in more detail. Chapter 1 offers an analysis of that social and intellectual climate in which Renaissance thinkers, painters, and writers tended to confound what they saw and what they wished to see. An exploration of ideas about the Renaissance prince and representations of him shows that what we might now conceive of as ideals were, for sixteenth-century minds, merely widely accepted standards. In this period, people seemed not at all inhibited by the obvious fact that a yawning gap frequently existed between visualizations of majesty, for instance, and political realities. On the contrary, some even argued that in adverse political conditions there was positive value in giving the prince an extraordinary presence in art and poetry. Chapter 2 sets out the nature and extent of the interactions between art and poetry in the French Renaissance, notes their common aesthetic language, and points to the benefits both poets and artists derived from the competitive atmosphere in which they lived. The essentially visual impact of Ronsard's poems and the frequency and length of the images are set in sharp relief by being placed in a context of display.

The second part of this book is concerned with the heroic forms that seemed so appropriate at a time when military strife was frequent and individual feats of arms still commanded admiration and respect. Even courtiers clung to deeds of prowess and their resplendent record, especially when the techniques of waging war seemed to be evolving away from individual performance. At a time when social and political currents threatened to undermine their status, socially advantaged individuals used art to bolster the high-flown image they had of themselves. And yet, however dominant their artistic display, it could not blot out the increasing evidence of visual horror and physical suffering that surrounded them. Classical literary sources were used to confirm and consecrate contemporary taste for iconic forms, studied in chapter 3; and these are illustrated as readily in sixteenth-century armour as in the poems of Ronsard and others. Icons were seen as sacred images ensuring protection against the passage of time, and princes were eager to appropriate such guarantees of immortality. In chapter 4, the widespread interest in ancient Rome, its atmosphere of imperial triumph, and its military virtues is discussed. For Renaissance minds, infected by the craze for ancient remains and antiquities, imperial Rome exerted an almost magnetic force, constantly attracting artists towards the reproduction of its triumphal forms. Examples of triumph littered the courts of Europe, figured on walls, in statues, on armour, and even on jewels, as if their presence had some talismanic influence and secured future recognition for their owners. Ronsard was perhaps the only French poet who was able to express in poetry those contemporary yearnings for the imperial heroic past, although his zeal in responding to them did occasionally affect his poetic performance adversely.

The final section of this book offers a study of ideal forms of beauty: women drawn in paint and by pen (chapter 5) and dancing forms (chapter 6), for which poets and artists drew heavily on classical and Italian sources. These dancing forms had a double significance: they seemed to grant ascendancy (in terms of expressiveness) to the moving power of poetry over the more static art forms and took Ronsard back to the fountainhead of poetry—to Hesiod, and they led him to make fundamental discoveries about poetic art as a form of initiation into the rituals of celebration.

At first contact, the word *ideal* might suggest remoteness. Certainly the timelessness of ideals offered consolation to writers and artists in the imperfect and insecure world of Renaissance France. What is remarkable about the Renaissance preoccupation with the ideal, however, is how writers and artists produced such rich variations and how, in their effort to give ideas permanence, they contrived to incorporate in them a sense of things living. Dynamism and physical activity animate the heroic forms, while shapes of beauty grow warm and ask to be touched and caressed. In the case of Ronsard, idealisation and seduction are always close, not only in his love poems, where one might expect overtones of sensuality, but also in poems cast in the heroic mould. This study attempts to explain the apparently paradoxical conjunction of the physical and the remote, and to show how the search for perfection in different modes of poetic discourse often relied for its expression on very specific social and political needs.

I

THE PERFECT PRINCE

Ilz ont de Dieu le portrait sur le front,
Dieu les inspire, et tout cela qu'ils font
Vient du grand Dieu qui darde le tonnerre.

RONSARD
Les Sereines

They have God inscribed on their brow;
God inspires them, and all that they do
comes from the great God who sends forth
the thunder.

As WE LOOK AT the Renaissance from the twentieth century, we tend to think that its art transformed the world and peopled it with exemplary figures; with models that represented standards of virtue, power, and beauty; with ideal forms intended as stimuli and incentives to kings and lesser creatures. We think of their artistic world as one that moulded and modified the real, shaped and perfected it, in order to impress. We would be wrong, however, to interpret as mere flattery or gross exaggeration the comparison of kings and their courts to the gods on Olympus. According to sixteenth-century thinking and to princely propaganda, mythological references that depicted the king as Jupiter and members of his court as lesser deities genuinely reflected their lofty notions of themselves and their functions. At this time, there was a clear and direct correlation between authority and the artistic forms chosen to clothe it. Idealisation was a norm in art and poetry; and princely magnificence was the imposing outward sign of real power and rule. When French kings, for instance, watched triumphant cars and gorgeous processions curling their way along the festival route on the occasion of their royal entries into towns, they were in fact contemplating a display of their own power, or so they wished to believe. The major artistic records that we have and that form the matter of this book suggest that their hopes and wishes were realities.

9

Before embarking on our analysis of praise and its contribution to art and literature, we would do well to remind ourselves that we are considering only one attitude and a somewhat one-sided artistic representation of society—albeit the dominant one. Beside the riches of princes and courts existed another kind of society, made up of some 80 percent of the population, who suffered war, ignorance, disease, deprivation, and prejudice and who left few artistic and literary remains. In the second half of the sixteenth century in France, the needs of this mass gradually began to infiltrate the minds of the powerful, who used the people's distress and legitimate complaints for their own selfish ends. Factions at court, secretly and then openly by the reign of Henri III, exploited each occasion (and these became more frequent) to undermine royal power;[1] yet, on the surface, splendid images of princes continued to be projected. If we are to believe Pasquier, kings were kept unaware of the appalling condition of most of their subjects, for no one told them the truth:

> Au millieu d'une infinité de graces et faveurs que les Roys reçoivent de Dieu, ils ont un particulier malheur, de n'entendre la vérité, s'ils ne s'y disposent d'eux-mesmes. Ceux qui ont cest honneur de les approcher; pour ne leur desplaire, se conforment du tout à leurs volontez; de maniere qu'un pauvre Prince assiegé de mille flateurs, ne cognoist jamais ce qui luy est bon, sinon lors qu'il n'en plus temps, et quand il est au-dessous de toutes ses affaires; car adoncques son infortune luy enseigne les fautes par luy commises pendant qu'il avoit le vent en pouppe.[2]

> Among the infinite graces and favours that kings receive from God, they sustain one particular ill—they never hear the truth, unless they are naturally disposed towards it themselves. Those who are close to them bend themselves to their will to avoid kings' displeasure; thus the poor Prince, besieged by a thousand flatterers, never knows what is good for him until it's too late and he is overcome; misfortune teaches him the mistakes he made when he was all-conquering.

Pasquier may well exaggerate the ignorance of kings in this passage in order (later) to stress his own honest demeanour. But, overstated or not, his words reinforce the point that interests us here: praise is an integral part of the condition of princes. To a consideration of that part we must now turn.

Some twenty years ago, Raoul Morçay was no doubt right to claim that few people read Ronsard's *Hymnes* because our democratic spirit had banished the taste for hyperbole and praise.[3] Since that time, however, lively critical interest in the many works of praise produced in France in the sixteenth century, especially in the works of Ronsard, has developed.[4] We now understand how close, synonymous even, were the terms *chanter*, *louer*, and *orner*; we recognise that *flageoler* meant 'flatter' and that if we are to appreciate the quality of achievement of both poet and artist at this time, then we must be clear about the nature and function of those modes of praise that so dominated their lives.[5]

The Necessity and Nature of Praise

Among the many writers who set out their ideas on the necessity of praise in art, Erasmus was perhaps the most influential. He touched on the subject many times. In a letter to the official orator of the University of Louvain (epistle 177) he wrote:

> Those persons who think Panegyrics are nothing but flattery appear not to know with what design this kind of writing was invented by men of great sagacity, whose object it was, that by having the image of virtue put before them, bad princes might be made better, the good encouraged, the ignorant instructed, the mistaken set right, the wavering quickened, and even the abandoned brought to some sense of shame. Is it to be supposed that such a philosopher as Callisthenes, when he spoke in praise of Alexander, or that Lysias and Isocrates, or Pliny and innumerable others, when they were engaged in this kind of composition, had any other aim but that of exhorting to virtue under pretext of praise?[6]

It is clear from these lines that both exaltation and exhortation have the serious purpose of raising the minds of rulers to an adequate view of their function. Nor was Erasmus's advice merely theoretical since he appended the *Panegyricus*, which he presented to Archduke Philip of Burgundy on 6 January 1504, to the 1516 printing of *Institutio principis Christiani*, in which similar sentiments are expressed. Furthermore, he defended this principle in another letter: 'No other way of correcting a prince is so efficacious as presenting, in the guise of flattery, the pattern of a really good prince'.[7] The importance that Erasmus attached to these ideas can be seen not only from the forthright way in which they are expressed and from the number of times they are repeated, but also from his insistence that 'they must be expressed, crammed in, and inculcated and in one way or another be kept before him [the Prince]'. Every means, he argued, should be used to hold before the monarch a splendid vision of his task 'now by a suggestive thought, now by a fable, now by analogy, now by example . . . they should be engraved on rings, painted in pictures . . . before him'.[8]

Erasmus was a realist, and his principal concern here was with princes. He recognised that training had given them an elevated notion of themselves and that while they expected to be judged by their actions—acknowledging the force of appearances—they counted on those actions being appropriately represented to the public. For these reasons, the great and powerful had to be impressed, encouraged, and enlightened by whatever means, and the most effective modes of influence available were, as Erasmus indicates, art and poetry. It was, therefore, the appropriate task of the poet and artist to act on the minds and emotions of their noble patrons by presenting them with heightened perceptions of themselves and of the world so that their pride might be satisfied and that they might strive towards greater deeds and a better life.

Perceptions that could elevate and satisfy the mind necessarily and naturally involved a process of writing or painting up. And this view was still widely accepted a century after Erasmus by no less a figure than Sir Francis Bacon, who, rather enigmatically, expressed it this way: 'By telling men what they are, they [artists and poets] represent to them what they should be'.[9] This paradox conflates the 'is' and the 'ought to be' and explains why artists and poets did not differentiate in their works what they saw from what they wished to see. In another work, Bacon expounds on the reasons that the poet, in particular, was engaged in this process of refining, of magnifying, and of perfecting. In order that the mind should be alerted and the emotions of man aroused, actual events had to be transformed.

> Because the acts or events of true history have not the magnitude which satisfieth the mind of man, poesy feigneth acts and events greater and more heroical: because true history propoundeth the successes and issues of actions not so agreeable to the merits of virtue and vice, therefore poesy feigns them more just in retribution, and more according to revealed providence: because true history representeth actions and events more ordinary, and less interchanged; therefore poesy endueth them with more rareness, and more unexpected and alternative variations: so as it appeareth that poesy serveth and confereth to magnanimity, morality, and delectation.[10]

Here, Bacon touches on the central spring of artistic creation: art requires something more than a straightforward projection of the ordinary; art is an act of celebration. According to Bacon, who speaks for most members of his and earlier generations, to be noticed and to be effective, the poet and artist must praise. However, the praise envisaged here is closely connected with the events it projects, and these are shaped not only to fulfil a solemn moral purpose but also to reveal insights into the nature of man and his environment, as well as the discovery that satisfaction in art has to do with the power to raise the spirit and free it from its earthbound body. The poet's task, then, was primarily to excite; the onus of judging the distance between the real event, the real person, and the ideal experienced in the poem or the canvas is placed on the reader or the spectator.

Wherever we look in the Renaissance, ideal types emerge. Poets and dramatists heeded Aristotle's arguments that characters in tragedy must be handsomer.

We in our way should follow the example of good portrait-painters, who reproduce the distinctive features of a man, and at the same time, without losing the likeness, make him handsomer than he is.[11]

Contemporary literary critics (especially in Italy) argued interminably about the means a poet must use in order to make events more striking or more delightful than they are in reality.[12] And theorists of painting were equally quick to point out that Plato had argued that artists should always aim at painting things more beautiful than they are. Even Leonardo followed this injunction since he consistently returned, at thirty years' distance, to his standard ideal types of the beautiful youth, the warrior, and the old man.[13]

The authority of Plato and Aristotle was, perhaps, reason enough for idealising to become the major form of artistic expression at this time. Another tradition, however, rich and unbroken, came to lend its support.[14] Over the centuries, models of the perfect prince had multiplied in innumerable treatises—*De regimine principum*—in mirrors of princes, and in Latin panegyrics, of which the most famous and the one that was to be used frequently as a model was Pliny the Younger's extended oration delivered at Trier in praise of the Emperor Trajan.[15] From these texts, rulers could discover the virtues as well as the magnificence appropriate to their office, and their subjects could learn of their own responsibilities towards their monarch.

As far as sixteenth-century France is concerned, two works belonging to this tradition were particularly influential, and my discussion will centre upon these since it is clear from surviving evidence that reigning monarchs attached some importance to them. The first, Guillaume Budé's *De l'institution du prince* (1547), was specifically written for François I and published in the first year of the reign of his son Henri II; a version of the second, Erasmus's *The Education of a Christian Prince*, was prepared by order of Catherine de' Medici for the use of her sons.[16] Both works stress the innate splendour of kings. Budé argues, for instance, that it is impossible for good kings (such as the kings of France) to hide their qualities since these will inevitably shine through, and, in any event, it is their duty to impress members of their court. These ideas were, of course, not new. From medieval times magnificence and munificence were considered necessary attributes of kings, as is made explicit in the following extract from a fourteenth-century manuscript:

Bons princes doit avoir la vertuz de magnificence et ceste vertuz est necessaire pour faire faiz grans et nobles, appartenanz à l'onneur de Dieu ainsi comme granz eglyses, granz offrandes et granz dons, granz maisons et granz edifices, granz convocations et granz mengiers pour couronnemens, noces et chevaleries ou par autres causes, granz dons aus personnes de la communité qui plus en sont dignes.[17]

A good prince must be magnanimous; his virtue is necessary if he wishes to achieve great and noble deeds, worthy of God, such as magnificent churches, large and great gifts, noble houses and rare edifices, magnificent assemblies and banquets for coronations, weddings, tournaments or for other reasons, and splendid gifts to those persons in the community who are most worthy of them.

By the beginning of the sixteenth century, these traditional ideas were given a practical twist. Jean Bouchet argued that princely liberality served artist, king, and the community at large.[18] Budé went much further. In his enthusiasm to project an image of François I and his entourage that would match his idea of their worth, he inflates his language and turns the court and its affluence into a showplace to be wondered at, 'un perpetuel spectacle d'honneur' (a lasting spectacle of honour); the court, he adds, is

le vray theatre des choses vertueuses, et de grande recommandation. Et est si ample, si renommé, si excellent, et si magnificque, et sentant sa grande principaulté, et grandeur pres que incroiable que lon ne la peult accomparer à aulcune Cour, ou assemblée de Princes de l'universal Monde.

(*De l'institution du prince*, pp. 39–40)[19]

the true theatre of virtuous things and of social reputation. It is so ample, so renowned, so excellent and so magnificent, aware of its own princely greatness and almost inconceivable powers that it cannot be compared with any other court or assembly of princes in the entire world.

The theatricality of the French court, its richness, and its ritual are assumed here to be the natural adjuncts of royal power, and most people would have unquestionably accepted them as such at a time when the king was believed to be God's representative on earth and when the annointing with holy oils at the coronation publicly proclaimed this belief as fact. Budé presses these points: like a second Solomon, the king of France is shown on his throne of justice and 'par son regard separe et dechasse de son Royaulme toute iniquité et tout désordre' (by his look identifies and banishes every ill and disorder from his kingdom); his supernatural gifts grant him the power to heal the sick and make his words 'comme oracles'.[20] At the time Budé wrote, and for decades afterwards (despite religious and political unrest), these would not have been considered outlandish claims. After all, power to do good and to maintain peace with dignity and justice were symbolised on the royal seal that displayed the king 'en son throsne royal, rendant et distribuant la justice' (on his royal throne, giving and distributing justice).[21] The image is repeatedly referred to, with evident approval, by many subsequent writers, though they rarely capture Budé's eloquence as he expands on the theme here:

> La Cour d'un Roy est le temple d'honneur et de noblesse: que sa maison est comme le sainctuaire de Maiesté, ie dy Maiesté dominante, et le domicile de Justice, qui tousjours doibt estre ouvert.
>
> (De l'institution, p. 83)

> The court of a king is the temple of honour and nobility; his house is the sanctuary of majesty, I mean all powerful majesty, the domicile of justice, and must always be open to all.

Budé's insistence on majesty is often encountered in *De l'institution du prince*, for he believed it to be the supreme concern of kings. He develops the idea with his usual panache, clothing it in metaphor to illustrate that majesty is a prince's condition and his principal occupation. It is inherent in his nature; and it is nurtured by the virtues of wisdom, justice, prudence, and eloquence

> car maiesté est revestue d'un manteau d'admiration, tissu de grandes vertuz, et d'honnesteté de coeur, dont les signes evidents sont en son maintien, en son régime, et en tous ses actes.
>
> (p. 155)

> because majesty wears a cloak of admiration, woven with great virtues and goodness of heart, whose signs are made manifest in its demeanour, its rule, and in all its acts.

The admiration that such a sight compels was further nourished by modes of display that could blaze forth its significance. An example of what Budé had in mind is Jean Dorat's hymn to majesty and the plate that accompanied it in the 1569 edition of his *Paenes* (fig. 1); there, *Imperium* with the crown, sceptre, and balance, flanked by justice, prudence, and victory, rises triumphant over rebellion.

This need to turn the French court into a theatre for majesty in order to instil its reality into the mind of spectators suggests both an attitude and a fear. It is interesting to note that as acute a political observer as Michel de l'Hôpital subscribed to Budé's view. According to him, kings had a veritable duty to display their power and their deeds 'comme s'ilz estoient à la veue de tous sur un théâtre représentez'[22] (as if they were displayed for all to see on a stage) so that future generations might profit from their virtues. In times of civil strife, it made sense to stress a strong moral line and to link it to a splendid display of power. Yet Michel de l'Hôpital's principal concern, in his speeches and in his writing, was to draw the vision of a

1. Engraving of *Imperium* (Majesty), first published in the
1569 edition of Jean Dorat's *Paenes sive Hymni* (sig. Biv) and
reproduced on the back of the title page of his *Magnificentissimi
spectaculi*, Paris, 1573 (British Library).

peace-loving and just monarch. This was the picture that was to be the
standard point of reference for commentators for the rest of the century.

> Nos roys . . . pour monstrer qu'ilz estoient, comme roys trèschrétiens, plus
> enclins au repoz qu'aux armes, ne se sont faicts figurer à leurs scels et ar-
> moiries, comme les aultres roys, grands princes et seigneurs, tout armez,
> ayant le glaive à la main; mais d'une figure et image de roys paisibles et ai-
> mant la justice, avec ung long manteau royal, qui est vestement de paix, ten-
> ant en leur main le sceptre, qui signifie puissance, et de l'aultre la main de
> justice, déclarant par là que le propre estat et office d'ung roy est de faire la
> justice à ses subjects, et de ne venir jamais aux armes sans grand besoing.[23]

> Our kings . . . in order to display what they really are, that is, as truly Christian kings more inclined to peace than to war, have had their seals and armorial bearings figured not as other kings, great princes, and lords, fully armed with sword in hand, but with the figure of peaceful kings and lovers of justice, dressed in long royal robes—the cloth of peace—holding the sceptre of power in one hand and the symbol of justice in the other, thus making clear that the fine state and office of a king is to be just to his subjects, and never to take up arms except in the greatest need.

The emphasis is laid on the outward show of justice—the throne, the sceptre, and the royal mantle, for these were accepted symbols of power, and from their outward splendour the onlooker learns about the sacred duties of a king.[24] It was Erasmus's contention that kings themselves should learn to philosophise about those very decorations with which they are adorned.

> What doest the anointing of the King mean, unless the greatest mildness of spirit? What significance has the crown on his head, if not wisdom that is absolute? What is the meaning of the collar with plaited gold around his neck, except the union and harmony of all virtues? What is symbolized by the bright rays of gems shining with many colors; if not the highest degree of virtue and that whatever is honorable ought to be found in a special degree in the prince?[25]

At a time when François I, Emperor Charles V, and Henry VIII sought to outdo each other in princely magnificence, perfect exemplars of good kingship proliferated. These monarchs and their children were made to seem like reincarnations of outstanding models from the past. Their portraits spoke modern aspirations. Solomon (as we have seen) was synonymous with justice and wisdom; his example—and that of Moses—was habitually used to embody the royal function and to emphasise the fact that kings are God's lieutenants on earth.[26] Such images of good majesty grew in number in France as royal power became frailer and as the art collections of rival princes enlarged. They were depicted on paintings, on walls, and on stained glass, and they were woven into tapestries. To cite but one example: in the art collection of the king's constable (the duke of Montmorency) there was a magnificent set of six hangings depicting the acts of Solomon; in 1556, he acquired a further set of eight pieces decorated with episodes from the story of Moses; the walls of his mansion at Ecouen were painted with little-known biblical scenes; and, in addition, he instructed artists to make a series of heraldic stained glass windows on which Moses played a dominant role.[27]

Inevitably, artists and writers had recourse to classical sources in their search for the ideal models that kings might emulate. They and their patrons were enthusiastic about Greek and Latin ideals, whose discovery

2. Agnolo del Moro, Giovanni Battista d'Angeli, engraving of
Henri II (Print Room Albertina, Vienna).

seemed still relatively recent. These heroes came clothed with virtuous
deeds and symbolic resonance. Their sublime afterlife, appropriated by
French kings and incorporated into their persons by writers and artists,
acted as a kind of guarantee of present greatness that could be projected
forward for future generations to admire. Thus, when justice and peace
are emphasised, the obvious comparison is made to Augustus, to his increasing antagonism to war, to his generosity to the arts, and to his appreciation of the moving power of eloquence. From the beginning of the sixteenth century this parallel of French kings with the Roman emperor was
a source of active contemplation (fig. 2). It provided the main inspiration
for Longueil's panegyric on Louis XII (1510),[28] and François I so favoured
the idea that he commissioned an artist, known only as 'Giovanni', to give
Augustus's features to the *gisant* figure of his father on his tombstone.[29]

Budé elaborated extensively on this comparison, which was later to be eloquently sung by Robert Garnier in his *Hymne de la monarchie* (1567).[30] It was also used, for obvious reasons, in innumerable prefaces dedicated to kings.[31] If war had to be fought, then the model changed, and the most inspiring and the most commonly used was that of Alexander, famous for his magnanimity as well as for his victories.[32]

Solomon, with all his gifts, and Alexander, with all his virtues, were expected to cohabit in the persons of ideal princes. However, a Renaissance prince's real ability to infuse his kingdom with harmony and peace came not so much from an imitation of past great performances—these were significant but secondary modes of emulation—but rather from the universally held view that:

> Ainsi qu'aux Cieux nous voyons le Soleil
> Representer de Dieu le grand ouvrage:
> Semblablement Roy usant de conseil
> En ce monde est de Dieu le vray image.[33]

> Just as in the heavens we see the sun displaying the great work of God: so, in this world, a king subject to counsel is the true image of God.

This assimilation of kings and gods was commonplace and seemed entirely reasonable at a time when most men accepted what historians have called the divine right of kings and when men thought that infinite analogies could be made between their little world and the cosmos. These correspondences had been established long ago in classical works, and they had become more detailed and more elaborate in late medieval and Renaissance writings. Desbordes's translation of Sacrobosco's handbook *De sphaera*, a copy of which was owned by Henri II, gives something of the flavour of these conceptions:

> Cest ordre et cours est avec grande raison: tellement que à tous ceulx qui attentivement contemplent les cieulx il semble qu'ilz voyent une police depeincte et descrite au ciel, tout ainsi que les poetes l'ont descrite dedans leurs oeuvres. Car le Soleil qui represente un Roy, est porté ou se pourmene au milieu de tous les cieulx environné et entouré des Senateurs, Saturne et Jupiter, du capitaine des guerres et batailles qui est Mars, et de l'ambassade Mercure, ayant pour ses domestiques et familieres La Lune et Venus.[34]

> This order and movement is bound by reason: so much so that for those who contemplate the heavens carefully, they seem to see a whole commonwealth drawn in the sky, just as the poets described it in their works. The Sun stands for a king and is carried on horses at the centre of the Heavens, surmounted and supported by his Senators Saturn and Jupiter, his battle leader Mars, his ambassador Mercury, and having, as his servants and familiars the Moon and Venus.

It will be seen that the elements are carefully matched and the tasks of government appropriately assigned. Order, harmony, and a centre of power radiating influences are the main factors in this parallel. Ronsard, unaware or unmindful of the cosmic revolution set in motion by Copernicus, developed step by step this idea of correspondence in a poem on the excellence of man's mind written to preface the 1559 French translation of Livy's works:

> Car, comme en une ville
> Où chacun garde bien la police civile,
> On voit les senateurs au premier rang marchans
> Tenir leur gravité; au second les marchans,
> Au tiers les artisans, au quart la populace;
> Ainsi dedans le ciel les astres ont leur place
> Et leur propre degré, grands, petits et moyens,
> De la maison du ciel eternels citoyens.

> (P 2:467, L 10:103)

Because, just as in a town where each preserves the civil rule, one sees the senators walking in the first rank sustaining their solemnity; in the second are the merchants, skilled workmen form the third, and the populace the fourth; so in the heavens, the stars have their places, their appropriate level, great, medium, and small in the house of heaven, its lasting citizens.

In these lines the poet has a ready-made set of references and harmonic resonances. He echoes oft-repeated sentiments about the composition of the world and is reenacting its stately pattern, just as another poet had done at Blois in February 1510, when in front of Louis XII, 'cler Phoebus' (bright Phoebus), there was acted out 'une momerie', in which seven planets danced as befitted their function, and travellers came from all corners of the globe to pay hommage to a monarch who, in fulfilling his proper duties, had brought peace to the world.[35] It comes as no surprise, therefore, to find that Orontius Finé depicted François I's device—a crowned salamander—at the centre of the sphere, and Symeoni, in like manner, centres Henri II among the signs of the zodiac (fig. 3).[36] The king-sun style continued unabated in France throughout the sixteenth century, finding its apotheosis later in Louis XIV.[37]

That these beliefs remained entrenched for so long is testimony to their strength and their political and artistic usefulness. Throughout the period that stretches from Louis XII to Louis XIV praise of princes was criticised both in courtiers' handbooks and by political and religious opponents.[38] Yet it survived. It dominated partly because it served as an essential contribution to the face of monarchy and partly because it joined a contemporary view of art and poetry that had been authorised by both the eminences: Plato and Aristotle. This does not mean that early writers were either uncritical or unaware. Claude de Seyssel had, in his biography of Louis XII, elaborated a familiar pattern of praise and a conception of glory, for, he unequivocally maintained, '[c'est] la gloire seule qui demeure en la fantaisie des hommes' (glory alone stays in the minds of men).[39] Likewise, Jean Bouchet's posthumous praise of François I was intended to be remembered and to act as 'le miroir, et l'exemple / De bien regner' (the mirror and example of a good ruler).[40] The twofold role of these panegyrics, which adapted the themes and style of formal *De regimine principum* to more personal accounts of monarchs, was to praise and—through praise—to counsel. Seyssel and Bouchet defended praise as fitting in an

3. Henri II at the centre of the zodiac; engraving from Gabriel Symeoni, *Interpretation grecque, latine, toscane, et françoyse du monstre ou enigme d'Italie*, Lyons, 1555, p. 41 (British Library).

address to great persons, and when they argued that it should never be construed as flattery, they referred hesitant readers to the, as yet unquestioned, authority of Claudian and Pliny. Their example had

> introduit anciennement et permis de louer et commander les vertus des empreurs, des roys·et aultres princes en leur propre presence et en public pour les inciter et stimuler a perseverer en oeuvres bonnes et vertueuses de plus en plus quant ilz entendent icelles ainsi estre prisees et magnifiees en eulx sans adulation.[41]

> of old, introduced authoritatively the custom of praising the virtues of emperors, kings, and other princes publicly to their face in order to stimulate them to persevere more intensively in their good and virtuous works as a consequence of hearing the latter praised and extolled without flattery.

Although praise was considered a political and artistic necessity, it was vulnerable to criticisms of excess and inappropriateness. Most sixteenth-century writers were aware of this fragility and sought to come to terms with it by stressing the ambivalent nature of praise. Seyssel, for instance, was aware that commendation in certain circumstances might seem misplaced. But, just as Mr Aglionby, when he welcomed Queen Elizabeth to Warwick in 1572, reminded her of the ambiguities present in 'thies panegyricae',[42] in similar manner, the French biographer warns Louis XII that the burden of judging whether a comment is appropriate or not belongs to the king's own conscience.

> Touteffois si en vous louant de quelque vertu je me suis plus estendu et en ay parle plus difusement que vostre conscience ne vous jugera . . . vous pourrez par continuation et perseverance bien aiseement parvenir a plus parfaite habitude dicelle que ie nay dit.[43]

> Nonetheless, if in praising some virtue I have extended my comments further than your own conscience judges appropriate . . . you can both by perseverance and persistance achieve that very act even more perfectly than I have indicated.

The Image of the French King

If we extend our enquiry into Ronsard's contemporaries' views of the perfect prince to include official assessments of the monarch's achievements and ritual presentations of the prince, we find that the theoretical statements and admonitions of Budé and Erasmus are fully realised in practice. On the death of a prince, the ceremonies were always prolonged and elaborate. The body of a dead French king was emptied and embalmed, his heart secured in a casket, and a lifelike effigy reposed for fourteen days in the 'salle d'honneur', suitably hung with rich tapestries from the royal collection that depicted the Acts of the Apostles. The appearance of the effigy dressed with all the attributes of royal power recalled sharply to those who kept watch and to those who mourned that though the king was dead, the power attached to his function lived on. Modern scholars have revealed to us the quasi-mystical beliefs that lay behind French royal funeral ceremonies;[44] the subjects of François I and Henri II no doubt took them for granted since the official mourners in their traditional *sermons funèbres* concentrated upon the virtues of the prince they had lost and the formidable duties of kingship.

As a rule, there were two formal orations. On the death of François I, Du Chastel first commemorated the life and deeds of the dead king, displaying his virtues as examples from which future generations might learn; then he offered general consolations.[45] On the death of Henri II in 1559, the same pattern was followed by Jerome de la Rouvere. On this occasion, the first speech (given on 12 August) was designed to bring the dead king back to life, with his 'presence pleine de maiesté et de grace' (his presence full of majesty and grace). This detailed evocation sought to imprint on the mind of the listener Henri II's virtue and goodness, his knowledge of and concern for the arts, his martial ability and his use of prudence, and, above all, his defence of justice against the brutal attacks of heretics. The image was meant to compel and to offer an obvious stimulus. The second oration meditated more generally on death and the hope for eternal life, proferring at the same time consolation to the mourners.[46]

Royal funeral orations, therefore, celebrated and preserved a life and praised and supported a function according to set rules and verbal ceremonies. They were an immediate monument to the dead. Future generations had, in theory, more artistic ways of remembering greatness and its function. We can still admire, for instance, Germain Pilon's elegant bronze urn, made to preserve the ashes of Henri II's heart, though the dead king's massive equestrian statue, designed first by Michelangelo and then by Daniele da Volterra, was never completely cast;[47] and Nicolas Hoüel's vast *L'Histoire de la royne d'Arthemise* (1562), which described the truly extraordinary funeral arrangements for King Mausolus (an allegory of Henri II)— with his effigy and tabernacle, the procession of accompanying nobles, the attendant soldiers and their triumphant cars, as well as the extensive funeral games—was never printed.[48]

Although such ambitious artistic remembrances did not go without criticism,[49] Henri II would have been disappointed by the nonappearance of these works. He seems to have been thoroughly convinced by all the arguments about display and, therefore, keenly concerned about the kind of impact that his own image had on his subjects. Appreciating that the greatest impact is normally achieved by the visual, this king, as his first act of authority, established in 1547 'un tailleur général des monnaies' (general engraver of coins).[50] His task was to design medals and silver and gold coins, embossed and engraved with the image of the king or with devices adequately extolling major political or military events. Such medals had helped to carry down through the centuries the fame of many a Roman emperor; therefore, for each year of his reign, Henri II decreed that first Marc Béchot (1520–57) and then Etienne Delaune (1518–95) should produce works that were both commemorative and signals of developing royal political aspirations.[51]

In the sixteenth century many people believed in the potency of images, and although we are inclined to think that royal crests and devices were somewhat arbitrarily chosen, it was believed then that qualities inherent in a person and in his function determined a particular figure. Henri II's device was the crescent moon, which already in 1540 appeared on the reverse of a coin showing his arms as dauphin, and it was kept as his official device once he became king.[52] The device was thought to be peculiarly appropriate to a king who took his role as pastor of his people so seriously. Throughout his reign he fought to maintain the power of the church against the encroachments of the Protestants, and, as he fought, the symbols became more insistent. His determination was considered well symbolised by the sign of the moon, which, in the words of the specialist Claude Paradin, 'Es sacrees escritures doncque la lune prefigure l'Eglise' (In the sacred scriptures then, the moon symbolises the church). Paradin develops this idea and its singular relationship to Henri II:

> La Lune est aussi sugette à mutacions, croissant et decroissant de tems en tems: ainsi est veritablement l'Eglise militante, laquelle ne peut demeurer longtemps en un estat, que maintenant ne soit soutenue et defendue des Princes catholiques, et tantôt persecutee des tirans et heretiques: au moyen de quoy est en perpetuel combat, auquel neanmoins la Royale Magesté, ou Roy premier fils de l'Eglise promet de tenir main de protection, iusques à ce que reduite sous un Dieu, un Roy, et Une Loy aparoisse la plenitude et rotondité de sa bergerie, regie par le seul Pasteur.[53]

> The moon is also the subject of change, increasing and decreasing from time to time; such is the true nature of the militant church that does not stay long in one state, now sustained and defended by Catholic princes and now persecuted by tyrants and heretics: and is thus in constant battle; yet His Royal Majesty or First Son of the Church promises his protection until the moment when the full size and force of his rule governed by one Shepherd appears controlled by one God, one King, and one Law.

The crescent moon device particularly attracted contemporaries, and it became the main focus for writers and artists who sought to give expression to the king's untiring and often dangerous efforts to extend the political dominions of the French.[54] The organisers of the entry of Henri II into Rouen in 1550 used it to develop the imperial aspirations they nurtured for their king;[55] in countless poems, its crescent shape grew into the round universe and thus confined the pretentions of the imperial eagle.

> Le croissant vient en rotondité
> L'Aigle à rebours ne peult passer plus oultre.[56]

The crescent grows to fullness, while the eagle, in contrast, cannot stretch beyond.

Etienne Perlin, in 1558, writing an account of the kingdoms of England and Scotland, argued that the moon device itself had magical properties that guaranteed Henri II as 'futur monarque et Empereur de tout le monde' (future monarch and emperor of all the world).[57] However excessive these claims seem, their very frequency commands our attention. Similar dynastic considerations were naturally uppermost in the minds of the king's engravers, such as Etienne Delaune. He knew that the images he wrought helped to condition the views of the general public and to promote royal interests abroad.[58] On the occasion of the Treaty of Vaucelles in 1556, for example, he made nine engravings to celebrate Henri II's victorious peace, using pagan mythology in combination with the king's device to convey the ideas. In one of them, Minerva and Mars hold the device aloft beneath an imperial crown (fig. 4). Another design presents the king himself (fig. 5): his features are drawn from life, and crowned with laurel leaves as a victorious emperor, he is seated on a world burgeoning with life, with all the paraphernalia of state. He is shown receiving divine inspiration, with whose help he can offer calm assurance against the evils

4. (*at left*) Etienne Delaune, design for a coin to commemorate the Treaty of Vaucelles (1556) showing Mars and Minerva holding Henri II's device aloft (British Museum).

5. (*at right*) Etienne Delaune, design for a coin to commemorate the Treaty of Vaucelles (1556) showing Henri II ridding the world of vice (British Museum).

of vice and ignorance, which are depicted at his feet attempting to destroy the world. These two examples typify the ways in which artists commonly expressed royal power and extolled the virtue of their prince.

Henri II seems often to have taken the initiative in promoting images of his power. From the first set of royal decrees that he promulgated, it is clear that the king set himself up to play a conspicuous religious role; and in the two remarkable and virtually unknown drawings that he commissioned in 1550 from the artist Jean Duvet, we have a startling presentation of the kind of image Henri II expected.[59] Figure 6 shows the figure of Majesty holding the sceptre of power, seated upon the world, and treading out vice with her feet. The idea of the picture is not unusual (see fig. 1), but the style is very strange, even idiosyncratic. On either side of Majesty appear

6. (*below*) Jean Duvet, a drawing of Majesty, one of three surviving designs commissioned by Henri II (British Museum).

7. (*at right*) Jean Duvet, a drawing of Henri II as royal French monarch; one of three surviving designs commissioned by Henri II; two are in Prints and Drawings (British Museum), the third design is in Dijon (Municipal Museum).

Wisdom and Fame with their usual attributes; between them, in a gesture that was characteristic of such works, they support the crown of France. The general impression is one of dignity, abstraction, and remoteness, despite the surrounding bustle of angelic *putti* with their bugles announcing the king's fame to the world. In figure 7 the specific application to Henri II is more marked. One of the attendant angels displays prominently the French royal crest—the fleur-de-lis—while the other holds the oriflamme, the banner carried by French kings as they led their armies to battle. The central figure, the king, has, around his neck, the chain of the principal military order of France—'l'ordre de Saint Michel'—with the triple crescent moons dangling from it. His crown is also surmounted by a triple crescent, set upon an H, at the centre of a larger crescent. Above the whole picture hovers the symbol of the Holy Spirit, indicating that the French king's powers come directly from God and that Henri II is fulfilling a sacred function when (as another Saint Michel) he undertakes a crusade against the Protestant heretics on whose writhing monster symbol he tramples with his feet. Both figures 6 and 7 have a biblical, almost apocalyptic, atmosphere about them.

8. Attributed to Niccolo da Modena, allegorical portrait of
François I (Bibliothèque Nationale).

Although Duvet's drawings were never realised in bronze nor transformed into paint, they represent a preoccupation with ways of projecting
the royal image that had less to do with the accuracy of rendering the
features of an individual as such but were more concerned to suggest,
through the portrait, the responsibilities of the kingly office. From the
time of François I, the state portrait became fixed in form. The royal portraits painted by Jean and François Clouet and by Corneille de Lyon show
how far its poses were calculated, its decoration ritualised, and its symbolism made obvious.[60] François I's official portrait, for instance, evolved
from the version with a fine head and broad shoulders painted in rich velvet and silk to the curious standing figure (attributed to Niccolo da Modena, fig. 8) of the king as a composite mythological deity, adorned with
the gifts of war and peace, eloquence and love, together with the bugle of
the hunt.[61] By the middle of the century we come to the power pose *par
excellence*, the equestrian portrait. François Clouet's painting of Henri II

9. François Clouet, drawing for equestrian portrait of Henri II (Chantilly, Musée Condé; photo Giraudon).

(now in the Uffizi Gallery) shows the king in full armour, on a richly caparisoned horse, grasping the sceptre of state; and, unquestionably, the painter has sought to imitate the gestures of the statue of Marcus Aurelius, which now stands on the Capitol in Rome. A drawing at Chantilly (fig. 9) shows Henri II in exactly the same pose. It is obviously copied from Clouet's painting of his father and thereby demonstrates the continuing preoccupation with imperialist intentions.[62] The same themes and symbolism were expressed in two medals of 1552. They were struck by Marc Béchot in order to commemorate the victories of the king against Protestant heretics. The first presents Henri II as another composite deity, triumphing over war and installing peace as the liberator of Italy and Germany; the second shows on its reverse side an imperial chariot, which transports the joys of peace (represented by the goddesses Ceres and Venus) with the figure of Good Fame driving the four horses and holding on high her trumpet decorated with the French royal crest.

In all these representations of the monarch, what seem uppermost are gestures that signify and symbols that crowd around the face and figure. Artists (keen on impressing the wearer and the spectator) seem less concerned with the details of feature or performance and more interested in projecting a view of power and its potential. The whole direction of such painting effort is summed up for us by Giovanni Lomazzo in his *Trattato dell'arte della pittura* where, having explained that idealising is fundamental to the arts, he concludes that

> the painter's skill in his art [is] to represent not the acts which by chance a certain pope or Emperor did, but those that he should have done, in accordance with the majesty, and the dignity of his estate.[63]

Although many Frenchmen could absorb the royal propaganda imprinted on coins and medals, few in the sixteenth century had the privilege of gazing on an expressive portrait of the king. There were, nonetheless, significant moments in a monarch's life when he presented himself directly to his people burdened with every possible symbol of his power. For instance, his first entry after his coronation into any town of the realm was marked by extended ceremonies as citizens sought, with shows and triumphs, to please their king who came in splendour and in force and whom they hoped would renew the city's privileges.[64] The most important ceremony of all, however, was the coronation itself.

Since the twelfth century the French king's royal and legitimate authority was made public at his coronation when, in the cathedral at Rheims, his subjects swore obedience to him, and, in the sight of all, he accepted the manifold duties belonging to a just king.[65] Magnificence and a sense of theatre dominated the occasion when the king and archbishop were chief actors, and the altar the holy stage on which a performance charged with significance was given anew. It was a time when the king's majesty was visibly reborn and when, according to ancient custom and belief, he had to be seen displaying its greatness and his own sovereignty through symbolic acts: assuming the cloak of majesty, accepting the sceptre of justice, and girding the sword of faith. Like the celebration of the mass with which they had many affinities, the ceremonies of the coronation were unchanging, its ritual fixed long ago. The climax of the reenactment and public establishing of majesty came with the anointing of the king with holy oils, which made him formally and publicly (so it was believed) God's representative on earth, with the power to heal the sick and with the sacred task of protecting the Holy Catholic church. After this consecration he was crowned.

Henri II's coronation is considered by experts as a model of the genre. The king, who was very sensitive to questions of precedence, took the matter so seriously that on the very day of his accession he ordered that all items that were to be used for the coronation be brought to Saint Germain so that he might inspect them. Finding them much deteriorated, he commanded that new and richer clothes be made.

En particulier il fait remplacer les camisole, sendales, tunique, dalmatica, et mantel de satin bleu azuré, et plus riches que n'estoient les vieux, restablir, rebrunir et renouveler les couronnes, sceptre, main de Iustice, espée, et esperons.[66]

In particular, he had the camisole, sandals, tunic, coat, and cloak of blue satin replaced, and the crowns, sceptre, hand of justice, sword, and spurs were made richer than the old and were refurbished, renewed, and brightened up.

Recognising their special significance, the king required each object and each item of clothing to be in a pristine state, appropriate to the majesty he was to display. Some idea of the theatricality of coronation ceremonies and of the ritual that controlled them can be gained if we remember that in the course of the service each item was given to the king by the appropriate member of his court. The archbishop of Rheims leads him to the high altar, where are set out the crown, the golden spurs, 'a sceptre of pure gold, with a golden rod, springing forth out of an Ivory hand: also a paire of hose, called *Sandanali* of purple collor . . . a coat, which is called *Dalmatica*, and a regall cloake'. The *sandanali* are put on by the Great Chamberlain, the spurs by the duke of Burgundy, and the archbishop offers the sacred sword. After the king is anointed, he puts on the royal cloak. Then the archbishop places on the middle finger of the king's right hand a ring saying, 'Take this ring in token of thy holy Faith, the firmnesse and soundness of the Kingdom'. Other symbols of royal power and virtue are laid upon the king before he is led 'unto a high throane, made and provided purposely for the King that he might be seene of all sitting in his Chaire'.[67]

This vision of majesty acknowledged and of splendour was the reality that stood behind Budé's fervour and Erasmus's enthusiasm; and it was the spectacle that artists and poets tried to re-create and perpetuate. It sufficed for a few people to witness these ceremonies and to see these gestures at Rheims for the majority of Frenchmen to believe in their efficacy. To drive home its reality, however, Henri II had a coin issued during the month of his coronation: one side showed his military strength, the other displayed his sacred function with the figure of a hand emerging from clouds that held aloft the sacred phial containing the oils of the Holy Ghost.[68]

Ideal Courts

The forms in paint and in words that, it was thought, might do justice to the feelings of awe aroused by the pageant of the coronation depicted the king and his court inhabiting a kind of paradise. In fact, in sixteenth-century France, Olympus could be encountered everywhere in art and poetry; since the early 1540s it had peopled the ceiling of the Galerie d'Ulysse in the royal castle at Fontainebleau (fig. 10).[69] It also appeared beneath the council of the gods in the frescoes that Noël Jallier had painted in the Grande Galerie at Oiron in 1550.[70] These gods at Fontainebleau and at Oiron were drawn according to the standard types, as far as we know; yet contemporaries had long been accustomed to read the face of their king into Jupiter and to assign other olympic roles to members of his court. Saint-Gelais, in his *Chanson des Astres* (1544), had systematically awarded the king, Henri his son, Diane de Poitiers, the duchesse d'Etampes, and seventeen other prominent figures their appropriate places in the heavens.[71] When we look at the enamelled dish that Montmorency had commissioned from Léonard Limosin in 1555, we see the gods assembled for a feast. At first, they seem merely copies of the figures Raphael had painted

10. Francesco Primaticcio, Apollo and the Muses, drawing for the fourteenth compartment of the ceiling in the Ulysses Gallery, Fontainebleau (Uffizi Gallery, Florence).

in his *Banquet of the Gods*, but closer inspection reveals that the olympic faces are individualised into clear images of Henri II (Jupiter) and his court. Ronsard celebrated the glories of this company in his *Hymne de Henri II de ce nom*, and this poem is thought to have inspired both Limosin's work and a matching fresco in the guard room at Tanlay (figs 11 and 12).[72]

Such idealising was standard practice in poetry. Olivier de Magny gave the king a new year's gift of a *chant poétique*, in which Mars, Mercury, Apollo, Juno, Minerva, Diana, the Muses, and the lesser gods do homage to Jupiter:

> Chacun depuis vous offrit sa personne
> Ses biens, sa force et repute à grand heur
> D'estre nommé subjet et serviteur.[73]

> Each one, since then, offered his person, his goods, his strength and reputation in happiness at the names of subject and servant.

Each deity, he makes clear, stands for a member of Henri II's court. The assimilation was felt to be so complete and natural that courtiers dressed as these same gods and planets moved in stately dance at the festivities for the wedding of Mary, Queen of Scots, and the Dauphin in 1559. An eye-witness in 1558 describes the setting for this dance of the spheres in terms that recall earlier theatrical visions of the French court. On this occasion the Louvre was

> si magnifiquement ouvré et paré, qu'on eust peu dire le champ Elisée n'estre plus beau ne plus delectable le Roy et toutte la Court (i'entends les plus proches du Sang Royal) [qui] s'asirent à la table de Marbre.[74]

> so magnificently worked and decorated that the Elysian Fields are not more delightful than the sight of the king and his entire court (I mean, especially the princes of the blood) who sat at the high table of state.

That other standard representation of the court—as an earthly paradise—was made fifteen years earlier in 1543 by Claude Chappuys, when he had claimed of the court:

> c'est ung paradis terrestre,
> Et estre ailleurs au monde n'est pas estre.[75]

> it's an earthly paradise; to be elsewhere is not to exist.

When poets tried to give fuller expression to this idea of a paradise on earth, they found inspiration in a particularly rich literary tradition, that of the pastoral. The affinities of panegyric and pastoral were evident and had, since Virgil, been demonstrated many times. Kings were thought to

11. The court of Henri II as Olympus; ceiling fresco at the Château de Tanlay (Arch. Photo. Paris/S.P.A.D.E.M.).

12. The court of Henri II as Olympus; ceiling fresco at the Château de Tanlay (Arch. Photo. Paris/S.P.A.D.E.M.).

find a natural habitat in nature, in an Arcadia where concord was supposed to reign. As a sixteenth-century commentary on Virgil's *Georgics* put it: 'Les plus grans comme roys et autres leurs dyademes bas mis et posez se tenoient aux champs herbus et floriz'[76] (The greatest of men, such as kings and others, laid down their crowns to live among the flowers and herbs of the fields). Kings are thus drawn to nature (so the argument ran) because, instinctively, they recognised their own attributes there: innate goodness, justice, and solid work, which was 'pas seulement Royal, mais plustost une occupation déifique' (not only royal, but rather, a divine occupation).[77] If one accepted this exalted view of the pastoral life, it followed that there was no incongruity for poets who wished to praise their kings to depict them as shepherds. After all, King David, Apollo, and an even more exalted Shepherd had been content to perform this role. Virgil's sixteenth-century interpreter had warned his reader what to expect beneath the guise of simplicity:

> Que le lecteur ne se méprenne pas sur l'identité de ces 'simples personnes'. Toutefoys soubz l'habit d'iceulx de simple maintien est veu comprendre les grans seigneurs potestaz et empereurs de Romme.[78]

> Let the reader be not mistaken as to the true identity of these 'simple beings'. Beneath this humble guise is hidden the greatest and most powerful princes and emperors of Rome.

Boiardo, for example, had so honoured Hercole d'Este in 1463; Telin had written his *Panegyricque pastourel* for François I in 1534; and in 1559, for the wedding of Philip of Spain to Henri's daughter Elizabeth, François Habert sang of their union in an *Eglogue pastorale*.[79]

In order to give a more precise view of how a major French poet in the sixteenth century filled out his picture of an ideal court, I propose to consider the *Bergerie* of Ronsard. It is important to recognise that it was composed in the middle of a civil war and that it was considered as a kind of antidote to strife and an exhortation towards virtue. In 1562, in his *Discours sur les misères de ce temps*, Ronsard had (at Catherine de' Medici's express command) first tried to intervene in the war and to bring Frenchmen to their senses.[80] Now he adopted another angle. Recognising the difficulties, dangers, and shortcomings of day-to-day politics, he attempts in the *Bergerie* to bring these into clashing contrast with timeless, arcadian harmony, striving not only to make his readers perceive perfection but also to surround them, overwhelm them even, with its special atmosphere.

In this extended poem of praise of the French court, the time is one of celebration, and the festival is given at Fontainebleau.[81] In that magnificent setting of marble fountains and formal gardens, in 'la grande salle du palais' recently beautified by the extravagant decorations of Primaticcio, Rosso, and others, Ronsard very consciously fills out the gentle harmonies of a pastoral scene—an Arcadia within a stately room. Trees, flowers, water, and calm breezes always commanded Ronsard's most lyrical notes, and his *Bergerie* attempts to bring alive a magical world where the rituals and ceremonies of shepherds and nature proceed peacefully. The art of compliment is at the centre of the pastoral mode, whose formulas were so well known in the sixteenth century that the slightest variation appealed to the connoisseur, while the musical and verbal contests indulged in by the shepherds were destined to call forth applause. Ronsard abides by the rules that Theocritus, Virgil, and, later, Sannazaro had formulated; but inside this essentially lyrical work in which he could embroider musical tapestries, he explores (as it was customary to do in the pastoral genre) political dimensions.[82]

The prologue sets an idyllic scene of shade, birdsong, rippling water, and the sound of music, in which choirs of shepherds and nymphs sing the praises of their gentle life. Then, the five principal shepherds—Orleantin, Angelot, Navarrin, Guisin, and Margot—enter to engage in poetic competition, according to an ancient rite. Their poems form the major part of the work. The proceedings are brought to a close by further choruses and the songs of two much-travelled shepherds.

From the outset, it is clear (as it is in most pastoral poems) that these are no ordinary beings: their song is described as sacred, their race as great and dignified, and virtue as intrinsic to their way of life. We are in the presence of the French court. We know that the five main parts were created for the king's two brothers and sister, and for Henri of Navarre and Henri de Guise, and that Catherine and Charles IX were the principal guests at this festival. It is an annual ritual, a time when shepherds come to pay homage to their ruler, when, in gratitude for their comfort and protection, they celebrate with dance and rivalry in song and strew flowers around the altar. The pledges they offer allow Ronsard to sing a slightly different tune each time. Orleantin's wager, for example, evokes the brilliant colours of the natural scene, and he brings to life tender and loving expectation, sweet shade, and leaves moving gently in the breeze in these melodious lines:

> Icy diversement s'émaille la prairie,
> Icy la tendre vigne aux ormeaux se marie,
> Icy l'ombrage frais va ses fueilles mouvant,
> Errantes, ça et là sous l'haleine du vent.[83]

(lines 91–94)

Here the fields are painted in diverse colours, here the tender vine embraces the elm, here fresh shade stirs her leaves, moving back and forth with the breath of the wind.

The rhythm stirs general and archetypal evocations of the beauties of nature and seduces the reader with its harmonies to the extent that, although we expect a political dimension in the poem, we are left totally unprepared for the sudden shattering of peace that occurs with Orleantin's vehement description of mercenaries invading France and of the discord that followed in their wake.[84] A scene peopled only with destruction and infertility is momentarily spread out before us; and then, as abruptly, there is a return to the blessings of peace, whose sweetness, brought about by Queen Catherine, is remarkably enhanced by the fierce reminder of recent troubles.

Aesthetically speaking, it was a bold stroke for Ronsard to break in on the enchantment he had created, and yet he dares still further. In the lines that follow he tries to hold two contrasting pictures in the same view: the distress of the real political situation and an imagined world of pastoral delights. Catherine and Charles IX were always the centre of the celebration, but until now the reasons for the honours done them had been allusively given—the conventional gestures of gratitude, reverence, and obedience from good servants to good kings in a public ceremony. In this next phase of the *Bergerie* (lines 322–448) expressions of praise are more precisely based. The songs echo quite accurately the political maneuvring that had been going on since March 1563, with the attempted French alliances with Spain, England, and Italy, made needful by the calamitous death of Henri II. Faithfulness in reporting of political and diplomatic dealings was no doubt essential in a work played before the knowledgeable court. Much more challenging, however, was the attempt to create, in parallel, a convincing vision of the attractions of peace and to make that vision so compelling that noble performers and spectators might be transported by it, and, as a consequence, be encouraged to prolong its effects in real life. Ronsard thus sought to bend his style to what had happened and to what should happen—Bacon's *is* and *ought to be*.

Each singer, therefore, passes from specific references to the contemporary political scene to his own version of an enchanted world embroidered with details drawn from a complex tradition of golden ages and of earthly and heavenly paradises.[85] The scene then moves from the pastoral joys of earth to a celestial vision of Catherine's late husband.

> Ainsi qu'un beau soleil entre les belles ames
> Environné d'esclairs, de rayons et de flames,
> Tu reluis dans le Ciel. . . .

(lines 471–73)

Like a splendid sun among good souls, surrounded with brilliant rays and rich colour, you shine out in heaven. . . .

Working with elements conventionally associated with paradise and through general suggestions, Ronsard tried (in expanding this idea) to convey a feeling of blessed tranquillity and of permanence. He evokes a world of joy where pure air, perpetual light, luminous colours, trees, flowers, and plants of a perfection unknown to man flourish eternally. A vision of the golden age follows (lines 511–86): a powerful evocation, presented nostalgically. Idealised in the past and promised for the future, Ronsard's golden age beckons invitingly; it represents a way of life to be sought after and made all the more desirable as painful remainders of present war and discord are interlaced and stand between a lost Eden and a hoped-for paradise. Many conventional touches enter Ronsard's projection of a land of leisure and plenty, glowing in sunshine, song, and virtue. There is no winter, no suffering, no work, no war, no disagreement, no legal dispute, and no vice; and since gods, men, and beasts commune freely together, there is abundant innocence, goodness, and liberty, and, above all, harmony and peace.[86]

It is not without significance that Ronsard juxtaposes this vision of the golden age with Margot's hymn on the glories of France, which surpasses 'cette vieille Arcadie':

Soleil source du feu, haute merveille ronde,
Soleil, l'Ame, l'Esprit, l'Oeil, la beauté du monde
Tu as beau t'éveiller de bon matin, et choir
Bien tard dedans la Mer, tu ne sçaurois rien voir
Plus grand que nostre France.

(lines 689–93)

O Sun, source of fire, o great round marvel, Sun, the Soul, the Mind, the Eye, and Beauty of the world, you might well wake early, and descend tardily into the sea, you will never see anything as great as our France.

These lines give some idea of Ronsard's expansive enthusiasm as he lists the mountains and rich pastures, the ripe fruits and broad rivers, the proud cities and the French race of heroes. Ronsard's purpose is twofold: to suggest that France is a country ideally suited to a return of some golden age and to prepare Charles IX for an extended lesson in kingship. Two shepherds end the *Bergerie* with songs of undisguised instruction on the familiar themes of virtue, justice, honour, faith, and liberality. The magical world was a necessary preparation for attempting to inculcate notions essential to a king if he was to accept the challenge of attempting to change the grim reality of civil war. With political conditions so appalling and a king so young (Charles IX was fourteen in 1564), Ronsard did not attempt to maintain the traditional anonymous voice of the pastoral poet.[87] His enterprise had, as we argued, a double purpose: on the one hand, to discover ways of giving listeners a share in a privileged world and of encouraging them through a participation in its delights to give some kind of permanency to its elevated existence. On the other, he felt obliged to state with stark clarity the conditions necessary for such an achievement and the terrible consequences of failure.

In other words, like all great artists, he sought to give his work a feeling of timelessness while injecting specific references to political events.[88] The ideal court depicted in the *Bergerie* has a fragile existence; conjured up entirely through lyrical effusion and painted set pieces (see chapter 5), its present life seems less secure than its past glories—an impression underlined by the urgent advice tendered by the shepherds at the end. It may well be that, in the final analysis, the *Bergerie* leans too consciously on the pastoral tradition and that it lacks the control and coherence of tone and the dramatic power to make of it a substantial work of art. Yet it has moments of great lyrical beauty and rhythmic power, and these coincide with evocations of the natural harmony that belongs to Ronsard's conception in the poem of an ideal court. It is crucial, therefore, for twentieth-century readers to see that this encomiastic poem is not a strange anomaly in Ronsard's corpus but that it expresses the political and poetic aspirations fervently held at the time. For the sixteenth century, praise does not constrain; it offers a challenge and a liberation. Certainly, contemporaries appreciated the festival. Catherine used the volume in which the *Bergerie* appeared in 1565 as part of her diplomatic overtures to Elizabeth I, and Nicholas Filleul borrowed lavishly from Ronsard when he mounted his celebrations before the king and queen mother at Gaillon in late September 1566.[89]

Poetry and Celebration

The *Bergerie* provides an impressive example of the kind of task Ronsard had set himself from the beginning of his poetic career. In the preface to the *Bocage* (1550) he had declared: 'C'est le vray but d'un poète lyrique de celebrer jusques à l'extremité ce qu'il entreprend de louer' (It's the true goal of a lyric poet to celebrate to the limit anything he undertakes to praise).[90] In stating this aim so firmly, he echoed the ideas of many colleagues. One thinks, for example, of Du Bellay's assumption that a poet's business concerns 'les louanges des dieux et des hommes vertueux' (the praise of gods and men of virtue) or of Pasquier's remarks: 'car, quant à la Plume du Poëte, elle doit estre vouée à la célébration de ceux qui le méritent' (because, as far as the poet's pen is concerned, it must be dedicated to the celebration of those who merit it).[91] Such affirmations justified the soaring images of flight that Ronsard and Du Bellay borrowed from Pindar;[92] but Ronsard was also (quite consciously) reiterating a view about the elevated nature of poetry that had been at the origin of Greek verse. For Hesiod or Pindar, the noble art of poetry was made to pour forth praises. *Chanter un poème* was then (as in the sixteenth century) synonymous with *celebrer, venerer, consacrer*, with *voler éternellement, beatifier, immortaliser*, and even *stellifier*; and such images are found in the writings of all these poets. Moreover, as we have seen, the extended theoretical discussions that surrounded Aristotle's *Poetics* (especially in Italy) supported these assumptions about poetry and celebration.[93]

If we consider poetic practice—Hesiod's *Hymn to the Muses* or Ronsard's *Ode à Michel de l'Hospital* and *Ode à Joachim du Bellay*—the claims do not seem exaggerated, as in each case the poetic enthusiasm soars. In Hesiod's ode, the muses breathed their inspiration into the poet 'that I might celebrate the things to be and the things that were before'.[94] Thus the role of the poet is seen as twofold: preserving and commemorating that which was already in being and creating the forms of the future. At the centre of the *Ode à Michel de l'Hospital*, Ronsard not only eloquently articulates the preserving and surviving power of poetry but also goes one step further and includes the power of moving listeners, and through these heightened feelings of transporting them onto a higher level of perception: 'levent en haut les hommes' (raise up the spirit of man).[95] In the poem this is the wish that is granted by Zeus to Calliope, the muse of poetry, when she asked for what all great poets yearn to have:

> Donne nous encor la puissance
> D'arracher les ames dehors
> Le sale bourbier de leurs corps,
> Pour les rejoindre à leur naissance.[96]
>
> (P 1:395; L 3:139)

Grant us also the power to snatch souls from the filth of their bodies and return them to the place of their birth.

This gift infused in poets and in their works a quality of life that was more vibrant than any lived experience, Ronsard argued in the ensuing stanzas. In the ode dedicated to Du Bellay, Ronsard extended yet again the potential he claimed for the poet. He maintained (as Hesiod had done) that the poet could glimpse the presence of virtue, discover it, and disclose its substance to the world. Of his friend's virtue, he wrote:

> Mais ma plume qui conjecture
> Par son vol sa gloire future
> Se vante de n'endurer pas
> Que la tienne en l'obscur demeure.
>
> (P 1:506; L 2:36)

But my pen by its flight anticipates its future glory, boasts that it will not tolerate that your own stays in obscurity.

The reading public had long been prepared to receive sympathetically these thoughts about the noble and uplifting role of the poet. Readers did not necessarily need to trace the Greek origins of such convictions in order to appreciate their usefulness. Such notions had percolated through the Neoplatonic tradition and had come to them in courtesy books and in Renaissance compendia and handbooks of mythology. The points had been clearly stated by Boccaccio, in about 1366.

> Poetry devotes herself to something greater; for while she dwells in heaven, and mingles with the divine counsels, she moves the minds of a few men from on high to a yearning for the eternal, lifting them by her loveliness to high revery, drawing them away into the discovery of strange wonders, and pouring forth most exquisite discourse from her exalted mind.[97]

Certain poetic forms were considered especially privileged. They had inbuilt heavenly connections. The ode (or hymn) reserved for great occasions—festival days or moments of sacrifice to the gods—was thought to be calculated upon movements of the spheres. According to this view, as poets recited their ode, with their own movements right and left, and through the strophe and antistrophe structure of the verse, they reflected the forward and backward action of the heavenly spheres.

> Il y ha d'autres choses, qui jamais ne se font, et si sont tousjours, c'est à sçavoir les celestes, eternelles et exemptes de tout inconstant changement. Ce que representoient les anciens poëtes Lyriques, qui, chantans aus sacrifices ou publiques ceremonies selon leurs religieuses institutions, se mouvoient au commencement à droite, à gauche, aus nombres et mesures des Strofes, et Antistrofes, refigurans la caduque inconstance, et les variables mouvemens de ça bas: puis quand ils addressoient l'Epode aus Dieus, ils s'arrestoient coy, pour donner entendre que la Divinité repose en lieu ferme, et non inconstant ou muable.[98]

> There are other things that are not created but simply are—that is to say, celestial eternal things, exempt from change. Ancient poets singing at public ceremonies according to religious custom and performing at moments of sacrifice gave them form by movements right and left following the number and measure of the strophes and antistrophes, representing the change and constant movement of the earthly planet; then, when they addressed their epode to the gods, they remained still, thus indicating that divinity belongs to a constant place without motion or variation.

Although this explanation, by Pontus de Tyard, seems unnecessarily complicated, it exemplifies the sixteenth-century belief in the sacred nature of the poet's power. In this context, it is not surprising that Du Bellay should plead with poets to begin to sing French odes,[99] for the ability to do so would, in itself, secure a sufficient status for the poet. Like poets of old, they would become the performers of a god-given art whose form had been designed in direct correspondence with that of the world's motion. By reenacting the movement of the spheres, they would celebrate creation and give expression to feelings of gratitude and admiration to the gods who had made it. Such praise, many writers claimed, such setting forth of 'leurs proüesse et vaillance, et les biens qu'ils avaient faits aux hommes' (their prowess and courage, and the good they have done to men) gave poets an intermediary role between gods and men. Praise was necessary and appropriate to the boons and blessings received; and it ensured that clemency and beneficence continued to be granted to man.[100] Small wonder then, as Sébillet suggests, that hearing the sweetness of the verses sung to the glory of the mightiest of gods, kings themselves 'prirent ensemble envie de s'égaler auz dieuz, et estre comme eux louéz et congnuz a la posterité par le carme de Poëtes' (collectively wished to be equal to gods, and, like them, to be praised and made known to posterity through the songs of poets).[101]

Kings and poets had discovered affinities, and Ronsard writes of poets as he writes of kings: they are both to be held 'en reverence, voire en singuliere veneration' (in reverence, even in singular veneration).[102] This is not mere bombast. Ronsard's purpose is serious: since the poet records the virtues of a great man 'afin que sa vertue soit connue' (in order that his virtue might be made known), he consecrates a reputation by animating virtue, and this, in turn, draws others into that sphere of high achievement. In this way, immortality and moral improvement go hand in hand. Henri II appreciated these matters. He called Ronsard 'sa nourriture', and by doing so, he hoped to earn for himself the reputation of a reign comparable with that of Caesar Augustus.[103]

Henri II and Ronsard

We have discussed sixteenth-century theories relating to the perfect prince, examined ritual presentations of the monarch in France, analysed typical ideal projections of the court, and tried to understand some of the revealing qualities of praise and compliment. It is fitting now to take up again the example of Henri II in order to study the evidence of the king's attention to artists' recording and promotional power, and to discuss the flavour of panegyric in two of the many poems that Ronsard specifically dedicated to him.

In his panegyric on Henri II, published one year after the monarch's death, the historiographer royal, Pierre Paschal, drew particular attention to the late king's love of architecture, in which he is said to have taken singular pleasure. Paschal reminded his readers: 'Tout ainsi qu'il aimoit la cognoissance de toutes choses honnestes, aussi se delectoit-il singuliere-ment de l'Architecture. Il fait bastir en plusieurs endroits, au temps de son regne' (Just as he loved knowledge of all things honorable, so he was par-ticularly fond of architecture. During his reign, he had buildings con-structed in many places).[104] Works had indeed flourished around him in all the royal palaces throughout his reign. Philibert de l'Orme extended the rooms at Fontainebleau and filled them with new paintings and with the king's ever-growing collections of arms and armour (fig. 13). He worked

13. Nicholas Beatrizet, engraving of Henri II (Bibliothèque Nationale).

at Chambord, completed the chapel at Vincennes (1551–53), transformed the Louvre, designed and built pavilions and a theatre at Saint-Germain (1558), and created the elegant château d'Anet (1547–52) for Diane de Poitiers. The king's love of sumptuous buildings was unrestricted, as can be seen from an early edict that commanded 'l'amplification et decoration des villes de son royaume' (the aggrandisement and decoration of all the towns in his kingdom).[105] Clearly, Henri II subscribed to the view expounded by Castiglione in the fourth book of *The Courtier*, that it is becoming and noble in a prince 'to make great buildings for his honour in life, and to a memorie of him to his posteritie'.[106] Many writers commented on the superb palaces built by recent French kings and deemed their magnificence such that 'l'antiquité mesme les pourrot admirer'.[107] According to Nicolas Hoüel, Henri II's knowledge of building (and, incidentally, the expertise of his wife on these matters) went far beyond what could be expected of a great prince.[108] Master builders, architects, and translators—Philibert, Sebastiano Serlio, and Jean Martin (who Frenchified Vitruvius)—eagerly dedicated their works to him; and successive Venetian ambassadors marvelled at the expense of his court.[109] Not only the profusion of palaces but the elaborate decorations within them emphasise the king's concern for visual display of power. Primaticcio's work in Henri II's ballroom at Fontainebleau provides an excellent example. The proportions of the room are immense, and mythological subjects swarm over the packed ceiling and around the walls. Fireplaces, window frames, and the minstrels' gallery are marked out with startling white stucco figures, and each compartment in ceiling and wall is edged with elaborate and fantastic arabesques as though some horror would be visited on any sign of vacuum, however small.[110] Colour and texture from gold-leaf embossed carvings added to the effect of splendour (fig. 14). Like words on a page, images were messages of royal power.

Henri II's tastes were generous: 'La libéralité te rend égal aux Dieux' (Generosity makes you equal to the gods; Ronsard, *Hymne de Henri II*); but his liberality was often the result of a corresponding favour from the courtier, artist, or writer. Apparently, he was the first French king to decree that a royal grant to publish would only be forthcoming after a writer had submitted a copy of his work 'imprimé en parchemin, de velin, riche et couvert comme il appartient luy être présenté' (printed on parchment and bound in rich vellum, as a king ought to have presented to him).[111] Ronsard's *Louanges du roi Henri*, 'un manuscrit en rime française, relié en parchemin' (a manuscript in French verse, bound in parchment), and 'Les hymnes de Ronsard en parchemin', found in the duke of Montmorency's small library of thirty books in 1556, were probably the kind of presentation copies of the *Odes* (1550) and the *Hymnes* (1555) that Henri II had in mind.[112]

14. Fontainebleau, *Salle de bal* (Château de Fontainebleau, Cliché Esparcieux).

Let us now turn to Ronsard's poems. The ode that begins 'Comme un qui prend une coupe' (Like one who takes a cup) is the second of the two opening poems dedicated to Henri II from the first book of *Odes*, published in 1550. Ronsard conceives the poem as a toast, as an appropriate start to his poetic banquet—five books of odes—which is to be abundantly laced with the wine of Pindar and sweetened with the honey of Horace:

Comme un qui prend une coupe,
Seul honneur de son tresor,
Et de rang verse a la troupe
Du vin qui rit dedans l'or
Ainsi versant la rousee
Dont ma langue est arousee

Sur la race des Valois
En son doux Nectar j'abreuve
Le plus grand Roy qui se treuve
Soit en armes, ou en lois.

(P 1 : 368; L 1 : 61)

Like one who takes a cup, sole honour of his treasure, and, according to
their rank, pours for each the laughing wine into the golden cup, thus pour-
ing the dew that flows from me onto the race of the Valois, in its sweet nectar, I drink to the greatest king that can be found whether in feats of arms or
in his laws.

The gesture of a toast allows us to glimpse the richness of his glass and the
joyous radiance of the wine, which, as it is savoured, brings delight as we
recognise (if we do) the echoes from Pindaric odes that praised the soaring
force of poetry. The poet's singing power and the grandeur of his theme—
the house of Valois, Henri II's martial prowess, and his regard for the
law—blend, as though naturally together, in the simple action of tasting
wine. The manner and implications of their blending are explained by
Ronsard's friend Jean Martin, who, in his commentary on the poem,
wrote:

Le poete est maistre du banquet, sa riche tasse est son hinne, parce qu'elle
reçoit toutes choses, le vin excelant c'est le don des Muses, le Roi, c'est son
hôte ou convié, abreuvé de telle liqueur.[113]

The poet is master of the banquet; his gold cup represents his hymn because
it accepts all things; the excellent wine is the gift of the Muses; the king is his
guest, celebrated by such a toast.

Obviously it is no vulgar toast, for (as Martin has made clear) the wine is
the drink of the gods. Further resonances add to the sense of celebration;
these are already established in the mind, for it so happens that at other
equally solemn moments, distinguished poets and poet-kings had raised
their golden glasses in joy and thanksgiving. Ronsard was doubtless thinking of Pindar, who had announced the poet in his seventh Olympiad:
'Comme un homme opulent prend en main une coupe, où bouillonne la
rosée de la vigne' (Like a rich man who takes in his hands the cup where
the dew of the wine bubbles) and of King David, who had expressed similar ebullience in one of his psalms:

Que ma coupe enyvrante
Est belle et excellente,[114]

How beautiful and excellent is my cup that brings excitement, where drink is the sign of overflowing contentment in those enjoying the fruits of paradise. Whether Ronsard intended us to pick up these allusions or not, there is no gainsaying that, in this opening stanza, he has sought to create an exceptional atmosphere—one of exhilaration and excitement.

The most complete exploration, however, that he gave to the ideal king set in his ideal court, is found in the *Hymne de Henri II de ce nom* of 1555, which, as we indicated earlier, might have inspired the ceiling frescoes at Tanlay.[115] The climax to this long poem is the extended comparison of Henri II and his court to that of Olympus; and Ronsard explains the parallel to the Muses, as 'pour dignement orner vostre frere mon Roy' (to provide decorations worthy of my king, your brother; line 22).[116] Henri himself, a magnificent figure at the centre of the pomp, is surrounded by Vulcan, Mars, Mercury, Apollo, and Neptune, by Pallas, Themis, Minerva, and Juno. Within the general structure of the poem, the comparison is made to appear as the natural culminating point, prepared from the opening lines of the hymn that introduce Jupiter and Henri as mirror images reflecting dignity and honour:

> Muses, quand nous voudrons des Dieux nous souvenir
> Il faut, les celebrant, commencer et finir
> Au pere Jupiter.
> . . . .
> Mais lorsque nous voudrons chanter l'honneur des Rois
> Il faudra par Henry, Monarque des François
> Commencer et finir.
>
> (lines 1–3, 5–7)

O Muses, when we wish to remember the Gods we must, in celebrating them, begin and end with Father Jupiter. . . . But when we wish to sing the honours of kings we must with Henri, king of the French, begin and end.

At first, it seems that Henri merely reflects a paler, earthly image of the celestial power enjoyed by Jupiter. However, as the poem unfolds, the same ceremonies and rituals due to the king of the gods, victorious against the warring giants, are enacted on behalf of the king of France. Ronsard takes on the role of Apollo to sing the praises of Henri's triumphant majesty; and his celebration assumes epic scale as echoing blocks of lines, organised according to the rhetorical rules of praise that Ronsard knew well, enthusiastically relate the qualities expected of kings and found in abundance, so the poet argues, in Henri II.

'Entré dans ton palais devant ta Majesté' (within the palace, before your Majesty; line 34): this is the strong visual impact of kingly magnificence that Ronsard holds out to arouse astonishment and fervour. The poet tries to make the visual splendour in the poem work in the same way as the sight of majesty at the coronation; both excite because, in sixteenth-century terms, both have symbolic power: they are the outward signs of harmony, justice and order in good government, and the virtues attaching to the good prince. The court is portrayed as Guillaume Budé had painted it, 'comme un lieu où il se fait un perpetuel spectacle d'honneur' (as a place where a perpetual scene of honour can be found); and, as the poet continues his epic account, he analyses in Henri II all those qualities that made of him the supreme courtier as well as the good ruler. Foremost among these virtues are the martial arts. A startlingly vivid picture of physical strength emerges as Ronsard relates Henri's athletic skills, his superior powers of fencing and of riding even recalcitrant steeds. The robust vitality of the king in action comes through immediately in the turbulent sweep of lines calculated to call forth again the sweat, the zeal, and the triumph and designed to please a king and a court that thought so highly of honour and revelled in physical combat:

> Quant à bien manier et piquer un cheval,
> La France n'eut jamais, ny n'aura, ton egal,
> Et semble que ton corps naisse hors de la selle,
> Centaure mi-cheval, soit que, poulain rebelle,
> Il ne vueille tourner, ou soit que, façonné,
> Tu le face volter, d'un peuple environné
> Qui pres de toy s'acoude au long de la barriere,
> Ou soit qu'à sauts gaillars, ou soit qu'en la carriere,
> Ou soit qu'à bride ronde, ou en long manié
> Ta main ait au cheval avec le frein lié
> Un entendement d'homme, à fin de te complaire,
> Et ensemble esbahir les yeux du populaire.
> D'une sueuse escume il est tout blanchissant,
> De ses nazeaux ouverts une flame est yssant,
> Le frein luy sonne aux dents, il bat du pied la terre,
> Il hannit, il se tourne, aucunefois il serre
> Une oreille derriere, et fait l'autre avancer,
> Il tremble tout sous toy, et ne peut r'amasser,
> Son vent entre les flancs, monstrant par un tel sine
> Qu'il cognoist bien qu'il porte une charge divine.

(lines 81−100)

For handling a horse and spurring him on—France has never had, and will never see, your like; your body seems to rise from the saddle, centaurlike, whether your rebellious steed refuses to turn; or whether, well trained and prepared, you make him jump before the assembled crowd that leans close along the wooden balustrade; or whether he leaps with lively gait along the course or with reins held tight or loosely threaded through, your hand commands, from the horse, it binds human understanding; in order to do your pleasure and to astonish the gaze of the populace, frothing with sweat, he seems all white, from his wide nostrils flames issue forth, the bit sounds against his teeth, his feet beat the ground, he neighs, turns, and sometimes cocks back an ear and thrusts the other forward, he shakes beneath his flanks, showing by these signs that he knows well that he carries a divine charge.

Ronsard has, I think, refreshingly activated a traditional picture. Henri II had already been given the conventional virtues of the perfect prince; liberal, hardworking, clement, listening to good counsel, obedient to the laws and traditions of his country, and reverent to his father and mother, who are shown gazing down from heaven with approval at their son's achievements. But in this passage, within a traditional frame of virtues appropriate to his function and alongside generalisations about good kings, Henri II is recognisably himself, and the military triumphs that Ronsard later recalls are real ones.

It is no inconsiderable achievement to have fused the function and the person without leaving a trace of contradiction. Henri's majesty, like Jupiter's, is stout and vigorous; and it, in turn, is made to correspond to the abundant energies of his people and to the riches of the lands that Ronsard has evoked in support of his vision of the olympic court. Rich towns, fertile crops, forests, good climate, craftsmen, poets, and artists crowd his empire, their efforts all struck in the single cause of doing honour to the powerful majesty of France, from whom all things are made and have their being:

> Pour toy le jour se leve en ta France, et la Mer
> Fait pour toy tout autour ses vagues escumer;
> Pour toy la terre est grosse, et tous les ans enfante;
> Pour toy, des grans forests la toison renaissante
> Tous les ans se refrise, et les fleuves, sinon
> Ne courent dans la mer, que pour bruire ton nom.[117]

(lines 56−62)

For you, day breaks in your France, and the sea for you makes its waves froth around; for you, the earth teams and every year gives birth; for you, the great forests every year renew their green leaves, and the rivers flow into the seas, only to sound your name.

Ronsard has expressed in these swelling, harmonious lines a dazzling and fervent picture of natural order, continuity, richness, and plenty, which fittingly belonged to France-Olympus. Through such lines, he has tried to transmit something of the amazing impact he experienced when he appeared before the king—'entré en ton palais devant ta Majesté' (once in your palace, before your Majesty). They fill out the nature of that majesty and carry into a larger marketplace the image that Budé had seen and that

Erasmus had so persistently advocated. The reader is swept along by a powerful current of enthusiasm, which projects a living image of an ideal prince. Such is the tone and flavour of Ronsard's panegyric. Such is the vision he has chosen, as poet, to satisfy the king's image of himself; to give moving and concrete expression to the counsels of political men like Budé, Erasmus, or l'Hôpital; and (perhaps, above all) to match the splendour of paintings and palaces. It is in the context of political and artistic aspiration that Ronsard's poems must be seen, and in the next chapter we will explore more specifically analogies between the arts and their relation to praise.

II

ART AND POETRY PARALLELS IN SIXTEENTH·CENTURY FRANCE

La poesie est une peinture parlante,
et la peinture une poesie muette.

BLAISE DE VIGENÈRE
Images de Philostrate

Poetry is a speaking picture and
painting is mute poetry.

A Common Aesthetic

In the middle years of the sixteenth century (1540–70) abundant were the links—both practical and theoretical—that drew together French poets and those artists who worked in paint and marble or who designed jewels and enamelled luxury goods. The pioneering studies of Lee and Gombrich and the later work of Hagstrum, Spencer, and Praz have made familiar the reasons that art and poetry were so intimately connected in sixteenth-century aesthetics and that interart analogies were commonplace.[1] Although poetry and art were not considered identical twins, they were thought of as sisters and brothers, with the same likenesses, differences, and rivalries as siblings.[2] Several factors had drawn them thus together. Classical and Renaissance critics consistently argued that both arts worked towards the same ends: both sought to imitate nature and, through their presentation, to instruct readers or viewers by stimulating their emotions. The power to move the mind depended, in turn, on the artist's or poet's ability to select details from nature and assemble them in a striking way, and these imitations were shaped and perfected according to rhetorical rules that both arts obeyed. A common system of patronage with its own demands for ideal performances seemed to tie the two arts even more closely together. The idea of their consanguinity is therefore not surprising, nor is the popularity of this idea, which can be gauged from Hagstrum's analysis of later writers' uses and distortions of classical ideas on this topic.[3]

Despite abundant evidence of the widespread acceptance of the notion of 'sister arts' in the sixteenth century, scholars have largely ignored France, even in theoretical discussions. In applied studies, too, there has been comparatively little investigation into the effect on a major poet, such as Ronsard, of contemporary awareness of the closeness of poetry and art. Two possible explanations for this neglect suggest themselves. Let us continue to take Ronsard as our principal witness. First, interest in Ronsard and the relationship of his work to the visual arts has been confined to two rather narrow issues: the wish, on the one hand, to determine how far the term *mannerist* might be a useful tool for the analysis of poetry; and the concern, on the other, to establish facts about Ronsard's biography and especially about his financial situation in comparison with that of contemporary painters and architects.[4] These approaches yield valuable insights but fail to relate Ronsard's concern with arts other than his own to an overall aesthetic strategy. Second, perhaps such comparative studies as have been attempted for other writers have, more often than not, exposed the difficulties of the task. For example, Praz and Hatzfeld on the whole make only rather loose thematic and general connections, while Pickering devastatingly expounds on the dangers and impossibilities of his undertaking in *Literature and Art in the Middle Ages*, warning scholars to beware distortion from overselection or removal from context.[5]

A further preliminary problem in comparative studies concerns the nature of the two arts: although both attempted to achieve the same purpose —that of imitating in paint or words what can be observed in the world— painting is a spatial medium and poetry a temporal form. We must always keep this difference in mind, holding before us the example of Michelangelo, whose sonnets in no way aid the study of his paintings. A final difficulty, our relative ignorance of sixteenth-century French works of art, has been partially remedied by recent scholarship. Research on sixteenth-century designs for tapestries, murals, jewels, and medals, and discoveries and positive attributions of drawings for armour and horse furniture now enable scholars to attempt an analysis of poetry in relation to this new mass of information concerning the decorative arts.[6]

New material makes such a study possible; aesthetic considerations make it imperative. For the very force and frequency with which poets and artists expressed their common functions, argued parallel claims, and spoke the same aesthetic language give an historian some confidence in pursuing this difficult approach, despite the problems outlined above. Let us examine these common thoughts.

Much of the discussion about artistic function revolved around the power of the visual image. Its central place in painting is obvious; yet, as early as 1435, Alberti sought to stress its significance and to argue its particular moving power in *Della Pittura*, a treatise whose structure and polemical tone were demonstrably borrowed from rhetoric.[7] If the immediacy of image and emotion could thus be brought together, then visual artists seemed to have a certain superiority in expressive power. Moreover, it was fairly generally accepted in the Renaissance that the eye was the noblest of the senses, 'le sens qui touche de plus près et a plus d'acointance et correspondance à nostre âme que nul aultre' (the sense that is the most acute and that corresponds, more than any other, to our mind).[8] The eye was also considered the most effective receiving organ of the body:

Segnius irritant animos demissa per aurem
Quam quae sunt oculis subiecta fidelibus.[9]

What enters through the ears, stirs the mind more feebly than what is placed before the trustworthy eyes.

Poets recognised the strength of such assertions and arguments, and assimilated them to their own art. In 1578, Blaise de Vigenère might well have been translating the same Neoplatonic ideas which had been borrowed by the painters when he wrote that images in writing 'nous introduisent les choses plus distinctement en l'apprehension; nous les approchent trop mieux du sentiment; et les impriment plus vivement en la congnoissance' (bring things more clearly to our understanding; impress them upon our emotions more sharply; and imprint them firmly into our memory).[10] The qualities that he claims here for the image—clarity, emotional density, and lasting power—are, however, those which French poets, since the 1540s, had sought to achieve in their works; and their efforts had had important consequences for poetry. The melodious simplicity and technical virtuosity of Marot, for instance, had by Vigenère's time been replaced by the large rhythmic harmonies and ornate tapestries of a Ronsard. Interestingly, this stress upon the importance and emotive power of the image parallels the prevailing views on political propaganda. When Henri II commanded his engravers Delaune or Béchot to produce images worthy of him, it was because he appreciated how powerfully the image could speak. Thus, the interests of kings, poets, and artists all converged towards the image as the best form of giving vividness to their impressions and, consequently, of ensuring that the reader or beholder would be adequately moved. Many are the accounts of the powerful exploitation of visual images, but perhaps a seventeenth-century historian of ancient art, Franciscus Junius, catches best the general tone of such remarks when he exclaims:

Both [poetry and painting] doe wind themselves by an unsensible delight of admiration so closely into our hearts, that they make us in such an astonishment of wonder to stare upon the Imitation of things naturall, as if we saw the true things themselves.[11]

Liveliness and truthfulness in the imitation are the elements that were thought to produce delight; and, indeed these criteria were used in any judgement of a good poem or painting. 'Rendre au vif' (making true to life) was an overriding concern. Since it is encountered everywhere in the sixteenth century, it suffices here to quote two of the more explicit statements to convey their generally confident tone. Dolce affirmed in his extended discussion of the resemblance of painting and poetry, in *L'Aretino* (published 1557), that 'the closer to nature a man comes in his work, the more perfect a master he is'; while Jacques Tahureau summarily asserted:

Les poëmes plus parfaicts
Doivent ressembler aux traicts
Du bon peintre qui prent cure
De rendre au vif la nature.[12]

The most perfect poems must resemble the marks of the good painter who takes care to make Nature lifelike.

The assumption that 'rendre au vif' was the main business of artist and poet brought with it signal aesthetic advantages. It enabled the painter to show off his skills in representation and to display his ability to select and project details and gestures that were realistic. But, in his re-presentation of the world 'au vif', in order to strike the onlooker, he was required to shape those details and those gestures. To make them affective involved a transformation or a painting up, and his presentation of the world became its illustration.[13] Similarly, the poet who saw his task as translating vividly into words the riches of nature, became more overtly engaged in the process of textual elaboration.

In this context, the full force of the title of Du Bellay's manifesto *Deffence et illustration de la langue françoyse* can be appreciated. The word *illustration*, with its twin meanings of 'explanation' and 'rendering illustrious', is a prominent sign of the central preoccupation of the poet. For Du Bellay clarity and richness of language were necessary starting points, while the resources of the French language had to be extended to meet the declared aims of re-presenting the world. Adjectives, comparisons, periphrasis and other rhetorical devices, and the use of myth were advocated as ways of achieving such an enrichment.[14] In his discussion of the varied figures and ornaments of poetry, Du Bellay stressed particularly the importance of giving a lifelike quality to forms. In order to explain his ideas of lifelikeness he used the term *energie* (*enargia*), which he borrowed from Quintilian and Denys of Halicarnassus,[15] a term that brings us back to the primacy of the image and again highlights the affinities of poetry and painting. Both classical writers could have been referring to either art in their explanations of this figure. Denys of Halicarnassus defines *enargia* as 'rendre les choses sensibles aux yeux par un style tout en images' (making things alive to the eyes with a style all made up of images), while Quintilian suggests that the best way of achieving *enargia* is 'by which the whole figure of an object is painted as it were in words'.[16]

Ronsard and Belleau both responded with fervour and enthusiasm (some would say with too much of both) to the challenge posed by Du Bellay.[17] Ronsard saw his role as the poet who describes, illustrates, decorates, praises, and amplifies; and, at the end of his life, he still clung to a view of poetry as an expansive and decorating art. He was, in fact, justifying his own earlier practice when he charged would-be poets to:

> Illustrer ton oeuvre de paroles recherchées et choisies . . . tantost par fables, tantost par quelques vieilles histoires . . . l'enrichissant d'epithetes significatifs et non oisifs. . . .
>
> (P 2 : 1017; L 16 : 337)

> Illustrate your work with learned, well-chosen words . . . now with fables, now with an old story . . . enriching it with important adjectives that signify. . . .

Ronsard was aware of the dangers inherent in a style so committed to elaboration, and his advice to poets includes a warning against overindulgence in the use of myths or periphrasis, pointing out how easy it is to render a work 'plus enflé et boufi que plein de majesté' (longer and inflated rather than filled with majesty).

Nonetheless, Ronsard's own bold conceptions were what commanded his contemporaries' respect and admiration. They saw in them two essential qualities needed for their approval: the accuracy and freshness of the representation, and the expressive power generated. Their esteem is cogently expressed by Du Bellay in his *Discours au Roy sur la poésie*, where he compares the work of the historian Paschal and the poet Ronsard. Both are true to their theme, but the latter by his art, by his language and through the use of myth dares and achieves more:

> Cestuy-cy [Ronsard] plus hardi, d'un art non limité
> Sous mille fictions cache la vérité,
> Comme un peinctre qui faict d'une brave entreprise
> La figure d'un camp ou d'une ville prise,
> Un orage, une guerre, ou mesme il fait les Dieux

La façon de mortelz se monstrer à noz yeux.
Tel que ce premier là [Paschal] est vostre Janet, SIRE,
Et tel que le second [Ronsard], Michelange on peult dire.

This one [Ronsard] is more audacious, through an art unbounded and beneath a thousand fictions hides the truth, like a painter who, out of the rude
battle, paints the shape of the camp or of the captured town, a storm, a war, or
even the Gods, he shows them as mortals to our eyes. As the first [Paschal] is
your Janet, Sire, so the second [Ronsard] is, one might say, Michelangelo.

The power to record accurately an event or a likeness is given to every
good historian, poet, and painter; but few have the genius that transforms
a mundane or even an important experience so it survives as permanently
significant. In his appreciation of Ronsard's dash or fire and of Michelangelo's force, Du Bellay claims for them here that immortality which Pindar had argued for those poets who could lift an event into timelessness.[18]

As Ronsard's own remarks indicate, he consciously sought a language
that would match such exalted ideas, a language made 'de belles et excel-
lentes paroles et phrases non vulgaires, qui te contraignent d'enlever ton
esprit *oultre* le parler commun' (of excellent, high-sounding words and
phrases, which oblige you to lift up your mind and speech beyond common parlance). Beyond the commonplace—he envisages the poet at work
in an elevated world, concerned to raise man's spirit to higher things. Thus
he advises the poet: 'esmouvoir les passions et affections de l'ame, car c'est
la meilleure partie de ton mestier' (move the feelings, stir the soul's passions, because that's the best part of your job).[19] In his vast poetic output,
however, Ronsard did not always control that great range of feeling which
Du Bellay argued the great poet must arouse:

Celuy sera veritablement le poëte que je cherche en nostre langue, qui me
fera indigner, apayser, ejouyr, douloir, aymer, hayr, admirer, etonner, bref,
qui tiendra la bride de mes affections, me tournant ça et la à son plaisir.[20]

He is the true poet I search for in our language who can make me angry,
subdued, joyous, sorrowful, bitter, full of hate, admiring, astonished; in
short, one who can hold sway over my passions, turning them hither and
thither according to his pleasure.

But Ronsard's very excesses testify to a determination to write in ways that
would move his reader deeply. Or, to express his endeavour in a fashion
more akin to his own thinking: by a renewal of forms and of language, he
sought to produce effects similar to those engineered by painters and
sculptors of ancient times. These are the effects admired by Junius, who
cited with approval Sallust's report that the 'great men of our city, were
wont to say, that they felt their mindes mightily inflamed to *vertue* when
they did but look upon the Images of their Ancestors'.[21]

It was inevitable that arts which claimed the same purpose and attempted the same rousing effects should see themselves sometimes as complementing each other and sometimes as rivals. The Renaissance habit of comparing the excellence of the various arts had turned artists' minds to competition,[22] so that Leonardo and Michelangelo, for instance, eloquently argued the superiority of painting and sculpture over all other arts, while Du Bellay, Ronsard, and a host of other poets set out similar claims of superiority for poetry. Arguments multiplied on the greater knowledge (technical and philosophical) needed for poet or painter, on whether painters and poets had equalled the achievements of Greek and Latin masters,[23] and on the status of each art. Should painting, for example, be classified as a liberal art, as Leonardo and Alberti claimed, or set down as a practical science, as Barthélémy de Chasseneux thought when he placed architecture alongside agriculture and trade in his *Catalogus gloriae mundi*, a point of view shared by Cardan and later by Vossius.[24]

The social conditions of poets and painters at court in mid-sixteenth-century France positively encouraged such competitive spirit. For obvious reasons, painters and architects saw their patrons as wealthy and aristocratic; and since grandees at the French court sought to follow the example of their king in financing the magnificent dwellings and commissioning expensive works of art, artists had ample opportunity to demonstrate their expertise. Usually, they were themselves amply rewarded with generous pensions and noble homes. In this context, a poet felt that he had somehow to create works which could successfully compete with those of painters and engravers. This sense of challenge explains the combative tone poets frequently adopted when writing about their art. From the beginning of his career, Ronsard, for example, saw writing as a competitive enterprise and his own performance as the winning of a race:

> Mais quand tu m'appelleras le premier auteur lyrique François et celuy qui a guidé les autres au chemin de si honneste labeur, lors tu me rendras ce que tu me dois.
>
> (P 2:971, L 1:43)[25]
>
> When you call me the foremost French writer of lyrics and the one who has guided others along the road of honest toil, then you will grant me what you owe.

Also, the readers he assumes for his poems have the same qualities of connoisseurship and courtliness and the same social standing as the artists' patrons; he calls them 'gentils esprits, ardans de la vertu . . . tels debonnaires lecteurs' (gentle spirits, ardent for virtue . . . such are [my] well-born readers)—adjectives he was to apply to Homer in his *Art poétique* (1565).[26]

Increasingly, claims and counterclaims became more extravagant. Sapet, for instance, argued that the poet is better than the painter because he is inspired: poets 'sont prophetes et truchemens des dieus . . . sont les Theologiens, ils sont des magiciens . . . Dieu les a surcités pour escripvre l'histoire de ses faictz' ([poets] are prophets and interpreters of Gods . . . they are theologians, magicians . . . God has given them being that they might write the story of his deeds).[27] Philibert de l'Orme, not to be outdone, drew impressive parallels between the creative powers of harmony achieved in architecture and those of the universe; but these he might have taken almost word for word from the elaborate claims of Louis le Caron in his *Dialogues*.[28] Martin, in contrast, in a preface to his translation of Vitruvius, wrote fervently of the public profit that comes to a kingdom through the work of painters and architects.[29]

It would be tedious to itemize the numerous examples of such excessive claims. In the competitive atmosphere of the court they were inescapable. However, the very need to defend and attack, the necessity of persuading a patron of their worth, led both artist and poet to an increased awareness of the nature of their work. Competition made them analyse more precisely what could be achieved through their individual skills; and this, in turn, brought about a considerable refining of their ideas about themselves. This refining process involved a closer examination of aesthetic norms and takes us to the heart of their artistic practice.

In attempting to define these norms poet and painter tended to borrow each other's terms. For example, Titian often exploited literary sources (especially Ovid) or he turned to the *Imagines* of the elder Philostratus, who had provided Renaissance artists with an extraordinarily rich fund of appreciation of ancient art.[30] The *Bacchanal of the Andrians* (1518–19), for instance, is specifically inspired by one of the Philostratus's descriptions (*Imagines* 1:25). Titian's appreciation of the programmatic nature of early wall paintings illuminates his thought about his own work.[31] His paintings told a story and were intended to be *read* as such, their myths unravelled and interpreted as in a narrative. He makes this clear in his correspondence with Philip II, where he consistently refers to the set of mythological paintings he was working on between 1554 and 1562 as *poesie* or *favole*, implying that his *Venus and Adonis* or his *Danae* were conceived of as painted poems or fables. Ludovico Dolce, too, in writing about Titian's work, speaks of them as poems.[32]

Critics largely respected the standards of the ancients in assessing any work of art; and certain key words—*grace*, the *natural*, *decorum*, and *variety*—constantly recur in their writing. Their first concern, it seems, was to judge whether an artist had achieved grace, as we observe in Giovio writing on art, Serlio describing a building, Dolce or Vasari commenting on a painting, Du Bellay or Sir Philip Sidney judging a poem.[33] Marot's work is favourably assessed by Guillaume Des Autelz as having 'une admirable douceur et naïve grace que les Grecs appellent Charité' (admirable sweetness and a natural simplicity that the Greeks call Grace), while Vasari praises Rosso's women as 'le femmine graziosissime' (the most gracious women) and commends the organisation of his paintings: 'e tutto conduceva con tanta facilità et grazia, ch'era una maraviglia' (the whole is achieved with such facility and grace that it's a marvel).[34] Grace, like the *je ne sais quoi* that it became in the seventeenth century, was generally defined through its effects on the reader or onlooker. Critics used different terms to capture its essential qualities; for most, it had to appear natural so that the observer could delight in lifelikeness; it had also to display that easy nonchalance Castiglione called *sprezzatura*, which he demanded of the good courtier. The term used by Vasari was, as we have seen, *facilità*, which he equated with *grazia*, and this was a sign of excellence for Dolce too: 'la facilità è il principale argomento delle eccellenza di qualunche arte, e la piu difficile a consequire: et è arte a nasconder l'arte' (facility is the chief criterion of excellence in any art, and the most difficult to follow: it's an art to hide art).[35] Dolce took this notion of hiding one's skills directly from Castiglione, and no doubt Du Bellay, who consistently argued that the court was the 'seule escolle ou voluntiers on apprent à bien et proprement parler', (the only school where painlessly one learns to speak well and properly) found his inspiration in *The Courtier* as well as in the advice of Cicero or Quintilian when he affirmed 'L'artifice caché, c'est le vray artifice' (Artifice that is hidden is the true artifice).[36]

At this time, the good painter was brought up to develop his natural talent through the acquisition of techniques that he was never ostentatiously to display; the good poet improved his gifts through study and imitation but in the way of producing 'une naifve et naturelle poësie'; while the courtier trained hard to behave with utter naturalness. These principles of painting, writing, and behaviour drew together painter, poet, and patron; and their mutual understanding of what was good was so well developed that writers and artists could take the appreciative judgement of the courtier for granted. Never had their several aspirations been so closely allied, and the consequences for art and poetry were incalculable.[37]

To know what was fitting, and how the parts slotted together, were other essential elements of any assessment of artistic worth. In behaviour these relationships were expressed by the terms *comeliness* or *seemliness*; in poetry and art, *decorum* or *appropriateness*. All these terms imply a knowledge of forms and general agreement about what constitutes them, so that any serious deviation from established norms could be recognised, then appreciated or rejected. In Dolce, *propriety* is closely linked to a need for order, for balanced proportions and for harmony achieved among all the parts. This was the standard view, established by Vitruvius and elaborated upon by Vigenère in 1578 in this way:

> Car ainsi qu'à un Poëte il ne suffist pas de sçavoir bien teistre un beau vers: Ny à un maçon de tailler proprement une pierre: Il les faut puis apres arrenger pour la structure d'un Poeme, ou d'un edifice; dont les membres viegnent à se correspondre, et les parties deüement se rapporter à leur tout, comme si ce n'estoit qu'une seule piece.[38]

> Because it isn't sufficient for a poet to weave a good line nor for a mason to shape a stone properly. Afterwards they have to arrange them to structure a poem or a building so that the parts correspond and harmonise with the whole as though it were one piece.

Whatever their significance, these criteria—grace, the natural, decorum, and proportion—did not of themselves ensure delight for the observer, nor did they collectively control the power to move the emotions. Indeed, they might only have produced a rather boring sameness without the basic imaginative principle to which every Renaissance critic, artist, and creative writer subscribed: the principle of *varietas*. Sebastiano Serlio was expressing everyone's thought when he wrote: 'La varietà delle cose è di gran contentezza all'occhio humano, et di sodisfactione all'animo' (Variety in things delights the human eye and produces great satisfaction of soul).[39] For Dolce, this variety had to be restrained and controlled; but for Vasari, *varietas* constituted perhaps the most important single factor in his assessments of works of art, just as it had been an absolute value for his predecessor Alberti.[40] Ronsard was acutely aware of its advantages and rather proudly asserted in the 1550 preface to the odes, 'Je ne fai point de doute que ma poësie tant varie' (There is no shadow of doubt, my poetry is infinitely varied). The pride comes from his knowledge that Pindar was noted for 'telle copieuse diversité', and that its creative force had been universally accepted in classical times.[41] Erasmus, too, had shown the creative force of *copia*, and his powerful influence had filtered into the thinking of most writers of the time.[42]

The extended comparison Peletier du Mans drew between painting and poetry provides a closer view of the elements that could constitute *varietas* for poet or artist:

> La Poësie̸ bien propre̸mant ę̈t compare̸ a la Peinture̸ pour beaucoup de̸ convenances qu'e̸le̸s ont ansamble̸: L'une que̸ le̸ Peintre̸ peùt libre̸mant fante̸sier sus son ouurage̸ an ordonnance̸, an habiz an qualitez de̸ pe̸rsonne̸s: an païsage̸s, arbre̸s, fleurs e autre̸s ambe̸lice̸mans: Comme̸ aussi le̸ Poëte̸ an disposicion, discours, digressions, e tant de̸ sorte̸s d'orne̸mans.[43]

> Poetry is properly compared to painting because of the many things they have in common. One might be that the painter can let his imagination roam in the ordering of his work and in the costume and qualities of his characters; similarly, the poet has free rein in the general ordering of his work, its language, and in all kinds of decoration.

As this passage shows, Peletier saw in both arts a process of ordering and embellishing. That his remarks have a rhetorical background is evident, but more interesting for our purposes is the emphasis on modes of decoration. Moreover, he seems to equate painterly and literary elements that we would now consider disparate, a guide to the strength of his conviction that the two arts were essentially similar.

Ronsard was much influenced by Peletier at a formative stage of his career and was undoubtedly attracted by his expansive view of poetry. When he himself turned to reflect upon the business of composing poems, and upon the fabric and elaboration of the alexandrine, Ronsard therefore depicted creative power as exploiting the principle of *varietas* in a continuous process of amplification and decoration. He takes up Peletier's suggestions, inflates them, and presents poetic descriptions as painted frescoes upon and around which the poet embroiders ornaments and rich borders on which he paints gold leaf and intertwines flowers and gorgeous figures. His verses are 'comme les peintures relevées' (like paintings in relief), and the poet must embellish his works:

> les ornant et enrichissant de figures, schemes, tropes, metaphores, phrases et periphrases eslongnées pres du tout . . . et les illustrant de comparaisons bien adaptées, de descriptions florides, c'est à dire enrichies de passements, broderies, tapisseries et entrelassements de fleurs poëtiques, tant pour representer la chose, que pour l'ornement et splendeur des vers.
>
> (P 2 : 1015; L 16 : 332)[44]
>
> decorating them and enriching them with figures, schemes, tropes, metaphors, phrases, and long paraphrases . . . illustrating them with well-tuned comparisons, florid descriptions, that is to say enriched with brilliants, embroideries, tapestries, and swathes of poetic flowers, both to give form to the subject and to serve as the ornament and decorations of the verse.

Ronsard is careful to insist that the ornament be appropriate, since (as he later maintains) when the building is done naturally and when ornateness and feeling are welded together, as in Virgil's rendering of the quarrel between Juno and Venus (*Aeneid*, bk 7), then 'tu n'auras cheveu en teste qui ne se dresse d'admiration' (there won't be a hair on your head that does not rise in admiration).[45]

Ronsard's description of the decorative qualities of poetry immediately conjures up the gilded mouldings and shapely arabesques with which

Rosso and Primaticcio had surrounded so many paintings and frescoes at Fontainebleau (fig. 14). And equally, his splendid conception of poetry offers us a powerful reminder of the context of praise in which poet and painter were working at that time. We cannot easily assess just how much the insistent demands of celebration conditioned this gorgeous view of art and moulded the ways of paint and poem so that the canvas almost disappears behind the brilliant froth of the ornate frame, and rich narrative set pieces sometimes stand out too prominently. Nor can we judge with any accuracy the extent to which the artist imposed his own vision on the prince and his court. However, it is clear that the king desired that perfected views of himself and his function should appear in paint and poem; that the courtier's ideal behaviour reflected the same aesthetic norms as those which belonged to good poems and excellent paintings; and that the artist's view of his craft showed remarkable affinities with both. Any attempt to establish true ownership is lost in a circular process. Patron, poet, and painter not only shared a common language but also had common needs.

When Ronsard tried to communicate a sense of the soaring expansiveness that he considered the true sign of poetic creation and that matched the ambitions of his patrons, he borrowed the technical language of the architect. Poets are unlike historians, he argued, since they

> ne cherchent que le possible, puis d'une petite scintille font naistre un grand brazier, et d'une petite cassine font un magnifique palais, qu'ils enrichissent, dorent et embellissent par le dehors de marbre, jaspe, et porphire, de guillochis, ovalles, frontispices et piedestals, frises et chapiteaux, et le dedans des tableaux, tapisseries eslevées et boffées d'or et d'argent, et le dedans des tableaux cizelez et burinez, raboteux et difficiles à tenir és mains, à cause de la rude engraveure des personnages qui semblent vivre dedans.
>
> (P 2 : 1021; L 16 : 340)

only seek the possible; from a tiny spark they make a huge bonfire; a little hut is turned into a magnificent palace that they enrich, decorate, and embellish—the outside with marble, jasper, with chequered patterns, oval shapes, columns and entrances, and capitals; the inside with paintings, tapestries in high relief embossed with gold and silver; paintings cut and burnished, nobbly to the touch and difficult to hold through the bold engraving of characters who seem alive within the paint.

Ronsard's tone is supremely confident. He appears not to doubt that the poet can achieve this progressive blending of magnificence and living quality. But, his building materials and his tools are those of the artist. Setting aside considerations as to whether these means are at all appropriate to the poet, we find Ronsard here clearly admitting (consciously or not) a dependence upon the artist; in an important argument about the status of poetry, he leans exclusively on the more developed vocabulary of architect, painter, and engraver.

Poet and Artist Collaborate

For reasons that are not altogether evident, Ronsard brought poetry and painting close together. Contemporary painters were, if possible, even more explicit about their dependence on poets; and, in this respect, Titian seems by no means unusual in having recourse to ancient tales for inspiration. Indeed, modern scholarship has increasingly revealed the extent of Renaissance painters' debt to literary and intellectual sources, and it could almost be argued that such researches have become too exclusive. However that may be, already in 1435, Alberti told painters that in order to be learned (as they must) they should seek out the work of poets; while over a century later Dolce roundly stated:

> The painter cannot possibly be in strong command of the elements that relate to invention—as regards both subject matter or propriety—unless he is versed in historical narrative and the tales of the poets.[46]

Dolce then shows how Raphael's *Roxana* was developed from ancient literary sources, and how his *Galatea* came from Poliziano's poem, insisting that 'it happens interchangeably that the painters often draw on the poets for their inventions, and the poets on the painters'.[47]

This interchangeability was common all over Europe in the sixteenth century. Among very many instances, Annibale Caro furnished Federico Zuccaro with the entire complex schema for the prolific paintings with which he festooned the walls of the Farnese palace at Caprarola.[48] Or, in France, N. Jallier drew heavily on the *Aeneid* for his wall decorations at Oiron, while Ovid's work furnished ideas for the panels painted in the castles at Villeneuve-Lembron and at Chareih-Cintrat.[49] We do not always know who was responsible for complicated programmes of wall decoration; and such questions of identity are especially tantalising when it is suspected (as at Fontainebleau) that the programmes may hide royal intentions and artistic comment thereon.

We do, nevertheless, have ample evidence of the interdependence and practical collaboration of painter and poet in other spheres. Particularly informative, in this regard, are the detailed descriptions of royal entries or of court festivities organised to commemorate significant political or military events. During his short reign Henri II made at least twenty-nine entries into towns outside Paris;[50] for each occasion, poets worked out appropriate welcoming themes, and painters hurried to carry out their instructions. At Lyons in 1548 Maurice Scève, the 'conducteur et ordinateur des ystoires et triumphes' (inventor and organiser of the legends and triumphs), with the aid of Guillaume Du Choul and Barthélémy Aneau, evolved an elaborate schema that transformed traditional ways of greeting a monarch and turned the event into a 'triomphe à l'antique' (a triumph in ancient mode). Bernard Salomon (better known for his book illustrations) did all the paint work according to the dictates of the poet.[51]

That Henri II regarded these public manifestations as important can be gauged not only from the number of entries he made but also from his having created in 1555 the post of 'maître de cérémonies' to ensure good order and adequate preparation. On certain occasions, however, the king gave very short notice of his wish for public entertainment. In February 1558 the citizens of Paris had only four days to prepare for his triumphal coming after the French seizure of Calais. Despite the haste, the city worthies must have felt confident since they had appointed that 'homme universel' Etienne Jodelle to do all the necessary work. He had presented himself to the public in this way:

> Je suis dedans Paris encor que j'en sois loing,
> Où je desseine, et taille, et charpente et massonne,
> Je brode, je pourtray, je couppe, je façonne,
> Je cizele, je grave, émaillant, et dorant,
> Je griffonne, je peins, dorant et colorant,
> Je tapisse, j'assieds, je festonne et decore,
> Je musique, je sonne, et poëtise encore.[52]

> I remain in Paris even when I'm far away; there I draw, carve, build, and shape; I embroider, paint, cut, and form; I chisel, engrave, enamel, and apply goldleaf; I write, paint, colouring and embellishing; seated, I weave, decorate, and ornament; I write music, play, and even sing poems.

According to Jodelle's self-assessment then, nothing was lacking;[53] and the king could hope for festivities commensurate with his military successes.

Four days' notice, however, necessitated the help of others; and, although Baptiste Pelerin apparently did an excellent job in painting the hall with the scenes ordered by Jodelle,[54] the costumiers, the actors, and even the musicians performed their tasks so badly that the unhappy author of it all could only describe the result as a *désastre*. Jodelle's elaborate explanation and defence of these unfortunate proceedings is interesting in many ways. It shows us something of the atmosphere of rivalry, one-upmanship, and downright unpleasantness that could prevail at court whenever a poet or artist failed to come up to expectations. He describes his self-interested critics as 'impitoyables' with 'leurs secretes reproches et leurs injustes injures' (their secret reproaches and unjust injuries); '[ils] tancent, reprennent, et conseillent, pour paroistre et non pour ayder' ([they] accuse, modify their thoughts, and advise not to aid me, but to show themselves off).[55] Jodelle's critics eagerly seized on this one disaster as proof of his general ineptitude; even his noble patrons, forgetting his earlier dramatic successes, withdrew their support. Moreover, since the artist's work is exposed to public gaze, and general opinion held that such entertainment was intended to influence, it was inevitable that Jodelle's failure should bring on both the general opprobrium and his spirited self-justifications.

Much more harmonious appear to have been the relationships between poets and painters for the 1571 entry of Charles IX and his queen into Paris. On this occasion Ronsard and Dorat invented the major themes of the entry and controlled the work of the painters and decorators. Ronsard's secretary, Jamyn, also contributed some of the verses, while the most talented French artists—Germain Pilon and Ronsard's friend Pierre Lescot—and the gifted Italian father and son Camillo and Niccolo dell'Abbate wrought in sculpture and in paint at the behest of the poets. Their orders were very explicit and were given in incredible detail, to judge from the financial accounts that survive in the *Registres de la ville de Paris*. One example will clarify the nature of this collaboration. The *Registres* declare that the statue of Gallia should appear thus:

> Et aura ladicte deesse le visaige semblant à la royne, au plus pres que faire se pourra. Et dessus sera escript: GALLIA. Ladicte deesse fera semblant d'en-hanner. Prés de ses piedz, fault mectre une grue, un daulphin, ung liepvre qui ayt les yeux ouvertz, et à ses deux costez, deux termes, qui seront de trois pieds de haulteur. Et la statue de ladicte deesse sera de cinq à six piedz de haulteur.[56]

> The said goddess will have the face of the queen, as far as can be managed. Above will be written—GAUL. The goddess labours hard. Beneath her feet should be a crane, a dolphin, and a hare (eyes wide-open), and on each side a pillar—three feet high. The statue will be five to six feet high.

Simon Bouquet's account of the entry shows that these instructions were faithfully carried out. The sculptors attempted to depict accurately the features of the Queen Mother, and they included the animals chosen to represent her political acumen and her vigilance.[57] The accuracy of the detail is also corroborated in a verse account of the scene written by an eyewitness, Charles de Navières:

> Au haut de la fontaine une Royne eslevée
> (Telle de Catherine est la face trouvée)
> . . . .
> Dessus son piedestal vers le senestre flanc
> Est l'oiseau de Pallas qui monstre de sagesse

Ceste Royne prudente avoir grande largesse
Pour penetrer l'obscur des secretz plus couvers,
A la dextre est un lievre aiant les yeux ouvers,
Près une grue aussi sur un pied reposante
Et levant avec l'autre une pierre pesante.[58]

Above the fountain, a Queen was placed (the visage just like that of Catherine). . . . Above her pedestal on the left side is Minerva's bird showing the wisdom of this prudent Queen and her generosity, her ability to penetrate the darkest secrets, on the right, the open-eyed hare, beside a crane with one foot stilled, the other lifting a heavy stone.

This example is typical of all the monuments erected or decorated for this entry. Clearly, the authority of the poet was in the ascendant on this occasion, although as historians we would perhaps think of the artist as having the greater role.

The importance of the poetic contribution is further underlined by the Parisian François Rose, who wrote a series of poems about the 1571 entry. On this occasion, he saw Paris transformed into a vision of Parnassus:

De là il vit le mont Parnassien
Hault eslevé ou le Pindarien,
Premier sonnoit sa harpe Vandomoise
Le saint honneur de la terre Françoise
Il vit Belleau, pinçant son Lucorin
Qui surmontoit le mi-poisson marin,
De son accord, et puis il vit Iodelle
Qui façonnoit la complainte mortelle
D'un triste roy qui ia contemplatif
Voyoit la mort: là il connut Baif
Corne beauté de sa damme Melinne.[59]

From thence he saw the Parnassian mount raised high, on which the follower of Pindar first sounded on his local harp the saintly honours of the land of France. He saw Belleau plucking his lute overcoming the sea monster with his harmony, and then he saw Jodelle who retold the mortal complaint of the sad king who already foresaw his own death: there, he recognised Baif trumpeting the beauty of his lady Melinne.

Rose extended the cortège to include Garnier and other members of the Pléiade. No painter or sculptor is mentioned, however, in this roll call of honour nor in another poem, which refers explicitly to Ronsard and Dorat, although its author—Navières—was anxious to show off his artistic knowledge by distinguishing Corinthian from Tuscan columns, and stiffening out his lines with such technical terms as *stilobate*, *plate perspective*, *cornice* and with references to 'Praxitelle'.[60]

15. Magestas, woodcut from Simon Bouquet, *Bref et sommaire recueil de cequi a esté faict . . . à la joyeuse et triumphante entrée de . . . Charles IX . . . en sa bonne ville de Paris*, 1571, between sigs. L^i–L^ii (British Library).

As the king progressed through the streets of his capital there unfolded before him a set of coherent themes that he could readily understand: expressions of French imperialism, which had been insistently stated under Henri II and which continued to be of primary concern to royal propagandists. For instance, the king's device—the twin columns of justice and piety—which in the early years of Charles IX's reign had appeared twisted, in this entry had been straightened. This might at first seem an insignificant detail. Yet the straightening of the columns represented a deliberate affront to the Hapsburg ambitions, since two straight columns, surmounted by eagles, had been Emperor Charles V's proud device. Now, the designers of the entry implied, imperial power had passed to the French.[61] The device not only appeared on all the arches, but it was also on the city's gift to the king, and it dominated what eyewitnesses considered the most remarkable scene: at the Châtelet, two upright columns went echoing back through the perspective behind the commanding figure of Magestas (fig. 15). Furthermore, the themes Charles saw also reflected ideas on the Trojan origins of France, ideas that Jean Lemaire de Belges had presented at the beginning of the century and that Ronsard had taken up again in *La Franciade*.

The Royal entry was always a means of promoting the power of the monarch; in 1571, it also became a propaganda channel for the poet.[62] The climax of the poet's aggrandisement was reached in the queen's banquet for which Dorat gave a fertile demonstration of how a poet's incredible learning might be turned to contemporary political and moral aspirations. Camillo and Niccolo dell'Abbate had been commissioned to decorate the town hall for the festivity, and Dorat issued minute instructions to them. The twenty-four pictures that were to form the frieze around the room and on the ceiling were based on a recently discovered poem, the *Dionysiaca* of the Alexandrian poet Nonnos.[63] The story of Cadmus with its themes of marriage, harmony, and peace seemed ideally suited to the needs of political strategy in 1571, when the king's recent marriage and the temporary lull in hostilities had given some slight credence to hopes for tranquillity at last. For a few moments, the French court could bask in the visible glories of poet and monarch, which were also made plain in the *sucreries* designed by Germain Pilon to represent the story of Minerva, the goddess who vanquished ignorance. Few could know that a massacre would soon come to demolish such political and artistic claims and achievements.

Source materials on the entry of Charles IX and his queen into Paris in 1571 have been preserved in unusual richness, and their accidental survival has allowed us to study fairly closely the dealings of poet and painter. Their collaboration on this occasion should, however, be seen as a culminating effort in a continuous experience of working together, an experience that stretched back to the beginnings of the century at least. The public favoured illustrated books, and through them it had developed the habit of linking poem and picture. The works were of many kinds; in emblem books the moral was impressed on the reader's mind through the effect of the image on the page, as in the many editions of Alciati's *Emblematum liber* or in the *Imagination poétique* of Barthélémy Aneau, who had helped Maurice Scève in the design of Henri II's entry into Lyons (1548).[64] Collections of verse set poems and pictures together in primitive couplings as in *La Fleur de la vraye poesie françoyse* (1540). Famous and favourite authors, Ovid or Ariosto, for example, appeared in beautifully worked volumes from the Lyons printing houses of Roville and Bonhomme, and Jean de Tournes with engravings such as the one shown in figure 16, from the *Metamorphoses*. The number of such editions testifies to their popularity. From these examples, we may conclude that sixteenth-century readers were thoroughly accustomed to seeing and seizing at the same glance a picture and a poem.

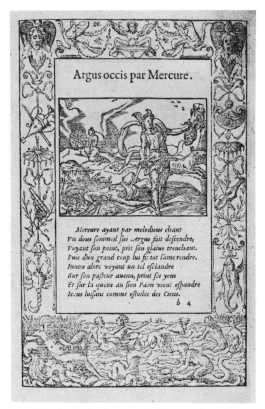

16. Woodcut of Mercury and Argus, from the
Jean de Tournes edition of Ovid's *Metamorphoses*,
Lyons, 1557 (British Library).

The same simultaneity of impression occurred when they looked upon
many tapestries or even upon stained glass windows of the time. The
forty-four stained glass windows depicting the loves of Psyche and Cupid,
which were commissioned by the *connétable* Montmorency in the early
1570s, featured below each image a short poem. The verses explained the
elements depicted in the pictures and, in addition, carried the narrative
forward to its next stage. Here are the lines given beneath the sixteenth
window (fig. 17):

Dedans la mer sur deux Dauphins assise
Se pourmenoit Venus environnée
De dieux Marins, et nymphes aornée,
Quand la mouette à son Oreille mise
Dist à Venus: d'un malheur je t'avise,
C'est que ton filz est au lict fort blecé,
Et toy icy: tout le monde en devise,
Qui sans toy est de grace delaissé.[65]

Dedans la mer sur deux Dauphins assise
Se pourmenoit Venus Enuironnée
De dieux Marins, & Nymphes aornée,
Quand la mouette à son Oreille mise
Dist à venus: d'vn malheur se t'auise,
C'est que ton filz est au lict fort blecé,
Et toy icy: tout le monde en deuise,   XVI.
Qui sans toy est de grace delaisse.

17. Engraving of the triumph of Venus, from the
1586 edition of *L'Amour de Cupido et de Psiché*,
fig. 16. The engravings are copied from the
woodcuts published in Paris (1546) by Jeanne de
Marnef Janot (British Library).

In the sea, resting upon two dolphins Venus is promenading, surrounded by
marine gods and decorative nymphs, when the gull flies close to her ear and
says to Venus: I come to warn you of misfortune: your son lies on his bed,
sorely wounded, while you are here; everyone is convinced that without you
his beauty is forever marred.

The beautiful goddess of love is shown drifting along with carefree gaiety
to the sound of marine music. This tranquil scene is abruptly followed, in
the next *grisaille*, by the anxious encounter of mother and son; and it is
the function of the verse to anticipate these sudden changes. Verse plays
the same role in the series of tapestries on the story of Diana prepared for
the château d'Anet between 1549 and 1552.[66] However, in this case the
text probably evolved from the medieval habit of strewing the image with
words ballooning from the mouths of the participants; the words seem
less concerned to describe the scene but rather, as in earlier examples, to

collect and transmit the thoughts and words of the characters depicted. This is well demonstrated by the figure of Diana (fig. 18), whose gestures imploring Jupiter to grant her the gift of chastity are commented on in the poem. Moreover, the royal application of the entire scene is emphasised by the device and motto of Henri II, which are displayed on both sides of the tapestry.

18. Tapestry for the Château d'Anet (ca. 1552), Diana pleading with Jupiter, after Etienne Delaune's design, which gave Diane de Poitier's features to Diana and those of Henri II to Jupiter (Musée départemental des antiquités, Rouen, France; photo Ellebé).

At a time when members of the French court had grown accustomed to comfort, artistic luxuries, and lavish surroundings, writers saw their opportunity to influence the kind of ornaments that would embellish noble rooms. For Diane de Poitiers's château at Anet, Pontus de Tyard suggested that stories be imported from respectable ancient authors and ideas 'tirées d'Homère, d'Ovide, de Diodore, de Pausanias, de Plutarque et autres anciens Autheurs' (drawn from Homer, Ovid, Diodorus, Pausanias, Plutarch, and other ancient authors).[67] As for the 1571 entry, his instructions are minute: he dictates the general shape of the work, sets out the distribution of figures on the canvas, and even details the expressions that are to be represented. He proposes twelve themes centred on the use of rivers or fountains. First, he explains the origins and symbolism of each myth; then, he charges the artist (in the fable of Narcissus, for example):

faudroit peindre une jeune fille morte, toute ressemblante à Narcisse et faudroit qu'en un paysage solitaire et écarté Narcisse fut couché près d'une fontaine en laquelle son image se representeroit, comme dans un miroir il seroit peint d'un visage mourant.

that he must paint a young girl, dead, much resembling Narcissus, and that Narcissus must be seen lying in a landscape bleak and lonely beside the fountain, which echoes his portrait as though a dying visage were reflected in a mirror.

A sonnet describing and interpreting this scene in a manner reminiscent of the Greek Anthology completes the lesson.[68]

Such literalness is fairly rare. When Nicolas Hoüel wrote his *Histoire de la royne d'Arthemise* in 1562 he sought to do no more than give pleasure to Catherine for whom he declared:

La lecture des histoires vous apportoit un singulier plaisir, et spécialement quant elles estoyent mises en bonne peinture, sculpture, broderie ou tapisserie.[69]

The reading of stories will bring you singular pleasure, and especially when they are recorded in good painting, sculpture, embroidery, or tapestry.

Antoine Caron and Camillo and Niccolo dell'Abbate drew scenes from this work (fig. 19), some of which were turned into tapestries.[70] Jehan de Mauregard attempted a similar feat the following year when he suggested to Charles IX that the twenty-six plates on the legend of the golden fleece (composed by Léonard Thiry and engraved by René Boyvin) might provide the patterns for tapestries in 'les sales de vos magnifiques palais' (the rooms of your magnificent palaces).[71] On this occasion, Jacques Gohorry

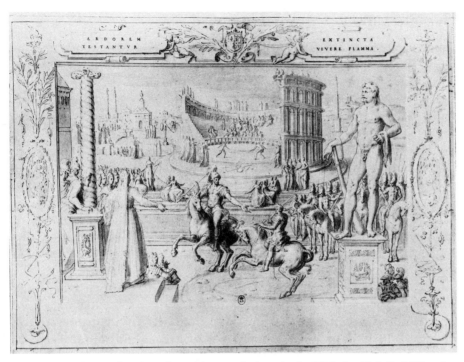

19. Antoine Caron, drawing of royal feats and triumphs for Nicholas Hoüel's *L'Histoire de la royne d'Arthemise*, 1562 (Bibliothèque Nationale).

furnished the verse that, discreetly set at the base of the work, rehearsed the main features of the story.

In all these combinations of poetry and visual art, features distinctive to each genre were given clear and separate representations. This simultaneous presence, and especially the amount of text that appeared side by side with the image or (as we have seen) in some cases, actually inside the frame or on the picture, suggests that collaboration between poet and artist was still a somewhat unbalanced affair. It also tells us something, perhaps, about the way sixteenth-century people looked at images. For, despite the powerful effects they believed were resident in visual images, sixteenth-century viewers needed help in order to understand them. It was not that painters were inadequate, but the images themselves had meanings that could neither be made nor elucidated without a text. To look at a painting satisfactorily was to know how to *read* it. In a very basic way, then, the sixteenth-century onlooker had to be a reader, and this gave a certain dominant power to the poet in most collaborative works. There were forms of writing, however, in which poem and painting are more thoroughly integrated, and the poet assimilated the artist's role. Let us consider the example of the pastoral tradition.[72]

The Integration of Art and Poetry

Thus far, we have considered the pastoral tradition as one that was eminently suited to the expression of the ways of kings or of ideal states of being. And, as our analysis (in chapter 1) of Ronsard's *Bergerie* revealed, the conjunction of simplicity and princely stateliness was managed, in the main, through the harmonies created by the lyrical power of the poet. Princes' affection for pictures and highly decorated luxury items also played an important role in this blending process. If we go back, for example, to Jacopo Sannazaro, who exerted considerable influence in France in the sixteenth century, we find that he drew together, somewhat paradoxically, an avowed nakedness of style and rich ornamentation. In his prologue to *Arcadia*, he argued that he was transmitting adventures 'just as naked of ornament as I heard them sung by the shepherds of Arcady'; but, this simple story is quickly surrounded by other painted narrative scenes. Such a scene of narrative simplicity was displayed above the entrance to the holy temple where naked nymphs were depicted drying their hair in the sun having successfully escaped the pursuit of satyrs. On either side were other pictures: Apollo guarding the sheep from Mercury; Battus revealing the latter's theft, despite the hundred eyes of Argus; Endymion asleep; or Paris in the act of judging the beauties of Venus, Juno, and Minerva.[73]

There was nothing haphazard about the placing of such painted scenes in the poem. Sannazaro used them to mirror the preoccupation of his shepherds. Pictures translated their thoughts and connected the reality of their simple world with the excitement generated by their anticipation of the temple's ritual and mysterious ceremonies. The paintings also give a status to their way of life by reminding the reader of the godlike shepherds of the past—Apollo and Paris. Sannazaro's work thus broke down the distinctions between two worlds, the painted world of princely heritage and the real work of shepherds tending their flocks.

This blurring process is present in most pastorals, and it is given particular strength in *La Bergerie*, written by Ronsard's friend and contemporary Rémy Belleau. But, whereas Sannazaro set his scene in a minutely described nowhere, in his poem Belleau explicitly puts the real château de Joinville at the centre of all the activity. Above the chimney in the sumptuous dining hall hangs a large painting on which the centrepiece is the château itself, 'les terraces, les galleries, les salles, les chambres, les antichambres, les cours, les offices, le ieu de paume' (terraces, galleries, halls, rooms, antichambers, courtyards, offices, tennis courts).[74] The inhabitants of the real castle thus see reflected in the painting the rooms through which they actually walk; and they see mirrored their own galleries and gardens. The painting is both a compliment to a noble home and an extension of that magnificence already suggested at the beginning of *La*

Bergerie. There, set out in the sun, the castle terrace, decorated with turrets 'tournees et massonnees à cul de lampe' (carved and turned into their lamp shape) and with carved stones intricately worked, is evoked as it sprawls along the rock face. At the far end from the enraptured gaze of the poet was a gallery:

> vitrée, lambrisee sur un plancher de carreaux émaillez de couleur: le frontispice, à grandes colonnes, canellees et rudantees, garnies de leurs bases, chapiteaux, architrave, frise, cornice, et mouleures de bonne grace et de iuste proportion.[75]

> windowed and wainscoated, with a coloured, tiled floor: the entrance, on large columns, ridged and hewn, complete with their foundations, capitals, architrave, frieze, cornice, and mouldings of great elegance and just proportions.

Belleau has absorbed current aesthetic criteria (*grace* and *juste proportion*) and is fully conversant with the builders' language. He seems intent on showing off this relatively new vocabulary in order to establish the architectural reality of the gallery and to praise the abundance and variety of its elements.

Joinville is shown as a special place, inhabited by a *dame* and her nymphs; a place where wall hangings throw back to the privileged occupants rich mirror images of themselves. Occasionally, the figures in the pictures are vitalised; they come to life, they speak and comment on their times as the three shepherds do at the beginning of the pastoral. This continuous blurring of the painted and the real is reinforced partly by the fact that some of the tapestries described (those of the seasons) were ones owned by the Lorraine family, and partly by the way in which the ladies of the house are called nymphs, suggesting quasi-mythological beings.[76] At this court, life is good; and the poet's purpose is to transmit to us the heightened feelings he experiences as a privileged witness of the significant family moments of the house of Lorraine. For this reason the occupations of the court at Joinville appear as gently controlled, and its ceremonies are performed with joy and reverence. Belleau strives to draw his readers into the cycle of events as though we were participants. Thus we see the military achievements of the Guise recorded in the third picture of the gallery, 'sieges et prises de villes, comme de Metz, de Calais, et de Thionville' (siege and surrender of towns like Metz, Calais, and Thionville);[77] we witness the touching prayers and the offerings of flowers and fruit by the nymphs of the household at the shrine of the dead hero François de Guise; we have a share in the solemnity and joy of the festivities that celebrated the union of the duke of Lorraine and Henri II's daughter Claude de France, events all depicted 'en plate peinture' in the rooms of the duchess;

and, finally, we are present at the rejoicings and impromptu mascarades that the nymphs designed to congratulate the duchess on the birth of a prince—le marquis du Pont.

Belleau slips, almost imperceptibly, from prose to poem and back again to prose as he works through this natural journey from death to birth, its aspects conjured now through narrative pictures, now through song, and now again through the graceful gestures of the ladies attendant upon the duchess. All these modes work together to convey the naturalness of the happenings as well as their stimulating power, which inspires the poet. There is no discrepancy between the world of nature, and especially its cheerful and benevolent aspects, which are threaded into the web of narrative, and the court life here presented in thoughtful, joyous, and fruitful mood. Their rhythms and qualities are shown to be the same: nature has a pattern of birth and decay, so does the life of man, however eminent his status. Nature enriches the earth with fruits and flowers, products of gaiety and goodness; a life in such a court is full of loveliness, good work, or a happiness of spirit from which burst spontaneously the dance and music of rejoicing. We seem in a fairyland, a miraculous world where sorrow, war, and death are absorbed and exorcised, and where 'douceur de vivre' sounds the dominant note.[78]

In the first day of *La Bergerie*, Belleau relied significantly on paintings and tapestries blended with songs to create these tones of sweetness and awestruck appreciation; and, sliding effortlessly from poetic mode to picture and back again, he achieved a rare fusion and demonstrated the benefits of working with the paint. If we turn again to Ronsard, we find that his practice is at once more complex and more ambiguous; and that his views, though often categorically stated, are frequently contradictory.

Ronsard's Spirit of Rivalry

Ronsard was not without friends and valued acquaintances from the art world. Among these figured François Clouet, Lescot, Denisot, and Delbene, to whom he dedicated works, a sign that he appreciated their talent.[79] For Lescot, seigneur de Clany, he wrote a *Discours* that accepted painting as a learned art dependent upon mathematics; but the climax to the poem concerns the poet's public image. The recognition of a painter's work gives way at the end to tones of self-praise as Ronsard draws attention to the story of the substitution of a trumpet for a lyre on part of the decoration of the Louvre 'exprès pour figurer la force de mes vers' (expressly to exhibit the force of my verse).[80] Whatever the truth of this story (apparently corroborated by Robert de la Haye),[81] for Ronsard artists were friends but subservient ones, and he had a fairly close knowledge of their work.

His poems written for Jean Martin suggest that he knew the French translations of Serlio and Vitruvius; while other poems show that he admired the three graces designed by Germain Pilon for the funeral urn of Henri II (fig. 20), and the battle reliefs that Bontemps had carved on the base of François I's monument.[82] In his biography, Claude Binet bears testimony to Ronsard's love of the fine arts; 'la peinture et la sculpture, comme aussi la musique, luy estoient à singulier plaisir' (painting and sculpture, as well as music, gave him singular pleasure).[83] Although Binet was not always entirely accurate in his remarks, in this instance at least he appears to be telling the truth, for when Ronsard spoke of the portraits of Corneille de la Haye before Henri III at the Académie du Palais, his knowledge and appreciation of the painter's work were obvious, as was his aesthetic judgement.[84]

20. Germain Pilon, the funeral urn for Henri II
(Louvre, département de la sculpture; Arch. Photo.
Paris/S.P.A.D.E.M.).

At the beginning of his career, in the first ode he ever wrote—*A son luc*—Ronsard acknowledged the force of painting:

C'est un celeste present
Transmis çà-bas où nous sommes,
De terrestre faix exent
Pour lever en haut les hommes.

$$(\text{P } 2:727; \text{L } 2:155)^{85}$$

It's a divine gift, transmitted to us here below, freeing us from earthly burden to raise up the spirit of man.

The ability to lift the spirit of man is the same as that power which Jupiter was to grant to the Muses of poetry in *L'Ode à Michel de l'Hospital*. Thus, in order to advance his own art, Ronsard willingly recognised the transforming power of paint. But, in lines such as these, he was also showing his awareness of contemporary interest in beautiful things and in fine buildings. A visitor to the court at Chambord or Fontainebleau could, for example, write with this kind of enthusiasm about royal palaces:

Sire, ces jours passés estant en vostre maison de Fontainebleau, ie me joué à regarder ce qui a mis souventesfois les espris des bons Architectes en admiration: et, entre les autres choses, vostre galerie, et les personnages qui y sont, faicts par telle dilligence, et si bien retirés au naturel, qu'à les bien voir l'on penseroyt que ce fust la nature mesme. D'avantage, si la peinture est belle, la decoration du stuc n'est pas moindre, par raison de ses fruits, estans plus plaisants que les naturels: d'autant que ceux-cy se despouillent de leurs fleurs, et, en changeant leur couleur, s'envieillissent et laissent leur beauté: et ceux là monstrent une primevere perpetuelle, et les fleurs immortelles: de sorte que ceux, qui s'en approchent, cuident recevoir l'odeur suave des fleurs et des fruits, recoyvent la senteur par grande visée. Là ne se treuve rien d'affecté, ny de trop, ny chose que l'on puisse reprendre.[86]

Sire, during these last few days, residing in your house at Fontainebleau, I delighted myself in the contemplation of all that which set architects' minds in such admiration; among other sights, your gallery and its characters fashioned with such skill and drawn so like to nature that in seeing them it's impossible to distinguish them from their natural state. Moreover, while the painting is beautiful, the stucco work is not less so, especially the fruits, which seem even more full of savour than real ones, especially those that have lost their leaves, and are changing their colour; they age and retain their beauty. Others, meanwhile, keep their green and seem immortal, so much so that those who look at them closely imagine they can smell the sweet scent of fruit and flowers, simply through the power of sight. In all of this, there is nothing affected nor extravagant, nothing that should be changed.

It is the decorative quality of the stucco work that particularly impressed this guest, the antiquarian Guillaume Du Choul. His gaze, diverted from the paintings in the long gallery at Fontainebleau, rests on their surrounds as he marvels at flowers formed to such perfection that they acquire a living quality so intense as seemingly to spread forth sweet odour.

Any stance that Ronsard chose to adopt towards the artist, favourable or antagonistic, had to take account of this context and of the beholder's excitement such powerful illusions generated. As Ronsard followed the court from Fontainebleau to Anet and from Chambord to Saint-Germain, he could not help being conscious of the evidence everywhere of princes' deep obsession with art.[87] Naturally and diplomatically, he too praised what he saw. Anet is a *belle place*, and the work done for the cardinal de Lorraine at Meudon is admirable:

> La grotte que Charlot, Charlot de qui le nom
> Est saint par les forests, a fait creuser si belle
> Pour estre des neuf soeurs la demeure eternelle.
>
> (P 1:955; L 9:76)

The grotto, that which Charlot (whose name is saintly in the forest) has made so deep to form the eternal domain of the nine Muses.

We notice, however, that even here Ronsard's admiration does not linger on the architectural achievements nor on the statues of Bacchus and Pallas that commanded entry to the grotto. He ignores the Roman emperors the cardinal had brought to inhabit his country retreat; instead, he concentrates his attention on the simplicity and appropriateness of a home built for the Muses of poetry, a residence that blends so easily into the beautiful surroundings provided by nature. Fauns and satyrs 'furent esbahis de voir' (were astounded to see)

> Le plan, le frontispice, et les piliers rustiques,
> Qui effacent l'honneur des colonnes antiques;
> De voir que la Nature avoit portrait les murs
> De grotesque si vive en des rochers si durs.

the structure, the front, and the rustic pillars, which obliterate the pride of ancient columns; the way that Nature had painted the walls with so lively a grotesque upon rocks so hard.

It is the case that Ronsard found it extraordinarily difficult to profer undiluted praise to his fellow artists, no matter how deep his appreciation of the value of their work. Compared to poetry, their art, however fashionable and however worthwhile, was inferior. In an early poem, *Hymne de France* (1549), he set out the natural and artistic riches of his native land.

Among them, he mentions the skills of 'noz imagers' (our picture makers). These he places fairly low in the hierarchy of the arts; they come after poetry and music, after mathematics and medicine, and are classified among the mechanical and technical skills, just as Chasseneux had traditionally listed them. This rather poor opinion is maintained by Ronsard even in poems in which he seeks to extol beautiful palaces or noble buildings; there, the compliment is often tempered by a very deliberate use of the mundane term *maçon* (artisan or craftsman) to describe the artist, as in

> Adjoustez y tant de palais dorez,
> Tant de sommets de temples honorez
> Jadis rochers, que la main du maçon
> Elaboura d'ouvrage et de façon.

(P 2:689, L 1:33)

Add so many gilded palaces, so many lofty and honorable temples that were once rocks, and that the mason's hand had conceived and modelled.

Occasionally, his tone is fiercely antagonistic, as in his envious denunciations of Philibert de l'Orme and unnamed 'peintres estranges' (foreign painters) in *Epistre à Charles*, and in a relatively early sonnet addressed to Aubert. Both these attacks, subsequently deleted from the *Oeuvres*, were inspired by Ronsard's firm belief that painters, and architects in particular, were grossly overrewarded for their work compared to the meagre resources made available to poets. The castigations sometimes assumed a more worthy tone, that of moral indignation, for instance, as in *Les Avaricieux, et ceux qui pres de la mort bastissent*. Here, through a play on the word *maison* Ronsard bluntly juxtaposed fine marble palaces and the approach of death: 'ta maison certaine / C'est de Pluton, la maison palle et vaine' (your certain home is the pale deathly abode of Pluto).[88] The satire here is traditional, but a later poem, which develops the same theme in even sharper tones, illustrates how abiding and deep-felt was Ronsard's antagonism towards building. The poem was addressed to Jehan Du Thier, secretary of state, a position that gave him more than adequate authority and ample funds to indulge himself and build a mansion commensurate with his purse. With strong irony, Ronsard praised his modesty and his restraint, and depicts the excavations of marble and the erection of proud palaces as a double injury to nature:

> Que sert de deschirer
> Le ventre de la terre, et hautement construire
> Un palais orguelleux de marbre et de porfire?
> Où peut-estre (ô folie) il ne logera pas.[89]

(P 2:397; L 10:38–48)

What does it serve to pull apart the centre of the earth; and to build there proud palaces of marble and porphyry where probably (O, folly) he might not ever live?

An acute sense of rivalry underlies such writing, yet Ronsard recognised the magnetic power of artists' work and envied their rewards. He saw that if the poet were to enjoy similar fortunes, he would be obliged to emulate in verse something of their style. And, indeed, Ronsard's poetry has an essentially visual impact.

At first, the urge to compete led him to borrow directly from narrative painting. In the *Peintures d'un paysage*, for example, he seems to be describing an actual scene (or scenes). This poem has seventeen stanzas, and into a single frame, 'Tableau, que l'eternelle gloire / D'un Apelle avou'roit pour sien' (Painting, which the everlasting glory of Apelles would admit to be his own; lines 1–2). Ronsard then packs together a variety of topics that seem to have no logical relationships: the cyclops at work in Vulcan's forge, the anger of Jupiter, a shipwreck, Juno's jealousy, Charles V's naval victory against the Turks, and Henri II's triumph over the Holy Roman Emperor. These are well-known themes, currently in fashion, engraved by Fantuzzi and others, and painted on multiple surfaces in royal palaces or among the works of art collected by French princes.[90] Ronsard's reader, therefore, would have had little difficulty in completing the scenes in his mind from the details supplied.

But if we think of the poem as an attempt to convey the content of a picture, we wonder how one frame could contain scenes so disparate in tone and subject matter. Perhaps Ronsard, despite his title, had no intention of conjuring up an actual painting. He may simply have been exploiting the reader's reactions to the *idea* of a composite painting in order to demonstrate the superior descriptive power of the poet. Notice that throughout the poem, he carefully places his readers as though they were looking at a real picture. In describing the cyclops in stanza 3, his indications are specific:

> Trois, sur l'enclume gemissante,
> D'ordre egal le vont martelant,
> Et d'une tenaille pinçante
> Tournent l'ouvrage estincelant:
> Vous les diriez qu'ils ahanent et suent,
> Tant leurs marteaux dessus l'enclume ruent.

Three, upon the groaning anvil, hit their strokes, each one in turn, and with gripping pincers turn the shining work of art. You'd say they heave and sweat, so heavily the hammers strike the steel.

There are three giants; their hammer blows fall rhythmically and noisily; and as they work the shining metal they groan and sweat. Movement, rhythm, and sound are, strictly speaking, not in the paint; they are the poet's reactions and additions. This interpretive process is intensified as the poem develops.

> Un peu plus haut, parmy les nues
> Enflées d'un vague ondoyant,
> Le Pere ses fleches cognues
> Darde aval d'un bras foudroyant:
> Le feu se suit et, saccageant l'air, gronde,
> Faisant trembler les fondemens du monde.

> Entre l'orage et la nuict plaine
> De gresle, martelant souvent,
> Un pilote cale à grand'peine
> Sa voile trop serve du vent;
> La mer le tanse, et les flots irez baignent
> De monts bossus les cordes qui se plaignent.

A little higher up, among the clouds that swell in a billowing wave, the Father with thundering arm sends down his well-known arrows: Fire follows fire, and blasting the air it growls, shaking the very fundaments of the world. Between the storm and the night, filled with frequently sounding hail, a pilot guides his boat with difficulty, its sail lies exposed to the wind; the sea beats it about, and the angry waves with huge mounds bathe around the complaining ropes.

Again, Ronsard scrupulously specifies that part of the picture we are to look at, 'Un peu plus haut' and 'Entre l'orage et la nuict', but the emphasis falls on the sound and movement—rather than direction—of the god's fury, on the beat of the hail, the screech of the ropes, and the swell of sails and waves. For any collection of scenes at first draws the viewer's attention to their pictorial and essentially static nature. A narrative picture composed of many episodes dotted over the canvas actually restricts and diminishes a painter's ability to depict movement and to give a living quality to things. In this poem Ronsard has chosen just such a circumstance. The painter is praised to the limits of his power, then the poet takes over and so animates these scenes that the last one can be drawn from a recent actual experience:

> Paris tient ses portes décloses
> Recevant son Roy belliqueur,
> Une grande nuë de roses
> Pleut à l'entour du chef veinqueur;
> Les feux de joye icy et là s'allument,
> Et jusqu'au Ciel les autels des Dieux fument.

Paris holds open its gates to receive its warlike king, clouds of roses rain down around the victorious chief, bonfires are lit here and there, and the smoke rises to the heavens from the altars of the gods.

Henri II had entered Paris triumphantly in 1549, a few months before Ronsard composed his poem. Six concentrated lines suffice to evoke the king's triumph, and they end the poem in a very different style from that of the preceding stanzas. They paint a picture, but one composed of highly selected elements; the essential symbols of triumph are present and they are enough. Gone are the precise details made to move and to sound. Of course, *Peintures d'un paysage* is not a great poem; it lacks coherence and, fashioned from an apparently arbitrary set of pictures, it appears unbalanced. And yet, it is a very revealing poem that lays bare Ronsard's preoccupations with painting. This poem's concern with visual art exceeds its thematic content.

In another early poem, *A son lict*, combative preoccupations are less dominant, and the evocation of a painting is more successfully woven into the emotional texture of the work:

> Qui vit jamais Mars et Venus
> En un tableau portraits tous nus,
> Des doux Amours la mere estroitement
> Embrasse Mars, qui laisse lentement
>
> Sa lance tomber à costé,
> D'un si plaisant venin donté
> Et la baisant presse l'yvoire blanc,
> Bouche sur bouche, et le flanc sur le flanc:
>
> Celuy qui les a veu portraits
> Peut sur nous contempler les traits
> De leurs plaisirs, lors que m'amie et moy
> Tous nuds au lict faisons je ne sçay quoy.

> (P 2:704; L 1:257–59)

Anyone who has seen Mars and Venus portrayed completely naked in a painting, the mother of sweet love closely embracing the god Mars, who slowly lets his lance fall to the side, overcome by such pleasurable poison, clinging tight to the white ivory limbs, he kisses her, lips against lips; he who has viewed them thus portrayed can also perceive the traces of those pleasures that my love and I enjoy in bed, doing *je ne sais quoi*.

There survives a drawing by Rosso of a corresponding picture made for François I in about 1530 (fig 21). The drawing depicts the naked couple surrounded by a whirl of joyous cupids delighting in having stripped Mars of his weapons. We do not know how closely the drawing resembles either of the two lost paintings on this subject that were housed at Fontainebleau, but it does communicate the same flavour of playfulness and enjoyment as Ronsard's lines.[91] More interesting than the parallel in theme is the use Ronsard makes of the picture. As the poet thinks of his bed, his mind plays on memories of the physical excitement he has had there, and since poetic and courtly decorum at the time discouraged overt and precise references to sex and physical contact, the poet uses painted versions of loving couples enjoying their intimacy in order to transmit his feelings to us. By transferring the experience into the realm of art, he could speak more frankly and could also exploit the favourable reception already accorded to the picture. At the same time, his own acts of love are exalted by these parallels to the very archetypes of passion.

As we saw in *Peintures d'un paysage*, Ronsard's subjects reflect the thematic preoccupations of contemporary painting. His narrative poems feature the same heroic and belligerent forms of Mars, Achilles, and Hercules; he rehearses the same exploits of the Argonauts; and he develops

21. Giovanni Battista Rosso, drawing of Mars and Venus (Louvre, cabinet des dessins; Arch. Photo. Paris/S.P.A.D.E.M.).

22. The education of Achilles, Galerie François Ier (Château de Fontainebleau, Cliché Esparcieux).

the historical significance of those same Roman emperors whom the king encountered in similar poses on arches, columns of buildings, and wall coverings, or engraved on armour and on plate, and set in jewels. A specific example is the theme of Chiron educating Achilles, which was painted in the first fresco of the Galerie François Ier in the early 1540s (fig. 22) and also used by Ronsard for François de Valois in 1544, and again for the *Institution* of Charles IX in 1563 (P 2:560–64; L 11:1–13). The poet's prodigious interest in subjects that permitted the gorgeous display of naked bodies, idealized in idyllic and luxurious settings, transposed and elevated into the shape and adventures of Apollo or Adonis, Venus or Juno, finds echoes in the paintings and tapestries of the time. Such thematic parallels in art and poetry are good indications of prevailing taste; they do not necessarily provide, however, evidence of the poet's conscious emulation of the artists' work. We must look, therefore, for closer ties.

Ronsard's references to art are extremely varied, and critics have frequently commented upon them. It has been argued that the structure of many of his love sonnets resembles that of an engraved 'tableau encadré' (framed picture),[92] which presents a scene accompanied by a tag of explication. Certainly, many of these sonnets do develop an event or a scene over eleven to thirteen lines before concluding with a short reflective comment, introduced by *ainsi* or *tout comme*. More pertinent, however, are Ronsard's explicit references to painting that are intended to explain his poetic purpose.[93] In *L'Hymne de l'Hyver*, for example, he explains the veiling techniques that the inspired poet invents to hide his discovered 'truths' from the incomprehending eyes of the ignorant.

La verité cognue, apres l'avoir apprise,
D'un voile bien subtil, comme les peintres font
Aux tableaux bien portraits, luy couvre tout le front,
Et laisse seulement, tout au travers du voile,
Paroistre ses rayons comme une belle estoile
Afin que le vulgaire ait désir de chercher
La couverte beauté, dont il n'ose approcher.

(P 2 : 252; L 12 : 71−72)

Known truths, once apprehended from beneath a subtle veil, just as artists achieve in well-drawn paintings, hide all their aspect and only permit its rays to shine through the veil, like some beautiful star, so that the ordinary man is prompted to probe for the hidden beauty that otherwise he fears to approach.

In other poems Ronsard took obvious advantage of his patrons' enthusiasm for building; in these he makes the composing process of architect and poet coincide. To write a poem for the cardinal of Lorraine becomes 'pour te bastir une gloire' (to build you a glory); to leave a record worthy of the protonotary Mauléon is 'basti[r] en l'univers / Les Colonnes d'une Mémoire' (to build in the world / the columns of a memory). Thus, evidently, he pampered a prevailing taste; but he was also declaring war. The mention of building a monument or erecting columns to perpetuate the memory of a public figure might make real architectural images spring to his reader's mind. However, if that reader was learned (and some were) he would have recognised verbal echoes of Pindar's hymns—'j'érige, comme un monument de la victoire que Théron a remportée à Olympie, cet hymne' (I build this hymn like a monument in honour of the victory achieved by Thieron at Olympus).[94] Then, like Ronsard, he would have conflated contemporary fashion and emulation of great models from the past.

By such conflations, Ronsard tried to make plain that poetry could do all that the visual arts could achieve. Its lines could transmit terror and fear by sculpting flesh into marble, as in the final words of love sonnet 58.

Telle enflure d'yvoire en sa voute arrondie,
Tel relief de Porphyre, ouvrage de Phidie,
Eut Andromede alors que Persee passa,
Quand il la vit liée à des roches marines,
Et quand la peur de mort tout le corps luy glassa,
Transformant ses tetins en deux boules marbrines.

(G, 417)

Just like a rounded figure of ivory beneath the circular vault, or a relief in Porphyry made by Phidias, such was Andromeda when Perseus passed by, when he saw her tied to the marine rocks, and when the fear of death froze her entire form, transforming her breasts into two sculptured balls.

Poetry's 'images bien tirées' (well-made images) were equal to those found in paint, metal, wood, or stone. In addition, poetry had musical qualities not found in the visual arts, qualities that penetrated right through to the soul of man, raising him up to a higher moral plane.[95]

Such views were by no means novel; in the Renaissance, they were repeated whenever a poet sought to establish a higher status for his art. What is perhaps remarkable about Ronsard, however, is the assertive and confident tones that always accompany his claims. When, for instance, he considered the representational power of his verses, as compared to paint or bronze, he claimed for the former a greater liveliness—'Ma peinture n'est pas mue / Mais vive' (My painting is not silent / but alive)[96]—and a heightened sense of presence:

Le marbre, et l'airain vestu
D'un labeur vif par l'enclume,
N'animent tant la vertu
Que les Muses par la plume.

(P 1:379; L 1:92)

Marble and bronze that wears the lively work of the anvil do not stimulate virtue as do the Muses through the pen.

The absolute nature of the statements seems to defy contradiction.

For further evidence of Ronsard's opinions on the superiority of poetry over all other arts, we may turn to his statements about the lasting power of verse. Poems triumph over time; they offer escape from contingency; and for those mortals lucky enough to figure in them, they grant the greatest gift of all—immortality. These points are made many times by Ronsard, formulated most succinctly in the following lines:

Ne pilier, ne terme Dorique
D'histoires vieilles décoré,
Ne marbre tiré de l'Afrique
En colonnes elabouré
Ne te feront si bien revivre.

Neither pillar nor Doric column, decorated with stories of old, nor marble brought from Africa worked into columns can thus well make your name live on.

Here, the noblest of Greek architectural styles, the Doric, and the most lasting of stones, marble, fail to achieve the durability of verse.[97] When we think of the ravages of time, when we consider the appalling conditions of insecurity, ill health, and war that even the richest men experienced almost daily at this time, we appreciate the extraordinary appeal of Ronsard's picture of his art.

An overwhelming attachment to the visual dominated France in the sixteenth century, and it brought poets and artists into close proximity. Whether they were competing or collaborating, their artistic objectives were similar and the criteria they used to praise a good poem or a picture extended even to the gestures of courtiers. All these factors conditioned poets' thinking about their work and powerfully influenced their compositions. Ronsard, for one, recognised the representational advances painters had made and clearly admired their illusionist techniques. To overtop these achievements, he argued for poetry magical powers—'C'est vouloir peindre en l'onde, et arrester le vent' (It's like striving to paint the waves or to arrest the wind; L 18 : 35 – 36)—straining for the impossible.

But although Ronsard was able to refine his aims and directions by contemplating the work of artists, he was not always artistically successful in practice.[98] In *Peintures d'un paysage*, for instance, we noted that he got too close to paint and failed to control the overall structure of the poem. On other occasions, similar urges to display poetic virtuosity and to pack too many visual references into inadequate space reduced the suggestive power so necessary to the poet. Nonetheless, contemporaries and successive generations of readers have always been impressed by the quality of his images. In subsequent chapters we shall explore his ability to give them life and lasting value in four distinct modes. As a fitting end to the present discussion, however, let us quote from the funeral oration that the Cardinal Du Perron gave in Ronsard's honour in 1586. There, in tones of passion before an approving audience, he praised the poet who had sought to praise the world:

> Nous ne t'adressons point des statues, des colonnes, des arcs triomphaux: car toymesme t'es érigé des images, des effigies et des statues par tout le monde; non pas des images muettes et inanimées, non pas des statues caducques et perissables, et qui tombent d'elles-mesmes dès le propre jour que meurent les personnes à qui elles sont dediées, comme celle de Hieron Roy de Syracuse, mais des images respirantes et cognoissantes, et des statues eternelles et perdurables.[99]

> We do not build you statues, columns, or triumphal arches: because you yourself have raised up images, effigies, and statues for everyone; not silent or lifeless images, not blunted statues that do not last and which begin to fall into ruins on the very day that those to whom they are dedicated pass away, like that of Hieron of Syracuse, but knowing and breathing images and permanent statues that last forever.

III

ICONIC FORMS

Picture portrayeth what is alreadie done,
What is adoing, and what as yet is to be done.
FRANCISCUS JUNIUS
The Painting of the Ancients

AMONG THE ORNAMENTS THAT decorated royal palaces and noble homes
in sixteenth-century France and within the increasingly rich scenes with
which poets adorned their works were images accorded particular status.
These images, whether painted by brush or pen, had common characteristics and functions derived from the same source. In order to convey something of their special (almost sacred) flavour, I am suggesting that we think
of such images as icons. Although sixteenth-century writers did not specifically attribute the same quasi-religious dimension to the words *icon* and
icones as we now tend to do, it is clear from the recurrence, placement,
and handling of certain images that they were considered as having exceptional distinction and were recognisable 'set pieces'.

These iconic images have easily identifiable forms. Although they were
usually rather small objects—a shield, a cloak, elements of a prince's armour, or a table utensil—they were laden, almost overladen, with decorative features that covered every available surface and crammed every space
with artistic significance. While creating a work worthy of a princely patron, the poet or artist was equally concerned to display his own skill at
overcoming the technical problems involved, for instance, in engraving immense scenes of battle upon a shield, or in interrupting the narrative flow
of a poem, as Homer did when he described the varied pictures of the
world and of life that Vulcan had wrought on Achilles' shield. The habit
of concentrating so much into such comparatively small space had important aesthetic consequences. For the artist, it drew explicit attention to
his craftsmanship and to his miniaturising power; for the poet, it high-
lighted his ability to describe elaborate and complex scenes 'with so much

89

evidence that they are almost to be seen with the eyes in our heads', as Mazzoni put it when he compared narrative poetry to a speaking picture.[1] In many respects, the poet's task was the more difficult, for he had not only to motivate his audience to admire the decorative qualities of his pictorial insets but also to persuade them that the interruption was a necessary and yet integrated part of his narrative.

Knowledge of a long tradition of classical writing had taught sixteenth-century readers to vary the pace of their reading. It had similarly given them time to visualise and ponder the 'significant' pictures that had been drawn, since such obviously and deliberately engineered set pieces contained meanings that had to be elucidated. The descriptions of shields or cloaks in narrative poems were, therefore, more than decorative interludes; they had symbolic functions. They might, as did Homer's description of Achilles' shield, act as a record of knowledge about the world and as a source of instruction. Or, they might (as in Virgil or Claudian) serve as potent indications of future events. Whatever their function, and in some cases several roles were incorporated into a single set piece, these iconic forms assumed a particular colouring. In narrative poems, they stood out from the rest and challenged poets of future generations to imitate their skill and their recording power; and in artefacts they were perpetuated. In Renaissance France especially, these forms blazed forth in the embossed shields and corselets of the parade armour so favoured by Henri II and members of his court.

Their attraction seems to have been at least twofold: on the one hand, the richness of their decoration provided another example of the prevailing taste for extravagant ornamentation; and on the other, the lasting power of these iconic forms, which make the events or personal deeds they record live again and again, made such image making singularly appropriate to a contemporary art and poetry so imbued with the need to praise. These artists and poets, who were ever preoccupied with establishing their own immortality, were quick to recognise that such forms could be exploited both for their own selfish ends and to accommodate the ambitions of their patrons. In an era when writers, thinkers, and preachers were preeminently concerned with the swift passage of time and with man's fallen state, and when the sight of misery around them emphasised even more eloquently the basic fragility of the human condition, it was a consolation and an excitement to hold on to those forms of artistic expression that seemed to give some kind of permanency to human endeavour and achievement.[2]

Moreover, writers and artists could assume that the well-educated among their patrons were familiar with the large number of pictorial set pieces that literary and artistic traditions had bequeathed to them. They could also take it for granted that any re-presentation of these iconic

23. Pierre Redon, the shield of Charles IX, gold and enamelled
(ca. 1570) (Louvre; Arch. Photo. Paris/S.P.A.D.E.M.).

forms would be keenly judged and assessed; and that innovations or variations on well-known themes would be appreciated by the noble connoisseur who delighted in learned reminiscences. Therefore, the poet trusted
that his description of the scenes encrusted upon a shield would conjure
up splendid contemporary examples (fig. 23) and recall earlier descriptions: Hesiod's shield of Hercules, Homer's shield of Achilles, Virgil's
shield of Aeneas, or the shield of Minerva made by Phidias, the marvels of

which were reported by Plutarch and Pliny. Since these classical examples exerted such an influence, let us consider them in some detail before we turn to sixteenth-century conceptions.

The Classical Heritage

One of the earliest examples of a painted inset in a classical text—Hesiod's fragment *The Shield of Hercules*—clearly exemplifies the educational value of such forms. The shield depicts two contrasting modes of life. First and foremost, it is an instrument of war. Painted in variegated colours, it speaks to posterity through dragons and serpents; through visages of tumult, fear, gloom, and courage; and with the appearance of Mars and his eager steeds, and of the battles of Lapithae and the Centaurs. These scenes were intended to provide the reader with an awesome and appalling reminder of brutality and strength, to bring alive the full horrors of war, and to act as a martial lesson. The second mode is represented by an assembly of gods. Hesiod evokes their sacred songs and their wealth, and depicts a city of peace and festivity, with sights of plenty in the fields and vineyards. Here suggested is a life regulated by the forces of harmony and tranquillity, a life that counterbalances the first horrid vision of fate clad in clothes gory with the blood of men. As a tool of persuasion, the shield both encourages the strong in muscle and offers an entry into an exalted world of plenty. Such an object forces the mind to contemplate alternative ways of being, and it suggests—but does not dictate—choice. Hesiod clearly intended more than the striking expression of warlike deeds or a beautiful existence.[3]

The educative purposes of such detailed description is even clearer in Homer's account of Achilles' shield (*Iliad* 18:478–616). On the shield Vulcan had hammered the contours of the earth, the constellations of the heavens, and the mighty ocean. In addition, two cities could be seen on the shield: the first, a blackened city under siege; while the second seemed alive with marriage celebrations, processions, festivals and games, the surrounding fields thick with crops and vineyards laden with grapes. This was the fair vision of the fruits of peace. The message here is obvious, but we notice that Homer has posited his two views of life within the more general frame of the world's structure, thereby demonstrating that poets were both counsellors and natural philosophers. Later generations of poets were to emphasise this cosmological dimension in their work. Ovid painted the world on his palace of the sun in the *Metamorphoses* (1:1–20), while Claudian had Proserpine weave a gift for her mother, on which she sewed the concourse of atoms, Jupiter's dwelling places, the ocean, and Nature in the process of ordering chaos into a harmonious world with hot and cold zones.[4] Thus, poets saw themselves as philosophers probing the mechanisms that brought the world into being, and having the duty of introducing their audience to discoveries about the workings of the heavens, the dispositions of the spheres, and the temperament and habits of mankind. Through their pictorial compositions they offered lively panoramas and an opportunity for those willing to ponder the fundamental principles of being and of behaviour. In this way, poets became discoverers.

Yet, their chief mode of communication was through the painting of images, and the effect of such painting was generally accepted as being dependent on degrees of craftsmanship. From the beginnings of narrative poetry, pictorial insets provided unrivalled occasions for the poet to display his skill to a level that touched divine performance. Indeed, most of the models we have mentioned so far were forged by the gods. Vulcan and the cyclops made the shields of Hercules and Achilles and the armour of Aeneas, while the visions of Olympus that Minerva and Arachne wove on cloaks in their celebrated contest are described by Ovid (the divine surrogate) as scenes that 'equalled the mists in their fineness'; both goddess and pupil marvelled at their respective skills (*Metamorphoses* 6:45–145). The attention here is focussed on the quality of the workmanship and on the refinement of observation and rendering. Other divine productions are revered for the forceful vitality of the scenes and characters depicted. In describing the cloak embroidered for Jason by Minerva, Apollonius of Rhodes says that the figures were so realistically worked that they seemed about to break into speech (*Argonautica* 1:721–78); Phrixus the Minyan appeared, for example, 'as though he were in very deed listening to the ram, while it was like one speaking'.

Thus these classical passages illustrate two complementary activities: the artist or poet has the all-important ability to grant life to things, and the beholder is to concentrate on the realism of the details. A shield that teems with multiple and decorative forms inevitably draws our gaze to consider first this figure and then that; their very quantity defies any serious consideration of their general disposition or overall coherence or of the interrelationships among individual elements. This classical standard of fine craftsmanship of minute details, faithfully rendered and pregnant with meaning, whether the object actually existed or was imaginatively created by the poet, continued to exert an influence on medieval and Renaissance art and literature.

Two examples, taken from a medieval and a Renaissance re-creation of a classical text, serve to illustrate the concern for detailed ornamentation for its own sake. As Ovid relates the adventures of Perseus in the fifth book of the *Metamorphoses*, he describes how Minerva comes to the rescue of her brother and protects him with her shield. The shield is merely mentioned. In a fourteenth-century French adaptation of the fable, however, the shield is the subject of a substantial pictorial inset, some 476 lines of the text.[5] Then, in Blaise de Vigenère's version, we are told that there was in Athens a colossal statue of Minerva sculpted by Phidias in gold and ivory. The shield seems to have aroused particular interest because of the quality of its workmanship. This is how Vigenère describes it:

> L'escu de laquelle estoit ouvré d'un très souverain artifice; assavoir sur le bord d'iceluy, qui se reiettoit en dehors, la bataille des Amazones contre les Atheniens; et au champ se reforçant en dedans le conbat des Geans et des Dieux; et au liège de ses pantouffles la meslée des Centaures et Lapithes. La moindre chose de tous ces petits enrichissemens estant très exactement recherchee et parfaite, à pair au visage de la Deesse.[6]

> The shield was worked with rare skill; that is, around its outer edge, the battle of the Amazons and Athenians; on the surface was spread the war between the Titans and the Gods; on the upper part of her slippers, the combat between the Centaurs and Lapithae. The tiniest element of all these embellishments was thoroughly researched and without blemish, equal to the face of the goddess.

Vigenère's idea of supreme craftsmanship—'très souverain artifice'—is an assemblage of myths that fill every inch of the surface with figures writhing in action (*la bataille . . . le conbat . . . la meslée*) and whose gestures, including minute marks of facial expression, are researched and accurately recorded.

The recording power of such sculptured or painted surfaces was an important function. In many classical writers, and notably Virgil, the decorated record stands not only as a challenge to the ravages of time but also as a text to be pondered by hero and reader, for it contains messages for the future. For example, in the *Aeneid*, there is a conscious interplay between past, present, and future events. In the opening book of the epic, just after arriving in Carthage, Aeneas comes upon a temple situated at the heart of a grove. Its walls are covered with pictures relating to the Trojan war (*Aeneid* 1:441–93). His gaze encounters King Priam, the contest of Greeks and Trojans, Achilles in his chariot, the tents of Rhesus, the armless Troilus, and Hector being dragged around the walls of the city. And suddenly, among these ghastly scenes he recognizes his own form: 'he knew himself, too, mingling in the fury'. This recognition of a different self, projected in paint and coming out of the past, has an overwhelming effect on Virgil's hero: it produces in him a state of mental stupefaction that dominates his first meeting with Dido. But equally significant, this vivid recall of terrifying events from the past keeps alive the pain and the excitement, and reminds the reader of Aeneas's mission. The painted inset, therefore, works in at least two ways: within the narrative it affects the hero's destiny, and to readers it offers a kind of moral permanency. In a sense, Virgil has frozen past experience in these painted scenes; yet, the draughtsmanship is so effective and the spectacle, as a result, so compelling that the mural stands out from the poem. The memories themselves are, of course, important, but it is the manner of their recording that emancipates them from the binds of time. By giving them iconic status, Virgil allows their reverberations to echo through successive centuries, thus making them forever available.

From the events of the past attentive readers could, as Boccaccio later suggested, infer the future.[7] Some authors made the signs very evident, and the painted inset served as an engraved prophecy. The most famous classical example is Virgil's description of the making of Aeneas's shield (*Aeneid* 8:608–731). Forged by Vulcan, its divine craftsmanship was impeccable. The lord of iron, endowed (like all immortals) with the gift of prophecy, engraved upon the shield the fortunes of Italy and the triumphs of Rome, carving into its surface the entire line that descended from Ascanius to Caesar Augustus, and detailing all the wars as in succession they were fought. As Aeneas lifted upon his shoulder this spectacle of his descendants' fame and fortunes, he admired the incredible artistry of the figures, though he comprehended nothing of their meaning. It is left to the reader to appreciate the traces of history that Vulcan has indicated, Aeneas having been denied the shudders of anticipation and horror that Proserpine experienced as she wove into her tapestry of the world the sighs and portents of her own gloomy fate: 'she embroidered the accursed seat of her uncle, Dis, the nether Gods, her destined fellows. Nor did the omen pass unmarked, for prophetic of the future her cheeks grew wet with sudden tears' (*De raptu Proserpinae* 1:246–75).

In this presentation of Aeneas's shield, Virgil is not interested in developing any serious emotional response from his hero. His concern lies elsewhere. Although as a craftsman he makes the most of the richness of the precious metals in this ornate narrative picture, which provides the culmination to book 8 of the *Aeneid*, Virgil's main purpose is to show himself as *vates*, as prophet and propagandist for Augustus's regime. Military prowess and dynastic considerations are central to the elaboration of Aeneas's shield. The aim is to celebrate Rome and, in particular, to praise and magnify the sacred role of Caesar Augustus. The emperor's dynasty is woven into that great sweep of historical circumstance that led inexorably to his threefold triumph: the climax of Virgil's description shows Caesar, seated beneath the snow-white portal of Apollo's temple, reviewing the offerings of the nations he had subdued and affixing them to the proud doors. So Aeneas's shield becomes a mode of panegyric.

Later poets exploited further this potential for praise contained in iconic forms. The most outstanding example, perhaps, can be found in the writings of Claudian, whose panegyrics were especially highly regarded in

24. Ecole de Fontainebleau, design for an
ornamental cup (Bibliothèque Nationale).

the Renaissance.[8] In the third book of *Stilicho*, Rome presents a consul's
cloak embroidered in heavy gold and silver designs, a blatant expression
of Stilicho's dynastic ambitions. On the cloth is figured a palace within
which is depicted his wife in childbirth, anxiously watched over by her
mother. In one part the stitches shape the child in the image of his father;
while in another, Stilicho is seen teaching his grandson—'the emperor that
is to be'—the science of war. The garment's narrative of implied praise is
completed when that child, grown to manhood, is shown in the act of
marrying the daughter and sister of an emperor. Thus Stilicho secures the
imperial throne for his descendants.[9] Claudian's description of the decorations on the cloak is deliberate and extensive; it halts the flow of oratory as
it seeks not to persuade but rather to make the listener visualise the actual
scenes of a dynasty coming into being. As with Aeneas's shield, the painted
inset replaces narrative currents with a static picture, and by that change of
pace and through the detailed elaboration the author gives to his painting,
it acquires exceptional status. It takes on all the qualities and concentrated
power of the icon.

I have dwelt long on these instances of iconic forms in classical literature
because they exerted such a powerful influence over Renaissance poets

generally, and because they illustrate the range and diversity of functions writers gave to decorative set pieces. As we have seen, they could be simply an occasion for exhibiting virtuoso narrative and descriptive powers. Simultaneously, they might concentrate learning and discovery, and provide lessons in virtue and resolve. As lively remembrances and engraved prophecies, they often became imposing modes of praise. These set pieces form the essential context in which the nature and import of some of Ronsard's more highly decorated poems of praise can be understood. Indubitably, Ronsard was at least as much inspired by these luxurious descriptions in classical literary sources as he was by the sight of contemporary armour and of elaborate drinking vessels (fig. 24).

Ronsard's Embroidered Cloaks

Ronsard describes three cloaks: Neptune's cloak made for the wedding of Thetis and Peleus in *Le Ravissement de Céphale* (1550); Châtillon's robe in *Le Temple des Chastillons* (1555); and the cloaks worn by Castor and Pollux in the *Hymne de Calays et de Zethés* (1556).[10] All three examples are embroidered around with elaborate scenes.

Although the classical tradition served as inspiration, the actual details of Ronsard's embroideries have no clear classical parallels. On Neptune's blue cloak is depicted the earth, a storm, a shipwreck, and a triumph of the king of the seas finally calming the raging waves.

> Au vif traite y fut la terre
> En boule arrondie au tour,
> Avec la mer qui la serre
> De ses bras tout à l'entour:
> Au milieu d'elle un orage
> Mouvoit ses flots d'ire pleins;
> Palles du futur naufrage
> Les mariniers estoient peints.
>   Desarmée est leur navire
> Du haut jusqu'au fondement,
> Ça et là le vent le vire
> Serve à son commandement;
> Le ciel foudroye, et les flames
> Tombent d'un vol escarté,
> Et ce qui reste des rames
> Vont lechant de leur clarté.
> . . . .
>   Neptune y fut peint luy-mesme,
> Brodé d'or, qui du danger

Tirant le marinier blesme,
L'eau en l'eau faisoit ranger;

. . . .

   Luy, les brides abandonne
A son char, si qu'en glissant
Sur la mer, ses loix il donne
Au flot luy obeyssant,
Et se jouant dessus l'onde
Se monstre seul gouverneur
Et Roy de l'humide monde
Qui s'encline à son honneur.

(lines 25–72)

True to life, the earth was here depicted its rounded ball shaped by the sea
that holds it all around in its embrace. In the centre of the cloth, a storm
poured forth its waves filled with ire; pale at the thought of the shipwreck to
come, thus were the sailors depicted. Their ship is shown disarmed. From
the top to the bottom, hither and thither the wind drives it subservient to its
command. The sky thunders, and flames fall in sideways flight, and all that
remains of the oars is seen licking through their light. . . . Neptune himself
is shown there; embroidered in gold, pulling the livid sailor, keeping back
wave after wave. . . . Neptune abandons the course to his triumphal car,
riding over the sea, commands the waves to obey him; thus disporting himself above the sea, he shows himself sole master and king of this watery
world that bows to his honour.

In these scenes there are certainly many verbal echoes of the *Aeneid* 1:
81–156, where Virgil describes the great storm that scattered the Trojan
ships and that was subsequently calmed by Neptune's words. In the visual
arts, however, the calming of the storm and the sea-god's majesty had become Renaissance topoi, and Ronsard could easily have been inspired by
the abundance of enamelled, engraved, embroidered, and painted stories
of Neptune's fame. His power to quell the storm was to be seen almost
anywhere: set in one of the arcades of the ballroom at Fontainebleau, engraved by Raimondi to serve as a frontispiece for Italian editions of Virgil's works (fig. 25), and copied many times by enamellers—René Reymond, Pierre Courteys, and the Péricaud jewellers set the theme on tazzas,
on saltcellars, ewers, and caskets. Androuet Du Cerceau gave circular form
to Neptune's triumph in his engravings—a shape that attracted many
goldsmiths, if we judge from the number of engravings that have survived,
although the splendid silver-gilt basin (now in the collection at Fitzwilliam
College, Cambridge) is the only finished example known to have escaped
holocausts and revolutions.[11]

Whatever the source of inspiration for Ronsard's elaborate description,
whether conscious emulation of earlier poets or competition with contemporary artists, his purpose, like theirs, appears to be to attempt magnifi-

cence. The material of the cloak is 'une soye non commune' (of unusual silk), and onto its golden colour Ronsard weaves contrasting hues—the blacks and blues of the billowing clouds pierced through the vermillion, gold, and green. As a painter would, Ronsard insists straightaway that his embroidery is true to life (*au vif*); but in the poem this lifelikeness is achieved not so much through the use of varied colours but rather through means more specific to poetry. Although he is undeniably concerned with richness and pictorial quality, the emphasis quickly shifts to movement, as the short, often broken lines imitate the uncertain swaying of the wind— 'ça et là le vent le vire' (hither and thither the wind drives it)—while strident verbs convey the violent sounds of activity: the crash of thunder, and the brilliance of the flames that lick the shattered oars with their light. The rapid rhythm is perhaps less appropriate, however, to Neptune's appearance as he slides into view in majesty.

Over and above his attempt to capture in words the visual power of the storm and its dreadful human consequences, Ronsard also seeks to emphasise the passage of time and to portray the apprehension of the sailors

25. Marc Antoine Raimondi, Neptune calming the storm, engraved after Raphael (Print Room, Albertina, Vienna).

'palles du futur naufrage' (pale at the thought of the shipwreck to come). In this short phrase Ronsard has concentrated a temporal sequence that a painter could depict only on a broad canvas, and probably by breaking the picture into a series of painted stories. Although the linear form of poetry has this narrative advantage, here Ronsard merely touches it in, directing all his energies towards an expansive and colourful unfolding of a highly decorated garment.

Yet, one might ask, what has this impressive embroidery to do with the stated subject of the poem—the rape of Cephalus? The poem is a kind of triptych, 'divisé en trois pauses' (divided into three sections). It is at first difficult to see how part 1 (Neptune's cloak and the Trojan war) and part 3 (Themis's prophecies about Achilles) relate to the centrepiece, Aurora's love for Cephalus. All three episodes of the poem, however, concern love between mortals and immortals; and, more significantly, parts 1 and 3 have oracular functions. The love matches described predate the collapse of Troy, but they serve to instruct the reader who needs to be reminded of these details in order to appreciate the poem fully. Thus, Neptune's cloak serves as recollection.[12] That Ronsard chose not to convey the information more succinctly shows that he was principally concerned with poetic display. Disregarding the likelihood of producing a lopsided poem, he crowded the borders of his work with ornament so that his own rich decorative power might amply be set forth.

Decoration and explication are also blended in Ronsard's description of the garments made by Leda for her sons, Castor and Pollux. In the hymn dedicated to two other Argonauts—Calays and Zethés—Ronsard interrupts his account of the heroes' embarkation to offer a decorative inset of some twenty-two lines (P 2:125–44; L 8:255–93). Thought by a seventeenth-century commentator to have been inspired by a painting, the poem develops a familiar theme.[13] Although many of its details are not in the obvious early sources—Apollonius of Rhodes or Valerius Flaccus—they appear in printed books and exhibitions on the Pont Notre Dame for the royal entry into Paris in 1549.[14] In Ronsard's poem, Castor and Pollux are shown emblazoned in gold and silk. Their royal purple robes are embroidered with the mountains and rivers of their birthplace and they show the Argonauts' divine provenance through a vivid representation of the broken egg that gave them being, which is seen lying beside Leda and the swan.

The principal function of this embroidered inset seems to have been to display divine ancestry, which itself already guaranteed the triumphs marked out for Castor and Pollux and which Phineus prophecies (lines 482–651). The divine presence is primarily established, Ronsard argues, through the living quality of the figures embedded in the silk:

Voloit an natural la semblance d'un cygne,
Ayant le col si beau et le regard si douz,
Que chacun eust pensé que Jupiter dessous
Encor' aimoit caché, tant l'image portraite
Et du Cygne et de Lede estoit vivement faite.

(lines 142–46)

There was flying, just as in real life, a swan, its neck so beautiful, its look so
sweet, that everyone guessed that Jupiter in love still lay beneath, so genuinely rendered was the representation of Leda and the swan.

Ronsard's poem, however, does not specifically celebrate the exploits of
Leda's offspring. Their divine status adds lustre in a contest of heroic
achievements against the odds (those of Calays and Zethés) and makes a
promise of future extraordinary deeds. In the closing lines of the *Hymne
de Calays et de Zethés* Ronsard deliberately recalls the sons of Jupiter and
Leda:

Je me veux souvenir de Castor et de Pollux,
Enfans de Jupiter, pour rendre leur mémoire,
Par les peuples François fleurissante de gloire,
Ils méritent mes vers.

(lines 701–4)

I wish to recall the memory of Castor and Pollux, the children of Jupiter, to
make known their memory and to keep it covered in glory for the people of
France; they are worthy of my verse.

Here, Ronsard joins the narration of legendary events and his poem's future; in doing so, he demonstrates how closely linked in his mind are notions of divine status, acts of renown, and the dignity of his poetry. The
children of Jove are worthy of his verse.

The past and the future so conjoined are also characteristic of the ornamentation Ronsard imagined for Châtillon's cardinal's robe (P 2:833–39;
L 8:72–84). In the *Temple des Chastillons* (1555) the robe, 'de mainte
belle histoire en cent lieux diaprée' (decorated in a hundred places with
many a beautiful story), was to be exposed on the heroic temple that the
poet dedicated to the entire Châtillon family. Although Ronsard has moved
from the world of legend into that of precise historical figures, the technique of decoration is hardly distinguishable, borrowing both from myth
and allegory as the poet seeks that double celebration of patron and self.
Châtillon's calling and his wealth of spirit are made manifest in the figures
on his robe that symbolize Truth and Faith, while allegories of Hope and
Love are threaded in to describe Ronsard's own feelings. Ronsard flat-

ters the learning of the Lorraine prince by describing as imprinted on the cardinal's robe the mountains and woods sacred to the Muses, with his somewhat obscure references to Ascra (the birthplace of Hesiod) and to Lebethra and Haemus (a fountain and mount frequented by the Muses).[15] The robe appears in company with portraits of Châtillon's two brothers depicted as in life in 'ce temple de gloire' (this temple of honour), built as a lasting monument to their honour and virtue. By erecting a temple, which was a time-honoured way of paying homage to a deity, Ronsard hoped to give permanent expression to his patron's noble example so that future generations might admire and learn, and simultaneously to exhibit his own talent for embellishment.

In these three examples of gorgeous embroidery, the decorative elements, although prominent, are neither entirely inappropriate nor irrelevant. Their elaboration served as explanation, and their designs recalled past events to give forms to the future, and often thereby to praise the present. The ability to appreciate these elaborate traceries also contained a touch of compliment, for the poet assumes that his patron and reader is a learned man who also responds readily to beauty. Ronsard's cloaks were embroidered with myths and erudite reminiscences, and with scenes and symbols that were very accessible to sixteenth-century audiences, since they also appeared on many surfaces susceptible to decoration. Although the three garments are individualised for specific purposes, the effect of their designs is of a fairly general nature, one that, as we have seen, has a timeless quality. In other instances in which Ronsard was undoubtedly inspired by iconic traditions, their meaning and their application are much more precise.

A Prince's Armour

In the commentary Ronsard wrote at the end of his life to serve as an introduction to his works—*Avertissement aux oeuvres* (1587)—he discoursed at some length on the ways of decorating and enriching verse in order to achieve the range and variety of theme and style that heroic poetry demanded. The poet, he explains, works on the terrain of 'le possible et sur ce qui se peut faire" (the possible and on that which can be created). There he builds his work

> tantost par personnages, parlans les uns aux autres, tantost par songes, propheties et peintures insérées contre le dos d'une muraille et des harnois, et principalement des boucliers. . . . Tu n'oublieras à faire armer les capitaines, comme il faut, de toutes les pieces de leur harnois.
>
> (P 2 : 1018, 1024; L 16 : 336–37)

26. Antoine Caron (attribution), pen drawing of the Siege of Metz, 1552 (Bibliothèque Nationale).

> sometimes with characters speaking to each other, then with dreams, prophecies or images, set against the wall of a building or into horse trappings, and especially displayed on military accoutrement. Don't forget to arm your captains properly, with every possible piece of their armoury.

In these lines, Ronsard admits the decorative value of painted insets, although in this context he is more particularly concerned with military accoutrement. His knowledge of the technical terms needed to describe the parts of a nobleman's armour is displayed in a number of poems, but his most sustained attention to these matters occurs in *La Harangue de très illustre Prince, François, Duc de Guise aux soldats de Metz* (1553).

The successful outcome for the French of Charles V's siege of Metz made a great impact and was celebrated by most contemporary poets and artists (fig. 26).[16] Ronsard's contribution in *La Harangue* chooses a prince's speech and the description of his armour as a way of congratulating François, duke of Guise and the entire Lorraine line on their outstanding military achievements. The poem begins with a pun:

> Quand Charles Empereur, qui se donne en songeant
> Tout l'Empire du monde, et qui se va rongeant
> D'une gloire affamée, et d'un soin d'entreprendre
> De vouloir, à son dam, contre nostre Roy prendre
> Les nouveaux murs François d'une foible cité,
> Où le Destin avoit son OUTRE limité,
> De gens et de chevaux effroya la campaigne. . . .

When Charles the Emperor, who in his mind attributes to himself the destiny of the world, and who rages forth thirsting for glory, taking care against his knightly cousin, to wrest from our king the newly built French walls of a defenceless city where fate had willed that his ambition should find its term, and with his people and his steeds set fright amid the countryside. . . .

Charles's motto *Plus ultra* (yet further) indicated the soaring territorial ambitions of that emperor, and Ronsard uses the phrase 'son OUTRE limité' to set the ironical tone that anticipates the imminent downfall of the imperious prince. The bulk of the poem, however, concerns the arming of the duke and his exhortation to the army:

> Lors ton frere de Guise, eslancé d'un plein saut
> Sur le rempart cognu, plein d'effroyable audace,
> Desfiant leurs canons s'arma devant leur face.

> (lines 30–32)

Then, your brother Guise, with a single bound on the ramparts was seen, sparkling with dreadful courage, and before their cannons and their very own faces publicly armed himself.

In contrast to the puny and ineffective motto of the emperor, the duke of Guise is presented as ostentatiously, and with incredible audacity, arming himself in full sight of the imperial hosts. He clothes himself from head to foot in glistening gold and silver metal, covered all over with engraved work. His shoulder pieces carry on one side the engraved portrait of Pope Urban II, while on the other could be clearly seen the visage of Godefroy de Bouillon. His breastplate shone with an ocean filled with three hundred ships of Christian soldiers returning in triumph from the pagan shores littered with graves and corpses. His shield, studded with the hundred eyes of Argus, blazed forth at its centre with a three-headed gorgon, while serpents twined their way around the edge decorated with the victorious deeds of the house of Lorraine, and especially those of Roi René and the Conte du Maine. His brilliant helmet sported the bitter and oft represented struggle between Hercules and the wrestler-giant Antaeus, who was squeezed to death.[17] His sword sparkled in the sunlight from the abundance and the brilliance of the many jewels set into its metal. Such were the glorious arms that Ronsard gave to the gifted favourite of the Lorraine house; and any witness to such splendour was supposed to respond as did the soldiers of the Greek general Philopaemen in Junius's retelling. These 'painted cassocks' evoked the proper military spirit in the Greeks: 'Magnanimitie and courage could be mightily enflamed by the very sight of such ornaments'.[18]

The learned Charles de Lorraine, to whom the poem is dedicated, would have had little difficulty in matching Ronsard's descriptive skill with other famous instances of highly decorated arms drawn from the strong literary tradition we have examined. In recognising the classical sources, however, he would have noted that the details of the Guise armour owed nothing to Homer's account of Achilles' armour, nor to Hesiod's lengthy description of the shield of Hercules. As far as the general design is concerned, he would have noticed certain affinities with the ideas of Virgil, who had pictured the fame and fortunes of Aeneas's descendants on his shield, and Ronsard's borrowing of elements from Homer's account of Agamemnon's armour—the gorgon on his shield and the colours of the rainbow.

The classical legacy thus includes some decorative elements and the notion that what a warrior displayed engraved upon his person represented a speaking picture of past force and a sign of future strength. The largest fund of inspiration, however, clearly derived from contemporary taste, which not only revelled in physical combat, tournaments, jousts, and naumachia but also favoured the reading of medieval romances. Early sixteenth-century encomia had, when appropriate, taken knowledge of arms and armour for granted. Once Ronsard had shown the aesthetic advantages of responding to the contemporary taste for the extravagantly decorated and had successfully set the heroic tone, other poets followed suit and filled their verses with descriptions of elaborate armour and martial feats. Baïf, for instance, even presented secretary Villeroy in 1573 with 108 lines of fifteen-syllable verse to describe Perseus's armour.[19] The hero's breastplate was engraved with the scene of the gods and the Titans doing battle, and, Baïf maintained, each figure displayed muscular strength and physical contortions worthy of the pictorial power of Giulio Romano.[20] Under the Valois, French court society, for all its pretentions to elegance and cultured conversations and for all its attachment to luxurious living, privileged war above everything and welcomed the opportunities it gave for display of physical prowess.

Henri II, who clearly thought of himself as the martial prince *par excellence*, was a skilled horseman, a good fighter, and an avid collector of *militaria*. It is therefore not surprising that he actively encouraged this fervour for war. He published edicts ordering town councils everywhere in his kingdom to foot the bill for the erection of lists 'pour iouster à la lance' (to joust with the lance) so that the young might learn the exercise of arms. At Fontainebleau, he moved his apartments in 1554 and had them and those of the duchesse d'Etampes redecorated with less lovesick themes—Niccolo dell'Abbate was later to paint a series on the deeds of Alexander to entertain the king's mistress.[21] Additionally, Henri continued to improve the fine collections of arms and armour inherited from his father through the

27. Niccolo della Casa, Henri II, engraved 1547 (Bibliothèque Nationale).

services of the brothers Caesar and Baptiste de Gambres, who made many magnificent suits for Henri and his sons. Their decoration of these armours is varied but reflects the same motifs carved in the wood panels of the château: masks and floral designs as well as military scenes. Indeed, this collecting craze seems to have continued beyond the king's death, for we find that work for the decoration of the armoury was still being carried out in 1562. His courtiers emulated his example: at Oiron, the master of the horse displayed painted images of the royal steeds along the entire wall space on the ground floor of his château; while Montmorency incorporated pictures of contemporary French victories into the decoration of his magnificent house at Ecouen.[22]

The official portrait of French rulers had, as we have seen, evolved markedly during the sixteenth century. Under Henri II, there was a distinct propensity towards portraying the monarch in full armour, a mode of representation most fitted to those holding the highest office and one customary among the Romans.[23] In the museum at Chantilly, for example, there is such a half-length portrait of Henri II, who is shown in the black armour, elaborately decorated in scroll work by the Gambres brothers; the suit itself can still be admired in the Musée de l'Armée, while an engraving of it adorns Pierre Paschal's printed oration on the king.[24] For another true life portrait of the king, this one projecting the powerful image of a Roman emperor, we may look at Niccolo della Casa's drawing of Henri II, made in the year of his accession, 1547 (fig. 27). It shows an impressively worked armour and helm. His shoulder pieces display a battle of sea monsters, the fall of the Titans runs down his arms, while the struggle of the Centaurs and Lapithae is stretched across his belly beneath the moon device of the king held aloft by two victories. The chain of the order of Saint Michel is just perceptible beneath the extravagant folds of the imperial cloak. Clearly, no incongruity was felt in this fusion of French, Roman, and ancient literary elements, for we see these blended together not only here but also on surviving suits of armour.

Visual records of belligerence were by no means confined to military objects. They could be viewed everywhere at Henri II's court: on the twenty-two magnificent tapestries woven with the triumphs of Scipio; on the enamelled plaques and caskets that recounted his triumphs or the works of Hercules;[25] on the marble blocks of François I's tomb; on the many historical paintings that adorned the walls of palaces; and even on jewels made after the designs of Etienne Delaune for Catherine de' Medici and her ladies (fig. 28). The court jeweller François du Jardin, for instance, often copied Delaune's designs. For a cameo with profile portraits of four Roman emperors, he added the same winged victory that appears on one of Henri II's helms;[26] while in the design for a mirror (preserved in the Print Room of the Victoria and Albert Museum) Delaune repeats his ideas

28. Etienne Delaune, design for a hand mirror, 1561, showing
the death of Julia (Bibliothèque Nationale).

on the death of Pompey's daughter Julia, ideas also used, as we shall see,
on Henri II's armour. Conversely, he used extravagant amorous themes
just as indiscriminately on designs for silver plate or armour, as can be
seen from a drawing for the decoration of a helm (preserved in the Kunstbibliothek, Berlin) where satyrs, cupids, and naked nymphs disport themselves among acanthus leaves and the twirling coils of stylised dragons.
Indeed, Delaune emerges as the major force in design at this time, whether
it be for trifles of personal decoration or the invention of suitable victorious scenes to be inscribed on Henri II's coins and medals, or for the
intricate and complex battle scenes and military figures and symbols that
were engraved on contemporary armour. As recent research makes abundantly clear, Delaune's designs were so universally admired that they were
equally exploited in Paris and Augsburg, thus making it difficult (even for
the expert) to distinguish suits and arms made in Germany, Austria, or
France between 1550 and 1580.[27]

Unfortunately, as far as I know, no example of a suit of armour made
for the Guise survives. However, a magnificent parade suit that belonged
to Henri II and that was designed by Delaune has been preserved for us in
perfect condition; along with some fine examples of his drawings for pageant shields and helms, it can be taken as typical of the kind of armour

Ronsard would have known and tried to reproduce in his *Harangue*. Indeed, an examination of the engravings on the king's parade armour illustrates sufficiently how faithful in the detail of his description Ronsard was to the taste of his time. The suit (fig. 29), now in the Louvre, is decorated with scenes that tell of the rivalry of Caesar and Pompey. Imprinted on the vizier is the death of Julia, on the back lies the battle of Durazzo;[28] the large shoulder pieces show Pompey refusing hospitality to the Mitylens and the death of his wife Cornelia; on the gauntlets, Pompey's arms are shown destroyed and Cato pronounces his funeral oration, while the figures of justice and victory adorn the armpieces; and on the breastplate,

29. Henri II's parade armour (1556–59) after Etienne Delaune's designs (Louvre; Arch. Photo. Paris/S.P.A.D.E.M.).

Caesar in triumph receives Pompey's head. The decorations are obviously analogical, for once inside the suit of armour Henri II's form filled out the scenes depicting Caesar, which were acknowledged as appropriate to his own military power. The same story is told upon one of the French king's shields (fig. 30) although the belligerent message is there tempered (as it could often be) by a moral inscription around the perimeter of the shield.[29] The moral instruction comments on the episodes of the lives of Caesar and Pompey depicted on the shield, warning those who gaze upon them of the dangers of ambition and of the evils of 'seeking for honours' without good cause.[30] Delaune modelled his designs partly on the engraved plates of Enea Vico and partly on decorative features found in the rooms at Fontainebleau.[31]

30. Henri II's shield, probably made from a design by Etienne Delaune (Windsor Castle, by gracious permission of Her Majesty The Queen).

From the hundreds of Delaune's designs (drawings and engravings)[32] it would be easy to multiply examples of armour, shields, and horse furniture that carry contemporary land and sea battle scenes (fig. 31), symbols of victory, the gorgon's serpents spreading out over the surface, a hundred golden studs, or the breathless struggle of Antaeus and Hercules. What is amazing is the balance attained in the decoration between classical heroic elements used metaphorically to anticipate present successes and representations of contemporary French victories.[33] The French shield in the Wallace collection, for instance, depicts the fight between the French and the English and the surrender of Calais in 1555; while the magnificent armour, covered with gold and enamels, which Pierre Redon made in wrought iron about 1572 for Charles IX, similarly depicts contemporary

31. Henri II's shield, from designs by Etienne Delaune (Louvre, département des objets d'art; photo Chuzeville; Arch. Photo. Paris/S.P.A.D.E.M.).

battle scenes (so far unidentified).[34] Ronsard achieves exactly the same kind of balance when using past examples of the crusading spirit of the Guise's ancestors to comment on and to extol contemporary belligerence —a relatively rare source of congratulation for a poet who in so many places shows how he hated war.

Just as his venerable ancestor Godefroy de Bouillon (a standard point of reference at the time in any attempt to extol the Lorraine princes)[35] had leapt to the side of Urban II in his call to defend the church in the first of the crusades, so the duke of Guise is engaged in a similar crusade—a holy war to support the Catholic cause against the excessive ambitions of Charles V, who fights with the support of the barbarian arms of German Protestants. The decoration on the Guise's armour, therefore, is not arbitrarily drawn—any more than that which so often adorned Henri II— nor is it taken haphazardly from epic sources. It is entirely appropriate to the present situation, and for anyone who has studied sixteenth-century armour, Ronsard's rendering has an authentic air about it.

This impression of authenticity is enhanced if we consider the harangue that the duke delivers in Ronsard's poem (lines 108−262). Throughout his exhortation, two themes are stressed: that God is on the side of the French and that the French soldiers should imitate their ancestors' feats against wrongful attack.

> Sus, courage soldats! sus, sus! montrez vous or'
> De la race d'Hercule, et de celle d'Hector.
> . . . .
>   prenez coeur, imitez vos ayeux;
> Encore Dieu vous aime, encore Dieu ses yeux
> N'a destourné de nous ny de nostre entreprise.
>
> (lines 108−9; 116−18)

Come on soldiers, courage! show yourselves of the race of Hercules, and of that of Hector . . . take heart, imitate your ancestors; God still loves you, he has not turned away his eyes from our endeavours.

These are the themes already resplendently indicated on Guise's armour. They are also, apparently, the very sentiments that François de Lorraine urged on his troops at the onset of the battle, if the record of the harangue preserved by Belleforest in his collection of model military orations is an accurate one. There, after praising the French troops' already proven strength and acknowledging the justice of their cause, the duke urges them to take courage, and he ends his peroration emphasising the crusadelike holy war on which they are engaged. Here are his final words:

> Courage (mes bons seigneurs, freres, compagnons et amys) courage, et nous asseurons de gaigner à ce tour un des plus grands honneurs que iamais autres

ayent emporté soutenans un siege . . . courons sur ces ennemys, la pluspart desquels que la France iamais n'a mieux estably son heur, que lorsqu'elle a deffendu la liberté, et pureté de la religion Catholique.[36]

Take heart, my good lords, brothers, allies, and friends; take heart and we are assured of achieving on this occasion one of the greatest honours that has ever been given to those engaged in a siege . . . let us throw ourselves on the enemy, against most of which France has never so well proved her happiness than when she has tried to defend her liberty and the purity of the holy Catholic faith.

Inevitably, he continues, Fortune will favour the just cause of 'un jeune Roy vaillant' (a young and valiant king) and bring defeat upon the excesses of an ageing emperor ('un Empereur grison').

This juxtaposition of the youthful vigour of the French and the tired and enfeebled emperor is precisely the theme with which Ronsard ends his *Harangue*. While the words of the fiery duke echo on, it is the glorious sight of his person that produces the instantaneous and dramatic defeat of the imperial eagle.

> Son panache pendant
> Terriblement courbé, par ondes descendant
> Sur le dos escaillé, du haut de la terrace
> Effrayoit l'Espaignol d'une horrible menace.
> Comme un brandon de feu le rond de son bouclair
> Escartoit parmi l'air un monstrueux esclair.
> . . . .
> L'empereur frisonna d'une si froide peur
> Voyant ton frère armé, que sur l'heure, sur l'heure,
> Du tout desesperé de fortune meilleure,
> Tourna le dos, honteux.
>
> (lines 265–70; 278–81)

His plumes hanging dreadfully bent, in waves flowing down his scaled back, from the height of the terrace dismayed the Spaniard with a horrible fear. Like a torch of fire, the circle of his shield sent forth through the sky an alarming light. . . . The Emperor shook with such cold trembling at the sight of your brother in arms that instantaneously, completely despairing of any better fate, he turned his back, shamed in defeat.

Thus Ronsard has brought his poem round full circle. By setting forth François de Lorraine's military magnificence, he has traced the decline and fall of Charles V, and at the same time found a supremely effective way of praising the French prince. The splendour written on the duke's armour offered the poet the chance to combine three essential features of heroic poems: descriptive power, quick comparisons, and vigorous rolling rhythms. Phrases such as 'le dos escaillé' trigger the reader's thoughts and evoke a clear vision of the scenes encrusted on the duke's armour. They also evoke historical and literary memories of ancient military pride and achievement, and bring once more into our sights the brilliantly packed surfaces of sixteenth-century arms and armour. The decorated French hero has thus acquired iconic status; he stands forth for all time as a double testimony: to France's military prowess and to Ronsard's ability to celebrate victory. Iconic forms, however, did not always take on this military guise in his poems.

The Lyre as Icon

In the poem *La Lyre* (composed in 1569) Ronsard gave such attention to its elaborate decorations that we cannot but see this musical instrument as expressing something beyond itself—as being, in fact, a kind of icon. The lyre is introduced halfway through the poem (at line 264) as a gift, divinely created to install again in France the rich power of poetry. Made of gold and ivory, the lyre's swelling form is densely engraved with mythological subjects: at its centre sit 'les plus hauts Dieux en festin delectable' (the highest gods, enjoying their banquet; line 273). Grouped around Apollo, they listen to his song, which recalls an old quarrel that raged between Minerva and Neptune and that is also recorded on the lyre. In another place, embedded in the ivory, lies the flayed body of Marsyas:

> Au naturel dans l'yvoire attaché
> Vit un Marsye au corps tout escorché.
> ....
> Vous le verriez lentement consommer
> Mort dans l'yvoire, et d'une face humaine
> N'estre plus rien qu'une large fontaine.

(lines 300–302, 304–6)

As in life, attached to the ivory, so lived Marsyas, his body in ribbons. . . . You see him dying in the ivory, slowly, and of a human face, there is nothing but a big fountain.

The imagination can paint such metamorphoses, and, as usual, Ronsard points to the lifelike nature of the figure. The lyre also displays its foremost executant—Apollo—shown now building the walls of Troy, now transformed into a shepherd and courting Admetus, and now the companion of Venus, the graces, and cupid. Bacchus, too, is drawn there, showering the fruits of abundance, holding the space between peace and war, and on the point of leading them into harmonious dance; while Mercury, inventor of the lyre, is shown composing its shape from a tortoise shell and assuaging Apollo's rage with his unique gift.

Multiple images, therefore, tumble onto the lyre's surface. Together they constitute that lyre of Apollo which Jean Belot, 'Bordelais, maistre des requestes du Roy,' brought to life again through his generous patronage to Ronsard and to other French poets. To Belot the poem is dedicated, and the lyre displays, through its decoration, the richness and variety of poetic inspiration that such generosity brings.

At this time, the lyre was considered a noble instrument, and the images that Ronsard strews across its surface are clearly intended to signal its high status. It is the instrument of the gods, created by one of them for their own delectation; this is the sight that forms the centre of Ronsard's design. As he seems to re-create the lyre before us, he is following a well-established view about its invention, its power, and its ornamentation.[37] He is also appropriating its use in the same way as Du Bellay had in *La Deffence*, when he had answered the charge that he was a 'presumpueux Marsye qui osa comparer sa fluste rustique à la douce lyre d'Apolon' (Overambitious Marsyas, who dared to compare his rustic flute with the sweet lyre of Apollo).[38] The lyre and Apollo are symbols of status.

Before studying their implications more closely, we should notice that Ronsard makes his own concern with status absolutely clear through the extremely personalised nature of the opening sections of the poem, which introduce the wonders of creative power as its chief theme. The poet marvels at the force that can suddenly impregnate his being when, after periods of physical and mental barrenness, divine inspiration stirs and overwhelms him. He depicts himself as one possessed, oblivious to the outside world, composing works for gods and for men before the power that controls him without warning abruptly leaves him. In diverse ways Ronsard tries to communicate the extraordinary nature of the feelings he experiences as inspiration soars and then suddenly contracts. The images he chooses—pictures of gods shown in the act of creation—themselves speak eloquently of his continuing exalted view of poetry. His creative intelligence and its maturing process are, for example, expressed by reference to Minerva, who issued fully armed from the head of Jupiter: 'C'est de l'esprit l'oeuvre toute nouvelle / Que le penser luy a fait concevoir' (It's the new work of the mind that thought has allowed him to make; lines 118–19). His sense of poetic seizure and the power to create and to foretell, he explains by evoking Plato's four furies.[39]

Bacchus, Amour, Les Muses, Apollon,
Qui dans nos coeurs laissent un aiguillon
Comme freslons, et d'une ardeur secrete
Font soudain l'homme et Poëte et Prophete.

(lines 39–42)

Bacchus, Love, the Muses, and Apollo, who in our hearts leave a pricking like to a needle, and from a mysterious source suddenly create man, poet, and prophet.

Such parallels assume that there are natural connections between poets and gods; by making these explicit, Ronsard simultaneously attempts to convey the experience of writing poetry and to glorify that activity.

These early sections of the poem are anticipatory. They prepare the reader's understanding so that when Ronsard comes to create the musical instrument that is to act as a consecration of poetry, little further elucidation is needed of the stories on its surface.[40]

Est Apollon, qui accouple sa vois
Au tremblotis de l'archet et des doits.
. . . .
Les corps tous nuds des trois Charites jointes
Suivant Venus, et Venus par la main
Conduit Amour.
. . . .
Vit un Bacchus, potelé, gros et gras,
Vieil-jouvenceau, tenant entre ses bras
Un vase tout plein.

(lines 275–76, 330–32, 339–41)

There is Apollo, who harmonizes his voice to the shimmering sound of fingers and bow. . . . The naked bodies of the Graces hand in hand follow Venus, and Venus by the hand leads on Love. . . . There is Bacchus, portly, fat, and plump, old yet young, holding within his embrace a well-filled vessel.

Because these gods couple poetic inspiration with prophecy, they are visually defined with considerable precision. Thus the lyre as an object does not merely constitute the speaking recollection of poetic frenzy; it also is a sign of the presence of creative power and of its availability to the poet. Such disponibility turns the lyre into a beautiful guarantee against those moments of personal incapacity when inspiration has inexplicably drained from the poet.[41]

The celebration of poetry in *La Lyre* takes on a highly integrated form, for this musical instrument fuses together the individual powers granted to the three arts of music, poetry, and painting. Through its shape, harmony is suggested; from its sound, divine inspiration is transmitted to man; and through the myths that decorate it, the creative arts are celebrated. The message of this work is the same as that so triumphantly sung in the *Ode à Michel de l'Hospital*. Yet here, the poet's confidence is born again. Inspiration is brought out of barrenness and given a secure form, and the tone of its shaping is as excited and fervent as in one of Ronsard's earliest poems, *A son lut*.[42] There too he wrote of poetry as 'un feu consumant' (a consuming fire), and although he had not yet developed the potential that iconic forms were to give him, he celebrated together music and poetry, praising the justice and grace of God who granted prophetic power to poets:

> Mais Dieu juste qui dispense
> Tout en tous, les fait chanter
> Le futur en recompense
> Pour le monde espouvanter.
> Ce sont les seuls interpretes
> Des hauts Dieux que les poëtes.
> Car, aux prieres qu'ils font,
> L'or aux Dieux criant ne sont.
> Ni la richesse qui passe,
> Mais un lut tousjours parlant
> L'art des Muses excellant
> Pour dessus leur rendre grace.

(P 2:726; L 2:158−59)

But the God of Justice who grants all that is, allows them in recompense to sing of the future, in order to astound the world. Poets are the only real interpreters of the gods. Since it is by their supplications and not with gold that they pray, not with ephemeral riches but with a lute that always speaks and excels in the art of the Muses with which, above all, they give grace to gods.

In thus promoting the lyre, Ronsard was not working in a vacuum. In *Les Images des deux Philostrates grecs* Vigenère recorded that he had seen many examples of decorated lyres, and not only in books and paintings. As he visited the art collections of prominent Italian figures—Cardinal Ippolito de' Medici, for instance—he had had the chance to admire such masterpieces, and he had heard reports of others. Of particular interest to us is Vigenère's view of the original structure of Amphion's lyre (an opinion he borrowed from Valeriano). The form of the lyre was conceived as embodying the structure of the universe itself. Its nine chords corresponded to the nine principal metals found in the earth and to the nine planets in the heavens (including the sun and moon). The significance of its structure is made clear in the decorations on its surface, which also offered a representation of the world and where were detailed 'les neuf estoilles dont est construitte la figure de cette lyre, sont les neuf Muses, ou Spheres mobiles' (the nine others of which the decoration of this lyre is made are the nine Muses, or moving spheres).[43] This lyre, therefore, similar to the one created by Ronsard, has the power to know the world and to transmit this knowledge to those who look upon its form or who play upon its strings. In other words, decoration and form have been fused.

Men and women in the sixteenth century also had other ways of becoming familiar with the image of Apollo and his lyre. He had appeared on the stage at Lyons as the apotheosis of *La Calandria* in 1548. He was seen again encased within a rock at the Rouen entry of 1550. Dell'Abbate placed him on the ceiling of the ballroom at Fontainebleau; and he was present in the woodcuts that adorned the fine mid-century Lyons editions of Ovid's *Metamorphoses*.[44] Enamelled platters made by Pierre Courteys from designs by Rosso and Delaune, or worked by Jean de Court from drawings by Luca Penni also carried his visage, and Germain Pilon (among others) carved him in stone.[45] Even tapestries and embroideries—such as the one for the bride's garments depicting a youthful Apollo with the graces and 'mille petits Amours', described by Belleau in the *Bergerie*—were apparently obliged to portray him. Indeed, the list is endless; Apollo and his lyre were ubiquitous.

When, towards the end of his life, Ronsard tried to locate the sources of pleasure, he argued in a speech delivered before l'Académie du Palais, that they could be found through hope, satisfaction, and remembrance. The most powerful of these, he claimed, was remembrance because it gave greater permanency to experience.[46] In the sixteenth century, poetry and painting built on this natural source of pleasure and developed forms that concentrated feeling and events; these, at the same time, evoked further reminiscences, which in their turn contributed to the sense of something special being preserved.

Ronsard wrote for a public of connoisseurs. When he brings to life the armour of the duke of Guise, he expects his sophisticated readers to think again of Homer and of Virgil, and to see the siege of Metz not only for what it was—a significant military coup—but also as a literary and military reenactment; he stirs their knowledge of classical norms and stimulates their appreciation of the slightest departure from them. When he interrupts and delays the narrative to present an embroidered cloak or a precious object, he is consciously remembering other similar riches found in books or seen in abundance on members of the court, in royal rooms, and on princely tables. Pleasure is found in ornament and in its variety, and Ronsard had no hesitation (if need be) in sacrificing the whole in order to fix our attention on the significant detail, which, he consistently maintained in all his theoretical writings, ensured enrichment and delight.

By the time he came to write *La Lyre* his use of iconic forms had evolved considerably. Clearly, he had always seen them as making important contributions to praise and to poetic elaboration, but he had never before envisaged them as dominating the entire poem and as coming to represent the power of poetry itself. Decoration had ceased to be a surface affair—it had become the centre and being of creative writing, as Ronsard made clear four years earlier in *L'Abbrégé de l'art poétique*, where he compared the make-up of the human body and the ingredients of poetry. Just as the human body, he wrote, in order to be 'beau, plaisant et accomply' (beautiful, pleasant, and well finished) cannot do without blood, veins, and muscle, so 'La Poësie ne peut estre plaisante, vive ne parfaitte sans belles inventions, descriptions, comparaisons, qui sont les ners et la vie du Livre' (Poetry cannot be pleasing, living, and perfect without beautiful inventions, descriptions, and comparisons, which are the very nerves and life blood of the book).[47] We have seen that decorative insets had many functions. But perhaps the outstanding service they provided for poets was very deliberately to draw attention to themselves, and thus to show off their powers of invention and performance.[48]

S. Augustum : fortuna tumet: Imppea Secundum.
Henricum titulus sors eademq. decet.

32. The triumphal car of Henri II, manuscript illumination of the king's entry into Rouen, 1550 (Rouen, Bibliothèque municipale, Ms. Y. 28 [1268]; photo Ellebé).

IV

TRIUMPHAL FORMS

C'est un travail de bon-heur
Chanter les hommes louables,
Et leur bastir un honneur
Seul veinqueur des ans muables.

RONSARD
Au seigneur de Carnavalet

It's a work of happiness to sing the praises
of men, and to build them honours that
alone survive the changing years.

THE LOOK OF A prince an hour before the battle, his portrait on coins and medals, his decorated arms and armour—all were accepted and effective ways of representing his power. These modes of display emphasised the personal capacity of the individual and set into particular relief his military potential (fig. 32). Both potential and eventual performance, however, had more general reverberations. These, we know, were sometimes already suggested in the pictorial designs, but they could also be given other forms such as magnificent buildings, stone monuments or arches littered with trophies of war, temples of honour and triumphal cars, all commonly associated with classical imperial might. These particular forms reemerged with increasing frequency in the sixteenth century, and they rapidly became the customary way to extend praise beyond an individual's achievements and to give a sense of solid and, it was hoped, permanent expression to a nation's pride.

Magnificent Buildings

Even in our own ruinous times, the building of a monument, whatever its form, seems a natural response to the desire to leave a firm and often expensive record of some significant human event. In sixteenth-century France, few had the resources to indulge such an urge, but those who did seem to have attached singular importance to the elevation of structures that might carry their names and that of their country forward into the future. Obviously, such edifices played a significant role in promoting artistic endeavour and in encouraging proper aesthetic appreciation. Androuet Du Cerceau was quick to explain these matters to Catherine de' Medici in the dedication of his *Des plus excellents bastiments de France* (1576), writing of 'le plaisir et contentement à contempler icy une partie des plus beaux et excellens edifices, dont la France est encore pour le iourd'huy enrichie' (the pleasure and delight there are in gazing on a part of the most beautiful buildings and edifices that still enrich the state of France today).[1] An architect is naturally enthusiastic about royal support and appreciation. Vitruvius had been equally so, some fifteen hundred years before, when he had dedicated his *De architectura* to Caesar Augustus. He argued that expansion of territory, the subjugation of foreign peoples, and other signs of military domination were incomplete without an imperial city whose buildings matched in form and splendour the triumphs that had been achieved.[2]

In sixteenth-century France more humble citizens, however, those who were neither architects nor prospective patrons, shared Vitruvius's view. Guillaume Michel, for instance, automatically assumed that magnificence, magnanimity, and generosity were the natural properties of princehood.[3] Or a certain François de Saint Thomas, who found himself in prison during the second civil war, occupied his hours of enforced leisure in writing a work in which he set out the conditions of a good king. Prominent among these was the necessity of magnificence. Saint Thomas developed this theme, with quotations from Aristotle and Cicero, arguing that:

> La plus grande magnificence et la plus digne du Prince magnifique se manifeste à faire bastir, dresser et eriger chasteaux, forteresses, palays, maisons de Plaisance et autres telz edifices.[4]

> The greatest magnificence and that which is the most worthy of a magnificent prince is to plan, build, and erect castles, fortresses, palaces, pleasure houses, and other like edifices.

Such magnificent buildings François I, Henri II, and Catherine de' Medici provided so generously that critics of the monarchy in the second half of the sixteenth century complained of their excess and profligacy.[5]

Despite opposition to building projects, which came principally from the Protestant sections of the community, when French subjects wished to express their respect to princes they employed architects and poets who created triumphal forms that were powerfully evocative of classical times. Vitruvius had set forth the advantages that accompanied such permanent records of triumph and of imperial power, using Sparta as his example:

Ces Lacedemoniens [qui] dresserent dans le portique, gallerie, ou prome-
noer nommé Persique, un trophee des despouilles de leurs ennemys, pour
exalter la vertu de leurs citoiens, et donner cognoissance de tele victoire a
ceulx qui viendront apres eulx.[6]

These Lacedaemonians who erected in a portico, gallery, or room for walking—called a *persique*—a trophy of the remains of their enemies, did so to
stimulate their citizens to virtue and to leave behind knowledge of such
achievement to future generations.

In sixteenth-century France, concrete examples of such forms were first
given to the French by an Italian, Sebastiano Serlio. He came to France in
1541 and began to publish a series of architectural works abundant in illustrations of actual buildings.[7] These structures inspired in ambitious
French builders visions of equal grandeur, which they thought would more
than adequately accommodate the French imperial claims that had seemed
quite realistic with Henri's successive victories in the early part of his
reign, and with the marriage of Charles IX to Elizabeth of Austria in
1571.

Serlio was also one of the first architects to describe in detail the ancient
buildings still standing in Rome, and to record the plans and shapes of the
more modern Italian temples and palaces that had been built according to
the principles of classical architecture. In addition to Serlio's drawings and
explanations, other works, equally specific, were mined for information
by French builders, artists, and poets. Typical are the researches of Guillaume Du Choul, who described Jupiter's temple on the Capitol thus:

Ce temple fut voué premierement par Tarquinius Priscus, et depuis edifié par
Tarquinius Superbus de forme quarrée: et là chascune de ses faces se mon-
stroit de deux cens pieds, ayant trois ordres de colonnes; comme l'a monstré
Traian par ses medailles, ou sont veus par le dessus du frontispice trophees,
chars triomphants, victoires, qui portent palmes, et chappeaux de laurier,
et plusieurs aultres sculptures, qui monstrent l'excellent ouvrage dudict
temple.[8]

This temple was first dedicated by Tarquinius Priscus and was then built by
Tarquinius Superbus in a square form: each of its sides were 200 feet long
and had three orders of columns; Trajan has shown it in his medals, whose
fronts display trophies, triumphal cars, goddesses of victory, carrying palms
and crowned with laurel, and many other sculptured things that demonstrate the excellent workmanship in the temple.

Precisely these features—columns, medallions, statues, trophies, triumphal
cars—were progressively accommodated to French political aspirations.
They were used on medals for Henri II;[9] in royal entries they replaced

those 'tableaux vivants' that had, until the 1540s, been used to praise French monarchs, to show them princely virtues, and to express civic and national pride. For the king's entry into Paris in 1549, for example, the organisers attempted to give the triumphal arches peculiar significance. Jean Martin, Thomas Sebillet, Jean Cousin, and Jean Goujon were all well versed in Greek and Latin, and they tried to make their arches resemble, as faithfully as possible, the neoclassical orders of architecture as they had been explained by Alberti. As a consequence, each monument, which still owed much to local traditions, was a mixture of old and new.[10] The first triumphal arch, for instance, showed the Gallic Hercules, but standing high on an arch of classical columns. The Argonauts 'vestuz à l'antique' (dressed in antique fashion) were sculptured into the niches of the classical arch that spanned the old bridge of Notre Dame. For the joustings and tournaments, which perpetuated medieval war exercises and which continued throughout the month Henri II was in his capital, an enormous edifice had been erected for the spectators. Built on Corinthian and Doric columns, it nevertheless carried aloft the figures of old national heroes, Brennus and Belgius.

As we have suggested, French princes needed little encouragement from their architects to indulge their passion for magnificent buildings; they turned to learned men to bolster their splendid views of themselves with parallel images and forms of triumph from classical times; and their passion for new construction was inevitably shared by their courtiers. The castle of Oiron, erected in 1550–52, provides a very vivid impression of how new elements blended with old and of how the accent in the decoration fell increasingly on triumph and pictures of heroism. Noël Jallier, who had spent some time in Rome, was responsible for the construction. In the decoration of the interior, he chose to cover the walls not with a rather heterogeneous collection of tapestries, which even in royal households still formed the principal mode of gorgeous wall display,[11] but rather with a coherent set of frescoes exhibiting newly learned effects. The castle belonged to Gouffier, master of the king's horse; it was, therefore, appropriate that the walls of the entire ground floor of the building be decorated with representations of horses from Henri II's stables. The decoration of the long gallery on the first floor—the *piano nobile*—was based solely on military encounters in the Trojan war. Fourteen action-packed scenes are spread around the walls in this attempt to rediscover the spirit of the Trojan war, from which emerged (according to the French legend that inspired *La Franciade*) the race of heroes who eventually founded the French nation.[12] Each scene has painted underneath the device and motto of Henri II, making explicit the application of the scenes of military heroism to contemporary French taste and achievements. The sixth panel (fig. 33), for instance, which shows the feats of Greeks and Trojans, communicates the vigour attempted by the artist. Patroclus's funeral pyre is displayed in the next fresco, while appropriate games to celebrate the death of a hero are played in the next. The ninth fresco shows the duel of Achilles and Hector (fig. 34), then come their deaths and the menace of the Trojan horse. In all the frescoes the artist has emphasised the expressive quality of the figures engaged in mortal combat. The style and the theme make the whole sequence seem both eloquent and very coherent.

33. (*above*) Noël Jallier, fresco depicting a battle of Greeks and Trojans (ca. 1552) (Château d'Oiron).

34. (*below*) Noël Jallier, fresco depicting the duel between Achilles and Hector (ca. 1552) (Château d'Oiron).

Little pictorial evidence of comparable quality survives elsewhere in France for this period.[13] Contemporary written sources, however, suggest something of the scope and richness of those noble buildings that no longer stand. Du Cerceau's *Des plus excellents bastiments de France* is tantalisingly schematic in its carefully engraved sections; but to find some idea of the building intentions of sixteenth-century princes, we must turn to *L'Histoire d'Arthemise*, by Nicolas Hoüel. Hoüel strove to re-create a world of triumphal edifices and matching deeds as a way of providing a fitting public monument to Catherine de' Medici's dead husband and to her work as Queen Regent of France. Hoüel's history (dated 8 February 1562) is in four books, each of which keeps in play three levels of concern: specific contemporary references to political events and to artistic achievements;[14] descriptions of the life and times of Queen Arthemise, especially her wars and triumphs; and justifications for the elaborate funeral ceremonies and monuments that she had erected to commemorate the death of King Mausolus and the victories of her people. The intention to create triumphal forms that could give visual expression to Catherine's conceptions of power and accomplishments is obvious. Hoüel gives particularly lengthy discussions of magnificent buildings; indeed, these form an integral part of his text and constitute a major preoccupation. Whole chapters are given over to the construction of pyramids, obelisks, ancient epitaphs, the temple of Diana with its twenty-five columns of marble, and to the architectural forms raised up for the queen's victories or for the marriage of her son. For each magnificent building, whether temporary or permanent, Hoüel explains its significance, describes the detail of its decoration and inscriptions, and points out the lessons it held for future generations.

The variety of structures he has imagined is perhaps not so excessive or astonishing when we reflect that his work was intended to be lavishly illustrated and to serve as inspiration for tapestry designs.[15] Hoüel gives us a fair indication of what to expect in his long preface to Catherine, where he warns:

> Vous y verrez les oedifices, les columnes, les piramides par elle construites et eslevées, tant à Rhodes qu'en la ville d'Halicarnasse, qui serviront de memoire pour ceux se souviendront de nostre temps et qui s'esbahiront grandement de vos oedifices et maison des Tuileries, de Monceux, de Sainct-Maur, et infinité d'autres que vous avez faict bastir et construire, enrichis de sculpture et belles peintures.[16]

> You will find here the edifices, columns, and pyramids that she had constructed and built both at Rhodes and Halicarnassus, which will serve as remembrances for those who reflect on our times and who will be astounded at your own buildings—the palaces at the Tuileries, Monceaux, and Saint-Maur, and the infinity of others that you have constructed, built, and embellished with sculptures and beautiful paintings.

35. Antoine Caron, *Porteurs de Trophées*, drawing for Nicolas Hoüel's *L'Histoire de la royne d'Arthemise*, 1562 (Bibliothèque Nationale).

This statement sums up very well the interplay between ancient and modern that is constant in the manuscript and in the surviving drawings.[17] Existing French buildings of note repeatedly appear side by side with descriptions of important edifices of the ancient world found in histories, such as those by Pliny. The 'Porteurs de Trophées' tapestry woven in the workshops of François de la Planche, and now in the Dijon Museum, gives an idea of the triumphal character that was envisaged and of the high level of imperial inspiration.[18] The tapestry also testifies to the concern for accurate rendering of classical structures (fig. 35), a concern further testified to in Caron's drawing for the king's circular mausoleum. He shows it crowned with a triumphal car and set beside a building erected on Corinthian columns, with an inscribed obelisk also in view. In composing this design, Caron drew on expert knowledge gleaned from at least three sources: Pliny's description of the mausoleum at Halicarnassus, elements from contemporary royal entries, and information about neoclassical structures and their proper use, such as could be found in Vitruvius, Alberti, or Serlio.[19]

If we take Oiron and *L'Histoire d'Arthemise* as indications of the chivalric and heroic taste dominant at Henri II's court and later in the cultural circles that formed around his widow, it seems clear that French builders and artists made a conscious effort to show off their learning and their expertise, and to reproduce in their own edifices and decorations the styles and significances that they attached to classical forms of triumph. Equally clear seems to be their patrons' affection for such magnificent monuments. In his otherwise sober account of the buildings worthy of notice in Paris in 1550, Gilles Corrozet wrote this of the contributions of François I and his son:

> Tout le temps du regne dudit seigneur Roy on ne cessa de bastir dedans Paris . . . un peu devant son trespas, feit commencer une grand' salle à mode des antiques, la plus excellente selon l'art d'architecture qu'on veid iamais: laquelle le Roy nostre Sire Henry 2e du nom, à present regnant, a fait parachever.[20]

> Throughout the reign of this king, they never ceased building in Paris . . . just a little before he died, he began to have constructed a large room modelled on the ancient style, the most excellent that was ever seen from an architectural point of view; King Henri II, who reigns at present, had it finished.

There could be no better witness than this to the nature of the building fever that struck French princes during this period, one that called for heroic gestures. Poets, too, tried to share in such splendid manifestations. They, too, imagined glorious edifices and resurrected others from the past, and they also imposed triumphal forms on the patterns of their poems.

Poets' Temples of Honour

Although poets naturally wished to explore their own ways of contributing to the general atmosphere of triumph and achievement, these ways were closely modelled on the triumphal forms developed by painters and architects. When Ronsard counselled young epic poets on the necessity of incorporating into their work 'conceptions grandes et hautes' (great and lofty ideas) he compared verbal realisation to wall decorations: 'Il fault imiter les bons menagers qui tapissent bien leurs sales, chambres et cabinets' (You must imitate the good housekeepers who line the walls of their rooms and cabinets with tapestry).[21] For him, elevated thoughts required such modes of display, and these, in turn, provided the poet with his opportunity to unfurl his own descriptive powers. In the same phrase, he connected the business of the poet and contemporary taste for splendour.

This coupling of magnificent, even heroic, fashion and aesthetic advantage was not new. A well-entrenched poetic tradition had undoubtedly lent strength to Ronsard's arguments, and a glance at Jean Lemaire de Belges's *Temple d'Honneur et de Vertu* is sufficient to convey this tradition's nature. Lemaire's long poem is a work of celebration, written in 1504 to commemorate the death of Pierre II, duke of Bourbon. The temple, dedicated to Honour and Virtue, was carved with the virtues contained in the name of the prince: *prudence, justice, esperance, raison, religion,* and *equité.* The temple served two functions. First, as the text explicitly states, it was an example to all young nobles: 'Mirez-vous aux faitz vertueux . . . pour estre bons en excellence' (To be good and perfect, mirror yourself in virtuous deeds).[22] Second, the temple was the site of the ceremonies for the 'glorieuse intronisation et celeste exaltation du tres bon duc' (glorious enthronement and divine celebration of the very good duke). Enthronement and exaltation are the key notes of the general mood of the poem, which seeks to encapsulate and to communicate that feeling of uplift that surged through those who assembled to consecrate the duke's memory and to meditate upon his exemplary achievements.

The architectural form Lemaire gave to the celebrations might well, as some say, have been suggested by the *Trionfi* of Petrarch, whose influence had percolated through manuscripts, painted *cassone,* and wall coverings.[23] The anecdotal writings of Valerius Maximus might also have inspired the notion of the temple's two purposes; but, then again, Jean Molinet's *Thrône d'Honneur* could have furnished a sufficient source, and poetic temples of praise were not uncommon. Lemaire claimed that his double structure resembled the temple built for King Solomon in Jerusalem, 'ou celluy de Dyane en Ephese' (or that of Diana at Ephesos; lines 713–14); and in his search for 'quelque hault chief d'oeuvre miraculeux' (some fine and miraculous work of art) worthy of the dead duke's triumphs, he also refers to the example of queen Arthemise. The source of Lemaire's inspiration matters far less than his multiple references to ancient and modern sources, which, along with those of his scholarly critics, indicate the persistence of triumphal customs in poetry. They also show how poets linked together celebration and modes of triumph.

By the middle of the sixteenth century concern with such forms of celebration became even more marked in France. Du Bellay associated the praise of gods and men of virtue with noble poetic forms such as the ode, and he claimed immortality and incorruptibility for the poet who could re-create in French the noble epic triumphs of Virgil and Homer.[24] In the same year that he published *La Deffence,* Du Bellay chose his monarch's own personal colours—black and white—when he planned to erect a marble temple of victory to Henri II. The temple takes on the shape of Henri's device, the crescent moon; and enriched with the painted attributes of Diana, it carries on golden columns a portrait of the king himself. Du Bellay's poem announced itself as a song of triumph relating to a particular event: *Chant triumphal sur le voyage de Boulogne 1549 au mois d'aoust.*[25] However, as the poem reaches its climax, whose images are architectural, the specificity of the occasion is turned into soaring and enthusiastic claims for victories not yet seen:

> Là mon grand Roy sera mis au milieu
> Sur pilliers d'or, qui tout autour du lieu
> Tesmoigneront sa louange notoire,
> Et sera dict le temple de victoire
> Là je peindray comme il aura donté
> Calaiz, Boulougne, et l'Anglois surmonté,
> Puis l'Hibernie, et tout ce qui attouche
> L'humide lict, où le Soleil se couche.

> There, my great king, will be set at the centre on pillars of gold, which all around the place will be witness to his extraordinary praise, and it will be called the Temple of Victory. There, I shall paint how he overcame Calais, Boulogne, and conquered the English, then Ireland, and all that country that touches the watery bed where the sun goes to rest.

The act of decorating is shown here as compulsive. Also implicit in these lines is the understanding that the poet has surpassed the architect, who merely recorded achievements. With his double power of inscribing truth and of anticipating future events, the poet stretches his canvas over time such that the building literally becomes the sacred house in which holy celebrations are performed, and the poet acquires that priestlike quality explicitly stated in the poem: 'De voz grandeurs le prestre je seray' (Of your greatness, I'll be the priest).

The same feelings of triumph and reverence are present in the poem Du Bellay wrote in 1555 to celebrate the temporary peace. And again, the form he chose to give expression to these sentiments is a triumphal ode. In the poem he depicts Henri II 'en habit triomphal' (in triumphal dress) seated on a throne of ivory within a triumphal car. Instead of defeated kings and princes with 'les braz liez au dos à la mode Romaine' (arms tied behind in the Roman fashion), he shows discord and the horrors of war following ignominiously behind. Spearheading the long cavalcade of all the provinces of Europe is the figure of Peace, who anticipated the king as he went to present the captured pagan standards 'dessus le grand portrait du sainct temple Romain' (above the great figure of the old Roman temple).[26]

Ronsard, especially in the 1550s, is even more conspicuous in his accommodation to poems of the architectural forms of triumph that found favour at court. In the second book of odes, the first poem is addressed to Henri II, and it begins:

> Je te veux bastir une Ode,
> La maçonnant à la mode
> De tes Palais honorez,

Qui pour parade ont l'entree
Et de marbres acoustree,
Et de hauts piliers dorez,
   Afin que le front de l'oeuvre
De premier regard decoeuvre
Tout le riche bastiment:
Ainsi Prince, je veux mettre
Au premier front de mon metre
Tes vertus premierement.

(P 1:430–32; L 1:167)

I will build you an ode, carving in the style of your proud palaces, which, for decoration, have the entrance embellished with marble and with tall golden pillars, so that the outward aspect of the work, at first glance, discovers the magnificent niches of the building. In the same way, my prince, I will put in the first facade of my poem your virtues, first of all.

Ronsard has here assembled the most prestigious elements in building—costly marble, golden pillars, and triumphal entrance—as suitable gestures to the magnificence and virtue of his king. Writing a poem is clearly seen by Ronsard as an elaborate building programme, embodying the richest materials. The form he has chosen is, as Du Bellay had advocated, the noble ode, which contains distinct verbal echoes of Pindar's poems of celebration. The vocabulary is fittingly elevated and the rhythms of the verse swell uninterruptedly over the two stanzas. It appears that the poet has tried first to attract the king's attention by appealing to his love of magnificent buildings, and then to display through measured, stately tones his own ability to control artistic creation and give it the form that belongs both to majesty and to Ronsard's exalted view of poetry.

The opening lines of *Le Temple des Messeigneurs* (dedicated to Odet de Châtillon) similarly demonstrate how conscious Ronsard was in his attempts to integrate triumphal forms into his odes.

Je veux, mon Mecenas, te bastir, à l'exemple
Des Romains et des Grecs, la merveille d'un Temple.

I wish my Maecenas to build you, following the example of the Romans and the Greeks, the marvel of a temple.

These lines seem at first like an expanded version of the earlier ode to Henri II, 'Je te veux bastir une Ode'. Closer examination shows, however, that Ronsard is not concerned so much to exploit the favour shown to contemporary artists, but rather to make specific explorations of classical models by following the rhetorician's injunctions about praising a prince through a display of the glories of his race, of his friends, and of his own particular successes.[27] He wishes to leave in verse a record of the Châtillon's achievement which might parallel that displayed in the stained glass windows at Ecouen and at Montmorency. The correlation between the house of Châtillon and the temple of praise is detailed and consistent: the virtuous exploits of Odet's father, of his uncle Anne de Montmorency, and of his brothers (Admiral Gaspard de Coligny and François de Coligny) form the stones, the columns, and the decorations of the building, suggesting to the poet thoughts of modern olympic victors and renewed sights of deeds worthy of Achilles. The white marble temple is set around with the engraved portraits of Odet's ancestors,

> Qui tous auront escrit aux pieds de leurs médailles
> Leurs gestes et leurs noms, et les noms ennemis
> Des chevaliers qu'en guerre à mort ils auront mis.
>
> (lines 14–16)

who will all have written at the base of their medals their deeds and their names, and the names of enemy knights whom they have killed in war.

Anne de Montmorency is at the centre of the structure and is figured just as he appeared on the ceiling fresco at Tanlay, or on the commemorative plaque that Léonard Limosin enamelled in the same year, 1555; that is to say, he appears as Mars. The praise of Montmorency is extensive: four noble pillars carry evidence of his deeds minutely recalled (lines 23–90), although their narration is delayed until Ronsard, attempting to rival painters, has rather painstakingly described the hoary head and beard of the river Rhône:

> Le Rhosne, d'autre part, dedans ses eaux couché,
> Laschant la bride longue à son fleuve espanché
> D'une cruche versée, ayant la dextre mise
> Au menton herissé d'une moustache grise,
> Et portant une rame en la senestre main
> Et une grand'fontaine au milieu de son sein,
> Chantera sa louange.
>
> (lines 63–69)[28]

On the other side, the Rhône, lying there among its waters, releasing the long stretch of his river that pours forth from the vessel, his right hand supports a hoary chin with its grey moustache, while the left brandishes an oar, and a great fountain flows from his breast, [this Rhône] will sing his [Odet's] praises.

The dedicatee of the poem appears within the work in his cardinal's robes embroidered with the figures of virtue and the Muses (lines 91–196).[29] His brother François is shown as an embattled and victorious Neptune (lines 117–173), while the emprisoned Gaspard de Coligny also stands out as 'l'un des Dieux de mon Temple' (one of the gods in my temple; line 177).

In his poem, Ronsard sought to give each of his heroes qualities consonant with their achievements in real life. Preserved in stone, they take on exemplary status; and yet, throughout, Ronsard emphasises the lifelikeness of the pictures he is painting. The heroes and armies, the cities, battles, and campsites are real persons and places sketched along the borders of France from Boulogne to Avignon; Ronsard cites Mezières, Attigny, Valenciennes, Béthune, and Avesnes; the Pas de Suze, Chimay, Rodemark, Montmédy, Danvillers, Hesdin, Yvoir-sur-Meuse, and Dinant. This persistent appeal to lifelikeness and the often clumsy naming of actual locations can, in some respects, be said to spoil the celebratory sweep of the poem. But such overpreciseness carried overt intentions of compliment, since Ronsard sought to justify the magnificence of his poetic temple by repeatedly turning the reader's mind to real happenings, thereby highlighting the poet's ability to transform events and to give a glorious record of them. By their very unevenness, these poems illustrate how strongly poets felt obliged to respond positively and specifically to the prevailing taste for heroic forms.

The taste had been encouraged by the king's evident fondness for majesty in all its shapes, and by his fatal personal preferences for war, for tournaments and duels in peace time, and for the collecting of arms and armour. More significantly perhaps, it had been inspired by a constant flow of information about heroic captains and events from the past,[30] and by a continuing craze for chivalric romances. Most of all, however, it was fostered by an acquisitive fever that seized prominent French noblemen as they viewed the quantities of newly discovered examples of classical statuary and heroic friezes in Rome and elsewhere in Italy and France.

The Power of Rome

In their wish to become outstanding connoisseurs and patrons of the arts, princes like Charles de Guise imitated their Italian counterparts. They used their time in Rome to have trunks filled with marble and bronze statues, ancient medals, and books and paintings.[31] Despite many local protests, Pope Julius III yielded to these powerful princes and granted official transit authorisation. Italian agents reported to the duke of Florence that 'le Cardinal de Guise s'applique à dérober le plus de médailles antiques et le plus de statues qu'il peut' (the cardinal of Guise applies himself to rob as many ancient medals and statues as he can), while French agents such as Lancelot de Carle were ordered to purchase paintings, and the cardinal himself bought the substantial library of cardinal Ridolphi.[32] Charles de

Guise's enthusiasm for Rome could almost be termed excessive. Elaborate funerals were much enjoyed by Lorraine princes, and the cardinal, impressed by the visual evidence of Roman funeral rites, employed the artist Pierre Woeriot to copy them so that future doleful ceremonies in the province might profit thereby.[33]

In addition, while negotiations about the sale and transport of marbles and books were going forward in Rome, at Meudon—one of the cardinal's country retreats—Primaticcio and Niccolo dell'Abbate (among others) were engaged in building and decorating a grotto designed to house the ancient treasures 'à l'imitation des anciens Romains, qui souloient bastir ainsi leurs edifices' (in imitation of the ancient Romans who used to build this way).[34] Apparently, the main room of the central pavilion formed a kind of gallery in which were displayed marble busts of Roman emperors and of Cicero and Demosthenes.[35] The effect of the entire building works at Meudon seems to have been remarkable. The house rapidly became a showplace and it appeared in all the guides with detailed indications as to its ambiguous character—half-artificial and half-natural —and the singularity of its architecture. Belleforest in his *Cosmographie* (1575) expounds its attractions thus:

> Il n'y a sorte d'antiquaille soit en colonnes, Architraves, soubassemens, Cornices, statues, Medailles et autres singularitez, ou en superbe et industrie de l'architecture (bien que ce soit une rustique) qui ne soit pratiquée en ce lieu, où ce grand Cardinal a comme renouvellé la gentillesse Romaine.
>
> (p. 278, col. 1)

> In this place, where this great cardinal has, as it were, renewed the beauty of Rome, no kind of antiquity is missing—columns, architraves, supports, cornices, statues, medals, and other singular things, with both the superb skill of architecture and in the rustic form.

Meudon aroused the interest of the curious for many years and attracted poetic comment as late as 1609.[36] It is Gabriel Symeoni's impression, however, recorded in 1558, that still carries something of the excitement Charles de Guise might have felt as he saw Meudon transformed by Italian artists. Symeoni, in a work dedicated to the cardinal, exclaimed:

> Retourné de Lyon à Paris, me print envie de visiter la Grotte admirable et tant d'autres belles choses faites par vostre commandement à Medon: auquel lieu voyant un si grand nombre de statues et marbres antiques, je ne l'eusse sceu plus honorablement saluer et louer qu'en disant: *Vive Roma Resurgens*.[37]

> Returning from Lyon to Paris, I was overcome by the desire to visit the marvellous grotto and to see all the other beautiful things that you have com-

manded to be made at Meudon. When I arrived, seeing such a large number of statues and marble, the best and most honourable way that I could salute them and praise them was to cry out, Here is Rome resurrected.

Charles de Guise's interest in Roman remains is typical of that shown by French princes. To cite but one further example: when the papal legate came to France in 1556, among the presents he brought to impress and please the king were fine marble statues and other antiquities.[38]

We know that these books and statues were not mere ornaments. Contemporaries report that some princes could be seen consulting their classical texts daily. Emperor Charles V, for example, claimed that he never went to war without Caesar's *Commentaries* and the deeds of Alexander ready to hand; Philip Strozzi, a favourite companion of Henri II, (according to a story related by Brantôme) was so addicted to his Caesar that he translated the *Commentaries* into Greek.[39] Further evidence is provided by Vasari, who on a visit to the castle saw twenty-four paintings of the life of Alexander mounted along the main royal staircase at Fontainebleau.[40] Books, statues, pictures of heroes and their deeds, battle scenes spread around the walls of a castle (at Trento or Oiron) were both sources of information and models to emulate. Sixteenth-century princes saw these as ways of stirring courage and desire for military glory as effectively as did the verses of Tyrtaeus, only recently made available in French.[41] In their eyes, such representations had the power of ancestral images; and, for this reason alone, princes accumulated and treasured them. Regardless of their size or even their authenticity, skilfully rendered art objects, images on walls, and models in books were considered of equal value since they all influenced men towards good. A tiny object could have a prodigious effect, like the miniature statue of Hercules, described by Statius; though but a foot high, it made the onlooker cry out:

This is the breast that crushed the ravages of Nemea, these the arms that bore the deadly club, and broke the oars of Argo: To think that a tiny frame should hold the illusion of so mighty a form: What preciseness of touch, what daring imagination the cunning master had, at once to model an ornament for the table and to conceive in his mind mighty colossal forms.[42]

Although French taste for the heroic was fairly indiscriminate at this period, and writers and artists were prepared to absorb influences from old traditions and from new discoveries as they presented themselves, their own persistent researches show that what impressed them most, and what they always came back to, was the vision of imperial Rome. When they came to express their enthusiasm for its buildings and their admiration for its triumphs their writing becomes lyrical and even exalted in tone. This

response is not inappropriate in that the Romans had sought to leave magnificent records of themselves, as Serlio points out at the beginning of *Des
antiquitez* (Paris, 1550):

> Les Romains par leurs magnanimes couraiges ont tousiours cerché de des-
> montrer choses à l'exaltation de leurs actes et puissances tant par mer que
> par terre.
>
> (f. 40ᵛ)

> Through their extraordinary heart, the Romans always strove to exhibit
> things that exalted their deeds and their victories either on sea or on land.

Moreover, the French recognised that triumphal remembrance played a
significant role in Roman religious beliefs. These were examined by Guillaume Du Choul in *Discours de la religion des romains*, a book finely illustrated with woodcuts of medals, statues, temples, and sarcophagi. Du
Choul offers careful analyses of these and other Roman solemnities, ex-
plaining, for example, that:

> C'estoit la coustume des Romains de consacrer et canonizer les Empereurs
> qui laissoyent leurs enfans successeurs quand ils venoyent à mourir, faisants
> certaines cerimonies, par lesquelles ils estoyent receus au nombre des Dieux
> immortels.
>
> (pp. 72–73)

> It was the Roman custom to consecrate and canonize their emperors who,
> when they died, instructed their successors to perform certain ceremonies,
> by virtue of which they were counted among the immortal gods.

His study elaborates upon these rites and tries to suggest something of the
religious fervour that surrounded them. Sixteenth-century French concern
for Rome and its ceremonies seems not at all surprising when we consider
how close a relationship they bore to similar rites performed in France.

While Du Bellay sat in Rome among the ruins and the splendour, and
thought with nostalgia of the smoke of home curling from the grey slated
chimneys of Anjou, poets and artists in France dreamed, wrote, and built
anew the heroic Roman past. The vision of Rome that they imagined had
various sources. Sebastiano Serlio, as we saw, inspired many to contemplate Roman remains and new Italian buildings and to copy them; even
Philibert de l'Orme (not noted for his generosity) recognised this and paid
him a tribute:

> [Serlio] a donné le premier aux françois, par ses livres et desseings la
> cognoissance des edifices antiques et de plusieurs fort belles inventions, es-

tant homme de bien, ainsi que je l'ay cogneu, et de fort bonne ame, pour avoir publié et donné de bon coeur ce qu'il avoit mesuré, veu et retiré des antiquitez.[43]

[Serlio] was the first to give to the French, through his books and drawings, a knowledge of ancient edifices and of several excellent constructions. He was a well-fortuned man, as I have known him, and a very good soul, who so generously has given to the public all that he had seen, measured, and drawn of antiquities.

In the 1530s and 1540s many French artists visited the imperial city and brought back home firsthand experience of its glories. Philibert, for example, used Rome as his standard of excellence and had measured for himself outstanding buildings, such as the Pantheon or Constantine's triumphal arch, some thirty years before. So, when he praises French buildings, such as the Tuileries, he compares the 'bonne grace et iuste proportion' (beautiful grace and just proportion) of its columns to their Roman antecedents. Noël Jallier, too, had been in Rome from 1540 to 1545, and the knowledge he gained there influenced the painting of the Trojan frescoes at Oiron.[44] Even Primaticcio had been sent to Italy in 1540 to make copies of famous antiquities—the statues from the Belvedere gardens and from several Roman palaces, the equestrian portrait of Marcus Aurelius, and the reliefs from Trajan's column.[45] Other notions of Rome came from books, which increasingly provided visual as well as verbal records of heroes from the past. Henri II showed a personal interest in these, and authorised Jacques de Strada to publish his *Tresor des antiquitez* (Lyons, 1553) 'pour le bien commun de nostre Republique' (for the general good of the commonweal). Strada was keen on accurate reporting, as was Du Choul, who frequently consulted him as to the exact size of buildings that he himself knew only from the medals in his possession.[46] Symeoni, too, devoted much attention to ancient monuments and Roman medals, stressing the need to reproduce them carefully since their detail could supplement the current imperfect knowledge of the image of what Rome once was.[47]

The most influential images, however, were drawn from the many engravings that found their way across the Alps in books, artists' folders, and prints. Throughout the 1530s, Agostino Veneziano had made copies of ancient Roman bronze vases, ornate ewers, urns, candleholders, and cavalry skirmishes on sarcophagi, as well as modern works by Giulio Romano and Raphael. These were distributed in large numbers and became the basis of enamellers' designs in France in the second half of the century.[48] In the 1540s, Enea Vico began his own drawings of the ancient and modern artworks to be found in Rome; as a consequence, dishes, plaques, and decorated cups were imprinted with images inspired by his

36. Henri II's covered agate cup, decorated with cameos of twelve
Roman emperors, and surmounted by an imperial crown (Louvre;
Arch. Photo. Paris/S.P.A.D.E.M.).

work, while other tableware and jewels were encrusted with the visages of
emperors and Roman ladies that Vico had engraved from medals.[49] A covered cup made for Henri II (fig. 36) may be taken as an example: it is set
with cameos of Roman emperors and the French royal crown. Another
example is a gem, restored by Cellini, that carries the profile portraits of
Julius, Augustus, Tiberius, and Germanicus Caesar.[50] Perhaps the most in-
dustrious engraver was Antoine La Fréry, who established himself in
Rome in 1544 and for the next forty years sent into France fine engravings
of the principal monuments of the city. These included some seventy-nine
engravings of antiquities and an equal number of subjects relating to Roman history, such as Trajan's column and the main triumphal arches, and
drawings of military trophies and of the equestrian statue of Marcus
Aurelius.[51] French interest in Rome clearly maintained itself into the final
decades of the century, despite the disturbances of the civil wars; in 1574
Etienne Du Pérac thought it entirely appropriate to dedicate to Charles IX
his representation of the imperial city with its surviving monuments accurately delineated.[52]

Veneziano, Vico, La Fréry, and Du Pérac were important contributors to that vision of Rome which so excited Renaissance princes and for whom representations of the twelve Caesars had, in particular, become an irresistible attraction.[53] In Italian palaces, the Caesars appeared as the chief decorative elements in rooms intended to display princely power: in cardinal di Trento's palace in Venice, for instance, and in the Palazzo del Te. Inspired by a set of Raimondi's engravings, the motif of the Caesars invaded France and was used to decorate the marble tables of Montmorency's *hôtel*. Reduced in size, as classical cameos they became hat jewels, or coat buttons; as coins they were considered indispensable to any self-respecting art collection, combining as they did artistic sense and princely achievement.[54] Even Elizabeth I showed her collector's pride when, in 1561, having been offered a set of the twelve Caesars in 'Corinthian brass most excellently executed', she, characteristically, found them too expensive, but was quick to add that her father's cabinets contained 'a great number of such monuments in gold, silver and copper'.[55]

In this general context of approbation for all things Roman, writers and artists could, with confidence, develop their notions of imperial forms. Of French princes, François I is probably the first to have shown warm interest in paralleling his achievements with those of a Roman emperor. His favourite imperial figure was Julius Caesar. In 1519, the king appears in this guise in three manuscripts entitled *Cesar Guerre des Gaules*, beautifully illustrated by the calligrapher Godefroy (fig. 37).[56] The text shows François as a 'second Caesar victeur et domateur des souyces' (second Caesar, victor and conqueror of the Swiss) encountering in the park of Saint-Germain-en-Laye his second self, Julius Caesar, who comes before him to answer questions on the first book of his *Commentaries*. As the discussion continues, the roles of the two men seem to fuse, and temporal disparities to fade, as Caesar's words and deeds are matched by parallel commentary on François's own exploits. The text figures Caesar burning a city (plate 1), receiving the Swiss ambassadors (2), attacking his adversaries in difficult mountain passes (3), building a bridge (5), and at work in the midst of the fray (8); yet alongside are references to sixteenth-century works (Budé's *De Asse*, for instance), and comments such as:

La similitude entre vous et Caesar mest admirable, Sire, car ainsi qu'il se vengea de l'oultrage faict à Lucius Piso pere de sa femme Aussi vous a Dieu donne puissance de vanger l'oultrage que les souycez avoient faict au Roy Loys XIIe voustre beau pere.

(f. 20ᵛ)

The similarity between yourself and Caesar amazes me, sire, because just as he avenged the outrage committed upon Lucius Piso, his father-in-law, so God has given to you the power to wreak vengeance on the Swiss on account of what they did to Louis XII, your father-in-law.

37. *Commentaire de César* (ca. 1559), illuminated by the calligrapher Godefroy. There are three manuscripts, one at Chantilly, one at the Bibliothèque Nationale, and one in the British Library, from which this illustration comes.

These parallel observations persist to the end of the work, when a lonely figure detaches himself and goes off to an unknown destination: 'Caesar sen alla tout seul ie ne sçay où, car il ne voulust quon luy feist compagnie' (Caesar went away alone; I don't know where because he did not wish for company). François's military schemes, the character of his battles, his negotiations and conference are commented upon as though they were exactly the same as Caesar's. In the end, the work reads less in the nature of homage due to a victorious and filial king than as an explanation of the nature and success of the king's strategy for France.

The degree of parallel elaboration is considerable, and I know of no other such consistent development in France before this date. Elsewhere in Europe, however, explicit comparisons with Caesar and reenactments of his triumphs were by no means novelties. In Florence, at carnival time, Lorenzo the Magnificent had regularly employed Francesco Granacci to give visual expression to his own poetic inventions, which were intended as displays of his power and as entertainments for the citizens.[57] These frequently took the form of triumphs with pageant cars sweeping through the streets of the city, bearing images of gods or glimpses of Caesar's triumphal entries into Rome, reconstructed from the writings of Plutarch, Suetonius, and Appian. In Rome, in 1500, Caesar Borgia celebrated one of the high points of his career with a similar triumph of Caesar; while the Emperor Maximilian has left extensive evidence of his own will to exploit the same triumphal forms for their prestige. More modest citizens had to be content with the friezes of ancient triumphs and triumphal cars that decorated their houses or their drinking vessels.[58] They could also turn to the many printed and engraved records, of both actual and imagined triumphs, that had become readily available: the decorated texts of Petrarch's *Trionfi*, the engravings of Burgmaier (1526), Colonna's *Hypnerotomachia Poliphili* (1499), and Geoffrey Tory's *Champfleury* (1529).[59]

François I's patronage and his grand ideas were clearly powerful stimuli. Yet it was not until the middle of the century that sustained attempts to recreate a Roman triumph in art and poetry were made in France. Despite the texts—ancient and modern—that could be consulted, despite the example of Maximilian (the symbolism of whose triumphs, incidentally, was still largely medieval), and despite reports of Italian festivals, all the essential prerequisites for such a reconstruction were fulfilled only during the reign of Henri II. First and foremost required was a poet or policymaker's clear perception of what was involved; second, a deliberate will to link policy and image making; third, adequate resources; and last, the presence of properly trained artists with sufficient technical evidence and actual models from which to work. As we have seen, all these conditions gradually came about, so that by the mid 1540s all was ready.

The final impetus of the French re-creations was the work of Andrea Mantegna, who exerted an overwhelming influence on French interpretations of the Roman triumph. He had become well known in France in a variety of ways: through the praise accorded to his work by authors of popular books, such as Sannazaro in the *Arcadia*;[60] through his own and others' engravings of the nine pictures depicting the triumphs of Caesar (now at Hampton Court but housed in the sixteenth century, since 1501, in the Palace at San Sebastiano);[61] and especially through the enthusiasm for Mantegna's triumphs shown by some French nobles. In about 1510 Georges d'Amboise, for instance, had had drawings made for his castle at Gaillon in Normandy and wished to see carved there

> tutto il triompho de Iulio Cesare, ne la forma ch'el famoso Mantinia lo depinse, de non troppo grande figura ma ben et con bona gratia intagliato.[62]

> the entire triumph of Julius Caesar, in the form as it was painted by Mantegna, not too large in size but well executed in elegant carving.

The principal means by which Mantegna's work was introduced into France, however, was the works of Serlio, who considered Mantegna's judgement and knowledge of ancient art to have surpassed that of all other artists, and thus frequently referred to his paintings.

In his first two books of architecture of 1545 (dedicated to François I), Serlio cites many famous artists whose inspiration he acknowledged—including Leonardo, Raphael, Dürer, Giulio Romano, Titian, and his own teacher Peruzzi—yet Mantegna is singled out precisely because of his style 'à l'antique'. Serlio's detailed appreciation of Mantegna's triumphs particularly fired the admiration of his French contemporaries. He describes them as projecting figures unlike any before seen, stretched out in the line of the triumphal procession, apparently in constant movement, without any one of them seeming to lose its function:

> Questa pittura i da celebrata, et tenuta in pregio grande: nella qual si vede la profundità del disegno, la prospettiva artificiosa, la inventione mirabile, la innata discretione nel componimento delle figure, e la diligentia estrema nel finire.

> (*Tutte l'opere* 4 : 192)

> This picture is celebrated and held in great esteem; in it can be seen the profundity of the design, the skilful perspective, the marvellous idea of it all, the refinement in the composition of the figures, and the extreme care with which it is all finished.

The remarkable nature of the design, the sureness of the perspective, its wonderful invention, its quality of understatement that draws the spectator in, and the care and finish of the painting—these commanded Serlio's respect and worked on the imagination of sensitive souls that they might rise up and shout just as Du Bellay did: 'La donq: Françoys, marchez couraigeusement vers cete superbe cité romaine: et des serves depouilles d'elle . . . ornez voz temples et autelz' (Go forth, then, Frenchmen, march with courage towards this grand Roman city, and from her ruins . . . decorate your altars and your temples.[63]

Thus Serlio established a taste for Mantegna's style, and subsequently French artists, like Jean Goujon, were quick to acknowledge their debt to both Italians. In his annotations on Vitruvius, Goujon praised among modern painters 'André Mantegna, non inferieur en son temps' (Andrea Mantegna, not inferior in his time) and he commended

> messire Sebastian Serlio, lequel à assez diligemment escrit et figuré beaucoup de choses selon les regles de Vitruve, et à esté le commencement de mettre teles doctrines en lumiere au Royaume.[64]

> Sebastian Serlio, who has carefully written and drawn many things, according to the rules of Vitruvius, and who was the beginning of our understanding of such doctrines in this country.

Even at the end of the century Mantegna's triumphs were cited by Blaise de Vigenère alongside Michelangelo's *Last Judgement* and Raphael's *Banquet of the Gods* as works for which their creators had been the first to tread an unfamiliar path.[65]

By the middle of the sixteenth century, even the cultivated French courtier who had not enjoyed a stay in the imperial city did have in his mind a clear vision of Rome, its power and its triumphal forms. As the imperial ambitions of the French monarchy sharpened, courtiers found themselves increasingly surrounded by artistic creations that purported to resurrect Rome and its spirit from their ruins. But the new city, however faithful the reproduction, was a place in which French citizens lived and thrived and where their aspirations and their deeds coloured the stones and inscribed the arches. The extent to which France had absorbed Rome unto itself could not have been made more obvious than in the scenes of royal entries that marked the opening years of Henri II's reign.

The French Royal Entry

In 1548 at Lyons, named by its citizens the new capital of the ancient world because of its many Roman ruins, as soon as Henri II had installed himself in a gallery specially prepared for him, he saw a sight that struck him as 'une nouvelle mode de combatre et si dangereuse, en sorte qu'il la voulut encor revoir six jours après son entrée' (a new way of fighting that was so dangerous that he wanted to see it all again six days after his entry).[66] What he in fact witnessed was a reenactment of gladiatorial combat as it had last been conducted in ancient Rome. The emphasis on military performance and Roman spirit is accentuated later in the entry when, as Henri progressed through the city, he was confronted by some 160 infantrymen, all dressed in 'sayes militaires romains' (Roman military costume). Their captain gave a quite remarkable show of horsemanship that thoroughly delighted the warrior king, who spent less time admiring the arches 'à l'antique' that had been erected at traditional stopping places in the town. One particular triumphal arch, however, attracted everyone's attention. The sixth on the king's route, it stood some sixty feet high at the Porcellet; with its bronze statues of Honour, Faith, Love, Victory, Fame, and Eternity, it represented the marriage of *Honneur* and *Vertu*, whose celebration could be seen carried on a continuous frieze around the top of the arch. Honour, seated in a triumphal car drawn by two elephants symbolising princely magnificence, had a military escort, while Virtue reposed in a car drawn by two unicorns and was accompanied by nymphs playing musical instruments.[67]

This was the kind of Roman inspiration that suffused artists in Paris for the king's entry of 1549. There Henri met the captain of the horse, who also rode forth in Roman military attire, and saw monuments made as replicas of classical forms. Ionic pillars with 'l'architrave, la frize et la cornice de proportion bien observée' (the architraves, frieze, and cornices in well-observed proportion), for instance, supported the triumphal arch at the Châtelet.[68] Spectacles such as these, and the attempt to record them in correct technical language, convinced learned observers that they were actually witnessing a Roman triumph. 'Antiquam speciem et imaginem triumphi Romani videre mila viderer' (I seem to see by the thousand ancient sights and images of Roman triumphs), exclaimed the Scotsman John Stewart.[69]

Although the edifices built and redesigned for the Paris entry were impressive in their classical character, the most consistent attempt at reconstructing a Roman triumph happened at Rouen in the following year.[70] The citizens chose to honour the king's most recent victories with triumphal chariots designed 'a l'immitation expressé des Romains triumphateurs, chose bien deue à ung si magnanime et victorieux prince comme est le nostre' (in express imitation of the triumphant Romans, a thing very appropriate to such a magnanimous and victorious king as ours). The epitome of the entry describes it as 'pareil triumphe à tous ceulx des Caesars' (a triumph like unto that of all the Caesars), yet it is clear from the text of the entry that the event was considered as more than a reconstruction and more than a simple fusing together of ancient and modern, as was the case with François I and Julius Caesar. It was the opinion of the organisers that Henri II had already performed in his short reign feats that required triumphs beyond those which were appropriate in the past, for unlike his distinguished antecedents, the king had brought about peace:

Il vous fault bien d'autres triumphans arcz
Que ceulx qui ont esté faictz pour Césars:
Car la paix plus grans font ses mérites
Que des Césars par cruels exercites.

You must have other triumphal arches, many more than those erected for the Caesars; because the merits of peace must be greater than those worthy of the cruel doings of the Caesars.

Hyperbole is not unexpected on such an occasion, and it is noteworthy that it is linked here to the message of peace—a message that Henri II was conspicuously to ignore.

Extreme attempts were made by the authors of this entry to give an authentic classical air to their account of the proceedings.[71] They couched their description of the arches, which they thought to be genuinely classical, in abstruse technical terms; they modelled the designs of the triumphal cars on general evidence taken chiefly from Plutarch, Suetonius, and Appian; and they filled in the detail of the clothes worn by the participants from copies of Mantegna's triumphs. Mantegna, indeed, appealed particularly to the devout Rouennais who applauded the king's spectacular and sometimes harsh demonstrations of devotion to the Catholic church.[72] For Mantegna not only stressed the quantity of spoils, their trophies and their richness, but also—in *The Vase Bearers*—communicated a sense of elation and religious fervour by painting vases steaming with incense and a tiny marble votive figure. This image was closely paralleled at Rouen by having the Virgin carried behind the *Char de Religion* (fig. 38). Moreover, Henri had special devotion for the Virgin Mary; on the morrow of his seizure of Boulogne, for instance, he had presented the town with 'une grande et excellente image de la Vierge Marie' (a large and excellent portrait of the Virgin Mary) in thanksgiving.[73]

The entry at Rouen falls into two parts: a procession of triumphal cars with hundreds of followers, and the king's own journey through the city, under the triumphal arches and heroic structures that bore the decorations appropriate to his recent victories. The arches were four in number. Two were constructed at each end of the bridge crossing the Seine: the first, in rustic style, showed Orpheus, the Muses, and Hercules in the act of destroying the Hydra; the other presented the golden age above Henri II's device of the crescent moon. In the cathedral square the figure of Hector in full armour was mounted on a platform held up by four caryatides, while

38. *Char de Religion* from Henri II's entry into Rouen, 1550. Woodcut from the printed account (Rouen, Bibliothèque municipale; photo Ellebé).

39. *Char de la Renommée* from Henri II's entry into Rouen, 1550. Illumination from the manuscript account (Rouen, Bibliothèque municipale, Ms. Y.28 [1268]; photo Ellebé).

at the Fontaine de la Crosse, flanked by Doric and Tuscan columns, François I stood. Four such arches, however accurately derived from classical sources their symbols and the columns on which they stood, could hardly transform into Rome the town of Rouen, still dominated by medieval turrets and wooden buildings. They did, nonetheless, provide sufficient monuments of triumph and signs of a victorious dynasty that extended back to the legendary Hercules and Hector.

The determination of the organisers to pull off a Roman triumph is given more convincing expression in the design of the triumphal cars and through the hundreds of Rouennais dressed 'à la romaine'. The first chariot, depicting Fame, was drawn by four winged horses (the manuscript shows elephants, fig. 39) and was decorated with battle scenes, spoils of war, and many representations of death; the second, enriched with statues, showed Vesta seated on a throne of honour and was dedicated to religion; and the third displayed the living image of the king himself, holding all the paraphernalia of state and receiving the imperial crown from the goddess Good Fortune. Each car was preceded and followed by a large company of foot soldiers, captains, cavalry, musicians, and standard-bearers. These came along in bands, dressed according to sixteenth-century notions of the appropriate armour of the Roman soldier or captain.[74] The woodcuts in the printed account of the entry show their weapons, standards, and garments heavily imprinted with the French king's device. Musical instruments seem to imitate the long tubular horns and trumpets of the Romans; and, as in Caesar's triumphs, elephants carried the weight of the booty. Banners and painted images of the countries they had vanquished were held triumphantly aloft; and there were laurel wreaths and palms, vases made from precious stones, torches of celebration, and pikes mounted with the spoils and armour of the captured, who came dejectedly behind in their chains. Priests followed with sacrificial lambs prepared for the slaughter, while Flora and her nymphs scattered sweet flowers of welcome. Wave after wave of excited citizens, so disguised, proceeded before the king, who, from his throne in the specially constructed gallery, viewed the long lines of triumph that culminated in his coming face to face with a second self. He clearly enjoyed the obvious parallel, for its echoes are consciously translated into art and poetry throughout his reign: his equestrian portrait on the *Belle cheminée* at Fontainebleau, flanked by Alexander and Julius Caesar; the triumph of Caesar enamelled by Pierre Reymond; or the medal designs of 1558 that showed Henri on horseback, enjoying Caesar's triumph and the spoils of war.[75]

When considering the intensity of this enthusiasm, it is well to remember that the taste for collecting heroic remains and for seeing contemporary achievements as faithful parallels to Roman feats of triumph was the preserve of princes and of the wealthy. Although their training had taught them to regard classical forms as models to emulate, other learned sixteenth-century Frenchmen (though they were few) were less responsive and were, indeed, more critical of Roman antiquities. Montaigne, for instance, during his visit to Rome, was characteristically more interested in people and their customs than in 'ruines';[76] while Estienne Pasquier actively opposed the idea that his son should use his time in Rome to study a deceased culture. He wrote on this topic to Paul de Foix, the French ambassador, in very firm terms:

> Et certes puisque sa fortune l'a conduit en ce lieu-là, je seray très aise *non* qu'il voye ces antiquailles de Rome, qui ne me semblent de grande edification sinon pour enseigner l'incertitude des choses humaines, mais bien qu'il considère les images vifves dont il pourra rapporter exemple et modelle de bien vivre à l'advenir.[77]

> Certainly, although his fortune has taken him to that place, I would be most pleased that he does *not* gaze at the antiquities of Rome, which seem to be edifying only as a lesson in the uncertainty of human affairs, but rather that he concentrates on images that are still alive, from which he can draw models and examples that he might live well by in the future.

No doubt, class difference and the need to carve out a suitable career provoked this view, which runs counter to all that artists and poets had argued and against all that princes evidently wanted. Pasquier's pragmatism (and perhaps his realism) did not accept that man-made artefacts could secure stability, or even immortality, in a fallen world; on the contrary, such things were eloquent signs of human vicissitude. For this celebrated lawyer, there was no practical advantage to be gained from wasting time on trying to revive what was dead. Yet the poet and the artist, if they were to thrive, had to do just that.

Ronsard's Triumphant Forms

Ronsard could not overlook the expressive power that triumphal forms gave to both personal and national sentiments. Indeed, his odes and hymns of the 1550s recall and helped to promote the heroic atmosphere that then prevailed. In his four hymns written to herald the seasons, triumphal cars are used to sweep powerful gods on or off the scene; the sun sets in motion the famous jewelled chariot made by Vulcan at the start of another day in *L'Hymne de l'Esté* (lines 131–49); and Bacchus dazzles Autumn with his triumphant youth and magnificent entourage as he races in on a chariot drawn by tigers:

L'Autonne en larmoyant s'en estoit en-allée,
Quand elle ouït un bruit au fond d'une vallée,
Et s'approchant de pres, elle vit un grand Roy
Que deux tigres portoyent en magnifique arroy;
Ses yeux estinceloyent tout ainsi que chandelles,
Ses cheveux luy pendoient plus bas que les aysselles,
Sa face estoit de vierge, et avoit sur le front
Deux petits cornichons comme les chévreaux ont;
Ses lévres n'estoyent point de barbe crespelées,
Son corps estoit bouffi, ses cuisses potelées,
Jeunesse et Volupté luy servoyent de voisins,
Et tenoit en sa main deux grapes de raisins.
Devant ce Roy dansoyent les folles Edonides:
Les unes talonnoyent des pantheres sans brides,
Les autres respandoyent leurs cheveux sur le dos,
Les autres dans la main branloyent des javelos,
Herissez de lierre et de feuilles de vigne;
Silene au rouge nez, sans mesure, trepigne,
Monté dessur son asne, et, comme tout donté
De vin, laisse tomber sa teste d'un costé;
Les Satyres cornus, les Sylvains pieds-de-chévre
Font un bruit d'instrumens: l'un qui enfle sa lévre
Fait sonner un haut-bois, et l'autre tout autour
De la brigade fait resonner un tabour.

(lines 370–393; P 2:248; L 12:63–64)

Autumn, full of tears, was on the point of leaving when she heard a noise in
the depth of the valley; going closer, she saw a great king whom two tigers
drew along in a magnificent cortege; his eyes shone like bright candles, his
hair fell below his shoulders, his visage was pale like a maiden's, and on his
forehead two tiny horns were placed as kids have; his lips carried no crinkly
beard, his body was well built, his thighs thick; Youth and Voluptas were his
companions, in his hands he held bunches of grapes. Before this monarch
danced the Edonides; some led reinless panthers along, others spread their
hair across their backs, while others brandished spears in their hands, covered with ivy and with vine leaves. Silenus, his nose red, made haphazard
progress mounted on his ass, and completely overcome with wine, he allowed his head to tilt; horned Satyrs and Sylvans with hooved feet played
musical instruments; one pouting his lips sounded the horn, while another
dancing around the entire troupe, banged the drum.

One might have expected the poet to promote the rhythmic power of his
verse by dwelling on the movement of the car. Instead, in these lines Ronsard's attention is lavished on a systematic presentation of the god's youth
and beauty. Bacchus seems almost serene amidst the excited bustle of his
companions, each one depicted by a typical feature or pose: the wild hair

40. Antoine Caron, *Le Triomphe de l'Hiver* (Paris, Collection Jean Ehrmann; photo Giraudon).

and dance of the Edonides, the tumbling gait of Silenus, or the musical instruments and cleft feet of the satyrs. Each characteristic gesture (and nothing significant is omitted) helps to complete the scene and bring it to life. This picture of Bacchus and his entourage shows the importance Ronsard attached to painting and to the selection of fitting details sufficient to allow the reader to visualize the whole.

It is helpful to set Ronsard's *chars de triomphe* beside those painted by Antoine Caron a decade or so later for his own celebration of the four seasons. His painting of Autumn has, so far, not been located, but in *Le Triomphe de l'Hiver* (fig. 40), for example, Winter is depicted in the foreground making her elegant progress across the canvas towards a temple flanked by triumphal arches, which forms the structural centre of the painting. Her approach is announced with music and by gods and goddesses—Janus, Apollo, Mercury, Minerva, Vulcan, and the cyclops—all of whom are identified by the attributes they carry. Both poet and artist expected their public to notice such indications and to interpret them with ease. There is, however, a fundamental difference of intention between Caron's painting and Ronsard's poetic picture. Caron's canvas has symbolic meaning: it celebrates peace, and Janus is on his way to close the doors of war; moreover, in the background lie the walls of sixteenth-century buildings and real people skate upon the ice. Ronsard's picture has no such immediate contemporary reference. He stays in the fantastic world of myth and makes a speaking picture that satisfies his descriptive powers. Unlike the painter, he is not bound by the exigencies of canvas space, so that when, in the same poem, he painted 'le palais magnifique où Nature habitoit' (the magnificent mansion where Nature lived), he could multiply the Phrygian pillars, imagine a hundred doors and porticos, and embellish at will with gold, silver, and bronze, furnishing a limitless supply of precious jewels.

In one instance at least, however, Ronsard's depiction does depend on a specific contemporary event, and there he reveals the extent to which he was concerned to reproduce the very forms of triumph that had given artists and propagandists such artistic scope, and that had proved so popular with princes. In his *Ode à Monseigneur le Dauphin* (1555), he makes explicit the inspiration he took from the illustrated accounts of Henri II's royal entries. The climax to the poem presents the heroic perspective of the dauphin François who, having inherited his father's military prowess, enjoys the popular recognition of a triumph that victories bring:

Ainsi qu'à Rome Cesar
Triomphant d'une victoire,
Haut t'assoiras dans un char
Dessus un siege d'yvoire:
Deux coursiers blancs haniront
D'une longue voix aigüe,
Qui ton beau char traineront
En triomphe par la rue.

(lines 217–24; P 1:481; L 7:50–51)

Like Caesar celebrating a victory in Rome, you will sit in your triumphal car high on an ivory throne; two white neighing steeds will sound the air with long, shrill tones and will draw along your beautiful car in triumph through the streets.

Ronsard might here be describing the living image of Henri II as he was depicted on the *char de triomphe* at Rouen in 1550 (see fig. 32).[78]

That Ronsard chose to praise the son by thus re-creating for him the Roman triumph that the town of Rouen had so faithfully mounted a few years before to honour his father—'pareil triomphe à tous ceulx des Césars' (a triumph like all those of the Caesars)—shows how sensitive he was to prevailing taste at court and how much he wished to match in poetic form the expansive gestures of court festivals. His poem evokes all the elements that composed the procession at Rouen. First, the royal chariot led by the goddess Fame and the dauphin-king, whose brow was circled with victorious palm leaves while his feet rest on 'les ferremens de Bellonne' (the spoils of war; line 228). Here Ronsard has conflated two images from the Rouen entry—*le char d'Heureuse Fortune*, where Henri II appears enthroned and crowned with palm leaves, and *le char de la Renommée*, where the goddess triumphs over death and the spoils of war. The procession seems endless as the bouncy rhythm introduces soldiers, trumpets, and musicians who acclaim their joy and the dauphin's glory as they contemplate 'en ordre les Rois veincus' (the conquered kings, according to their rank) who drag themselves along

> en diverse mine
> Trainez dessus leurs escus
> Devant la pompe divine.

(lines 249–53)

with varying thoughts on their faces, kings and their shields are drawn along at the head of the divine pomp.

Just as the soldiers at Rouen who bore Henri II's device of the crescent moon had carried aloft models of the forts they had conquered and painted canvasses of the towns they had subdued (figs 41, 42), so for the dauphin's triumph, other victorious soldiers proudly brandish models and pictures of their conquests.

Deniēte Capteq, vrbes Spolia atq. Trophea
Gestantur, flamen. Victima pivgvis adest

41. *Porteurs de Trophées* from Henri II's entry into Rouen, 1550. Illumination from the manuscript account (Rouen, Bibliothèque municipale, Ms. Y.28 [1268]; photo Ellebé).

La premiere bande.

L A premiere bande des ſix portoit
ſur demies picques ſemées de fleursde lys d'or, les fortz reduitz
au petit pied, q̃ le Roy noſtre ſouuerain ſeigneur auoit nagueres
pris au pays de Boullónoys, par ſa magnanime vertu & puiſſáce,
leſquelz fortz eſtoiét ſi bien fillez par art de maſſonnerie, aprochás de la choſe
repreſentée, que ceux qui auoyét eſté preſentz à la prinſe diceulx pouuoyét fa
cilemét lès recognoiſtre, par le deſſaing qui en eſtoit lors porté, ſouz le plan de
chaſcun fort pendoyent floquartz & feſtons proprement entrelaſſes qui don-
noient vn grand enrichiſſemét à lembaſſement de le difice.

42. *Porteurs de Trophées* from Henri II's entry into Rouen, 1550. Woodcut from the
printed account (Rouen, Bibliothèque municipale; photo Ellebé).

Là seront peints les chasteaux,
Les ports et les villes prises,
Les grands forests et les eaux,
Et les montagnes conquises;
Le vieil Apennin sera
Portrait d'une morne,
Le Rhin vaurien cachera
Entre les roseaux sa corne.

(lines 265–72)

There will be painted the castles, the captured harbours and towns, the great forests and waters, and all the vanquished mountains; ancient Apennine will be drawn in melancholy mood, and the wicked Rhine will have to hide its head among the reeds.

Henri II's procession had terminated at the high altar of the cathedral at Rouen to offer thanksgiving and to remind the king, his entourage, and the people that kings of France held their virtues and their authority direct from God. In similar fashion, Ronsard's lines bring his son to another 'palais venerable' in order that he might be seen thus:

Là t'assoyant au milieu
Sur des marches eslevées
Tu rendras graces à Dieu
Pour tes guerres acheveés.

(lines 325–29)

There, seated at the centre on the steep steps, you will give thanks to God for all your successful wars.

The prophecy that ends the poem also calls sharply to mind aspirations expressed in stone and in gold at the Rouen entry. Ronsard in his role as prophet, 'chantre divin', has the power to foretell the peace and justice that the dauphin's happy fortunes are destined to bring to his people. He prophesies:

Tu feras egal aux Dieux
Ton regne, et pour ta contrée
Fleurir la Paix, et des cieux
Revenir la belle Astrée.

(lines 333–36)

You will make your reign equal to the gods, and in your country peace will flower, and from the heavens beautiful Astraea will return.

These final lines give to the son the same goal as had the father who passed through the arch of the age of gold set upon the bridge that crossed the

Seine, the only feature of the entry which the Rouennais left as a permanent reminder of the coming of Henri II. They had referred to him as the 'Monarche terrien [qui] / Restituera l'eage d'or a Saturne' (the earthly monarch [who] will restore the golden age to Saturn). Ronsard's lines also recall the gold statue of Astraea 'accomodé à la Royne de France' (seen in the likeness of the queen of France) offered by the citizens of Rouen to serve as a parting gift worthy of her judgement. The poet blends together again two significant elements from the Rouen triumph to round off his own hymn of glory to Henri II's son.

The grandiloquent tone and the lordly rhythms of Ronsard's odes and hymns are, I believe, heard to their full advantage when set beside the achievements of court painters and architects, but in the *Ode à Monseigneur le Dauphin* Ronsard has substituted for the static, detailed picture-building of the *Ode à Henri II* or the *Temple des Messeigneurs* a moving triumphal form, a procession, that allows him to emphasise an essential quality of poetry—its music. The need to infuse movement into the verse was overwhelming. For this reason Ronsard later deleted all the detailed references to Henri II's victories from his ode to that king, replacing them by more abstract compliments of triumph; and he changed the focus of the poem so that the simple record of past achievements recedes into the background giving more prominence to 'la gloire / De sa future victoire' (the glory of the future victory).[79] In the ode to the dauphin, the singing power of poetry is given particular emphasis not only through the verses' pronounced rhythmic beat but also through Ronsard's inclusion of himself in the procession, his praises placed alongside and granted equal weight to those of Fame:

> Devant ton char bien-tournant
> Marchera la Renommée,
> Qui ton bruit ira cornant
> De sa trompette animée;
> Et moy qui me planteray
> Devant ses pieds pour escorte,
> Comme elle je chanteray
> Ta louange.

> (lines 273–80)

Before your smooth rolling car will march Reputation, who will sound your praise from her vigorous trumpet, while I myself will be her escort; in front with her I shall sing your praises.

Through two elements especially characteristic of triumphal forms—processions and 'chars celestes'—Ronsard gives full development to the musical power of his verse, a power that no other French poet before the end of the sixteenth century could match. Only the glittering chariot of the Sun and of Bacchus are held still while Ronsard paints the sumptuous metals that Vulcan forged and engraved for Apollo and depicts the excitement that surrounded the youthful appearance of the god of wine. In all other cases—that of Mars, for instance (*L'Hymne de Henri II*), or even the chariot that carried Marguerite de Navarre's soul to heaven on its four wheels representing the cardinal virtues—Ronsard emphasises the way his figures move. Marguerite floats on a gentle rhythm; and Mars, suitably accompanied by fury and fear, bustles his noisy way across Europe.

The urge to give life and motion to the poet's painted forms of triumph and to outdo his fellow artists by adding a musical dimension that was, perhaps, finally denied to the brush of the painter or to the chisel of the architect or engraver, can be seen in *L'Hymne de l'Eternité*, offered to Marguerite de Savoie in 1556.[80] Here, Ronsard works on celestial painting in an effort to 'attaindre à la louange / De celle qui jamais par les ans ne se change' (to attain the praise of her whom the years cannot change; lines 5–6)—by which he seems to imply both Marguerite and Eternity herself. As in countless medieval portraits of the Blessed Virgin, shown in glory at the height of heaven, he sets Eternity in royal robes on a golden throne. In her hand she holds the sceptre of justice. Below her throne swirl the nine spheres of the heavens; and far below is suspended the world 'comme une boule ronde' (like a round ball). In this description little differentiates Ronsard's work from that of a painter.

However, as Ronsard assembles the other elements of his picture, he begins to animate the whole. Eternity's companions—Youth and Age—are actively in conflict; while Power is equipped and braced to exterminate Discord,

> qui ses forces assemble
> Pour faire mutiner les Elemens ensemble
> A la perte du Monde.

(lines 62–63)

who assembles his forces to arouse all the elements to mutiny in order to destroy the world.

Then, the image billows out into a procession of magnificent beings who walk in Eternity's wake: 'Nature te suit' (Nature follows you); Saturn comes next, 'marchant tardivement' (walking slowly); while the sun, 'qui vient à grands pas' (who comes with its great strides), accelerates the movement that culminates in the busy circuit of the year, 'qui, tant de fois, tourne, passe et repasse' (that so many times turns, comes, and goes). Ronsard presents this animated picture of celestial splendour simultaneously as a gift worthy of the queen and as an exploration and explanation of the secret workings of the universe. This view is corroborated by the opening lines of the poem, in which the superior, oracular power of the poet is established.

> Tourmenté d'Apollon, qui m'a l'ame eschaufee
> Je veux, plein de fureur, suivant les pas d'Orfée
> Rechercher les secrets de Nature et des Cieux.

> Troubled by Apollo, who has warmed my soul, and filled with inspiration, I wish to follow the steps of Orpheus and discover the secrets of nature and of the heavens.

It is to the poet, inspired by Apollo and taught by the musician-bard Orpheus, and not to the painter, that the gods have given the heightened powers of imaginative perception needed for such a task. And although Ronsard begins by attempting to match the painter's craft, the musical, orphic influence predominates:

> Afin que ma chanson soit vive autant de jours
> Qu'éternelle tu vis sans voir finir ton cours.
>
> (lines 19–20)

> That my song might live as many days as eternity, which you perceive without seeing the end of your life.

This aspiration for immortality, thus expressed at the beginning of the poem, seems to find an appropriate echo later in the figure of Eternity, whom the poet describes as

> Vive tu te soustiens de ta propre puissance,
> Sans craindre les cizeaux des Parques.
>
> (lines 98–99)

> Alive, you sustain yourself with your own power, with no fear of the Fates' scissors.

Thus, Ronsard tries to fuse together representations of immortality and the power of the word.

Ronsard's odes and hymns show clearly that he was seduced by the decorative qualities he saw in the work of artists around him. Tempted by their glitter and their popularity, he was drawn to reproduce ornaments from buildings and frescoes 'faits à l'antique' and to borrow the symbolism and triumphal elements of the royal entry and other heroic forms that progressively turned to Rome for inspiration. That he found such a complete transference possible in only a few poems, and that ultimately he found this technique wanting, is also clear. He was attracted by forms of celebration that so happily coincided with his elevated view of poetry and with his way of seeing poems as coming into being through an expansive and continuous process of elaboration. In this context, art undoubtedly provided a forceful stimulus. Notwithstanding that influence, in order to satisfy the essential rhythmic demands of verse and to convey a greater sense of presence, Ronsard transformed what he borrowed and infused into his triumphal forms the harmonies appropriate to poetry.

V

LA BELLE FORME

For Thethys, the sea nymphs with such beauty bright,
And the painted Island of angelic kind,
Are nothing more than honours which delight,
Whereby life is exalted and refined.

CAMOENS
The Lusiads

THUS FAR WE HAVE traced the heroic fortunes of the great in artistic forms
that crowded every line and every inch of space with incident, with representations of power, and with stirring symbols of virtue. We now turn to
other forms of praise, equally plentiful in sixteenth-century European
courts, which gave poets and artists the opportunity to apply their embellishing skills to the full. Since political power was then considered synonymous with magnificence, any court occasion was remembered by chroni-
clers for the splendour of the ceremonies, the beauty of the participants,
the richness of the costumes, and the brilliant colours of the jewels. It was
the duty of the artist and the poet to give proper expression to the spectacle of Catherine de' Medici's *escadron volant*, for example, a group of
some eighty young girls chosen for their grace and beauty, or to the appearance of Queen Elizabeth's handsome youths got up in curls and frills,
their persons set off with delicate ruffed lace and garments strewn with
jewels and flowers. The portraits by François Clouet or, later, by Nicolas
Hilliard give some idea of the continuing taste for gorgeous decoration.
Beneath the effervescent surface of display can also be detected the artistic
concern, frequently expressed, to render the portrait lifelike and the effort
to compose a picture combining grace and proportion with symmetry. Renaissance poems about beauty and beautiful women actively invite us to
read them against such a rich pictorial background, and the qualities of

159

the lady are usually presented by poets with such portraits in mind. Before we consider them in detail, however, we must establish more particularly the nature of sixteenth-century views about beauty.[1]

Ideal Beauty

For Ronsard (as for most of us) beauty was a source of pleasure. It aroused within him a 'doux, gratieux et amiable mouvement, amy et familier de nature, qui agite, pousse et incite les sens' (sweet, gracious, and amiable movement, kindly and familiar in nature, that stirs, stimulates, and incites the senses).[2] Thus he spoke in a discourse delivered before Henri III at the Académie du Palais in about 1583. To amplify what he meant by pleasure, he referred to the paintings of Corneille de la Haye—known as le Flamen, 'the Fleming'—who had worked for the French court between 1540 and 1570, and whose portraits clearly constituted an ideal for Ronsard.[3] Ronsard's explanation to the king continues:

> Quand vous voyez, Sire, un excellent tableau du Flamen bien proportionné où les couleurs sont bien mises et les lineamens bien tirez, et que les parties de la peinture, par une belle et ingenieuse symmetrie se rapportent l'une à l'autre, avecque un air de perspicacité qui vous contraint soudain de l'admirer, et tout ravy le contempler et attacher vos yeux sur la peinture, telle peinture vous chatouille, parce que le sujet qui se présente à vos yeux est bien proportionné, vous esmeut et agite incroyablement le sens de la veue.

> When, sire, you look at an excellent painting by the Fleming, so well proportioned, where the colours are well applied and the lines well drawn, and whose parts harmonize with each other through a beautiful and ingenious symmetry, all in such a telling way that you are immediately obliged to marvel at it, fully entranced with gazing at it and keeping your eyes on the picture, that picture charms because the subject it offers to your gaze is so well made that it rouses you and unbelievably stirs your sense of sight.

It is noteworthy that Ronsard here, at the end of his life, describes an ideal consonant with classical canons, an ideal that belonged to his youth. Not for him are the elongated forms and attenuated figures of Antoine Caron or Claude Deruet, which covered canvasses in the 1580s. He remains faithful to the standards approved by (among others) the most celebrated commentator on art in the sixteenth century, Giorgio Vasari.[4] The picture that Ronsard praises is fashioned in symmetry; it is well proportioned and lifelike; and it has the ultimate quality—grace, 'un air de perspicacité'— that comes from facility and skill in representation. These are the qualities that constitute beauty and that rouse the poet to pleasure. They are also the same qualities that had impressed Catherine de' Medici when she visited the artist's studio in Lyons and found a full-length portrait of herself, in which she appeared, according to Brantôme,

> peinte très bien en sa beauté et en sa perfection, habillée à la francèze d'un chappeau avec ses grosses perles, et une robe à grandes manches de toilles d'argent fourrées de loup cervier, le tout si bien représenté au vif, avec son beau visage qu'il n'y fallait rien plus que la parolle . . . elle mesme s'y ravit en la contemplation, si bien qu'elle ne put retirer ses yeux de dessus.[5]

> well painted at the height of her beauty and perfection, dressed in the French manner with a hat decorated with large pearls, and in a dress with wide sleeves in silver cloth lined with white fur; the painting showed her so well drawn to life with her lovely face that only words were lacking . . . when she saw it she was so delighted that she could not take her eyes off it.

An extant portrait of the queen (fig. 43) greatly resembles Brantôme's description: she is shown in a velvet gown, crisscrossed with chains of pearls and precious stones, and with wide bands of ermine on her sleeves. This portrait exemplifies what queen, poet, painter, and chronicler thought of 'la beauté en sa perfection'.

This view of physical perfection, which commanded such enthusiasm, had evolved from poetic and painted models, and through a rich heritage of theoretical writings. Painted models were present in abundance. There was the oft-cited example of Zeuxis, who in his pursuit of beauty had conflated the most excellent parts of the body from several models. And there was Parmigianino's striking rendering of the courtesan Antea, which appears to have been very influential.[6] Or again, there were the men of genius, like Michelangelo, capable of carrying 'in their mind an uncorrupt image of perfect beautie' of which their works offered glimpses and 'certaine glimmering sparkles'.[7]

Supplementing such visual material were written definitions of perfection that systematically listed (from head to toe) desirable shapes and colours, measuring exact proportions and discoursing at length on the harmony that blended the separate beautiful parts into an ideal type; as Agnolo Firenzuola put it: 'la beauté est une grace qui naist de l'agencement de plusieurs membres' (beauty consists of that grace which comes from the harmonizing of several parts).[8] Such handy sources of perfection are almost too numerous to count in the sixteenth century. Among the most influential, apart from Firenzuola, are Agostino Nifo's *De pulchro et amore* (Rome, 1531) and Federigo Luigini's *Il libro della bella donna* (Venice, 1554). These works rapidly became material for comment and argument, as Brantôme's memoirs show; and, encouraged by the kinds of conversation developed in Castiglione's *Il Cortegiano*, they formed the

43. Corneille de la Haye (or de Lyon), Catherine de' Medici (Uffizi Gallery, Florence).

basis of games played by court ladies and their admirers, games that writers like Innocenzio Ringhieri collected for further use.[9]

In all these works the relationship between beauty and excitement is a very close one, which afforded poets and lovers a language of description, amplification, and analysis. The following extract from the French adaptation of Marsilio Ficino's *La Diffinition et perfection d'amour* (Paris, 1542) exemplifies such discourse, its excessive attention to detail and use of amplification.[10]

> Quelle chose y au monde qui resiouysse plus l'homme que veoir une belle femme à grand quantité de cheveulx deliez et longs? le fronc large, yeulx en plaine teste, beaulx et rians, luysans comme à faulcon tire de mue, le nez droit et traitif, face en escusson de beau tainct, petite bouche, bau lievres deliées par mesure et coulourées, menton forchu, le col blanc, gorge pollye, blanches dentz, mains et doigz longs, petites mamelles rondes et fermes, relevées sur hault et large estomach, corps délié, bien assise, les cuysses grossettes et rondes en agrelissant de souffisante longueur, à cuyr delié, genoulx fossus, la raine longuette à belle greve et pommeau trossé, les chevilles des piedz petites et piedz proportionnez avec arthaulx et ongles unyes. Un amant diroit louant sa dame, face angelique, cheveulx dorez, sourcilz de hebene, yeulx luysans comme estoilles, gencives de roses purpures, levres de courail, dentz d'yvoire, estomach allabastrin, mamelles rondes, mains nayves et ongles de perle, figure plaisante qu'on ne scauroit enrichir.

> (ff. 48–49)

> What thing in the entire universe delights a man more than a beautiful woman with abundant long and free-flowing hair? a wide forehead, lovely laughing eyes well set and shining with the keenness of a falcon, a nose finely drawn and straight, a face beautifully shaped of lovely complexion, a tiny mouth, lovely lips well coloured and formed according to measure, a dimpled chin, a neck white like alabaster, white teeth, hands with tapering fingers; small, firm, and rounded breasts above her high-lifted stomach; a well-delineated body, firmly set; plump thighs smooth and burnished, which grow slender at the neat knees, the leg long and slender too with beautiful ankles and tiny feet, beautifully proportioned, showing veins and even toes. A lover would say of his sweetheart, angelic face, golden hair, ebony brows, eyes shining like stars, a mouth the colour of roses, coral lips, teeth of ivory, body of alabaster, rounded breasts, pure hands with nails of pearl—a pleasing picture that cannot be improved.

The comparisons continue over several pages. It is easy to imagine how fawning and obsequious courtiers would be attracted by such a display of verbal power. Many works, including Ficino's, as its title suggests, are really concerned with defining how passions are aroused; they move, therefore, from an analysis of beauty to a discussion of love; and, with Ficino, on to considerations of divine love.

Indeed, diluted Platonic notions about the inspirational force of beauty are found everywhere in these theoretical writings; they occur as readily in Firenzuola's work as in the various adaptations and translations of Ficino.[11] Definers of beauty were essentially moralists, concerned to promote the view that physical perfection was a source of virtue and spiritual uplift. After all, man had been made in God's image. Firenzuola expressed their conviction this way:

> La beauté est le plus grand don que Dieu aye iamais élargi à la créature humaine, veu par la vertu d'icelle nous dressons l'esprit à la contemplation, et par la contemplation au désir des choses celestes.

> Beauty is the greatest gift that God vouchsafed to man, since through beauty our minds are raised to contemplation, and through contemplation to the desire of celestial things.

Such sentiments were, naturally, a marvellous way of justifying the work of both painters and poets. Edmund Spenser in his *Hymne in Honour of Beautie* could, in this context, happily claim 'That Beautie is not, as fond men misdeeme / An outward show of things that onely seeme'.[12] Contemplation of beauty brought such rewards of virtue and meditation that praise of lovely women could easily be legitimised.

Some writers went even further. With the support of respected moralists like Lactantius, they maintained (as the preceding long citation from Ficino implies) that the human form was at its most perfect when naked: 'Nakednesse itselfe doth wonderfully helpe pulcritude', wrote Junius, expressing a generally held view. Indeed, the poet Charles Turrin explicitly advocated that the way to higher things is through the sight of a beautiful naked body:

> Le moyen pour renouveller la memoire de ces choses spirituelles, est de choisir la perspective d'un beau corps, et le miroir d'une belle ame qui nous puisse representer ceste premiere et plus elegante beauté.

> The way to bring back the light of spiritual things is to choose the perspective of a beautiful body and the mirror of a fine soul, which can reshape that first, most perfect beauty.

Given the moralists' description of the naked body as a source of admiration and edification, poets and artists were quick to take advantage. They eagerly took upon themselves the duty of presenting their audiences with a vision of beauty whose perfections could adequately arouse feelings of awe that would carry them on to higher things. Poets and artists can and should improve on Nature, as Brantôme quite categorically explains:

Jamais nature ne sçauroit faire une femme si parfaitte comme une ame vive et subtile de quelque bien-disant, ou le crayon et pinceau de quelque divin peintre la nous pourroient représenter.

Nature could never make a more perfect woman than that presented us by the subtle and lively mind of a good speaker or the pencil or brush of some divine painter.

Brantôme adds that he intends this observation to correct what might seem a criticism of Ronsard and his methods of idealisation:

M. de Ronsard me pardonne, s'il luy plaist, jamais sa maistresse qu'il a faite si belle, ne parvint à cette beauté, ny quelque' autre dame qu'il ait veu de son temps ou en ait escrit . . . mais il est permis aux poëtes et peintres dire et faire ce qu'il leur plaist.[13]

May Ronsard forgive me, but his mistress, whom he made so beautiful, could never have had that beauty, nor any lady whom he might have seen or written about . . . but, poets and painters are both allowed to say and do what they like.

Brantôme's comments lead us to the artists' central preoccupation: when even the apparently most unadorned of beauties, the naturally beautiful woman, appears in poem or in paint, there is embellishment. The beauty evoked by Ronsard surpasses and thereby intensifies the original. This double process of idealising and intensifying is achieved through freely acknowledged artistic licence, which controls both the emotional response of the onlooker and prescribes the excellence (or otherwise) of the artist-poet.

Poetic licence, however, was constrained to a degree by the standard forms of feminine beauty that had been elaborated in earlier poems. For example, Boccaccio's panegyric on Emilia in the *Teseida* was enormously influential. Her physical perfections are painstakingly described: long, blond, flowing hair; a wide forehead; fine, black eyebrows; dark, luscious eyes, shining like stars; a tiny, pointed nose; cream and rosy cheeks that were delicate and full of grace; a dainty and laughing mouth; pearly teeth; a snow-white throat and long neck; well-set, milk-white shoulders; breasts small yet prominent; slender hands with tapering fingers and tiny feet.[14] The literary portrait of beauty is here fixed, and no subsequent poet could ignore its settled features. Boccaccio's details are repeated some hundred years later by Ficino, among others, and Ariosto remembered them in his evocation of the enchantress Alcina in *Orlando furioso* (canto 7). He recorded the same sequence and the same colours—blacks, whites, and reds—the serene delicacy and the just proportions; but he sought to intensify the brilliance of his picture by interspersing within his account of feminine perfection references of more general relevance. Thus, around her two dark eyes, 'Love seemed to flit, frolicksome'; and her nose—'Envy herself could find no way of bettering it'. Of her mouth, with its inevitable 'double row of choicest pearles', Ariosto expanded: 'Here was the course of those winning words which could not but soften every heart, however rugged and uncouth. Here was formed the melodious laughter which made a paradise on earth.'

For both artists and poets Ariosto's Alcina became the new standard. Dolce recommended, for instance, that 'if painters wanted to find a perfect example of feminine loveliness', they should consult those stanzas of Ariosto that describe Alcina; then, they would appreciate 'the degree to which good poets are also painters themselves'. Concerned to demonstrate their own descriptive powers, successive generations of poets did turn to Ariosto's account. Sannazaro gave the same qualities to his shepherdess Amarantha who was 'merveilleusement belle et de bonne grace' (wonderfully lovely and beautifully graceful), whereas Tasso attempted the more generalised effects of beauty in his vision of Armida's wondrous form.[15]

Thus it is evident that the challenge to any poet, and the measure of his excellence, was his ability to exploit these known examples of perfection. Since the poet knew that pictorial and poetic versions had made his court audience almost as familiar as himself with ideals of female beauty, and since he also knew that pleasure for the connoisseur comes largely from recognition, he found himself faced with two major alternatives. Either he could accept the challenge and outdo the canon by a virtuoso offering of his own, or he could succumb to the temptation to be different. The existence of a strong tradition of examples throws into relief considerations important for anyone interested in creative processes. It seems to privilege virtuosity, to emphasise poetic awareness, and to highlight in particular the art of embellishment. Ronsard was eminently conscious of these benefits that could be derived from conforming to this tradition, and it is to his poems that we now turn.

Ronsard's Poetic Idealisation

Throughout his career Ronsard is an idealiser in his love poems. If panegyric of the kind we have been considering did initially suggest itself to him as a way of presenting Cassandra in his first cycle of love poems, *Les Amours* (1552–53), then it is immediately apparent that he was interested in varying its use, and that this way of writing continued to attract him even to his last lyrical pieces in the *Sonnets pour Hélène*. His idealising plan is already suggested at the very outset, with the frontispiece to the 1552 edition of the *Amours*, which carries the well-known portraits of

44. Engravings of Ronsard and Cassandra from Ronsard's *Oeuvres*, 1623 (British Library).

Ronsard and Cassandra (fig. 44). Beneath each engraving, a quatrain comments on their appearance; that of Cassandra reads:

L'Art la Nature exprimant
En ce pourtraict me faict belle
Mais si ne sui-ie poinct telle
Qu'aux escrits de mon amant.

Art expressing Nature, makes me beautiful in this portrait, but then, am I not such as my lover paints me in his poems.

The portrait thus acknowledges that Cassandra's beauty is a creation of her poet-lover and that its true qualities can only be found in his writings.

Although the sonnet form requires concentration and speed, we encounter in Ronsard's sonnets the same elements of praise that had been adumbrated by epic poets. As an example, we may consider the eighteenth sonnet of the *Amours* (1552):

Un chaste feu qui les cuoeurs illumine,
Un or frisé de meint crespe annelet,
Un front de rose, un teint damoiselet,

Un ris qui l'ame aux astres achemine:
Une vertu de telles beaultez digne,
Un col de neige, une gorge de laict,
Un cuoeur ja meur dans un sein verdelet,
En dame humaine une beaulté divine:
Un oeil puissant de faire jours les nuictz,
Une main forte à piller les ennuiz,
Qui tien ma vie en ses doitz enfermée,
Avecque un chant offensé doulcement
Ore d'un ris, or d'un gemissement:
De telz sorciers ma raison fut charmée.

(G, 14)

A chaste flame that enlightens the heart, gold curled with many and many a ringlet, a delicately coloured brow, a youthful complexion, a smile that lifts the soul to heaven; virtue worthy of such beauty, neck and throat as white as milk, a heart already ripe beneath that young breast, in human form a divine beauty; eyes capable of making night into day, strong hands to stir up suffering, fingers that hold my life in their grip, with a song sweetly offered, the sound of laughter or of complaint—with such charms my reason was bewitched.

Speedily and economically, Ronsard has piled up known features of beauty, fusing them together into a luminous mass of colours—curling gold, rose tints, and snow-white—that, the poet asserts, dazzles the onlooker. Her smile lifts him to the heavens and allows him to perceive that exceptional quality and divine beauty can reside 'en dame humaine'. Thus the first two quatrains end well within the convention and rest on the transformational power of smiling beauty, which often preoccupied Ronsard and which he described many times. In the sonnet 'Avec les liz, les oeilletz meslez' (With lilies and pinks blended together; *Amours*, sonnet 43), for example, after a somewhat routine account of Cassandra's beauty, her smile produces such magical effect that:

Et ça et là par tout où elle passe,
Un pré de fleurs s'esmaille soubz ses piedz.

(lines 7–8; G, 28–29)[16]

And here and there wherever she goes, a field of flowers springs up beneath her feet.

The magic is maintained in this poem, but in sonnet 18 Ronsard ended the list of compliments at line 10, where gentle, slender hands and tapering fingers assume a strong grip that bewitches, holds, and emprisons its prey—a condition most unlike the admiration Boccaccio accorded his elegant heroine Emilia. Ronsard here upends the convention to emphasise the pain of his helpless submission to beauty. 'Une main forte à piller les ennuiz' stands out in forceful contrast to all that has gone before and alludes to a physical state of quite another order from the beautiful surface that produced it.

The epic poet can stop to gaze and paint at leisure a panegyric set piece, and he remains distanced from the perfection he is creating. The lyric poet, in contrast, is immediately drawn into the emotional zone that surrounds an object of beauty. This kind of personal involvement can be observed at the centre of sonnet 23:

> Ce beau coral, ce marbre qui souspire,
> Et cest ébenne ornement d'un sourci,
> Et cest albastre en vouste racourci,
> Et ces zaphirs, ce jaspe et ce prophyre,
> Ces diaments, ces rubis qu'un zephyre
> Tient animez d'un souspir adouci,
> Et ces oeillets, et ces roses aussi,
> Et ce fin or, où l'or mesme se mire,
> Me sont au cuoeur en si profond esmoy,
> Qu'un autre object ne se présente à moy,
> Si non le beau de leur beau que j'adore,
> Et le plaisir qui ne se peult passer
> De les songer, penser, et repenser,
> Songer, penser, et repenser encore.
>
> (G, 16–17)

This beautiful coral, this marble that breathes, and this ebony that decorates the brow, concentrated in alabaster, these sweet sighs, this jasper and prophyry; these diamonds and rubies that sweet breath keeps alive with its soft sound, these pinks and roses, too, and this fine gold so bright that gold can see itself—All produce such a profound disturbance in my heart that nothing else can affect me beyond the epitome of that beauty I adore and the delight that is everlasting as I think and contemplate and think again; think, contemplate, and reflect yet again.

Here the evocation in the first eight lines is vaguer, more abstract and generalised. It assumes that the reader can visualize the model of perfection and that the colours, the riches, and the flowers are sufficient cues to our imagination. The poet, by concentrating their cumulative effect upon his own person, breathes life into them just as the gentle breezes of the warm west wind stir colours in nature and bring them to our notice. In addition, the uninterrupted, rhythmic sweep of the poem carries this vision right into the emotional disturbance so that the final impression of the poem is, once again, not so much centred on the portrait of beauty but diverted to its effect on the poet who remains contemplative, rapt in pleasure, concentrated.

In *Les Amours*, Ronsard draws many variations in the relationships between poets and beauty. Through consummate control of the movement of his verse and skilful changes in his rhetorical approach, he seems able to expand and reduce at will the distance that separates him from the ideal of feminine perfection. And that distance affects the tone of the poem. In the sonnet we just examined, the poet absorbed the vision into his own feelings, and contentment at 'le beau de leur beau' is the result. In sonnet 55 (*Amours*, 1552), the same elements that composed 'leur beau' in sonnet 23 are used to create 'dea beaultez'; yet, as the apostrophes accumulate and the rhythm accelerates, the vision seems to slip away. Naming the fragments that constitute the epitome of beauty paradoxically take her out of his grasp, and the poet is left evoking them and imploring their touch.

> O doulx parler, dont l'appast doulcereux
> Nourrit encor la faim de ma memoire,
> O front, d'Amour le Trophée et la gloire
> O riz sucrez, o baisers savoureux.
> O cheveulx d'or, o cousteaulx plantureux
> De liz, d'oeilletz, de Porphyre, et d'ivoyre,
> O feuz jumeaulx dont le ciel me fit boyre
> A si longs traitz le venin amoureux.
> O vermeillons, o perlettes encloses,
> O diamantz, o liz pourprez de roses,
> O chant qui peulx les plus durs esmovoyr,
> Et dont l'accent dans les ames demeure.
> Et dea beaultez, reviendra jamais l'heure
> Qu'entre mes bras je vous puisse r'avoyr?

> > (G, 36)

O sweet speech, whose honeyed bait yet nourishes my memory's hunger; O sweet smiles, savoury kisses; O golden locks, rich banks of lilies, pinks, porphyry, and ivory; O twin fires whose amorous poison the heavens make me drink in such long draughts; O red lips enfolding their pearls; O diamonds and lilies, coloured with rose; O songs that can move the harder hearts and whose tones stay embedded in the soul. And goddess of beauty, will the hour ever come that I can hold you again within my arms?

When Ronsard changes Cassandra for Marie, although the poems tend on the whole to prize simplicity and naturalness, he is still interested in attempting new variations in his poetic idealisations of women. In the celebrated sonnet 10 of the 1555 edition of *Amours*, he constructs a fairly systematic account of Marie's physical delights:

Marie vous avés la joue aussi vermeille
Qu'une rose de mai, vous avés les cheveus
De couleur de chastaigne, entrefrisés de neus,
Gentement tortillés tout-au-tour de l'oreille.
Quand vous estiés petite, une mignarde abeille
Dans vos levres forma son dous miel savoureus,
Amour laissa ses traits dans vos yeus rigoreus,
Pithon vous feit la vois à nulle autre pareille.
Vous avés les tetins comme deus mons de lait,
Caillé bien blanchement sus du jonc nouvelet
Qu'une jeune pucelle au mois de Juin façonne:
De Junon sont vos bras, des Graces vostre sein,
Vous avés de l'Aurore et le front, et la main,
Mais vous avés le coeur d'une fiere lionne.

(G, 177)

Marie, you have cheeks as red as a rose in May, you have hair the colour of chestnuts, newly curled and twisted around your ears. When you were young, a delightful bee gave to your lips its sweet, delicious honey; Love left his mark in your severe eyes, while Python gave you an incomparable voice. Your breasts are like two mounds of milk, curdled white as snow under the reeds at which the maiden works in the month of June: your arms come from Juno and your bosom from the Graces; Aurora gave you brow and hands; but, despite all that, your heart is that of a fierce lioness.

Here, the poet mingles details taken direct from nature ('chastaigne', 'mignarde abeille', 'lait caillé') with learned reminiscences of the *Greek Anthology* and with standard mythological parallels. Until the last line, the poem seems entirely serious—a conventional poem of compliment to female beauty—but that last line changes everything by introducing a playful note of reproach that deflates all the grandiloquent praise which had preceded. Ideal beauty is here set in an ironic perspective which, by suggesting that the portrait is in some way superfluous, or at the very least insignificant compared to the fierceness that lives beneath the surface beauty, actually draws attention to the poet's descriptive skills.

In a longer poem written one year later—'Je ne veulx plus que chanter de Tristesse' (I wish only to sing of melancholy; G, 243–46)—Ronsard gave himself more scope. This time, the portrait is, as it were, interiorized. Absent from his mistress,

Qui dans mes yeux, et dans l'âme frappée
Par force m'a son portrait engravé

(lines 31–32)

who has forcibly engraved in my eyes and in my very soul her own image, his mind unremittingly draws her picture wherever he finds himself. If he wanders through fields of corn, the sheaves take on the shape of her 'beaux cheveux de soye' (beautiful silken hair); the smooth planes of 'quelque table carrée d'yvoire' (a broad table of ivory) brings her beautiful forehead into being; her arching brow is instantly present when he looks at the crescent moon; stars become her burning eyes; the rose, her vermillion lips; and the flowers of the field with their grace opened to the sun, her lustrous colouring. Even the trees, found in the wilderness, simulate her person:

> Si j'apperçoy quelque chesne sauvage
> Que jusqu'au ciel esleve ses rameaux,
> Je pense veoir en luy son beau corsage,
> Ses pieds, sa greve, et ses coudes jumeaux.

> (lines 61–64)

If I see a wild oak lifting its branches up to heaven, I think I see there her beautiful form, her feet, her flank, and her twin elbows.

Here, Ronsard has broken open the traditional mould. He follows the established pattern of praise, but, in his total absorption, draws out and expands it to the extent that the whole world is engaged in painting the beauties of Marie. Natural elements and parts of her body interpenetrate. Between the two beauties—Nature and the woman—there is a perfect match.

Inevitably, when a poet decides to describe the individual elements of beauty, he has recourse to ways of seeing and to terms that belong to the domain of the visual artist. 'Je ne veulx plus que chanter de Tristesse', for example, is structured upon regular reiterations of 'je pense veoir' and references to colour and to planes or surfaces. Although Nature serves here as the intermediary, it was but a short step for a poet who saw beauty in such plastic terms and in such detail to implicate the painter himself. In fact, Ronsard's most extensive treatment of the female form occurs, as is well known, in his *Elégie à Janet* (1555), in which he tells the king's painter, François Clouet, those excellent features that he wishes to see portrayed in the picture he is commissioning.[17] His instructions follow the now familiar pattern. Yet the poem's structure (a conversation piece in which he can expound, explain, elaborate, and illustrate) obviously gives him more room for variety than does a sonnet. In trying to see the beautiful figure in terms of actual painting, he discourses on the lines and expatiates on the colours; and through his own impatient presence that criticises, applauds, and changes its mind, he gives a marvellous liveliness to the whole. 'Ha, que fais-tu? tu gaste ton ouvrage' (Ah! what are you doing? you're spoiling your work; line 177), he exclaims to the painter. Then he expostulates excitedly at the prospect of beauty complete:

> Ha, je la voy! elle est presque portraite,
> Encor un trait, encor un, elle est faite,
> Léve tes mains, Ha mon Dieu je la voy!
>
> (lines 189–91)

Ah! I can see her; she's almost made; just another touch, and another, and she is done. Take your hands away; Ah! my God, I can see her.

At times, it is difficult to know who is creating the picture—poet or painter—and whether it is a true painting at all, since so many alternatives are offered to achieve this surpassing vision. For instance, is her hair long or gathered up in fantastic knots and coils?

> Fai luy premier les cheveus ondelés,
> Noüés, retors, recrepés, annelés.
> Qui de couleur le cedre representent,
> Ou les demesle, et que libres ils sentent
> Dans le tableau, si par art tu le peus,
> La mesme odeur de ses propres cheveus.
> D'un crespe noir sa teste soit voilée,
> Puis d'une toile en cent plis canelée,
> Telle qu'on dit que Cleopatre avoit
> Quand par la mer Anthoine elle suivoit,
> Et qu'elle assise au plus haut de sa poupe
> Au bruit du Cistre encourageoit sa troupe.
>
> (lines 11–22)

First, paint her waving hair, knotted, curling, twisting, and full of ringlets; make it cedar coloured; or let the curls hang loose and free in the picture, and (if your skill can manage it) paint the scent of those very curls. Let her head be shaded in a black veil, and her garment pressed with a thousand pleats, just as Cleopatra used to wear when she followed Antony across the sea and when set high on the prow of her ship she entertained her company with the sound of the cittern.

Ronsard here offers Clouet et least two distinct possibilities for his painting; at the same time, he seems to be promoting his own poetic skills at portrayal. In a single portrait, the artist can paint the hair either coiled or loose, but the poet can depict multiple sights, which even stretch back over time to a vision of Cleopatra and the barge she sat in; moreover, he can also suggest the very smell of his mistress' hair. On this last point, for the painter, Ronsard seems to nourish some doubt—'si par art tu le peus'. The doubt persists; for, as the poem unfolds, it is clear that the poet is fundamentally concerned about intensity of feeling and that the painter is the poet's agent.

Throughout this elegy Ronsard seeks to infuse into every part of the woman's body the myriad feelings that each has aroused in him. Her eyes, for instance, are described over some eighteen lines (47–64). 'Que l'un soit dous, l'autre soit furieus' (Let one be kind, the other terrible), the poet demands; the one created under the cruel influence of Mars while beneficent Venus has made the other. Ronsard then uses myth and fable to elaborate their meaning: one eye must be pitying and forlorn, like Ariadne's gaze as she searched for the departed Theseus; the second, full of joy, must bring back thoughts of Penelope's look as she recognised the returning Ulysses. However strange two warring eyes might appear on a canvas, they had nonetheless ample literary pedigree. Her mouth presents further difficulty for the painter, as Ronsard suggests that it be painted as though belonging to one of the Graces, smiling and yet as if speaking, imbued with that persuasiveness which suggests 'un milion / De ris, d'atrais, de jeux, de courtoisies' (a thousand smiles, loveliness, games, and courtesies; lines 100–101). Thus, while transferring to the painter the responsibility of painting an actual portrait, the poet is left free to describe the several visions of beauty that come into his view. Ronsard questions the painter's ability to capture the mobile attractions of his mistress, which the poet can record, overfilling his verse with every trait, gesture, or expression that has ever affected him.

Description Becomes Evocation

Ronsard's renderings of beautiful women are as much evocative as descriptive. We have already noted how he quickly abandoned unalleviated and direct description and that even within the particular convention of a systematic shaping of loveliness, he saw differing manners and tones of perfection.[18] Oblique approaches to praise, which he effected by concentrating on emotional responses to beauty or by evoking parallel exquisiteness, are taken further in poems in which he exploits the rich resources of mythology. As we know, the gods of the firmament had totally infiltrated the court of Valois, and no incongruity was felt in depicting the French court as Olympus (at Tanlay), Queen Catherine as Juno (in a painting at Anet), or Henri II and Diane de Poitiers as Mars and Venus (on an enamelled cup made in the workshop of Pierre Reymond). Nor did it seem at all discordant to present the marriage of Mary Stuart and François II allegorically, with Mary combining the virtues of both Diana and Venus, or to depict a lady of the court as Flora.[19]

In poetry, there were powerful aesthetic reasons for extending this process of assimilation to any beautiful form. Mention of any familiar goddess not only obviated the need to describe her, it also removed the requirement of arguing for status, fairness, radiance, style, grace, or charm. Mere names sufficed. Thus, in sonnet 183 (G, 116) Cassandra's physical perfection is given sufficient presence in two lines: 'Pour qui Juppin reprendroyt le plumage, / Ore d'un Cygne, or le poyl d'un toreau' (For whom Jupiter would assume the feathers of a swan or the hide of a bull; lines 7–8). Equal economy, and greater intensity of feeling, are achieved in sonnet 20 as Ronsard absorbs to himself well-known stories of the loves of the gods.

Je vouldroy bien richement jaunissant
En pluye d'or goute à goute descendre
Dans le beau sein de ma belle Cassandre,
Lors qu'en ses yeulx le somme va glissant.
Je vouldroy bien en toreau blandissant
Me transformer pour finement la prendre,
Quand elle va par l'herbe la plus tendre
Seule à l'escart mille fleurs ravissant.
Je vouldroy bien afin d'aiser ma peine
Estre un Narcisse, et elle une fontaine
Pour m'y plonger une nuict à sejour:
Et vouldroy bien que ceste nuict encore
Durast tousjours sans que jamais l'Aurore
D'un front nouveau nous r'allumast le jour.

(G, 15)[20]

Would that I could as a rich shower of gold, drop after drop fall into the bosom of my Cassandra just as her eyes close on the point of sleep. Would that I could transform myself into a white bull that I might take her as she walks alone on a remote path delicately picking her way among the herbs and thousand flowers. Would that I could be Narcissus and alleviate my pain as she becomes a fountain in which I might plunge for the night. And would that night might last for always, without the new face of a dawn ever bringing back the light of day.

Nobility and urgency are here combined through myths that draw a decorous, yet transparent, veil over passion.

In these examples, we see Ronsard's recognition that he could meet the challenge to conjure up beauty and its perfections by means that took him beyond extended descriptions or detailed comparisons. Allusions brought riches, and myths were themselves embellishments. He was, of course, aware that Homer had refused to describe Helen, preferring to leave her beauty to the imagination and to reflexions on the ravages it caused, and that Virgil had similarly refrained from detailing the passion and charm of Venus (a fact much admired by Montaigne).[21] Their examples carried weight, and however ambitious Ronsard's own poetic enterprise, he would ultimately have conceded some truth to Ripa's statement that 'il n'est rien de si obscur à l'esprit humain, ny rien de quoy la langue des hommes puisse parler plus difficilement que de la Beauté' (nothing is less clear to the human mind, and there is nothing about which the human tongue speaks with greater difficulty, than beauty).[22] Ronsard's concession might well have been self-interested, since it would doubtless have drawn attention to the marvels he himself managed when he came to compose beauty through significant detail and suggestiveness.

With these considerations in mind, it is instructive to consider how Ronsard tackled the challenge of leaving a record of the principal ornament at the French court—Mary, Queen of Scots. The difficulty was not to persuade everyone to agree about her accomplishments; this, they all did. Cardinal de Lorraine's praises, expressed in a letter to his niece (1552–53), bespeak the common view:

> Vostre fille, est tellement creue et croist tous les jours en grandeur, bonté, beauté, saigesse et vertus, que c'est la plus parfaicte et accomplie en toutes choses honnestes et vertueuses qu'il est possible.[23]

> Every day, your daughter matures and grows in height, goodness, beauty, wisdom, and virtue, such that it is not possible to find one more perfect and accomplished in all honourable and virtuous things.

These sentiments were corroborated by foreign ambassadors; for example, the Venetian Jean Capello called her 'très belle, et qui est douée de qualités admirables' (very beautiful, and endowed with admirable qualities).[24]

The problem for Ronsard, therefore, was to give adequate expression to her beauty; to outvie the lavish praise already bestowed upon her owing to her position and sojourn at court. How was he to compose her beauty and grant it a presence that would be distinguished and moving? Among several poems he wrote for Queen Mary, there are two, in particular, in which he attempts to capture her beauty and qualities.[25] Both evoke this image by describing scenes after her departure from France. *Discours à elle même* begins:

> Le jour que vostre voile aux Zephyrs se courba,
> Et de nos yeux pleurans les vostres desroba,
> Ce jour, la mesme voile emporta loin de France
> Les Muses.

(P 2:290; L 12:277)

The day that your veil bent beneath the breath of the west wind and your weeping eyes left ours behind, that same day, the same ship took the Muses far from France.

Within this perspective of loss and deprivation Ronsard sets his portrait of the queen. The image he paints seems very familiar, despite the fact that the parts of beauty are given in a different order and have a new focus. Her lips are 'un beau jardin d'oeillets' (a beautiful garden of pinks); her mouth, the home of pearls and rubies; her starlike eyes make night into day; and her forehead is like alabaster. We are well acquainted with such charms, and their disappearance, of course, enhances their value. But, their effect is rendered much more poignant because Ronsard views their loss as contributing to the civil strife that erupted into war in the very month that he was composing his poem.

> Quand vostre front d'albastre et l'or de vos cheveux
> Annelez et tressez, dont le moindre des noeux
> Donteroit une armée, et feroit en la guerre
> Hors des mains des soldats tomber le fer à terre;
> Quand cest yvoire blanc qui enfle vostre sein,
> Quand vostre longue et gresle et delicate main,
> Quand vostre belle taille et vostre beau corsage
> Qui ressemble au portrait d'une celeste image.

(lines 25–32)

When the alabaster of your brow, the gold of your intricately waved hair, whose slightest curl would defeat an army and in the midst of battle would make soldiers lay down their arms, when this white ivory that rises at your breast, when your long, thin, and delicate hand, when your beautiful form and lovely shape, so resembling the sight of a celestial image. . . .

This portrait of the queen incorporates all the conventional aspects of loveliness, but it seems less a routine rehearsal of ideal qualities than such direct reference to tradition might suggest. For the context of war provides a vivid contrast to the beauty Ronsard is painting, and having brought the physical perfections into such sharp perspective, he then with great simplicity states: 'Las! ne sont plus ici' (Alas! they are no longer here; line 35).

A elle-mesme, written four years later, goes further: it conveys not only the queen's delicacy but also something of the magic of her person, the aura that roused such admiration in her contemporaries. 'Le trait de votre belle face' (The sight of your beautiful face) is drained of the vivid colours, of the gold and the jewels, to produce an unexpected apparition, clothed in simple white 'sa blancheur naturelle' (line 14). Thus the Mary who stirs in his mind is unadorned with artificial ornament, as in the portrait drawn

45. François Clouet, drawing of Mary, Queen of Scots, in mourning, ca. 1562 (Bibliothèque Nationale).

by Clouet in the early months of her widowhood (fig. 45), dressed in the white simplicity of royal mourning, which startles into relief her natural beauty.

Et la beauté de vostre gorge vive
N'a pour carquan que sa blancheur naïve.
Un crespe long, subtil et delié,
Ply contre ply retors et replié,
Habit de dueil, vous sert de couverture
Depuis le chef jusques à la ceinture,
Qui s'enfle ainsi qu'un voile quand le vent
Soufle la barque, et la single en avant.

(lines 17–24)

And the living beauty of your throat has as its only ornament its natural whiteness. A long veil, fragile and flowing, folded and shaped into pleat after pleat, as your cloth of mourning it covers you from head to waist and billows gently out, just as the sail filled by the wind as it blows forth the boat and the tide carries it along.

There is a touch of innocence and virtue as well as compelling attraction inherent in the whiteness. The delicate, transparent veil winds and swells about her form in company with Ronsard's long, slow, smooth phrase that opens it out until it billows into the sails of the ship, that vehicle of sorrow which took her away from the 'sweets' of France. The usual aspects of beauty and their colouring are absorbed beneath the gossamer whiteness, into which coalesce several separate perceptions of the queen. As the wind catches at her garments and blows them gently out into the sails of the ship, Ronsard recalls the sight of Queen Mary, her eyes dimmed with sadness, as she walked at dawn and at dusk along the stately, ordered paths of the gardens at Fontainebleau, reflecting forlornly on her fate and on the journey to come.

> Tous les chemins blanchissoient sous vos toiles,
> Ainsi qu'on voit blanchir les rondes voiles
> Et se courber bouffantes sur la mer.
> . . . .
> Lors les rochers, bien qu'ils n'eussent point d'ame,
> Voyant marcher une si belle Dame,
> Et les deserts, les sablans et l'estang,
> Où vit maint cygne habillé tout de blanc,
> Et des hauts pins la cyme de verd peinte,
> Vous contemploient comme une chose sainte,
> Et pensoient voir, pour ne voir rien de tel,
> Une Déesse en habit d'un mortel
> Se promener, quand l'Aube retournée
> Par les jardins poussoit la matinée,
> Et vers le soir, quand desjà le Soleil
> A chef baissé s'en alloit au sommeil.
>
> (lines 33−35, 41−52)

Every path whitens beneath your step, just as one can see whiten and bend the rounded veils blowing on the sea. . . . When the rocks, though they have no soul, saw such a beautiful lady walk forth, and the deserts and the sands and the marshes where many a snow-white swan finds its home, and the tall pines, their summits painted green, they all looked upon you as a heavenly thing, and, though they had never seen such a thing, they thought they saw a goddess walking abroad in the shape of a mortal, whether at dawn when the light lit up the gardens or towards evening when the sun had bowed its head to rest.

Mist and whiteness dominate, and a power radiates through them, imposing awe and respect upon the elements of nature that, shrouded and muted, seem to understand her sorrow and, of one accord, to grant her a divine status 'comme une chose sainte' (as a heavenly thing). Ronsard's elevated, white harmonies have animated the still figure of the queen, whose static beauty had, in the earlier poem, stayed within the traditional definitions. Such formulae are now consciously rejected, and the effect is a totally remarkable picture, infused with infinite feelings of wistfulness. The intensity of the regret generated by so vivid a spectacle recalls, in contrasting spirit, another white vision of Mary on her way to her wedding with the dauphin. Then, she was

> vestue d'un habillement blanc comme Lis, fait si sumptueusement et richement qu'il seroit impossible de l'escrire: duquel deux ieunes Demoiselles portoient la queüe longue à merveilles. A son col pendoit une bague de valeur inestimable, avec Carcans, Pierreries, et autres richesses de grand pris. Et sur son chef portoit une couronne d'or, garnie de Perles, Diamans, Rubiz, Saphirs, Esmeraudes et autres pierreries de valeur inestimable; et par especial au milieu de ladite couronne pendoit une Escharboucle estimée valoir 500,000 escuz ou plus.[26]

> dressed in a garment as white as the lily, so sumptuously and richly made that it's impossible to describe; its remarkably long train was carried by two young ladies. Around her neck hung a pearl of inestimable value, with decorations, stones, and other riches of great price. On her head she carried a crown of gold, ornate with pearls, diamonds, rubies, sapphires, emeralds, and other stones of extraordinary value; in particular, in the centre of the crown was a stone valued at 500,000 crowns or more.

Ronsard's evocation of Mary's stateliness and sorrowful dignity is enhanced by the memory of the splendour of a royal marriage so recently performed, and it also brings into view the dreadful fate that eventually greeted such queenly loveliness. It is easy with hindsight, of course, to make such conflations of three visions separate in time; in doing so, however, we are responding to layers of experience already indicated in the poem, and we are reflecting in ways well known in the sixteenth century. When, for example, the archbishop of Bourges, in 1587, delivered the queen's funeral oration in Notre Dame, he too called up from the past her wedding:

> Beaucoup de nous ont veu au lieu où nous sommes aujourd'huy, ceste Royne que nous desplorons maintenant, le iour de ses Nopces parée de son accoustrement Royal, si couverte de pierreries que le Soleil n'estoit pas plus luysant, si belle et agreable, que iamais femme ne le fut tant.[27]

Many of us have witnessed in the same place as we are today this queen, whom we now mourn, on her wedding day, dressed in her royal garments, so covered in precious stones that the sun does not have more lustre, so beautiful and delightful as a woman never was.

La Difficulté Vaincue

Visual and emotional transformation were powers that belonged to beauty, but, Ronsard maintained, beauty herself is rarely given to us for long. In *A elle-mesme* and in an earlier work dedicated to this same queen,[28] the cruel and jealous waters of the sea claim the vision in white, just as, in different circumstances, they had taken Europa as she rode joyously on the bull's back (fig. 46). The rape of beauty was an exciting and popular topic in art and poetry in the Renaissance, partly because Ovid and others had left celebrated examples that writers were keen to emulate, but principally because the theme's sensuality and violent activity were difficult to render through pen or paint. If an artist or poet wished to draw attention to his virtuosity—and in a patronage system such a wish was inevitable—then, the choice of a theme that posed artistic difficulties was almost a duty.

46. Leonard Limosin, oval dish depicting the rape of Europa (Herzog Anton Ulrich Museum).

47. Jean Cousin, *Eva Prima Pandora* (Louvre, département des peintures; Arch. Photo. Paris/S.P.A.D.E.M.).

Of course, there were in French art tranquil scenes or pictures of submission like the *Danae* of the Galerie François Ier, or the *Eva Prima Pandora* (fig. 47) and the beautiful naked woman representing an allegory of peace—both by Jean Cousin. More often, however, one saw the female figure surrounded by or engaged in lively activity: the Flora of an unknown French master set amid a profusion of flowers and cupids on the wing (fig. 48), or Jean Goujon's nymphs on the Fontaine des Innocents, who remove their heavy veils to reveal their lovely forms, while waves, cupids, and sea horses join in admiration (fig. 49). Deliberately, artists chose challenging subjects impregnated with desire and movement. They turned to topics in the *Metamorphoses* that obliged them to represent the act of transformation, and they searched for similar ideas in lesser-known works. For instance, the romance *Leucippe and Clitophon* of Achilles Tatius offered extensive descriptions of Europa's physical charms, which might be copied to arouse pleasure and appreciation at the artistic difficulties overcome. Ronsard would have seen many representations of Jupiter's amorous exploits: at Fontainebleau, painted in the *salles des bains* and in the Galerie François Ier; or at the château de Madrid on one of the chimneys; or again, worked into an enamelled cup designed by Pierre Reymond, after an engraving by the artist known only as Maître L.D.[29]

48. Maître de Flore, *The Triumph of Flora* (Fine Arts
Museums of San Francisco, Roscoe and Margaret Oaks
Collection).

49. Jean Goujon, nymphs on the Fontaine des Innocents (Paris; photo Giraudon; Arch.
Photo. Paris/S.P.A.D.E.M.).

At the very outset of his poetic career, Ronsard elected to compete in this formidable game, and he chose a subject that was perhaps even more celebrated than the rape of Europa: Leda and the swan. This daring topic had by the 1540s received various artistic treatments in many different kinds of materials, and their sheer quantity is an indication of Ronsard's concern both to take advantage of the topic's popularity, and to demonstrate his confidence in being able to give a good performance. Leonardo and Michelangelo had established for the curved and twisted Leda figure a kind of canonical status, an ideal, and a norm of gracefulness. They had been interested in the elegant variations of line and form that the subject suggested, and in the harmonizing of the girl's flesh and the bird's texture. Innumerable copies of their work made their ideas well known throughout northern Europe.[30] François I had an original painting of Michelangelo's *Leda and the Swan* displayed in the *cabinet des peintures* at Fontainebleau, and another 'Leda accompagnée de Jupiter en Cygne' (Leda with Jupiter disguised as a swan) in one of the *salles des bains*; while in 1542, Aretino wrote to the duke of Urbino about the beautiful copies that Vasari was making from the original drawings of Michelangelo.[31] Such copies found their way into the art collections of both princes and artists.[32] Similarly, Benvenuto Cellini recognized the opportunity the theme gave him to show his consummate skill in working a complicated myth into hard materials such as metal, precious stone, or marble. He made it into jewels; he restored an antique cameo representing Leda, the swan, and Cupid, and set in gold and adorned with enamels, diamonds, and rubies; he sculptured it on the low relief at the base of the colossal silver Jupiter that he cast for François I; and he made a marble group of Leda with the swan and four children.[33] His success encouraged French engravers, goldsmiths, and jewellers to follow suit.[34] In parallel to this artistic profusion flourished printed explanations of the theme: engraved for the first time in a printed work in Francesco Colonna's *Hypnerotomachia Poliphili* (1499), the subject then appeared in Maurice Scève's *Délie* and in the many Latin and French versions of the *Metamorphoses* in the sixteenth century.[35] Although Ovid's version of the tale had been rather bare, through artists' imaginative embroidery the myth had become more and more elaborate.

It is within this rich vein that Ronsard chose to work, knowing that these varying representations of his topic were already well established in the educated man's mind. Unashamedly dedicating the explicit title *La Défloration de Lède* to his mistress Cassandra, he gives the theme an immediately personalised look, though as in painted versions, the use of myth by convention ensured a certain decorum.[36] The poem has three parts or 'pauses'. The first (lines 1–72) expresses the poet's lust and describes the swan; the second brings Leda onto the scene and depicts her union with the swan (73–200); and in the third Jupiter prophesies her fortunate destiny (201–32). Thus by far the largest section of the poem is given over to the most difficult and the most audacious part of the myth.

Even within the first 'pause', the poet's interest in rendering the difficult is apparent, as Ronsard quickly shifts the focus from extreme statements of raging need to Jupiter's transformation. The king of the gods slips gently into his disguise, which is skilfully and very economically evoked through mere colour and speed.

> En son col mit un carcan
> Taillé d'artifice, où l'oeuvre
> Du laborieux Vulcan
> Admirable se descoeuvre.
> D'or en estoyent les cerceaux
> Piolez d'esmail ensemble;
> A l'Arc qui verse les eaux
> Ce bel ouvrage resemble.
>   L'or sur la plume reluit
> D'une semblable lumière,
> Que le clair oeil de la nuit
> Dessus la neige premiere.
> Il fend le chemin des cieux
> D'un long branle de ses ailes,
> Et d'un voguer spacieux
> Tire ses rames nouvelles.
>
> (P 1:515–21; L 3:67–80)

Around his neck, he put a collar artfully made, where the admirable skill of hardworking Vulcan can be seen. The circles were of gold, flecked with enamelled colours; this work of art was like the rainbow as it falls to the water. The gold of the down shone with a light equal to that reflected on the first snows by the bright rays of the moon. The swan swoops down through the skies with a great startling of its wings, and a spacious traveller starts on a new labour.

An intensity of snow-white plumage lit up by a golden collar as the bird flashes through the air is sufficient indication to create the swan's presence.

Ronsard then had to transmit a convincing vision of that beauty which had compelled Jupiter so to disguise himself. He found his inspiration and his strategy in Moschus, a little-known Greek bucolic poet who had lived in Syracuse in the second century B.C. Moschus had left a number of poetic fragments, among them an account of the rape of Europa in which, instead of discoursing in detail on the maiden's looks, he transferred the sense of beauty to her activity of picking 'odorous lily-flowers' and 'springing roses', and then to his heroine's flower basket. This 'was of gold, an admirable thing, a great marvel and a great work of Hephaestus' on which 'were wrought many shining pieces of cunning work'. The basket, in fact, carried scenes prophetic of the maiden's wooing by Jupiter, which is then related with evident pleasure.[37]

Ronsard seized on this oblique approach to beauty, and he transfers Leda's unconscious grace to another source of loveliness that he inscribes upon her basket.

> Du haut du panier s'ouvroit
> A longues tresses dorées
> Une Aurore qui couvroit
> Le ciel de fleurs colorées;
> Les cheveux vaguoient errans,
> Souflez du vent des narines
> Des prochains chevaux tirans
> Le Soleil des eaux marines.

(lines 73–80)

On the top of the opened basket, with her long golden tresses, emerged an Aurora who covered the sky with bright flowers. The sea horses rode freely on the waves, touched by the breath of their companions who drew across the sea the chariot of the sun.

Here, admiration is transposed as Ronsard creates in our minds a correspondence between Aurora and Leda. We glimpse a maiden with her golden hair blown by the wind amid a whirl of flowers, and this image seems to melt into the vision of the goddess of the morning, spraying the sky with colour and light. On the basket are other images of great portentousness; each one tells the story of a struggle, and the poet emphasises the realism of the scenes depicted. Thus he assimilates to his own art the painter's skill in representation. For instance, the veins on the necks of the sun's steeds stand out realistically:

> Les nerfs s'enflent aux chevaux,
> Et leur puissance indontée
> Se roidist sous les travaux
> De la penible montée.

(lines 85–88)

The nerves of the horses grow hard and prominent as they work up the steep slope, their power undaunted.

And the waves are painted so artfully that 'un pescheur ne ni'roit pas / Quelle ne fust naturelle' (even a fisherman would not deny that they are real; lines 91–92). All the scenes presented on the basket are violent, and

50. Giovanni Battista Rosso, Leda and the swan, a copy of the lost Michelangelo painting (Royal Academy of Arts, London).

all—whether lighthearted or potentially more serious—show signs of the amorous struggle to come.

Only at this point, well over halfway through the poem, does Ronsard use the rich painted tradition of the myth. In this connection, it is instructive to compare the poem with Rosso's beautiful drawing (fig. 50) copied from Michelangelo's lost picture of *Leda and the Swan*, which belonged to François I. In the drawing, delicate yet distinct lines clearly etch out the contours of the girl and the bird, who are shown together, fused, all physical urgency spent and only remembered in the swirl of draperies that surround the couple. The painter has concentrated on the single most significant moment of the story; whereas the poet, within a linear form and in the realm of myth, can be more explicit in presenting details of courtship and conquest. Ronsard stresses the gentleness and pleasure of the preliminaries, as he lingers on the bird's song and on the delicate preparations of plume and flowers.

> Puis d'une gaye façon
> Courbe au doz l'une et l'autre aile,
> Et au bruit de sa chanson
> Il apprivoise la belle;

La nicette en son giron
Reçoit les flames secrettes
Faisant tout à l'environ
Du Cygne un lict de fleurettes.

(lines 153–60)

Then, in a delightful way, the swan bends its form, gathers first one wing, then the other, and charms the beautiful girl with the sound of its song. The girl feels the secret flames in her heart and prepares all around the swan a bed of tiny flowers.

Sweet anticipations are, however, rudely shattered as the bird suddenly bursts into audacity, stretches forth its flowing neck, and, holding the girl close within its wings, overpowers her:

De son col comme ondes long
Le sein de la vierge touche,
Et son bec luy mit adonc
Dedans sa vermeille bouche.
  Il va ses ergots dressant
Sur les bras d'elle qu'il serre;
Et de son ventre pressant
Contraint la rebelle à terre,
Sous l'oiseau se debat fort,
Le pince et le mord, si est-ce
Qu'au milieu de tel effort
Sentit ravir sa jeunesse.

(lines 165–76)

Its long wavy neck touches the virgin's breast, and its beak enters her rich red mouth. Standing on its hind legs, it holds fast the girl's arms, and with its own urging breast forces the rebellious one to the ground; beneath the bird she fights, pinches, and bites, and in the midst of the struggle feels her youth stolen away.

By a deliberate change of pace, and by piling up in six short lines a series of strong verbs—*serre, pressant, contraint, se debat, pince, mord, ravir*—the poet has achieved a tremendous sense of thrust and physical violence.

In this early poem, Ronsard left aside one order of difficulty to tackle another. The presentation of ideal feminine forms has been displaced by a concentration on the overwhelming physical effects that such forms arouse. As the comparison with Rosso's drawing shows, the poet had an advantage over the painter in that he could present more frankly and without embarrassment intimate and violent physical activity, and one might assume that Ronsard was consciously exploiting such an assumed ascendancy. The change of focus in his depiction of beauty, however, corresponded to certain contemporary preoccupations in art. Luxury tableware, painted baskets, drinking vessels, cups, ewers, and vases in rich metals, enamelled in brilliant colours and studded with precious gems, were signs of princely wealth and extravagance. The packed scenes of erotic love play, naked figures, satyrs, or bacchic frolics that so often crowded their surfaces gratified their owners with a blend of sensuality and richness. The value of an object was assessed by three criteria: the quantity of encrusted jewels, the brilliance of the colours, and the boldness of the scenes displayed.[38] Cellini makes this abundantly clear in his extended descriptions of the extravagant saltcellar he made for François I; and a mere glance at the drawings of Etienne Delaune (fig. 51), Du Cerceau, Rosso, or Salviati,

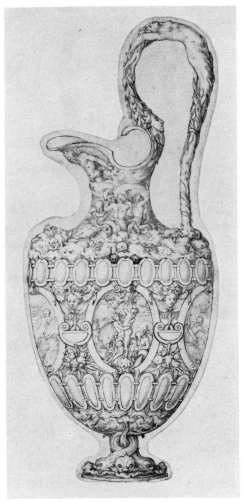

51. Etienne Delaune, design for an ornate ewer (Windsor Castle, print room, by gracious permission of Her Majesty The Queen).

52. Pierre Woeriot, design for a sword hilt (Bibliothèque Nationale).

or at the engravings of Boyvin, Fantuzzi, and Woeriot (fig. 52) show just how ambitious and complex designs became.[39] Their drawings also show extraordinary similarities, which point both to a community of taste and to a spirit of competition that ruled their artistic lives. One-upmanship was a serious matter when the connoisseur-patron expected to appreciate and to applaud the virtuosity of the artist. Such is the context into which Ronsard's poem must be placed.

To find such luxury objects in writing, we must look to the pastoral tradition. There, in the form of the various wagers that shepherds offered as prizes for their singing skills, poets could exercise their love of display and their zest for competition. In any single pastoral poem, customarily the minute presentation of wagers delayed the narrative or ceremony while the poet exhibited varied descriptive talents and crowded onto the surface of the object pictures of strenuous activity. Navarrin's wager in Ronsard's *Bergerie* (1565), for example, seems a match for any goldsmith's piece. It is a vessel made of wood, elaborately worked with a scene that shows the rape of a nymph by a satyr, attended by three naked cupids, who try to help the girl, and a heifer who looks on. The nymph's struggle is vigorously and explicitly described thus:

Son couvrechef luy tombe, et a, de toutes pars
A l'abandon du vent ses beaux cheveux espars,
Dont elle, courroucée, ardante en son courage,
Tourne loing du Satyre arriere le visage,
Essayant d'eschapper, et de la dextre main
Luy arrache le poil du menton et du sein,
Et luy froisse le nez de l'autre main senestre;
Mais en vain: car tousiours le Satyre est le maistre.

(P 1:922–23; L 13:85–87; lines 185–92)

Her headdress falls to the ground and her beautiful flowing hair is blown all about in the wind; in anger, full of fire and courage, the nymph turns her face away from the satyr, and, trying to escape, she tears with her right hand at his beard and breast, while with her left she pummels his nose. But, all in vain, the satyr always remains supreme.

Ronsard pays a price for attempting this degree of realistic description. First, the passage seems too long: and second, the effort to detail each despairing gesture of the nymph becomes almost painstaking. In eclogue 5, written two years earlier, Ronsard had shown a similar preoccupation with rendering an object so faithfully that we could see naked flesh, the colour of a garment, or the muscles and the sweat of physical exertion. Xandrin's drinking cup is minutely described, with its trailing vine around the edge, its wine harvest, and the picture of two drunk satyrs enraptured by a near-naked 'nymphe blonde',

A cheveux deliez, qui se couvre le flanc
Et le corps seulement d'un petit linge blanc.

(P 1:981–90; L 12:146–63)

with flowing hair that hangs down to her thighs, her body covered merely with a tiny white cloth.

The figure of a fisherman crowns the goblet, 'ses muscles grands et gros / S'enflent, depuis son chef jusqu'au bas de son dos; / Tout ce front luy degoutte' (his big, fat muscles ripple from his head right down his back; his forehead drips with sweat). Here, more scenes are piled on than the surface space credibly allows; paradoxically, the care Ronsard lavishes on each fragment is intended to make each appear absolutely true to life. Great artifice combined with detailed realism is the impression that he seeks; if he has succeeded, then he has indeed matched the luxury achievements of contemporary goldsmiths.

'Overcoming difficulty', which involved a use of insistent detail (as opposed to evocation or artistic transposition), might strike us as producing a somewhat laboured effect. We must remember, however, that Navarrin's vessel and Xandrin's drinking cup are incredibly accurate transmissions of earlier descriptions of works of art, and for this very reason such reincarnations were held in particular esteem. Navarrin's vessel is literally translated from Sannazaro's *Arcadia*, where it belonged to Elpino; while Xandrin's goblet comes straight from the creator of pastoral poetry, Theocritus.[40] Ronsard's fellow poets, such as Du Bellay, who had enthusiastically advocated such a process of assimilation ('innutrition', as he called it) would undoubtedly have applauded.[41] And here we begin to see the entangled sources of inspiration and response that the poet absorbed and revised from an established and well-loved tradition that gave freedom to decorate, to be licentious at will, and to gratify a taste for effusive ornament—activities that coincided with Ronsard's own view of poetry as an embellishment.[42] The extent of Ronsard's description and detail are always prominent features, but they never reach the fantastic hyperbole of Belleau's mirror in his *Bergerie* with its mouldings and cartouches festooned with every possible fruit, leaf, animal, and insect; his mirror is

> enrichy de mille petits animaux marins . . . élabouré de petites vignettes, lieues où rampent mille petis animaux, comme frélons, mouches guespes, sauterelles, cigales, lezars, et mille sortes de petits oysillons.[43]

> enriched with thousands of small marine animals . . . decorated with tiny vignettes where thousands more tiny animals move around, such as fireflies, wasps, crickets, grasshoppers, lizards, and many many tiny birds.

Sheer quantity in decoration is as much a characteristic of Belleau's style or of that of his contemporary Jacques Béreau as it is of Delaune's designs for mirrors and frontispieces, or Fantuzzi's and Du Cerceau's engravings of cartouches with their swathes of fruit and vegetables held in place by a crowd of fluttering cupids.[44] By comparison, Ronsard's depiction of luxury objects is more controlled and less repetitive. Although our modern eye may not at first see restraint in a poet so patently attracted by the idea of painting-up forms and of pushing descriptive powers to their limits of expression, nevertheless there is evidence here of such artistic discipline.

Portraits of Venus and Naked Idealisation

Thus far we have considered poetic *belles formes* that either projected contemporary taste for beautiful things or embodied qualities specifically attributed to named individuals. Let us now turn to the inspiration and to the rich source of poetic performance that Ronsard discovered in the goddess of beauty herself.

Throughout the winter of 1552–53, with his colleagues Muret and Baïf, Ronsard worked hard at his Greek, studying poems that described artworks belonging to the rich Greeks of Alexandria of the sixth and third centuries B.C., and to Romans living towards the end of the Republic.[45] These poems were collected into a volume called *The Greek Anthology*, a work that exerted significant influence upon both Belleau, who translated much of it,[46] and Ronsard, who found there new examples of *la belle forme*. Originally, the poems were painted around vases or were engraved on the base of drinking cups, and their purpose was to bring alive the statues—of Aphrodite, Bacchus and his followers, Eros, or the youth Bathyllus—that were painted there. Three of the four themes that predominate in the *Anthology*—Venus, Bacchus, and Eros and Bathyllus— were precisely those that aroused such enthusiasm among poets and painters in the Renaissance. They were, artistically speaking, the most challenging, partly because they had been represented so often before and partly because they were not easy to portray satisfactorily.

The artistic variations inherent in such themes were quickly recognised by the classical poets themselves, and in the course of the *Anthology* figures like Venus, Bacchus, and Eros were progressively transformed. Venus-Aphrodite, at first a clothed, serene, and remote figure to be revered, gradually became sensuous, a composite, naked ideal of beauty, frankly displaying all the perfections of the female form. The crowd of satyrs and bacchantes surrounding Bacchus became increasingly expressive and wild; while Eros developed as a playful, changeable figure given to mimicry and irresponsibility.[47] Occasionally, fuller treatment was given to the naked form. A good instance is Anacreon's portrait of Bathyllus, an ideal of youth in which we can recognise many of the parts that composed the Renaissance view of woman's perfect beauty. The youth has flowing blond hair:

> Laisse libre son poil meslé,
> Frisé, retors et crespelé,
> Comme il voudra, errer en ondes,
> A l'entour du col vagabondes.[48]

> He let his hair flow freely, at will, in its waving locks, curled, twisting and burning round his neck.

He has dark eyes and eyebrows, a broad forehead, a smiling mouth, and an ivory neck—and so the description goes until it encompasses all extremities. Given such licence, it is not surprising that poets were excited by these poems, especially if they appreciated what Dolce calls 'Titian's poem on the subject of Adonis', which was regularly cited as achieving Apelles' notion of a masterpiece—an amalgam of handsomeness and grace.[49]

While Ronsard and his companions worked at their Greek, coincidentally in Rome, as we have seen, the craze for unearthing classical statuary showed no signs of abating. Rediscovered were actual examples of Greek and Roman art that seemed replicas of those described in the *Anthology*, findings that gave yet further impetus to poets and artists as they sought to emulate and then to outdo the artistic triumphs of the ancient world. Philibert de l'Orme (among many, even including Montaigne) waxed lyrical on the wonders in the Belvedere palace gardens:

> Un lieu accompagné d'une infinité de beaux ouvrages et statues de marbre, comme aussi autres belles antiquitez et signament d'un Laocoon et d'un Apollon, qui sont très admirables à voir pour estre divinement bien faictes. Il y a aussi un Hercules, une Venus, et plusieurs autres Statues antiques de marbre colloquées dedans des nyches.[50]

> A place where there is an infinite number of beautiful works of art and marble statues; with wonderful masterpieces from antiquity, namely a Laocoön and an Apollo that are wonderful to see, being of such divine workmanship. There is also a Hercules, a Venus, and many other ancient statues made of marble and set within the niches of stone.

Many factors seemed to conspire to spread this interest in the representation of naked human forms. Collectors were eager to own new finds of marble or sculptured reliefs, which were regularly attributed to masters such as Praxiteles or Phidias. Among many such examples, there was the remarkable head of Venus—duly marked 'Opus Phidias'[51]—that cardinal du Bellay had sent from Rome as a contribution to the decorations at Anet. If originals or even copies were not available, then princes made do with modern masterpieces of beautiful nakedness, such as the profusion of bathing scenes like this one, in *Diane au bain* by François Clouet (fig. 53).[52] It was a taste François I had inaugurated in France at Fontainebleau. There, in the long gallery, he had given unimpeachable royal approval to such works: above a view of the château can be seen Venus and her nymphs going to the baths (fig. 54). The mother of love and the goddess of beauty was thus given her natural place at the centre of the court. The fresco was very influential; copied and adapted many times, as in an engraving by Mignon (fig. 55), it could be found by 1563 even in bourgeois households and in furniture design alongside other paintings of Venus seen either in the company of the Graces or in amorous play with Mars or Cupid.[53] That a work such as Bronzino's *Venus, Cupid, Folly, and Time* entered the royal collection in 1540 is a further indication of the French love of colourful display and variety in naked forms.

Brantôme was in no doubt about the infinitely disturbing effect on a man's feelings that came from looking at 'une Vénus toute nue, couchée et regardée de son fils Cupidon; l'autre d'un Mars couché avec sa Vénus;

53. François Clouet, *Diane au Bain*, Ecole de Fontainebleau (Rouen, Musée des Beaux Arts; photo Giraudon).

54. Fontainebleau, Galerie de François Ier, fresco of Venus going to the baths (Château de Fontainebleau; Cliché Esparcieux).

55. Jean Mignon, engraving of fresco *Venus Going to the Baths*, from the Galerie François Ier, Fontainebleau (Bibliothèque Nationale).

l'autre d'un Leda couchée avec son signe' (a recumbent Venus, all naked and admired by her son Cupid; and another of Mars lying with Venus; and another of a Leda resting beside her swan).[54] The disturbance, however, was willingly sought and given. When, in 1548, Giorgio Vasari was anxious to please a patron with a work depicting the most beautiful form, he received the following advice from Annibale Caro:

> I would think that Adonis and Venus would form an arrangement of the beautiful bodies you could make, even though this has been done before. And as to this point it would be good if you kept as closely as possible to the description in Theocritus. . . . Should you want to do more than one figure, the Leda, particularly the one by Michelangelo pleases me beyond measure. Also that Venus which that other worthy man [Botticelli] painted as she rose from the sea would, I imagine, be a beautiful sight.[55]

Both poet and painter are noticeably relatively unconcerned about the originality of theme. Their chief interest was to return to the fountain-heads of beauty and to astonish the connoisseur with new spice: some new arrangement, more variety, a novel manner, or some unknown technique.

While almost all poets and painters were, as we have seen, attracted by the aesthetic benefits of imitation, a few writers were more critical; but these tend to be among those after the first generation of enthusiasts had gone into decline. Vigenère, for instance, was tired of the procession of copies of the known masterpieces of Zeuxis or Apelles; he preferred originality and extolled those who opened up new territory rather than, as he said, 'plusieurs mediocres ouvriers [qui] ont pu fort heureusement contrefaire les Centaures de Zeuxis: la Venus d'Apelles naviguant à bord dedans une conque' (several mediocre workmen who have happily managed to counterfeit the Centaurs of Zeuxis and the Venus of Apelles riding on her shell-ship).[56] Despite this view of what artists should attempt, all the surviving evidence indicates that in the 1550s and 1560s a majority— including the all-important patrons—inclined to the opinion that new approaches to old themes were what was wanted.

This competitive process can best be illustrated by a study of one of the very numerous examples of Aphrodite: the Venus Anadyomene created by Apelles, bought by Augustus, and later placed in the temple of Julius Caesar. This famous picture became the standard to emulate; four epigrams in the *Anthology* celebrate its uniqueness, and their adulation undoubtedly affected the many poems and works of art in the Renaissance that were inspired by the original picture. In this context, let us consider Ronsard's sonnet 'Quand au matin ma déesse s'abille' (When, at dawn, my mistress begins to dress; *Amours*, 1552–53, poem 42; G, 28). In his commentary on this sonnet, Muret mentions Apelles' Venus Anadyomene, noting that

> Sur ceste peinture ont esté faits beaucoup d'Epigrammes Grecs: desquels j'en ay mis icy un de Leonide qui m'a semblé merveilleusement gentil.

> Many Greek epigrams have been made about this painting; here I cite one from Leonidas that seemed to me to be especially good.

Muret then cites the Greek text of the epigram, which Vitry rendered as:

> La féconde Cypris sortait du sein de sa mère, couverte encore d'écume frémissante. Apelles la vit et rendit sa beauté qui fait naître les désirs, non pas en peinture, mais réelle et vivante. De ses mains effilées, elle presse sa chevelure avec grâce; avec grâce brille dans ses yeux un calme désir et son sein qui annonce la jeunesse et la force se gonfle doucement.[57]

> Fecund Cypris, born from the breast of her mother, came into the world still covered with shimmering foam. Apelles saw her and recorded her beauty that rouses desire not in paint, but as real and living. With her tapering fingers, she arranges her hair gracefully; in her eyes a calm desire elegantly shines and her gently rising breast promises both youth and strength.

From Muret's remarks, it is reasonable to assume that Leonidas's epigram was one of the poems of the *Anthology* that he and Ronsard discussed together in their studies. At all events, echoes of Leonidas can be traced in many of the poems Ronsard wrote in praise of feminine beauty. In his commentary, Muret is explicitly reminded of the *Anthology* in both 'Soit que son or se crespe lentement' (Whether her golden hair gently curls) and 'Ecumiere Vénus, reine en Cypre puissante' (Foaming Venus, powerful queen of Cyprus).[58]

A comparison between Leonidas's epigram and Ronsard's poem 'Quand au matin ma déesse s'abille' demonstrates the links between the two. Both poets stress the flow and movement of the hair, which at times seems to screen completely the naked body, but which at other moments, as it curls gracefully through the comb or about the twisting fingers, threatens to reveal the beauties beneath.[59] Rapture comes from the active qualities of beauty described in the Greek epigram as 'réelle et vivante . . . presse sa chevelure' and in Ronsard's poem thus:

> Quand au matin ma Déesse s'abille
> D'un riche or crespe ombrageant ses talons,
> Et que les retz de ses beaulx cheveux blondz
> En cent façons ennonde et entortille. . . .
>
> (lines 1−4)

When, at dawn, my mistress begins to dress, and her rich curling gold covers her heels, and the beautiful locks of her blond hair curls and twists in a thousand ways. . . .

Her qualities are presented so powerfully that the comparison with Venus —'Je l'accompare à l'escumiere fille' (I compare her to the daughter of the foam; line 5)[60]—seems a natural extension of all the admiration felt. The combing movement of her fingers, which was rendered by Leonidas as 'De ses mains effilées, elle presse sa chevelure', is accentuated by Ronsard, who associates her action of curling her hair with a vision of Venus rising on her shell-ship as it comes into shore:

> Qui or peignant les siens jaunement longz,
> Or les ridant en mille crespillons
> Nageoyt abord dedans une coquille.
>
> (lines 6−8)

Now combing her long, golden hair, now curling it into a thousand ringlets, she road ashore on her shell-ship.

Ronsard's lines immediately conjure up Botticelli's famous picture the *Birth of Venus*, which was copied and engraved many times in the sixteenth century, and a stucco replica of which is situated at the base of the last fresco, *L'Ignorance chassée*, in the Galerie François Ier at Fontainebleau (fig. 56).[61] The reference to the shell, not found in Leonidas's por-

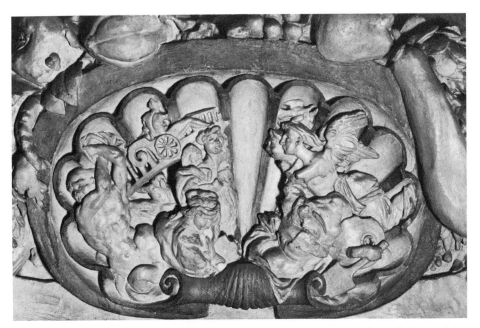

56. Fontainebleau, Galerie François Ier, the birth of Venus in stucco from the base of the fresco *L'Ignorance chassée*.

trait of Venus, thus illustrates how Ronsard relied on an interesting complex of verbal and visual reminiscence to strike the reader with the power of beauty that has overwhelmed him. He does, however, in the last version of the poem, try to attenuate the obvious specific reference by changing the direction of the scene in line 8 to a weaker statement 'Passoit la mer portée en sa coquille', (crossed the sea, carried on her shell).[62]

In a second sonnet, 'Soit que son or se crespe lentement' (Whether her golden hair gently curls; *Amours*, 1552–53, poem 90), instantly striking is the way in which the poet has fused the motifs of waves of hair, waves of the sea, and those of the body.[63] All seem to flow voluptuously together in a slow, wayward, yet insidious movement, which leads without pause to the the almost breathless satisfaction of 'je me contente en mon contentement' (I'm happy in my happiness; line 8). The first quatrain recalls the *Birth of Venus*:

> Soit que son or se crespe lentement
> Ou soit qu'il vague en deux glissantes ondes,
> Qui ça qui là par le sein vagabondes,
> Et sur le col, nagent follastrement. . . .

Whether her golden hair gently curls, or whether it flows down in two shimmering waves that float here and there across her breast or nestles gently in her neck. . . .

57. Ecole de Fontainebleau, *Dame à Sa Toilette* (Dijon, Musée des Beaux Arts; photo Giraudon).

But the next lines bring a second vision: that of another Venus, one whose portrait had been drawn several times by painters from the so-called School of Fontainebleau. There are many versions of this lady at her toilet (fig. 57), whom Ronsard described as 'd'une Vénus imitant la façon' (imitating the style of a Venus).[64] In these paintings, except for her jewels, the lady-Venus is naked. Instead of the natural flowing hair of Botticelli's Venus in an outdoor scene, here we have an interior setting and the lady's elaborate hair creation of coils and precious stones chosen from a rich casket open before her; her dressed-up beauty is reflected in a mirror. Ronsard's second vision is similarly wrought:

> Ou soit qu'un noud [*sic*] diapré tortement
> De maintz rubiz, et maintes perles rondes,
> Serre les flotz de ses deux tresses blondes . . .
> Je me contente en mon contentement.

> > (lines 5−8)

Or whether tied in a knot twisted and studded with many a ruby and many a pearl, which bind the waves of her two golden plaits . . . I'm happy in my happiness.

Hardly has this new sight been absorbed when a third portrait intervenes:

> Quel plaisir est ce, ainçoys quelle merveille
> Quand ses cheveux troussez dessus l'oreille
> D'une Venus imitant la façon?
> Quand d'un bonet son chef elle adonize.

> > (lines 9−12)

What pleasure is better, what wonder is greater than the sight of her with her hair lifted above her ears, imitating the style of a Venus? When she turns herself into an Adonis as she places a bonnet on her head.

The description of her hair looped over her ears brings into view almost a copy of Léonard Limosin's coiffed and bonneted Venus, with which he adorned several works, including the enamelled dish he titled *Venus et l'Amour* (fig. 58).[65]

These and many other poems that Ronsard wrote about Venus show his awareness and appreciation of the wide range of pictorial and textual sources available to him. Beauty always seems to have aroused deep feelings in Ronsard, and, as though part of a circular process of artistic creation, when he tries to communicate beauty's power and to move his audience to wonder, he awakens his readers' erudite memories of earlier texts and works of art. In the two sonnets we have examined, the ideal figure emerges composed of highly selected elements. Interest is almost entirely focussed on the hair: on its richness, on its playful, undulating movement,

58. Leonard Limosin, *Venus et l'Amour*, enamelled dish (Louvre, département des objets d'art; Arch. Photo. Paris/S.P.A.D.E.M.).

and on its power to hide or to reveal. In *Amours* 42 the long tresses, emphasised by the soft lyrical flow of the verse, are all that is needed to suggest the whole body. Ronsard had here found the advantages of not naming or drawing all the parts, in contrast to the Renaissance portrait painter's virtual obligation to do so. Ronsard had discovered that absence communicates, and that if he allowed the onlooker a larger dimension of imaginative play, then his pictures of beauty would have the same elevating effects as those of famous artists.

Ronsard could so build his poems on the fame of artists and their works that in another sonnet on the same theme two words—'Ecumiere Venus' (foaming Venus)—suffice to conjure up the beautiful goddess within her marine view (*Amours*, 1554, poem 9; G, 148–49). Thus Ronsard relies on multiple received pictorial impressions, and he uses a kind of shorthand that takes beauty for granted; as a result, in the rest of the sonnet, he is free to explore other aspects of the myth of Venus, ones that, incidentally, would be difficult to convey through paint. The poem also illustrates how Ronsard's preoccupation has changed from the evocation of extraordinary beauty and its effect upon him to much more generalised considerations of the good consequences of appreciating loveliness. His interest is both philosophical and moral, in that he examines the nature of the power that Venus wields over all creatures. His analysis takes the form of a celebration of the functions of the goddess before the sonnet appears to fall away into self-preoccupation.

> Ecumiere Venus, roine en Cypre puissante,
> Mere des dous amours, à qui toujours se joint
> Le plaisir, et le jeu, qui tout animal point
> A toujours reparer sa race perissante,
> Sans toi, Nimfe aime-ris, la vie est languissante,
> Sans toi rien n'est de beau, de vaillant ni de coint,
> Sans toi la volupté joïeuse ne vient point,
> Et des Graces sans toi la grace est desplaisante.
> Ores qu'en ce printans on ne sçauroit rien voir,
> Qui fiché dans le coeur ne sente ton pouvoir,
> Sans plus une pucelle en sera elle exente?
> Si tu ne veus du tout la traiter de rigueur
> Au moins que sa froideur en ce mois d'Avril sente
> Quelque peu du brasier qui m'enflame le coeur.

Foaming Venus, powerful queen of Cyprus, mother of sweet loves, who always joins pleasure and play, who stimulates every animal constantly to repair its dying race. Without you, O nymph, lover of laughter, life is wearisome; without you, joyous pleasure does not come; and without you, the grace of the Graces does not please. Let it be that in this springtime, nothing can be seen which does not reflect your power that penetrates the heart. A maiden, will she be exempt? If you do not wish to treat her rigorously, at least, in this month of April, let her coldness be warmed just a little by the flames that fire my heart.

The poem gives a dense impression, and the wealth of erudition that underlies the beautiful rhythm of its opening lines is suggested by Rémy Belleau, who first appended his comments to the 1560 edition of the *Amours*.

Ce Sonnet est fort aisé de soy, dedans lequel est compris un bel hymne de Venus, que rien sans elle (comme a chanté Lucrece) ne peut estre ny plaisant, ny beau: et que c'est elle qui incite tous les animaux a conserver leur espece, et que la mesme Volupté, ny les Graces ne sont point douces, ny gracieuses, sans leur maistresse Venus, qui est le plaisir d'engendrer, et de faire une chose semblable à soy. Nostre Poëte l'appelle Escumiere, du nom Grec ἀφροδίτη, qui signifie escume: car tout sperme, dont se fait la generation, est humide, blanc et escumeux. Il a esté dit par cy devant, comme Venus fut née de l'escume de la mer, et des parties honteuses de Saturne. Si tu veux lire plus amplement sa naissance, voy Hesiode en sa Theogonie.[66]

This sonnet is easy of itself, in which is comprised a beautiful hymn to Venus, without whom (just as Lucretius sang) nothing can be pleasant or lovely: and it's she who incites all animals to preserve their race, and even Voluptas and the Graces are not sweet or beautiful without their mistress

Venus, who is the principle of creation and of the desire to make a being like oneself. The poet calls her "foaming" from the Greek word for foam: for all sperm, which stimulates life, is damp, white, and foamy. It has been said before how Venus was born from the foam of the sea and from the private parts of Saturn. If you want to know more about her birth, consult Hesiod in his *Theogony*.

As a fitting climax to this study of *la belle forme*, let us examine the *Ode à la Fontaine Belerie* (1553), which in some ways constitutes the most complex interweaving of praise and detail of loveliness that Ronsard ever attempted (P 1:620–25; L 5:233–42). In this poem are blended themes favoured by contemporary court painters: the bathing scene; the naked sleeping form of a woman stretched out in the open air; and the combination of nude bodies and a scattering of flowers.[67] Although the poem purports to celebrate a fountain, its centre is the naked presence of Cassandra, whose lovely aspects are itemized in the familiar visual sequence that starts with her head and ends with secrets that cannot be named. Each part is idealised with sustained references to divinities—for Cassandra, like Pandora, has received all the heavenly gifts.

As the poem gains momentum, it becomes apparent that Ronsard is trying to do more than offer an admiring description of a beautiful woman. He is making love to her, and water is the medium for doing so. First, it mirrors her form; then, it washes and bathes her; and finally the water 'A cent fois baisé les brins / De ses boutons cinabrins' (a hundred times kissed the tips of her red nipples; lines 73–74). By giving the water the role of lover, Ronsard succeeds in maintaining a double perspective;[68] while the onlooker is never distracted from the delightful picture of a naked woman bathing, he is made acutely aware all the time of the poet's own sensual commitment, especially in lines of blatant titillation:

C'est toy qui tâtes sa hanche
Sa gréve et sa cuisse blanche,
Et son, qui ne fait encor
Que se frizer de fils d'or.

(lines 80–83)

It's you who touch her hips, her loin, and white thighs, and her . . . which just begins to show its golden hair.

The transfer of the lover's role is sustained throughout the ode as water's edge, summer heat, and a breeze that mingles its own soft breath with the gentle movements of Cassandra's breathing all combine to keep sensuous preoccupations in the foreground. Even the birds are affected and in their excitement they rain down flowers so plentifully that human loveliness and the flowers' sweetness seem indistinguishable:

Si bien qu'on ne peut sçavoir,
A la voir, et à les voir,
Laquelle, ou de la fleurette,
Ou d'elle, est la plus douillette.

(lines 113–116)

So much so that in seeing her and them, one cannot tell which—the maiden
or the flower—is the most sweet.

Stylized versions of this topos were painted several times by the Maître de
Flore (fig. 59), and they appear elsewhere in Ronsard's writing.[69] They are
rarely accompanied, however, by the degree of exuberance present in this

59. Maître de Flore, allegorical painting (Louvre, département des
peintures; Arch. Photo. Paris/S.P.A.D.E.M.).

ode. Ronsard himself seems aware of it, for he takes over the initiative and orders ritual sacrifices to be made in honour of the fountain, whose status has been elevated to that of a god by its contact with a divinity: 'Front en qui ma Cytherée / A sa face remirée' (brow in which is reflected the face of my Venus; lines 163–64).

In this poem, the process of idealisation of woman is complete. Painted and formal reference to tracts of erudition stretching back to the Greeks of Alexandria have here been dissolved into a disarmingly natural song whose seven-syllabled lines, with their words and sounds frequently echoing each other, trip happily along. Notions of beauty are as recognisable as ever, but the items are softened and absorbed into the play of water, which is the principal agent of transmutation. Human beauties are transformed by the fountain; these, in turn, create a magical atmosphere that draws all the elements of nature into concerted gestures of praise. Cassandra and Cythérée have become one, and although the applause goes from the poet to the fountain, Ronsard ends the ode with specific reference to his own role in the idealising function, as—through wordplay—fountain and poem are fused:

> Je vous pri', ma Fontelette,
> Ma doucelette ondelette,
> Je vous pri' n'oubliez pas
> Dés le jour de mon trespas
> Contre vos rives de dire
> Que Ronsard dessus sa lyre
> N'a vostre nom desdaigné,
> Et que sa Dame a baigné
> Sa belle peau doucelette
> Dans vostre claire ondelette.

> (lines 187–96)

I beg you, my fountain, my sweet flowing waters, I pray you, from the very day of my death, not to forget, as you sound against the banks, that Ronsard did not disdain to sing your praises, and that his mistress bathed her sweet, soft skin in your clear water.

Tradition had bequeathed to poets and artists a notion of beauty that was to be constituted simply by an enumeration of its parts. We have seen how Ronsard recognised the limitations of mere recitation and how quickly he moved to a recognition of the poetic advantages of evocation. Yet his poems on *la belle forme* continued to oscillate between powerful suggestions of beauty and lavish descriptive performances. Reliant as he was on a public of connoisseurs, he could take much for granted and create visions of perfection that rested on unsaid pictorial and textual sources. His public, however, was also impressed by colourful display and variations on difficult topics, so the dependent poet, all too easily sometimes, succumbed to virtuosity. With the *Ode à la Fontaine Belerie* we have an example of the penetrative force of sensuality; and here, in 1553, Ronsard transformed his pleasure into a painted, breathing presence, just as some thirty years later, at the Académie du Palais, he was to turn to painting in order to elucidate his idea of joy.

Artists might occasionally produce a jewel fit to set beside the Fontaine Belerie; there was, for example, the fountain jewel that could be seen in the mid sixteenth century at the château de Pau, described as follows in the inventory of 1561–62:

> Une fontaine où il y a une femme blanche qui se baigne devant ung mirouer en sa main, le fondz de la fontaine semé de perles, les fillets d'eau de perles, le bassin faict d'une pierre verte, son couvercle d'or faict à jour esmaillé de rouge; une terrasse d'argent doré esmaillé de vert. . . .[70]

> A fountain where a lily-white lady bathed, a mirror in her hands, and the depths of the water littered with pearls; its waters, strings of pearls; the basin made out of green stones; its golden cover latticed and enamelled in red; its parapet of silver was gilded and enamelled in green. . . .

Beside such feats of the goldsmith's art, Ronsard was supremely confident of his own superior power to beautify, and thereby to grant immortality to those he admired. More than once he expressed this conviction, but rarely in tones ringing with such certitude as these:

> C'est lui [Ronsard] Dame, qui peut avecque son bel art
> Vous afranchir des ans, et vous faire Deesse:
> Prométre il peut cela, car rien de lui ne part
> Qu'il ne soit immortel, et le ciel le confesse.
>
> > (*Amours*, 1555, poem 18, lines 5–8; G, 182)

> It's he [Ronsard], O lady, who with his great art can set you free from the years' limits and make of you a goddess; he can promise you that, because nothing flows from his pen that is not immortal, and the heavens admit that.

60. Jacques de Bellange, costume design for a shepherdess
(Louvre, Collection de Rothschild).

VI

DANCING FORMS

Le bal est une poësie muette, et
la poësie un bal parlant.

PLUTARCH
Oeuvres morales, translated by Amyot

Dancing is mute poesy, and
poetry a speaking dance.

Beauty on the Move

Ronsard had discovered in his triumphal odes that his reader's feelings could be most sharply affected by verse that conveyed a sense of images in motion; his poems in praise of the human form demonstrate a similar awareness. Let us consider for a moment the song of farewell that Ronsard wrote on the departure to Savoy in 1559 of the beautiful and talented sister of Henri II, the princess Marguerite.[1] The poem is cast in a pastoral mode, and its opening lines paint a natural scene whose simplicity is consciously contrasted with the pomp of life at court, although, as Bellange's drawing shows (fig. 60), shepherdesses could be seen there. Into this idyllic context, Ronsard sets Marguerite, a person of such exceptional qualities, the poet argues, that she can both decorate the rich rooms of a royal palace and light up the humbler beauties of the fields. These qualities are the measure of the loss that all sustain, and in his attempt to convey an appropriate depth of feeling, Ronsard speaks not in his own voice but acts as the chronicler of another's plaintive song. The climax of the poem occurs with the appearance of Marguerite herself, who is described thus:

Elle, marchant à tresses descoiffées,
Apparoissoit la Princesse des Fées;
Un beau surcot de lin bien replié,
Frangé, houpé, luy pendoit jusqu'au pié,

Et ses talons, qui fouloient la verdure,
Deux beaux patins avoient pour couverture;
Un carquan d'or son col environnoit,
Et son beau sein sans branler se tenoit,
Pressé bien haut d'une boucle azurée,
Telle qu'on voit la belle Cytherée.

(lines 115–24)

She walked, her hair flowing behind, and seemed like a fairy princess. A
lovely linen overskirt, pleated, fringed, and hooped, fell down to her toes;
and on her feet, as they stepped across the grass, were two lovely slippers. A
golden chain circled her neck, and her firm beautiful breasts sat high above a
blue-toned broach, similar to that which Venus always bears.

It is clear from the outset that we are seeing something singular: the apparition of a fairy princess. Such a naming, one might have thought, would
suffice, but Ronsard goes on to give her substance. The portrait is very precise; her walk, her hair billowing freely behind, her simple, hooped dress
picked out with a single rich ornament, her shoes, and her quiver—all are
detailed and characterised as beautiful or precious. What makes the vision
remarkable, however, is that the fairy seems to move with the slow, stately
rhythms of the verse; or, as the poet says, it is as though Venus treads the
grass. Just as he had earlier suggested that Princess Marguerite could inhabit any atmosphere, rich or simple, so Ronsard's lines blend stateliness
with a rural prospect.

Movement and simplicity were the two striking elements in Ronsard's
evocation of Henri II's sister, and both were significant factors in a tribute
that he wrote fifteen years later—to another princess Marguerite, the
same king's daughter.[2] This second Marguerite was particularly renowned
for her beauty and her accomplishments. When she was seven years old,
the Venetian ambassador Jean Capello predicted:

Si elle conserve cette grace, cette beauté, cet esprit que je lui ai vus, il n'y a
pas de doute qu'elle ne devienne une très-belle et rare princesse.[3]

If she keeps this charm, this beauty, and that loveliness of mind which I've
seen in her, there's no shadow of a doubt she will be a most beautiful and
rare princess.

Brantôme's fervent admiration of Marguerite is typical. He filled many
pages of his works with exclamations on her qualities. At one point he
claimed that compared to this princess, 'toutes celles qui sont, seront, et
qui jamais ont esté, près de la sienne sont laides' (all those that are, will be,
or ever were set beside her appear ugly). He also offers this slightly more
measured analysis of her individual grace:

Soit qu'elle veuille monstrer sa douceur ou sa gravité, il [son beau visage] sert d'embrazer tout un monde, tant ses traicts sont beaux, ses lineamens tant bien tirez, et ses yeux si transparents et si agreables qu'il ne s'y peut rien trouver à dire; et, qui plus est, ce beau visage est fondé sur un corps de la plus belle, superbe est riche taille qui se puisse voir, accompagnée d'un port et d'une si grave majesté qu'on la prendra tousjours pour une déesse du ciel.[4]

Whether she shows sweetness or severity, her beautiful face lights up the world, so beautiful are her features, her lines so well drawn, and her eyes so clear and so delightful that one is left speechless; and, what is more, this lovely face is set on a body so beautiful, of a form so rich, and she carries herself with such grave majesty that she is always taken for a goddess.

Clouet's portrait of the princess at the age of sixteen (fig. 61) already indicates her seriousness.

61. François Clouet, drawing of Marguerite de Valois (Chantilly, Musée Condé; photo Giraudon).

In his tribute to her noble bearing and her dignity, Ronsard depicts the princess moving in stately procession through the Tuileries gardens back to the Louvre, outshining her courtly companions, who are richly dressed like herself:

> Des divines beautez le patron eternel
> Revenoit des jardins du Palais maternel.
> . . . .
> Elle, race des Rois, marchoit en gravité
> Au milieu de sa troupe, et passoit les plus belles,
> Comme l'Aube la Nuict de ses flames nouvelles.

(lines 29–30, 34–36)

The lasting pattern of divine beauty made her way back from the gardens of her mother's palace. . . . Of the race of kings, she walked gravely amidst her troupe and outdid the most beautiful, just as dawn overcomes the night with her new light.

The night scene, words that mark her exceptional status—*patron eternel, race des Rois, troupe*—and the stress on movement and emergent light, all contribute to the poem's dazzling effect. In his own portraits of the princess, Brantôme remembered Ronsard's poems of nocturnal rapture, and even claimed to have suggested the comparison with dawn.[5] Far removed from the rustic setting created for the duchess of Savoy, this second Marguerite is a queenly model: 'Elle . . . marchoit en gravité', and she sparkles, though the glitter of dress and jewels are only implied through the comparison with dawn. Despite their surface differences, both portraits are impressive because their beauty of form, animated by the movement and by the flow of garments, has been caught in all its liveliness. And yet, the two ladies remain aloof. Seen from afar by shepherd and poet, they are presented with respect and even reverence.

In poems that describe other moving forms of beauty, ones drawn from a less elevated sphere and for whom the poet has closer and more personal association, Ronsard's admiration and desires are excited and expressed in similar ways. In *Le Voyage de Tours, ou les amoureus Thoinet et Perrot*, the same attention to setting frames the joyful aspect of beauty stirring. We find also the same heightening power of distance and the same self-absorption of the maiden:

> C'estoit en la saison que l'amoureuse Flore
> Faisoit pour son amy les fleurettes esclore,
> Par les prés bigarrés d'autant d'aimail de fleurs
> Que le grand arc du ciel s'emaille de couleurs:
> Lors que les papillons et les blondes avettes,
> Les uns chargez au bec, les autres aus cuissettes,

Errent par les jardins, et les petits oyseaus,
Volletans par les bois de rameaus en rameaus,
Amassent la bechée, et parmy la verdure
Ont souci comme nous de leur race future.

(lines 13–22; G, 279; L 12:214)

It was the season when the enamoured Flora made the flowers open to
please her lover, and the fields were enamelled with colours as varied as
those that the rainbow sprays across the sky; when butterflies and golden
bees, some filling their mouths, others their loins, wander through the gardens, and little birds fly through the trees from branch to branch, filling
their beaks, and amid all the greenery think, like us, of their future race.

With these exuberant lines Ronsard evokes a season of pleasure and fertil-
ity, when colours are at their brightest and nature buzzes with a movement
and life of its own. With the words *comme nous* man is introduced almost
as an afterthought, while nature, independently, creates an atmosphere of
celebration and happy anticipation. The occasion, however, is also a country wedding; and among the guests are Ronsard and Baïf, with their
sweethearts Marion and Francine, who join in the dancing:

Là Francine dançoit, de Thoinet le souci,
Là Marion balloit, qui fut le mein aussi.

(lines 43–44)

Francine, Thoinot's trouble, was dancing; Marion, who was mine, also
danced.

Ronsard's direct and economical statements are unusual, but they are sufficient to describe the source of his passion. Movement arouses his desires,
it also intensifies them as he catches sight of the boat that, without warning, carries Marion off down the Loire.
    While the beginning of *Le Voyage* shows man almost as an intruder in
nature, from line 197, the poet tries to turn the natural world to magic and
to become a controlling part of it.

Que les bords soient semez de mille belles fleurs
Representant sur l'eau mille belles couleurs,
Et le troupeau gaillard des gentiles Nayades
Alentour du vaisseau face mille gambades,
Les unes balloyant des paumes de leurs mains
Les flots devant la barque, et les autres leurs seins
Descouvrant à fleur d'eau, et d'une main ouvriere
Conduisant le bateau du long de la riviere.

(lines 207–14)

May the river banks be covered with a thousand flowers reflected in the water with a million colours, and the joyful troupe of gentle naiads around the boat perform many a game: some making the water dance with their hands and making waves before the prow, others just on the surface of the water displaying their breasts as their hands worked to drive the boat along the river.

The poem is still descriptive, but wishes and imaginary scenes are conjured up and used by the poet as a way of exhibiting, and in part satisfying, his passion. Denied a place in his lover's journey, he invents one; he fills the scene with beauty, gaiety, and excitement at the centre of which is the moving boat with Marion, whose own attractions seem enhanced by the attention and by the presence of beings such as naiads. Once liberated, the poet's imagination tries not only to mould natural elements to his own purposes but also to transform them so that the branches of the elm tree embraced by the vine, for example, might seem (even to Marion) her own arms clasping Ronsard to her:

Où Marion voirra, peut estre, sur le bord
Un orme, des longs bras d'une vigne enlassée,
Et la voyant ainsi doucement embrassée,
De son pauvre Perrot se pourra souvenir,
Et voudra sur le bord embrassé le tenir.

(lines 224–28)

Where Marion will perhaps perceive, on the riverside, an elm, its long branches embraced by the vine, and seeing it so sweetly held will also remember her poor Pierrot and will wish to take hold of him as she comes ashore.

The final stage in this process of transformation is reached when Ronsard actually envisages the complete fusing of his self and the liquid element that carries his precious cargo. The water that he seeks to become gives freedom to privacies and satisfactions withheld from him as soon as he returns to the real world, though the geographical locations of that world—'la chapelle blanche' and 'Bourgueil'—are also present in his creative dream. In the world of make-believe, the beautiful woman moves according to his bidding:

Que ne puis-je muer ma resemblance humaine
En la forme de l'eau qui cette barque emmeine!
J'irois en murmurant sous le fond du vaisseau,
J'irois tout alentour, et mon amoureuse eau
Bais'roit ore sa main, ore sa bouche franche,
La suivant jusqu'au port de la Chapelle blanche:

Puis, forçant mon canal pour ensuivre mon vueil,
Par le trac de ses pas j'yrois jusqu'à Bourgueil,
Et là, dessous un pin, sous la belle verdure,
Je voudrois retenir ma premiere figure.

(lines 233–42)

Oh! that I might change my human shape to become the water that drives
that boat along. I'd go sounding beneath the vessel, I'd move all around it,
and my loving water would bathe now her hand, now her generous mouth,
following her right up to the white chapel: and then forcing my channel to
fulfil my wish, I'd go on to Bourgueil following the traces left by her feet,
and there, beneath a pine and under its lovely green, I'd like to recover my
first form.

His imagination gives him such a power of transmutation that the remote,
resistant beauty seems almost conquered. The victory, given a force and
sense of reality through the insistent rhythms and the bold words, is nearly
sure, although the reiterated use of the conditional tense implicitly recog-
nises that the surges of excitement and anticipation are only in the mind.

In the previous chapter we noted how closely Ronsard associated excitement and movement (particularly that of water); and here we see again
how elements intrinsic to poetry—sounds and rhythm—make significant
contributions to the increased power that movement gives to form and
feeling.[6] A taste for forms shown on the move has never been confined to
poets, and ample evidence proves that Ronsard's fellow artists had been
attracted by the lightness and elegance of the dancing figures that picked
their way around the broad base of Greek vases or across sarcophagi.
Veneziano had recorded many such pieces in the series of vase designs engraved from 'ancient sculptures in bronze and marble' (as he says), and
their qualities of grace and of delicate shifting draperies were emulated by
many sixteenth-century artists. These figures reappeared, for instance, on
tableware such as the French or Italian gilt saltcellar (fig. 62) on which a
frieze of dancing maidens of pure classical taste travel below a border engraved with mauresques.[7]

Dolce, whose views have guided us in elucidating mid-sixteenth-century
attitudes towards art, also praises figures on the move as being more lifelike; of one of Titian's paintings, for example, he wrote:

[in the] poem sent by the divine Titian to the king of England . . . one sees
Adonis moving, and his movement is easy, vigorous and gentle in its temper,
for one has the impression that, with a burning desire to go off hunting, he is
stepping out in order to take his leave of Venus.[8]

Movement is indeed dominant in the picture; on one side, Venus's imploring gestures of restraint, and on the other, Adonis's forceful determination

62. Sixteenth-century saltcellar, French or Italian (Victoria and Albert Museum).

that is handsomely controlled. For French examples, we can consider the buoyant folds of transparent cloth that cling to the shapely limbs of the nymphs sculptured by Jean Goujon on the Fontaine des Innocents (fig. 63). These forms, whose beauty is accentuated by the use of prominent lines and a marked flow of movement,[9] were designed in 1571 for the entry of Charles IX into Paris, at about the same time that Ronsard was composing his expansive tribute to Marguerite de Valois. With Goujon's nymphs, however, the space allotted to each seems barely adequate to contain the bouncy folds of her garment. The constrained space precludes the movement from becoming too violent or too disturbing. It is as though a current is set in motion sufficient to arouse emotion and to enclose it.

In contrast, the solemnity and seeming timelessness of the static court portrait suggest that, on formal occasions at least, artists fought shy of leaving a record that might in any way imply mobility or its companion, instability. Affairs of state required a different kind of idealising. When times for jubilation came, however, artists could, and did, give rein to impulses that created the floating garments designed for festivals, and worn by the ladies and gentlemen of the court. Relatively few designs survive, but Primaticcio's drawings for Thalestis and Alexander (now in the Tessin

63. Jean Goujon, nymphs from the Fontaine des Innocents, Paris (photo Giraudon).

64. Francesco Primaticcio, designs for ballets, Thalestis and
Alexander (National Museum, Stockholm).

Collection in Stockholm, fig. 64) give a clear view of the airiness of the
conception and freedom of movement needed for the complex figures of a
court dance.[10] Before we look specifically at the nature of court ballet,
which under the Valois acquired a clearly defined form and purpose, it is
illuminating to consider the connections that a poet such as Ronsard already saw between the art of dancing, perceptions of beauty, and degrees
of feeling.

Dancing: A Mode of Elevation

Dancing is a natural expression of joy, and poets repeatedly are drawn to
its simple, spontaneous pleasure.[11] More significant for our present purpose, however, is the extent to which the dance served as a magnet and
a signal of beauty, attracting attention first to the graceful steps of the
dancer and subsequently producing in the poet a sense of wonder and ele-

vation. Poets certainly did not need Bembo to tell them of the penetrating charm of glimpsing someone for the first time in the act of dancing.[12] On numerous occasions Ronsard writes of how he has been startled at such a sight: in a love poem of 1569 he exclaims, 'Et des le jour qu'en dansant je vous vy, / Je meurs pour vous, et si en suis bien aize' (And from that day when I surprised you dancing, I would die for you and I'd be happy). In an early poem (1552–53) the flavour of the *Roman de la Rose* still lingers in the allegory:

> Hà, Belacueil, que ta doulce parolle
> Vint traistrement ma jeunesse offenser
> Quant au premier tu l'amenas dancer,
> Dans le verger, l'amoureuse carolle.[13]

Ah, Belacueil, your sweet voice strikes insidiously upon my youth when you first led her out to dance in the orchard, with the songs of love.

Because of its magnetism and powerful effect, dancing played a significant role on special occasions: in celebrations for a peace treaty or an important alliance, and in the festivities that accompanied lowly or princely marriages. Every major poet of the sixteenth century has left some record of such ceremonies, whether in the form of verses that were sung or recited during the proceedings, or as delighted reminiscences.[14]

As an example, one might cite the marriage in 1559 of Claude de France (daughter of Henri II) to Charles, duc de Lorraine, for which Ronsard composed an *Eclogue* that transferred the pomp and riches habitual to the court into fresh-air ceremonies.[15] High points of this occasion were a feast that lasted through the night, and a ball of naiads and other beings that went on through the day. Or, there is the *Chant de liesse*,[16] which celebrated the Scottish and Spanish marriages of the same year, and in which Ronsard recalled the jousts, the music, the joyous manifestations of the people, and, above all, the resplendent banquets, games, mascarades, and ballets—which (somewhat predictably) he likens to the solemn ceremonies on Olympus:

> Et par-sus tous de voir la gravité
> De ta tres-haute et grande Majesté?
> Voir au Palais les tables solennelles,
> Ainsi qu'au ciel les tables eternelles
> De Jupiter, quand au Palais des cieux
> Il se marie, ou festie ses Dieux,
> Et qu'au milieu de la celeste Troupe
> La jeune Hebé luy presente la coupe?
> Hé! quel plaisir voir danser et baller.

(lines 77–85)

And, above all, to see the solemnity of high and royal majesty, to see the superb banquetting tables in the palace, just like the eternal tables of Jupiter when there's a wedding in the heavens or when he entertains the gods, and amid the celestial troupe young Hebe presents the cup to him. Ah! what a pleasure it is to see the dancing.

Mortals always extend to the domain of the gods the most pleasurable of their activities.[17] To such special events, Ronsard's imagination responded vigorously, and his lines evoke the richness and glamour of the Valois court, otherwise miraculously recorded for us in the famous Valois tapestries.

So far we have touched upon the scenes of festivity, to which the dance frequently marked the climax, and in which it is evoked in very general terms, with *danser* and *baller* used vaguely and interchangeably. Other poems have a more specific direction and convey a greater personalised effect. Listen to the intimate yet elevating tone that Amadis Jamyn communicates in six lines from a poem describing one of the most popular social dances of the sixteenth century, the *volta*:

> Ha que ie sens l'effect de ton essence,
> Quand aux flambeaux la Provençal danse
> Me fait jouir de ton corps ambrassé
> Flanc contre flanc pres du mien enlacé!
> Je porte au dos des aeles inconnuës
> Qu'Amour m'attache, et vole dans les nuës.[18]

Ah! I can feel the effect of thy spirit, when, beneath the torchlight, we dance the volta, and I enjoy our proximity, your body held tight, limb against my limb in close embrace. I feel that I have wings that Love gives to me, and I fly through the skies.

Most striking here is the immediate power of transportation and metamorphosis attributed to this particular dance, whose steps bring the couple into proximity. Jamyn concentrates his interest exclusively on his own passionate response. In contrast, Ronsard gives a fuller expansion to the transforming power of the dance. His art allowed him, even obliged him, not merely to record the splendour of a special court occasion but also to bring the event alive again, to make the reader feel that he is taking part in the excitement, experiencing the dazzle and the noise, responding to the music and the rhythms of the dance. In this domain, his art is superior to the recording power of the painter or the engraver; for the poet can describe both detailed incidents within a general scene and the feelings and thoughts of the dancers and spectators. In the few pictorial examples that remain to us of such brilliant occasions, the artist transmits a general idea of the crowded scene and concentrates attention on surface splendour and

65. Ball at the court of Henri III (Louvre, département des peintures; Arch. Photo. Paris/S.P.A.D.E.M.).

on the costly gowns and jewels of the dancing couples; such examples include an engraving of a ball at the court of Henri II, or the painting in the Louvre that is thought to depict one of the balls given at the marriage of the duc de Joyeuse in 1581 (fig. 65), or again the Valois tapestry showing the festivities given for the arrival of the Polish ambassadors in 1573.[19]

If we turn from these general remembrances of grand occasions to the poem *La Charite* (G, 363–68), which Ronsard dedicated to Marguerite de Valois, we instantly recognise the rich halls of the Valois court, but, in addition, we are taken into its midst. The poem, which depicts the princess dancing on the eve of her marriage to the king of Navarre, is conceived as a compliment to Marguerite's loveliness. What seems a fairly routine assignment for a poet is turned by Ronsard into something remarkable. He has planned a staged approach to the projection of beauty. First, status and attraction are combined as Cupid reports Marguerite's beauty to Venus; then, we catch our first sight of the princess reflected through the eyes of Pasithea, the nymph sent by Venus to investigate the miracle of Marguerite's form. The nymph herself is described minutely, in terms and in an order now very familiar to us: from her head to her heels she represents, in every part, the sum of beauties. Ronsard uses her arrival to introduce us, without other intermediaries, to the specially charged atmosphere of a court ball, where excitement is generated by the dance and

the music, by the bright lights and glistening frocks, by the precious jewels
and the flash of gold and silver.

> Il estoit nuit, et les humides voiles,
> L'air espoissi de toutes parts avoyent,
> Quand pour baller les Dames arrivoyent,
> Qui de clairté, paroissoyent des estoiles.
>   Robes d'argent et d'or laborieuses
> Comme à l'envy flambantes esclattoyent;
> Vives en l'air les lumieres montoyent
> A traits brillans des pierres precieuses.

(lines 109–16)

It was night, and its damp veils and the thick air of dusk had invaded all
parts, when the ladies arrived for the ball, so lit up they seemed like stars.
Their frocks were worked with gold and silver as if their sparkle rivalled
that of flames; high into the air the light of their precious jewels leapt with
brilliant rays.

At the centre of this rousing spectacle that is alive with sparkle, anticipation, and virtual intoxication, Ronsard sets the princess. There is no need
to describe her person, as Pasithea's divine intuition immediately recog-
nises Marguerite as the only being in that vast hall whose form can inhabit
her own.

Although this miraculous fusion of two exquisite forms seems a sufficient climax to Ronsard's staged compliment, he goes yet further by fixing
attention on the extraordinary effect of a dancing princess; her brother,
Charles IX,

> Serrant sa main la conduit à la danse;
> Comme une femme elle ne marchoit pas,
> Mais en roulant divinement le pas
> D'un pied glissant couloit à la cadence.
> . . . .
>   Le Roy dançant la volte Provençalle
> Faisoit sauter la Charite, sa soeur
> Elle suivant d'une grave douceur,
> A bonds legers voloit parmy la salle.

(lines 149–52, 157–60)

Holding her hand, led her out to dance; she walked not as a woman, but
guiding her step as though some divine impulse led them out to dance. . . .
The king danced the volta, accompanying her sister, Grace; she followed
with a light step and danced with elegant tread in every part of the hall.

It is a *volta* that Marguerite performs with her brother; and in a dance not
noted for its elegance, the poet stresses her lightness and grace, and the

supernatural ability of her performance. In an attempt to translate into words the sensational effect of such sweet nobility of bearing, Ronsard turns, in the next lines, to the spectators' response:

> Elle changeoit en cent metamorphoses
> Le coeur de ceux qui son front regardoyent;
> Maints traits de feu de ses yeux descendoyent,
> Et sous ses pieds faisoyent naistre des roses.

(lines 165–68)

She transformed the hearts of those who looked upon her a thousand times, many fiery sparks came from her eyes, and beneath her feet sprouted roses upon roses.

Here, the poet shows the entire assembly electrified by the inspirational and transforming powers of her dance: warm lights seem lit up everywhere, and the ground is strewn with roses.

The atmosphere of a court ball has already something special about it, and Ronsard worked to capture the general feeling of intoxication so that Marguerite's ability to give a further dimension of magic to this world seems not incredible but the natural consequence of all the excitement felt. The powers of elevation and transformation that beauty and the act of dancing grant to the princess in this poem resemble similar forces given to the poet, as we saw in the imaginative sweep at the end of the *Voyage de Tours*.

It is especially appropriate that Ronsard, when he wished to praise the future queen of Navarre, chose to depict Princess Marguerite in the act of dancing, since she was apparently a singularly gifted performer. On a number of occasions Brantôme refers to her skill; he recalled, for instance, the time when an honourable French gentleman, having seen her dance, suggested that le sieur des Essars might have referred directly to the princess when he portrayed Nicquée (the heroine of *Amadis*) rather than indulging in 'tant de belles et riches parolles pour la despeindre et la montrer si belle' (so many beautiful and rich words to paint her and display her loveliness). Moreover, the admiring Brantôme continues, a truly accurate impression of the princess's beauty can be gained from Ronsard's poem *La Charite*; and in a slightly later passage, he outlined the range of dances and intricate steps that she executed perfectly, with movements marked by gravity and majesty. Whether she danced the admirable *pavane d'Espaigne*, the *vazzemeno d'Italie*, or a simple *branle*, according to Brantôme, the company could not take their eyes off her nor, he claimed, could any dancer (of common stock or princely rank) approach the quality of her performance.[20]

Whether Ronsard addresses a poem to queen or simple lady of the court, there is no discernible discrepancy in his mode of writing. In the sonnet beginning 'Le soir qu'Amour vous fist en la salle descendre' (The evening that Love enticed you down into the ballroom), inspired by the sight of Hélène de Surgères dancing, he focusses immediately (as in *La Charite*) on the dazzling impact the dancer makes on all present in the room:

> Le soir qu'Amour vous fist en la salle descendre
> Pour danser d'artifice un beau ballet d'Amour,
> Voz yeux, bien qu'il fust nuict, ramenerent le jour,
> Tant ils sceurent d'esclairs par la place respandre.

The evening that Love enticed you down into the ballroom to dance with skill, the wonderful dance of Love, although it was night, your eyes brought in the day, they knew so much how to send their rays through the place.

Succeeding lines of the sonnet move from an analysis of the effect of dancing to a depiction of the actual nature of the ballet; the meandering verse seems to convey the very rhythms, steps, and figures of the dance:

> Le ballet fut divin, qui se souloit reprendre,
> Se rompre, se refaire, et tour dessus retour
> Se mesler, s'escarter, se tourner à l'entour,
> Contre-imitant le cours du fleuve de Meandre.
> Ores il estoit rond, ores long, or estroit,
> Or en poincte, en triangle, en la façon qu'on voit
> L'escadron de la Grue evitant la froidure.

(lines 5 – 11)[21]

The dance was divine; it kept its momentum, breaking, rejoining, and time and again blending, separating, and turning yet again, imitating the flow of the river Meander; now it was circular, now long and then narrow, now pointed, as a triangle, just as one sees the flight of the cranes as they go to avoid the cold.

Here, the woman's beauty is taken for granted as the poet concentrates on the movements and the geometric patterns that made sixteenth-century dancing both graceful and more significant than a simple social ritual. The patterns inscribed on the floor of the ballroom or stage were not haphazard; they had divine effects.

> Je faux, tu ne dansois, mais ton pied voletoit
> Sur le haut de la terre: aussi ton corps s'estoit
> Transformé pour ce soir en divine nature.

I mistake myself; you did not dance, but rather your foot touched the summits of the earth; and your body was transformed, for that night, into a divine nature.

The movement to higher planes of being is exactly the same as in *La Charite*: dancing effects the elevation.

It might be argued that these lines describing this degree of seduction are mere poetic hyperbole; that comparisons with divinities were *de rigueur* in such a context; and that Ronsard was doing nothing more than offering a view of a delightful beauty, excited by the dance, and dressed rather as in the portrait by an unknown French artist that shows a lady of the court around 1580 in the guise of a nymph of Diana (fig. 66). Although such arguments are not without merit, nonetheless, in the sonnet

66. Portrait of Diana, perhaps as dressed for a ballet, ca. 1580 (private collection).

we have analysed Ronsard has undeniably established close bonds between beauty, graceful movement, and intense emotion. Moreover in this study, generally, we have grown to be more cautious about easy dismissals of apparent extravagance. An examination of one or two French court ballets and of the ideas behind such performances will reward such caution by revealing the serious purpose of dancing forms.

Court Ballet

At Bayonne in 1565, Catherine de' Medici organised a series of festivities to entertain and to astonish representatives of the Spanish court who had crossed the border into France to accompany Catherine's daughter Elizabeth, the queen of Spain, who came to see her family.[22] One of the days was set aside for the pastimes arranged specifically (and in great secrecy) by the Queen Mother, who in these affairs prided herself on the unusual and the extravagant. After a journey by barge to the island of Aigueneau, enlivened by songs of tritons and sirens and by nautical diversions of all kinds, her guests enjoyed a magnificent banquet followed by a ballet 'de toutes les provinces de France' (of all the provinces of France). The only details of the dancing are provided by Princess Marguerite herself, who in her memoirs writes that:

> Chaque trouppe [dansait] à la façon de son païs: les Poitevines avec la cornemuse; les Provençales, la volte avec les timballes; les Bourguignonnes en Champenois avec le petit haut-boys, le dessus de violon et tambourins de village; les Bretonnes dansans leurs passe-pieds et bransles gais; et ainsi toutes les provinces.[23]

> Each troupe [danced] according to the custom of its country: the people from Poitou with their pipes; those from Provence, their *volta* with their drums; and the Bourguignons with their horns, viols, and village tambourines; the Bretons danced their *branles* and foot dances; so each according to the habits of his land.

These purely social dances (known, loved, and performed at other times by Marguerite) were evidence of the lively variety of dance tunes and movements that existed throughout France. Catherine's pride in them and in the occasion can be judged by their appearance in one of the Valois tapestries. These social dances were intended to be followed by a more complicated ballet, 'un beau ballet', to be danced by nymphs so richly attired that they resembled 'des artificielles lumières' (artificial lights). In preparation for this spectacle, a huge tribe of satyrs entered the arena on a luminous rock; having tuned their instruments, they awaited the arrival of the dancers. The proceedings, however, came to an abrupt end when thunder and lightning struck and rain poured down; thus we shall never know what was envisaged. The occasion, although marred by the weather, is nevertheless of significance, since it was the first time (to our knowledge) that the two kinds of dancing that Ronsard has evoked in his poems—the social and the geometric—came together in a festival.

Something similar seems to have happened during the wedding festivities for Marguerite when twelve nymphs from the Elysian Fields 'se mirent à danser un bal fort diversifié, et qui dura plus d'une grosse heure' (began to dance a very varied dance that lasted more than an entire hour).[24] After the dreadful days and nights of massacre that followed, no one wished to remember the patterns of nuptial dancing. We do have some information, however, about the entertainments invented the next year for the pleasure of the Polish ambassadors who had come to lead their new king Henri to his kingdom. In these entertainments we find distinct echoes of the style and atmosphere that so affected Ronsard. Brantôme writes, for example, of the ballet of sixteen ladies who represented the sixteen provinces of France (fig. 67). Unlike the regional social dances performed at Bayonne, this time the dancing was an altogether more complicated affair. Accompanied by the music of at least thirty violins, 'la plus melodieuse qu'on eust sceu voir' (the most melodious that one could ever hear), the ladies performed

> un beau ballet si bizarrement invanté, et par tant de tours, contours et destours, d'entrelassemens et meslanges, affrontements et arrets, qu'aucune dame ne faillit se trouver à son tour ni à son rang.

> a lovely ballet, strangely designed, and with so many turns, twists and movements, figures and exchanges, meetings and pauses, and yet no lady missed a figure or her place in the dance.

According to Brantôme, the smoothness and intricacy of this studied ballet amazed all who saw it. Again, the dancing lasted over an hour, and the one figure of the dance, engraved in Jean Dorat's account, shows the formal and calculated pattern that was being attempted.[25] Each set of rhythms and each successive figure naturally and harmoniously evolved out of the previous grouping; movements and gestures intertwined; and steps went in and out just as Ronsard had described them in 'Le soir qu'Amour vous fist en la salle descendre'.

The most developed form of this distinctive style of dancing is found in the famous *Balet comique de la reine*, performed in 1581 during ten days of festivities organised to mark the wedding of the king's favourite, the duc de Joyeuse, to the queen's sister.[26] At two moments in his account of the performance, which went on for five hours, Balthazar de Beaujoyeulx

67. *Ballet des Polonais*, woodcut from the printed edition of
Jean Dorat's *Magnificentissimi spectaculi*, 1573.

(who may also have created the ballets performed in 1572 and 1573)
pauses in order to describe the figures that the dancers' feet inscribed on
the floor of the Salle de Bourbon in the Louvre. The first interruption concerns the ballet of the twelve naiads, who covered the entire floor area
with diverse movements, sometimes circular, then triangular in shape, and
sometimes threading their serpentine way across the room. Before the en-
raged enchantress Circe put a temporary end to their dancing, they had
accomplished 'douze figures de geometrie, toutes diverses l'une de l'autre'
(twelve geometrical figures, each one different from the last). The interest
in careful patterning of steps, which changed with each new movement in
the music, is evident in Beaujoyeulx's account of the first figure:

Au premier passage de l'entree estoyent six de front, toutes en un rang au travers de la salle, et trois devant en un triangle bien large: duquel la Royne marquoit la premiere poincte, et trois derriere de mesme: puis selon que le son se changeoit, elles se tournoyent aussi, faisans le limaçon au rebours les unes des autres, tantost d'une façon, tantost d'une autre et puis revenoyent à leur première marque.

In the first movement of the entry, six faced the audience, all in line across the stage, three in front arranged in a big triangle, of which the queen was at the foremost point, and three others behind in the same position; then, according to the changes in the music they also turned, snaking their way across each other, first with one step and then another until they came back to their point of departure.

An even more complex choreographic invention was reserved for the *grand bal* at the end of the entertainment: forty different figures constantly formed, broke, and reformed, danced by four dryad nymphs (of whom one was Hélène de Surgères) and by the twelve naiads finally released from captivity. The progress of the forty dance passages, or figures géométriques', were thus described by Beaujoyeulx:

Icelles toutes iustes et considerees en leur diametre, tantost en quarré, et ores en rond, et de plusieurs et diverses façons et aussi tost en triangle, accompagné de quelque autre petit quarré, et autres petites figures.[27]

These were all exactly measured and worked out, sometimes as squares or in circles, and in many other forms, also as triangles accompanied by small square formations and other tiny kinds of figures.

Ronsard's own appeal to geometrical patterns suggests that he had in mind the sort of dance movements that Beaujoyeulx describes. Moreover, the structure of the sonnet 'Le soir qu'Amour vous fist en la salle descendre' throws into relief the power of transportation and metamorphosis residing in the dance, as line 12 suddenly breaks off with the exclamation 'Je faux', giving the impression that the poet has radically changed direction and thereby reinforcing his point:

Je faux, tu ne dansois, mais ton pied voletoit
Sur le haut de la terre: aussi ton corps s'estoit
Transformé pour ce soir en divine nature.

I mistake myself; you did not dance, but rather your foot touched the summits of the earth; and your body was transformed, for that night, into a divine nature.

The precision of 'pour ce soir' also emphasises that some magical operation has on this specific occasion taken place, and that its effects are somehow related to the act of dancing. Dance is a transformer; it enhances beauty and, through this improvement, not only provides material for poetic inspiration but also itself becomes a form of perfection.

Ronsard's response to the sight of beautiful women dancing is further elucidated and supported by sixteenth-century theories about the performing arts. Although musicologists now think that Ronsard was not terribly knowledgeable about music, he did nevertheless consistently promote the virtues of combining music and poetry, for example, in *La Lyre*. In his preface to the *Meslanges* of 1560, dedicated to Charles IX, he furnishes a summary of accumulated thinking about the ethical character of music, and the power and therapeutic effects of such an alliance.[28] Sensitivity to music is the sign of a naturally noble spirit 'de ceux qui se sont montrez vertueux magnanimes, et veritablement nez pour ne sentir rien de vulgaire' (of those who have shown themselves virtuous and magnanimous, and truly born not to be tainted by anything vulgar), and for more authoritative opinion Ronsard refers the king to Plutarch and Boethius.[29] As a close friend of Antoine de Baïf—one of the founders of the Académie de Poésie et de Musique—he could not but be acquainted with the latest developments in 'musique mesurée à l'antique' in which words and melody were harmonized, and modes and intervals carefully calculated and manipulated in order to produce the therapeutic effects known to the ancient world.[30] Some effort along these lines is evident in the homophonic choruses of the *Balet comique*, in which Beaujoyeulx and his collaborators sought to invite favourable influences to fulfil the moral and political purposes outlined in his dedication to the king and developed in the four allegorical explanations appended to the printed account. In his note to the reader he reminds us that in antiquity no one recited verse without musical accompaniment and that Orpheus, for example, 'ne sonnoit iamais sans vers' (never played without words). Despite this evident concern to blend together poetry and music in the *Balet comique*, Beaujoyeulx gave the principal role to dancing, as he announces unequivocally: 'J'ay toutesfois donné le premier tiltre et honneur à la dance' (Nevertheless, I gave the first title and principal honour to dancing).[31]

Beaujoyeulx, among others, thought that by adding the further dimension of dancing to the harmonies already orchestrated through poetry and music an equivalent increase in effects could be achieved. Plutarch had been one of the first to set out connections between poetry, music, and dancing; in trying to elucidate his meaning, sixteenth-century writers carried his ideas further.[32] They believed that cosmic influences could actually be drawn to affect human affairs, and they thought that by playing on the emotions of an audience through harmonies and movements finely calculated to echo those of the heavenly spheres their listeners and spectators could be moved to act peacefully.[33]

Though perhaps incredible to us, this conviction was founded upon well-articulated and generally accepted notions about the nature of the universe. As Ronsard put it to Charles IX, 'toutes choses sont composez d'accord, de mesures et de proportions tant au ciel, en mer, qu'en la terre' (all things are composed through harmony, measurement, and proportion in the heavens, on the sea, and upon the earth). This perception of harmony shaped the approach to all the arts. When the learned Julius Caesar Scaliger linked the Pindaric ode, heavenly motion, and the singing and dancing of the Greek chorus, he was expressing what others had long thought; all over Europe in the sixteenth century, poets, choreographers, musicians, and artists were supremely confident in this view.[34] Even Cornelius Agrippa's antagonistic tirades did nothing to undermine their assurance. He had ridiculed the Greeks and their arrogance in connecting the dance with the origins of the world:

Ils ont donné à entendre qu'elle [la danse] a prins son origine dés le commencement du monde sur le patron des mouvements celestes des astres et planettes, de leurs tours naturels ou retrogrades, des conionctions, et en somme de l'ordre d'iceux, qui n'est qu'une danse mesurée et bien acordante.

They understood [the dance] to have taken, from its first inception, the pattern of heavenly movement of the stars and planets, their natural motion and contrary movements, their conjunctions; in short, the order of the heavens is nothing more than a well-ordered and harmonious dance.

But Agrippa's very words, as so often in the *Declamation sur l'incertitude, vanité et abus des sciences*, perpetuated the beliefs he was trying to crush. They were excerpted, expanded, and used to prove that through the harmonious measures of the dance order was made out of primary chaos. As Louis Le Caron put it: 'Tout dance au ciel, ioueux d'estre sorti / D'un tel chaos' (Everything dances in the heavens, delighted to be freed from such chaos). Or as Jean Dorat said: 'Le monde est faict par discorde accordance . . . / Dansons ainsi pour n'avoir discordance' (The world is made from discord accorded . . . dancing thus so as to have no discordance).[35] Sentiments such as these were much elaborated upon at the end of the century by Sir John Davies in *Orchestra* (1596), where he aptly describes the nature of dancing as 'The fair character of the world's consent'.[36] Thus, according to such writers, dancing and the harmony of the heavens are at one, and expressions such as the 'danse des sphères' and 'le bal des astres' became commonplaces.[37] Beneath these general terms, which we tend to take for granted, were hidden rich and complex notions about the nature of the world, its elements, the seasons, the turning of night into day, and man's own nature and social forms. Davies, for instance, in the ninety-six stanzas of *Orchestra*, perfected a complete account of the workings of man and of the universe, all brought alive through the dynamics of the dance:

> For what are breath, speech, Echoes, musick, winds
> But Dauncings of the ayre in sundry kinds?
> . . . .
>   All learned Arts, and every great affaire
> A lively shape of Dauncing seemes to beare.
>
>   (stanza 43)

The whole world had danced in similar fashion exactly fifty years earlier in Béranger de la Tour's poem *Choréide*, which also provided a systematic account of the universe in terms of the dance. If dancing was natural to all living things in this way, then it was indubitably the responsibility of man (so sixteenth-century reasoning went) to maintain that harmony intact. Furthermore, if movement unconsciously produced such a degree of order, how much more effective must be those dances that have been artificially devised; such was the rhetorical question Béranger posed:

> Si donq tant de bien nous depart
> Le mouvement cru, et sans art,
> Combien plus nous en recevons
> De celui qui par reigle avons?
> Combien plus nous convient et duit
> Celui qui par art est conduit.[38]

If, thus, such good comes to us from basic natural movement, how much more might we receive from that which we organise according to rule? How much more becoming and appropriate that which is led by art.

Court ballet sought to put such theoretical notions into practice. The famous acrobat Arcangelo Tuccaro, in a vigorous defence of the art, maintained that any dance movement had, of itself, some correspondence with a similar movement in the heavens, whether the movement was consciously wrought or unconsciously performed. He expounds this theory at great length, and his argument provides an especially detailed example of sixteenth-century beliefs in the incantatory power of the dance, while also furnishing remarkable verbal parallels with Beaujoyeulx's prose and Ronsard's language of geometry.

> La diversité des mouvements faicts à l'opposite l'un de l'autre par ceux qui dancent n'est qu'une generale imitation de divers mouvements des cieux, et le retour qu'on faict en arriere au bal et à la danse n'est autre chose que vouloir imiter honnestement la retrogradation des planettes . . . et puis ces

belles et diverses retraictes, droictes et obliques, qu'on exerce avec tant de grace, sont les mesmes conionctions et oppositions triangulaires et quadrangulaires voire sexangulaires qui interviennent quasi tous les jours entre les planettes et leurs spheres celestes.[39]

The diversity of movements made by those who dance facing each other is merely a general imitation of the varied movements of the heavens, and the return movement that one makes in dancing is nothing more than wishing instinctively to imitate the retrograde motion of the planets . . . and then, those lovely diverse withdrawals, straight or slanted, that are done with such grace have their same counterparts in the conjunctions and contrary motions, triangular or quadrangular (even sexangular), that happen every day between the planets and their heavenly spheres.

Against the background of sentiments that granted such nobility and status to the act of dancing, it is hardly surprising that writers—additionally inspired and supported by the authority of Lucian of Samosate—made as extravagant claims for the wisdom of choreographers as for poets and artists.[40] In the dedicatory poems to his *Balet comique*, Beaujoyeulx received undiluted praise; he was called 'geometre, inventif, unique en ta science' (geometrician, inventor, unique in your knowledge) for having known how to snatch from oblivion 'des vieux monuments de la Grèce' (the old monuments from Greece).[41] Yet, over and beyond its cosmic implications, the dance was thought able to reflect and influence the workings of the mind. 'Le bal est le propre de l'ame' (Dancing is the character of the soul), Béranger de la Tour wrote in 1556; a century later, the first historian of court ballet stated that dance 'va jusqu'à exprimer la Nature des choses et les habitudes de l'âme' (can even express the nature of things and the habits of the mind).[42]

As we begin to understand the beliefs that gave such power to the art of dancing, we also begin to appreciate the significance of certain events. We discern more clearly, for instance, why at a court anxious for durable peace and harmony, the wedding of the dauphin to Mary, Queen of Scots, was celebrated by a ballet of the seven planets, dressed very precisely, according to the instructions of the poets.[43] Similarly, we begin to comprehend why the central panel of the ballroom ceiling at Fontainebleau shows a dance of hours flanked on either side by a banquet of the gods, and by a view of Parnassus with Apollo and the Muses. We understand, too, why Beaujoyeulx explained so meticulously the nature of the geometric dancing, and why he and Ronsard (whose reading on the subject in ancient and modern sources was very extensive)[44] should both associate the act of dancing with the divine. Dancing's power of elevation came from a source more remote and altogether more potent than the simple vision of a beautiful form on the move.

Inspiration and the Muses' Dance

Sixteenth-century notions concerning the workings of the universe and man's relationship to it thus underlie the conception of dance as an emanation of the divine. Ancient authority, too, had given particular emphasis to the dance, positing that dance predated other art forms in the festivals arranged in celebration to the gods, for whom song and dance were natural expressions of their being. In the fourteenth olympiad, for example, Pindar wrote of the dancing Muses and of their natural and central place on Olympus beside Apollo, god of music. The Homeric hymns had granted them a similar lofty role; the second hymn, which celebrates Apollo, opened with the evocation of a scene of olympic contentment whose high point is reached when to the singing and dancing of the Muses, Apollo steps out to dance:

> Le dieu lui-même, Phébus Apollon, toujours touchant sa lyre, marquant le pas descend dans le bal. Le scintillant éclat de ses pieds et celui que jette sa tunique fine, le font paraître enveloppé de lumière aux yeux des dieux émerveillés.[45]

> The god himself, Phoebus Apollo, continually playing his lyre, gives the beat and comes down to take part in the dancing. The dazzling brilliance of his shape and that which shimmers from his light robe make him appear all wrapped in light, to the gaze and wonder of the other gods.

Passages such as these, from poems recorded at a time so remote as to be almost undateable, persuaded sixteenth-century poets that the spectacle of dancing was not only deeply moving but also a source and a manifestation of poetic inspiration much more fundamental than a mere aesthetic response to beauty on the move.

Poets were greatly excited by the prospect of a dancing Olympus and reproduced in their own works parallel scenes of gods in jubilation. Ronsard's *L'Hymne de l'Hiver* may be cited as an example.[46] They were equally impressed by variations on this scene that gave poets themselves access to such powerful harmonies, variations that linked together the act of dancing, poetic inspiration, and the annual process of natural renewal. Horace first made these connections in his ode to Sextus (*Odes* 1 : 4), and Renaissance poets used the dance of the Muses to give material expression to poetic inspiration. Thus, Du Bellay in *Les Regrets*, having at one time worn the mantle of Apollo, complains of adverse fortune and loss of poetic power in this way:

> Où sont ces doulx plaisirs, qu'au soir soubs la nuict brune
> Les Muses me donnoient, alors qu'en liberté

Dessus le verd tapy d'un esquarté
Je les menois danser aux rayons de la Lune?

(Poésies 2 : 172)

Where are those sweet pleasures that the Muses used to grant me, when in
the evening beneath the darkened sky, in a lonely spot, I led them out to
dance on the green carpet lit up by the rays of the moon?

In the *Discours à Pierre Lescot*, Ronsard similarly visualizes inspiration
as a dance. The magnetic attractions and strange feelings of excitement
that he feels in the heat of creation are transmitted through the vision of a
rare company of nymphs and satyrs who, in dead of night, far from the
eyes of the common run of men, dance familiarly together. The poet is
shown at the centre of all the activity, whose mysteries seem deepened by
the darkness, the fearful secrecy, and the distance.

Je n'avois pas douze ans qu'au profond des vallées,
Dans les hautes forests des hommes reculées,
Dans les antres secrets, de frayeur tout couverts,
Sans avoir soin de rien je composois des vers;
Echo me respondoit, et les simples Dryades,
Faunes, Satyres, Pans, Napées, Oreades,
Aigipans qui portoient des cornes sur le front,
Et qui ballant sautoient comme les chévres font,
Et le gentil troupeau des fantastiques Fées,
Autour de moy dansoient à cottes degrafées.

(lines 85−94)[47]

I was but twelve years old when, in the depths of the valleys, in the tall forests distanced from the life of men, in dark caves punctuated by fear, careless
of all other things I composed my verse. Echo replied to me, the simple dryads, fairies, satyrs, pans, napeans, oreades, or aigipans, who have tiny horns
on their heads and who dance around like young goats, and that sweet company of fantastic fairies would, in great freedom, dance around me.

Here, Ronsard, an initiate in the joyful ceremonies where beings of un-
believable form dance uninhibitedly, stresses the strangeness of an experience that couples awesome feelings with intimate access. Ronsard consistently maintained that it was a rare privilege to be present 'voir les Muses
baller dans une antre de nuit' (to see the muses dance in a cave at night);[48]
but in this passage he claimed singular status: it was the greatest gift to a
poet to be allowed to participate in their effusions, and (Ronsard is keen to
persuade) he had enjoyed that permission since the age of twelve!

In attempting to translate for the noninitiate the feelings of excitement
and sense of uplift that poetic composition brought to him, Ronsard here

abandons the crude descriptions of physical effects that he had carried almost to the point of ridicule in some early poems. The opening stanza of
the ode addressed to Catherine de' Medici, for example, contrasts sharply
with the lines we have just read:

> Je suis troublé de fureur,
> Le corps me fremist d'horreur,
> D'un effroy mon ame est pleine.
> Mon estomac est pantois,
> Et par son canal ma vois
> Ne se desgorge qu'à peine.
>
> (P 1:369; L 1:65)

I shake with inspiration; my body trembles with awe, and my mind is filled
with terror. My whole frame shudders, and my voice scarcely disgorges
sound from its light channel.

These lines may be an accurate rendering of actual feelings; nonetheless,
they seem overstated and too literal with their very specific references to
parts of the body and their functions, and with the abstract nouns *fureur*,
horreur, and *effroy*. How much more convincing is the transfer of poetic
fury and its soaring power to the dancing figures of the Muses. The special
atmosphere that this transposition creates no longer depends on violent
physical reactions in the poet, but rather on the assimilation of the exceptional writer to a privileged world. It is natural, therefore, that when Du
Bellay sought to praise Ronsard's poetic accomplishments, he showed him
controlling the sacred dance of the Muses; and as a special touch of hyperbole, he even congratulates them on their luck: 'Nymphes, heureuses vous,
à qui la nuict aggree / Mener soubs tel Sonneur vostre danse sacrée'
(Nymphs, happy you, to be granted the right to perform your sacred
dance in the shades of night, and led by such a player!).[49]

Dancing, with its powers of elevation, was considered to be more than
an act of celebration. Poets placed it at the very heart of poetic inspiration,
and they argued that poetry (among all the arts) had uniquely the ability
to capture and give life to the twisting, wavy patterns of the dance, to its
expressions and its gestures, and to its renewing movements. The most expansive account of this inspirational power is given by Ronsard in a well-
known passage from the opening section of *L'Hymne de l'Automne*.

> Le jour que je fu né, Apollon qui preside
> Aux Muses, me servit en ce monde de guide,
> M'anima d'un esprit subtil et vigoureux.
> . . . .
> Me donna pour partage une fureur d'esprit,

Et l'art de bien coucher ma verve par escrit.
Il me haussa le coeur, haussa la fantaisie,
M'inspirant dedans l'ame un don de Poësie,
Que Dieu n'a concedé qu'à l'esprit agité
Des poignans aiguillons de sa Divinité.

(lines 1–3, 7–12; P 2:239; L 12:46)

The day that I was born, Apollo, who is in charge of the Muses, also guided me in the world by animating my mind with subtlety and vigour. My share was a soul inspired and the art of putting that inspiration into writing. He lifted up my heart, sharpened my imagination, enspiriting my soul with the gift of poetry that God has only granted to a spirit moved by the acute shafts of his divinity.

Here, the poet has confidently listed the gifts with which Apollo has infused his spirit and which have awakened his imagination to stirring sights and intuitions. Into the centre of such gifts that fire the mind and put it in touch with things and forms known only to the gods, Ronsard plants the dance of the dryads. As we have seen, the intensity of feeling and mental apprehension that accompany poetic composition could not successfully be communicated directly. The experience is transferred such that the poet becomes a hunter, and inspiration his prey. Through deep forests, through empty landscapes of rock and desert, and through dark caves of fear, the poet stalks the dryad emanations of divinity in order to surprise them in their dance, 'Afin de voir au soir les Nymphes et les Fées / Danser dessous la Lune en cotte par les prées' (in order to see the nymphs and fairies dance in the fields at night, their light dresses reflected in the moonshine; lines 37–38).

Alone at night, in this heightened state of sensitivity, he finds them and witnesses their dance with feelings of awe and exhilaration. Then comes the moment when the poet seeks to convince himself that inspiration has indeed come upon him:

J'allois apres la danse, et craintif je pressois
Mes pas dedans le trac des Nymphes, et pensois
Que pour mettre mon pied en leur trace poudreuse,
J'aurois incontinent l'ame plus genereuse,
Ainsi que l'Ascrean qui gravement sonna,
Quand l'une des neuf Soeurs du Laurier luy donna.

(lines 43–48)

After the dance, I followed and placed my feet in the traces left by the nymphs, and having set my foot in their marks still in the dust, immediately my mind (I believed) would be made more noble. It was thus that Hesiod could solemnly sing when one of the nine sisters crowned him with laurel.

Through the placing of his feet in the marks left by the dancers, Ronsard gives physical expression to poetic intuition. And the comparison with Hesiod serves to reinforce the idea of a transfer of power from muse-nymph to poet, since the opening lines of Hesiod's *Theogony* assume divine collaboration:

> Begin we to sing with the Heliconian Muses, who keep safe the spacious and divine mount of Helicon, and also with delicate feet dance about the violet-hued fount and altars of the mighty son of Cronos.[50]

Vigenère's commentary on this exordium is illuminating. He explains that the movements of the Muses are inspired as an act of praise to the gods, that their measures imitate the direction and harmony of the heavens. To the poets who participate in the celebration, or who are in some way associated with it, the Muses communicate these exact rhythms and intervals. Thus the structure of the lyrical odes that the poets are later inspired to compose corresponds exactly to the Muses's perceptions of the dance of the heavenly bodies.

> à l'imitation du mouvement des cieux, et des astres accompagnez de l'harmonie qui en precede comme pour leur servir de note. Les trois couppes des odes nous en font foy, lesquelles se danssoient avec beaucoup de conformité à quelques bransles des nostres.[51]

> in imitation of the movement of the heavens and of the stars whose harmonious sound gives them the beat. The triple division of odes can serve as a guarantee to us that they danced them much in conformity with some of our own dances.

To Ronsard's mind there was no doubt about the reality of the dryads' dance, and as though to prove his conviction, in his poetry he has given their form flesh and blood. Sixteenth-century readers of poetry would, in any case, have had little difficulty in recognising these nymphs. They were characterized by Mantegna, who showed them dressed in flowing garments and dancing in a circle around an oak tree. This image was diffused throughout Europe in Raimondi's copies of the painter's own engraving. A dance of dryads appears, for instance, beneath the eleventh fresco in the Galerie François Ier (fig. 68), which represented a religious festival and the moment of sacrifice.[52] This particular rendering seems to have had unsurpassed appeal in the sixteenth century. It was engraved by Pierre Millan (fig. 69), and so became a popular focus of decorative interest. Over a thousand copies have been traced in the archives, and it can still be seen today, in stucco form, in the central panel of the ornate chimneypiece in the Star Chamber at Broughton Castle in Oxfordshire, and carved in wood on a Renaissance *secrétaire* preserved in the Rijksmuseum.[53]

68. Fontainebleau, Galerie François Ier, painting of dancing dryads, depicted below the fresco *Le Sacrifice* (Château de Fontainebleau, Cliché Esparcieux).

69. Pierre Millan, *Danse des Dryades*, engraving inspired by the Galerie François Ier, painting of dancing dryads (Bibliothèque Nationale).

In our preliminary considerations of the fourth of the modes of idealisation prevalent in Renaissance art and poetry, it seemed that the dancing form was little more than an extension of beauty or a superlative means of compliment as the poet brought the Muses down from their Parnassian mount to dance with him in celebration of the daughters of a king.[54] We have seen, however, that for the sixteenth century (as for generations of ancient Greek poets) the art of choreography had a loftier purpose: it embodied the essential nature and behaviour of beings vital to poetry, and it came to represent inspiration and expressive power. Thus, in a deceptively simple ode dedicated to the Muses, Ronsard includes them all in his appeal that they join with him in the dance of poetic creation:

> Vous, Graces d'une escharpe ceintes,
> Qui dessous les montaignes saintes
> De Colche, ou dans le fond du val
> Soit d'Amathonte ou soit d'Erie,
> Toute nuict sur l'herbe fleurie
> En un rond demenez le bal;
>   Et vous Dryades, et vous, Fées. . . .
>
> (ode 18, lines 13–19; P 1 : 557–58; L 7 : 108–10)

You, O Graces in your floating veils, who beneath the holy mountains of Colchos or in the depths of the vales of Amathonte or Eria, all the night through the flowering fields, dance your rounds; and you, dryads and fairies. . . .

In this ode, as in many other poems, Ronsard is secure in the thought that this 'bal des muses' confers immortality; its springing form is more durable than any metal:

> Si tout ravy des saults de voz carolles
> D'un pied nombreux j'ay conduit vostre bal
> Plus dur qu'en fer, qu'en cuyvre ou qu'en métal.
>
> (G, 3; L 5 : 102)

Completely overcome by the sight of your dance steps and by the sound of your song, I led your ball with a measured step, stronger than iron, brass, or any other metal.

Many readers are shocked by the arrogant tone and inflated assertions that Ronsard made so frequently about his name and his work; for example,

> Je suis, dis-je Ronsard, et cela te suffise
> . . . .

Bien cognu d'Helicon, dont l'ardant aiguillon
Me fist danser au bal que conduit Apollon.[55]

I am, I tell you, Ronsard, and let that suffice . . . I'm well-known on Helicon, whose penetrating shafts take me into the dance led by Apollo.

Statements such as these must be set, however, in their historical context, which acknowledged the high status of the poet and which recognised in his art the power to play again the harmonies of the universe and to reveal its secrets. As an intimate associate of Apollo and the Muses, Ronsard became a creator; having danced to their measures night and day, he was assured that his reputation and his name would flourish forever: 'Vostre nom fleurira; / L'âge de siecle en siecle aura de vous memoire' (Your name will flower forever; from age to age, each century will have memories of you; *Ode en dialogue*, lines 14–15; P 2:830–31; L 7:307–9).

Conclusion

In *La Deffence et illustration de la langue françoyse*, Du Bellay argued that if poets were to leave pictures of nature that matched the excellence of those presented in the ancient world, then they would need to rebuild the entire fabric of poetry.[1] Such rebuilding would involve the bringing together of the resources of the French language, considerably extended, and a profound knowledge of Greek and Latin works. In the event, Ronsard was the only sixteenth-century French poet who fully achieved the aims outlined in his friend's manifesto. His vast knowledge of ancient literary sources enabled him to recall for his readers their flavour and characteristics, even as he introduced into the forms borrowed from Latin and Greek the habits of thought, the ideals, and the aspirations of his own time.

We have seen in this study that the *vive nature* of which Du Bellay and other poets and artists wrote so frequently was, in artistic practice, an idealisation of the natural. This is what poet, artist, and patron all sought. Titian's *Adonis* is praised by Dolce because its pictorial qualities surpass those commonly offered by a natural scene; the picture 'includes a painterly piece of landscape of such quality that the reality is not so real'.[2] The sixteenth-century audience sought a nature that was filtered, shaped, beautified in rich metals, and decorated with precious stones. Thus, when Ronsard came to depict Nature's palace in *L'Hymne de l'Automne* he pictured it built by Vulcan on pillars of Phrygian marble; its ceilings were of gold and silver, its hundred doors made of loadstone and set with diamonds, rubies, and sapphires:

> Le Palais magnifique où Nature habitoit,
> Sur piliers Phrygiens elevé se portoit;
> Les voûtes estoyent d'or, d'or estoit la closture,
> Et d'argent affiné la haute couverture;

Là cent portes estoyent toutes faites d'aymant;
En-contre les parois reluist meint diamant,
Meint rubi, meint saphir, que le boiteux manoeuvre
A luy-mesme attachez, ingenieux chef-d'oeuvre.

(lines 328—35)

The magnificent palace of Nature was built on Phrygian pillars; its ceilings and walls were of gold, of fine silver was the high roof. The hundred doors were all made of metal: the walls shone with a profusion of diamonds, rubies, and sapphires, which Vulcan created and applied himself into a marvellous masterpiece.

Nature's home is remarkable, not for the abundance of life or vital elements that might be found there, but by virtue of its rich materials, ingeniously worked. It is an artefact, an 'ingenieux chef-d'oeuvre', and in thus re-presenting it Ronsard is offering evidence of the kind of artistic skill admired by his patrons and by ancient writers.[3]

Idealising was, however, a complicated business, especially for a poet as versatile as Ronsard. If we return to the example of the grotto at Meudon, we note that Primaticcio and Niccolo dell'Abbate had tried to 'outdo' nature by simulating natural elements in paint and stucco. The place was

tout recouverte d'émail, pavée de mosaïques, et de porphyre moucheté de couleurs diverses . . . murs décorés d'arabesques et de compartimens de stucs, de coquillage et de coraux, ornés de fontaines, de reliefs et de peintures.[4]

completely covered with enamel, paved with mosaics and porphyry shot through with diverse colours . . . the walls were decorated with arabesques and stucco frames, with shells and coral, ornate with fountains, reliefs, and paintings.

Impressed by the simulation, Ronsard's own vision paints a home of the Muses where only wild things grow. Nature and the reader's everyday experience provide the decorative elements: the ground, a carpet of moss, flowers, and sweet-smelling mint; the stone is covered with ivy that twines in and out of trailing vines, while rustic pillars become the home of bees and fireflies:

Tousjours tout à l'entour la tandre mousse y croisse
Le poliot fleuri en tout temps y paroisse;
Le lierre tortu, recourbé de maint tour,
Y puisse sus son front grimper tout à l'entour,
Et la belle lambrunche ensemble entortillée
Laisse espandre ses bras tout au long de l'allée;

L'avette en lieu de ruche agence dans les troux
Des rustiques piliers sa cire et son miel roux,
Et le freslon armé qui les raisins moissonne,
De son bruit enroüé par l'antre ne bourdonne.

(lines 135–44; P 1 : 958; L 9 : 82–83)

All around grow soft mosses, at all times the bright poppy appears, the twisting ivy, turning and circling around climbs up the facade and all around. The lovely wild grape stems, twisting around each other, stretch their arms along the entire alleyway; the bee, instead of a hive, finds its home in the holes of the rustic pillars and makes its wax and red honey; the buzzing sound of the wasp who harvests the grapes is heard nowhere in the cave.

Inside this essentially 'natural' dwelling, however, are preserved the vast collections of Roman antiquities brought into France by the cardinal of Lorraine, described by François de Belleforest as 'amoureux de tout ce qui est rare, exquis, singulier, et gentil en la nature et imitation d'icelle' (a lover of all that is rare, exquisite, unusual, and pleasant in nature and in its imitation).[5] The cardinal's acquisitive genius is such that Belleforest remains perplexed when he comes to describe the place. It is artificial but also quasi-natural: 'cette Grottesque artificielle, et à demy naturelle de Meudon' (this artificial grotesque and half-natural style at Meudon). Nonetheless, his hesitation helps us to define the character of ideal forms. In their production, we have the fusing together of the best from every source of experience—literary and lived experience. The best of one source is easily fused to the best of another, so that the work of art (poem, statue, painting, or palace) is seen as more natural—because more ideal—than nature itself.

This fusion, which informs every attempt to give idealistic expression to feelings and observations, brought a blurring in artistic consciousness. Praise involved working between two worlds—between the artificial and the natural, between a real scene and a painted canvas—and maintaining both together in the mind of the observer. In order to praise the created or artificial object, it therefore became a formula to describe it *as if* it were natural or lifelike. Of the 'chevaulx artificielz' (artificial horses) designed to be led around the banquetting hall at the wedding supper of Mary, Queen of Scots: 'on eust dict iceulx estre vivans' (one would have said that they were alive); and the fountain that sprang from the large beech tree at Bayonne on Catherine's special day was 'faite de tel artifice qu'il sembloit qu'elle fust naturelle' (made with such skill that it seemed natural).[6] Conversely, in order to praise the natural, impressions of wonder were transposed. Thus Aretino describes the sight of the Grand Canal in Venice as though it had been composed and painted by the brush of Titian:

Vizualize it while I describe it. First the houses which though of real stone seemed to be made of artificial material. And then imagine the air as I perceived it, in some places pure and vivid; in others turbid and dull. . . . Oh, with what beautiful strokes did Nature's brush move the air back, separating it from the palaces the same as Titian does in his landscapes. In some part a bluish green appeared, in others a greenish blue. . . .[7]

Yet again, in order to praise a prince artists and poets deliberately blurred the distinctions between real and fictional. As a compliment to Lucrezia Borgia, Ariosto makes the beautiful women on the fountain indistinguishable from real ones (*Orlando Furioso*, canto 42), while Ercole d'Este's own embroidered pavilions are woven into canto 35. This mirroring technique is the same as that used to show François I's face in one of the frescoes in the gallery at Fontainebleau, or, similarly, Ronsard's marvellous fusion of Pasithea and Princess Marguerite in *La Charite*.

Poets and artists were decorators and transformers, sharing and constructing a complex and tangled web of reciprocal sources, aims, and influences. And it was their proven ability to create artistic illusion through such decorative means that roused worries in the minds of some. The *trompe l'oeil* of the painters, with their mastery of perspective, and the visions and imaginative distortions of the poets were profoundly disturbing to writers like Agrippa, for instance. In his view, poets and painters had equal power to feign and to represent the world, and to bring it alive almost to the touch. Yet such power, Agrippa concludes, is essentially dependent upon the systematic falsifying of the facts of vision, which painters, in particular, sometimes carried to excessive lengths.

Ainsi dit-on que la Peinture n'est autre chose qu'une poësie muette, et la poësie une peincture parlante, tant sont bien alliees l'une avec l'autre: Car et peintres et poëtes feignent egalement les uns comme les autres des fables ou des histoires, et representent toutes choses: la lumière et splendeur, les ombres, les hauteurs, les abbaissements, montagnes, et plaines. Davantage la peinture a cela, qu'elle deçoit la veuë par un mesme object, faisant voir et paroistre en diverses sortes, une mesme figure, selon le changement de l'assiette ou d'icelle ou des regardans, ce qu'elle emprunte de l'optique et passe plus outre que la sculpture ou statuaire, en ce qu'elle contrefait le feu, les rayons la lumière, les tonnerres, foudres, le poinct du jour, le Soleil couchant, l'entre iour et nuict, les nuages, fait apparoistre les passions et affections de l'homme, et presque fait parler les figures et par fausses mesures elle raccourcit les choses, et fait apparoistre ce qui n'est point comme s'il estoit, ou autrement qu'il n'est.[8]

Thus one says that painting is nothing other than mute poetry, and poetry a speaking picture, so closely are they allied to each other. Because both poets and painters feign stories and fables and represent things: light and magnifi-

cence, shades, heights and valleys, mountains and plains. Moreover, painting has that capacity which allows it to deceive sight by taking the same
object and making it appear in different guises, the same figure made different according to a change of site or of the perspective from which it is
viewed; a capacity borrowed from optics that takes painting beyond sculpture or statue work, since it can counterfeit fire, rays of light, thunder, moving light, the setting sun, twilight, clouds, the feelings and passions of men,
and can almost make figures talk; by false ways, it foreshortens things, and
makes them appear not as they should be and certainly not as they are.

Thus, far from contributing to our well-being, as artists and poets regularly claimed, the arts of poetry and of painting especially are vain and
unreliable, the moralist Agrippa objects.

Even in this attack on the two arts, however, they are considered as
similar in aim and in performance. In Renaissance Europe, for political
and social as well as aesthetic reasons, artistic disciplines converged, and
poet, artist, and patron spoke the same normative and idealising language.
To appreciate the nature of Renaissance artistic endeavour, therefore, we
must cross disciplinary boundaries and, despite the critical problems involved, explore the analogies between the arts. This study of ideal forms
has attempted such an exploration by concentrating on sixteenth-century
France, where the convergence was unusually pronounced. Social and political forces combined to encourage painters and poets in the exploitation
of similar themes and common sources, which can be traced by juxtapos-
ing the production of heroic poems with armour, frescoes, and royal festivals, and by tracing affinities between love sonnets or poems of compliment and jewels or painted and sculptured images of beauty.

In promoting their respective interests, each of the arts often imitated
the others, and through their specific means put forth converging messages. Such attempts brought both aesthetic benefits and pitfalls. It has
been said that Ronsard was at times overly enthusiastic in the attention he
paid to artists and to the painted inset; that, as a result, his reliance on the
decorative elements in poetry became too exclusive. As we have seen, he
was quite firm and explicit about decoration being an activity fundamental to poetry, a conviction apparent in his poetic practice and in his theoretical writings. In the *Abbrégé poétique*, for example, he draws together
three key concepts for sixteenth-century aesthetics: imitation, invention,
and imagination.

L'invention n'est autre chose que le bon naturel d'une imagination concevant
les idées et formes de toutes choses qui se peuvent imaginer, tant celestes
que terrestres, animées ou inanimées, pour apres les representer, descrire et
imiter.

(P 2:999, L 14:12–13)

Invention is nothing other than the good natural operation of the imagination conceiving the ideas and the forms of things that can be imagined, terrestial or celestial, animate or inanimate, to re-present them afterwards, to describe and imitate them.

Here Ronsard's emphasis moves from the initial perception of the widest range of things ('tant celestes que terrestres, animées ou inanimées') to the artistic process of reproducing them in verse ('representer, descrire et imiter').[9] In his poems, the picturing forth was no straightforward mirroring of observed phenomena, but rather (as we have noted) their beautifying. The art of sacrifice, so notably present in the French poems of Du Bellay,[10] was not for Ronsard. He turned his painted canvasses into flamboyant pieces that earned the praises of contemporaries such as Belleforest:

Et avec quel art il paint les choses qu'il descrit, les mettant si dextrement devant l'esprit par ses vers, qu'il semble que les yeux corporels voyent les choses descrittes.[11]

And with what art he paints the things he describes, putting them so skilfully with his verse before the eyes that it seems that real eyes see the things described.

Ronsard showed everything, and his peers clearly admired his approach. Yet sometimes, by clinging too closely to the notion of painting, his verse became excessively static. Such a want of dynamism is particularly present in *La Franciade*, where Ronsard so concentrated his care on painting scenes and characters that he failed to sustain a developing narrative argument.[12]

Nevertheless, in other works, Ronsard demonstrated the aesthetic benefits that accrued from his combining picture-making with extraordinary lyrical power. These works illuminate the way Renaissance poets and artists captured moments of heightened perception and gave them some kind of permanent resonance. For by celebrating that which is best in nature—whether in forms heroic and triumphant, or beautiful and moving—they created highly decorative modes into which they poured force and vibrant sensuality. At the centre of the magnificent *Ode à Michel de l'Hospital* (1550) Ronsard places a vivid description of the mastery they achieved over such combinations. He borrowed the terms from Plato (indeed, the very ones Baudelaire used three centuries later, when he tried to explain the central purpose of *his* art). Art, he says, has

   la puissance
D'arracher les ames dehors
Le sale bourbier de leurs corps
Pour les rejoindre à leur naissance.

                    (lines 361–64)

the power to snatch souls from their filthy earthbound bodies, to give them back their state at birth.

This study of ideal forms in the French Renaissance is, of course, only one approach to sixteenth-century art and writing. But it is a fruitful one, especially for the study of poetry, and it could be extended to other domains. Three or four centuries ago, most thinking people approved of arts that, by painting up experience, improved their audience's minds. Montaigne related such idealising to strong emotional effects and wrote admiringly of it:

> C'est l'office des gens de bien de peindre la vertu la plus belle qui se puisse; et ne nous messieroit pas quand la passion nous transporteroit à la faveur de si saintes formes.[13]

> It's the job of worthy men to paint virtue in the most splendid colours possible, and it is not inappropriate when passion moves us to favour such saintly forms.

Some years later, even greater claims were made. The Reverend Father Nicolas Caussin saw in the phenomenon of praise and in the fusing of beautiful form and knowledge of the world or of the soul, a sign of civilisation at its highest point of development:

> L'art de l'éloge, qui allie la transmission du savoir philosophique ou religieux à une forme luxueuse et délectable, est le signe d'une civilisation parvenue à son dernier degré de développement.[14]

> The art of praising, which brings together the transmission of philosophical and religious knowledge and splendid and delightful forms, is the sign of a civilisation that has reached the brightest point of its development.

By 1605, however, the process of incomprehension had begun. In that year, the geographer royal, Antoine de Laval, published in Paris his *Desseins et professions notables et publiques*, to which he appended a discourse on the kind of paintings worthy of decorating the new gallery in the Louvre. Recalling the magnificence of François I's building projects, he has this to say about the famous gallery at Fontainebleau:

> Ie m'estonne comme il [François I] ne fit pourtraire en quelque lieu de ses beaux Palais un subject tout propre et particulier à ses predecesseurs Rois et à soy-mesme: sans aller emprunter l'erreur mensonger d'Ulisse, pour les ioüees et entredeux des fenestrages de sa gallerie de Fontainebleau, et pour la voute ceste fabuleuse invention de l'adultere de Mars avec Venus en la presence de toute ceste folle troupe des Dieux.[15]

> I'm astonished that he [François I] did not portray in some place in his pal-
> aces an appropriate subject which becomes his predecessors and himself,
> without filling up the space between the windows of his gallery at Fon-
> tainebleau with lying stories taken from the legend of Ulysses, and choosing
> for the ceiling the theme of the fantastic invention of the adultery of Mars
> and Venus before the entire foolish company of the gods.

The mind of the moralist is uppermost here, but also revealed is an observer who is unable to understand the mythological world he saw before
him, who cannot penetrate the political allusions there displayed. He stands
outside and therefore does not perceive how social reality and mythological fiction are blended in these paintings. His reaction, based on inadequate knowledge and on a lack of integration, exemplifies the response of
those who come to Renaissance poetry with similarly entrenched ideas
and attitudes. It has been the purpose of this book to try, as far as possible,
to reintegrate author, work, and patron, and thereby re-create the conditions that prevailed for a sixteenth-century public.

Notes

Introduction

1 On rhetorical training, see Alex Gordon, *Ronsard et la rhétorique* (Geneva, 1970). Grahame Castor has studied Petrarch's influence on Ronsard's love poetry in a number of articles, principally, 'Ronsard's Variants: "Je vouldray bien richement jaunissant"', *Modern Language Review* 59 (1964): 387–90; 'Imitation in Ronsard: O de Nepenthe . . .', *Modern Language Review* 63 (1968): 332–39; and 'Petrarchism and the Quest for Beauty in the *Amours* of Cassandre and the *Sonets pour Hélène*', in *Ronsard the Poet*, ed. Terence Cave (London, 1973), pp. 79–120. The aesthetic arguments have been examined by Terence Cave in his book *The Cornucopian Text* (Oxford, 1979) and in a number of substantial articles: 'Ronsard's Bacchic Poetry: From the *Bacchanales* to the *Hymne de l'automne*', *L'Esprit Créateur* 10 (1970): 104–16; 'Ronsard as Apollo: Myth, Poetry, and Experience in a Renaissance Sonnet Cycle', *Yale French Studies* 47 (1972): 76–90; 'Mythes de l'abondance et la privation chez Ronsard', *Cahiers de l'Association Internationale des Etudes Françaises* 25 (1973): 247–60; 'Ronsard's Mythological Universe', in *Ronsard the Poet*, pp. 159–208; and 'Copia and Cornucopia', in *French Renaissance Studies*, ed. Peter Sharratt (Edinburgh, 1976), pp. 52–69. I am deeply endebted to Dr. Cave's work, as will be clear from the developing argument in this book.

2 Guillaume Des Autelz, *Replique aux furieuses defenses de L. Meigret* (Lyons, 1551), pp. 71–72.

3 Blaise de Vigenère, *Les Images des deux Philostrates grecs* (Paris, 1578), ff. 158–158ᵛ.

4 Blaise de Vigenère, *Les Commentaires de Jules Cesar* (Paris, 1589), p. 101.

5 Joachim Du Bellay, *Poésies françaises et latines*, 2 vols, ed. E. Courbet (Paris, 1918), 1:5.

6 Estienne Pasquier, *Choix de lettres*, ed. D. Thickett (Geneva, 1956), p. 88.

7 Ibid., pp. 58–59.

8 See H. Schutz, *Vernacular Books in Parisian Private Libraries of the Sixteenth Century* (Chapel Hill, N.C., 1955); and Annie Parent, *Les Métiers du livre à Paris au seizième siècle* (Geneva, 1974).

9 Daniel Ménager, *Ronsard: Le Roi, le poète et les hommes* (Geneva, 1979).

10 Dorothy Gabe Coleman, *The Gallo-Roman Muse* (Cambridge, 1979); and Dorothy Gabe Coleman, *The Chaste Muse: A Study of Joachim du Bellay's Poetry* (Leiden, 1980).

1. The Perfect Prince

1 Ivan Cloulas, *Un Portrait de Catherine de Médicis* (Paris, 1979), has an extensive and up-to-date bibliography on growing criticisms of the court, pp. 628–94.

2 Estienne Pasquier, *Lettres historiques*, ed. D. Thickett (Geneva, 1966), pp. 307–8.

3 Raoul Morçay and Armand Muller, *La Renaissance* (Paris, 1960), p. 318:

> Les Hymnes ne sont pas la partie la plus vivante de l'oeuvre de Ronsard. L'hyperbole dans la louange déplaît à notre esprit démocratique et à notre goût; les scènes mythologiques développées longuement . . . nous paraissent lointaines et bien étrangères; trop souvent, les considérations que nous offre le poète ressemblent à de froides dissertations. On lit peu ces deux livres aujourd' hui.

> Hymns are not the most lively part of Ronsard's work. Hyperbole in praise displeases our democratic mind and our talk; mythological scenes developed at length . . . seem strange and distant to us; too often, the poet offers us considerations that seem like cold dissertations. These books are rarely read today.

4 See the work of Terence Cave, cited in n. 1 of the Introduction; and G. Lafeuille, *Cinq Hymnes de Ronsard* (Geneva, 1973).

5 Françoise Joukovsky has analysed these synonyms in *La Gloire à la Renaissance* (Geneva, 1969), pp. 133–36. Her study should be consulted as an important source book for attitudes towards the stimulating power of praise.

6 Erasmus, epistle 177, in *The Correspondence*, ed. R. A. B. Mynors and D. F. S. Thomson, 2 vols to date (Toronto, 1975), 2:71; also quoted in James D. Garrison, *Dryden and the Tradition of Panegyric* (Berkeley, 1975), p. 21.

7 Erasmus, epistle 179, in *Correspondence* 2:52–55; for Erasmus's Latin antecedents, see Lester K. Born, 'The Perfect Prince, According to the Latin Panegyrists', *American Journal of Philology* 55 (1934): 20–35.

8   From Erasmus's *Apologia pro panegyricis*, trans. and ed. Lester K. Born as *The Education of a Christian Prince* (New York, 1936), pp. 144–45.

9   'Of Praise', in *The Works of Francis Bacon*, ed. J. Spedding, 14 vols, (London, 1860), 6:501.

10   Bacon, *The Advancement of Learning*, in *Works* 4:307.

11   Aristotle, *On Poetics*, ch. 15, in *Works*, 2 vols, ed. Robert Maynard Hutchins, (Chicago, 1952).

12   Baxter Hathaway, *The Age of Criticism: The Late Renaissance in Italy* (Ithaca, N.Y., 1962), p. 138, cites Trissino, Varchi, and many others on the process of idealising; later, pp. 142–43, he relies principally on the work of Robertello.

13   E. H. Gombrich, *The Heritage of Apelles: Studies in the Art of the Renaissance* (Oxford, 1978), p. 65.

14   For details on treatises concerning perfect princes, consult Theodore C. Burgess, *Epideictic Literature* (Chicago, 1962).

15   See Born, 'The Perfect Prince', although it was Pacatus's panegyric on Theodosius (A.D. 389) that Florent Chrestien translated to compliment Henri III in 1578. I have used Gallatier's edition of the *Panégyristes latins*, 2 vols (Paris, 1949).

16   The influence of Erasmus is easily traceable in the works of Rabelais; see Nicole Aronson, *Les Idées politiques de Rabelais* (Paris, 1973); and—to cite a little-known writer—in J. P. de Cermenate, *Discours de la droite administration des royaumes et republiques* (Lyons, 1561). That of Budé can be seen, for example, in Jehan Breche de Tours, *Premier Livre de l'honneste exercice du prince* (Paris, 1544). The *Institution* receives special commendation from Du Bellay in *La Deffence et illustration de la langue françoyse* [Paris, 1549], ed. H. Chamard (Paris, 1904), pp. 333–34. Among other important writers who expressed similar views and attitudes, Sir Philip Sidney refers several times in his *Apology* to 'notable images of virtue [which] draw us to as high a perfection as our degenerate souls can be capable of'; and later 'to lift up the mind from the dungeon of the body to the enjoying his owne divine essence' (*An Apology for Poetry*, ed. G. Smith [Oxford, 1959], 1:160–61). The handwritten version of Erasmus's work (ca. 1553–54) is at Chantilly; see Fricke Dietmar, *Die Französischen Fassungen der Institutio Principis Christiani des Erasmus von Rotterdam* (Geneva, 1967). In a letter to her son Charles dictated on 8 Sept. 1563, Catherine outlines 'ce que j'estime aussi nécessaire pour vous faire obéir à tout vostre royaume' (What I esteem is necessary to ensure that you are obeyed in your kingdom). Her principal argument seems to be that Charles should match his father's mode of life and the magnificent daily habits of his court: these involved having balls twice a week and knightly exercises:

> Car, j'ay ouy dire au Roy vostre grand-père qu'il falloit deux choses pour vivre en repos avec les François et qu'ils aimassent leur Roy: les tenir joyeux et occuper à

quelque exercise; pour cest effet, souvent il falloit combattre à cheval et à pied, courre la lance.

> (*Lettres de Catherine de' Médici*, 5 vols,
> ed. M. Le Cte. Hector de la Ferrière
> [Paris, 1885], 2:92)

Because, I heard it said to the king, your grandfather, that two things were necessary to live peacefully with the French and to make them love their king: keep them happy, and give them plenty of exercise; for this reason, they must often have experience of feats of arms, on foot and on horseback and running with the lance.

17 Cited in Dora M. Bell, *L'Idéal éthique de la royauté en France au Moyen Age* (Geneva, 1962), pp. 67—68.

18 Jean Bouchet, *Epistres morales et familieres du Traverseur* (Poitiers, 1545).

19 Guillaume Budé, *De l'institution du prince* [Paris, 1547] facsimile ed. (Farnborough, 1966). Subsequent references are to this edition.

20 Ibid., p. 79. This view of French kings has been amply explored by Marc Bloch in *Les Rois thaumaturges* (Strasbourg, 1924).

21 Jean de la Madeleine, *Discours de l'estat et office d'un roy, prince, et monarque* (Paris, 1575), p. 29; see also Le Frère de Laval, *L'Histoire de France sous les rois Henri et François II, Charles IX, et Henri III* (Paris, 1581), and his report of the Etats d'Orléans, Dec. 1560.

22 Michel de l'Hôpital, *Oeuvres complètes*, 5 vols, ed. P. J. S. Duféy (Paris, 1824—26), 5:10.

23 Ibid., 2:29. Echoes of these sentiments can be traced in François de Belleforest, *L'Histoire des neuf roys Charles de France* (Paris, 1568), pp. 427—28; and in Louis Le Caron, *Panegyrique ou oraison de louange au roy Charles IX* (Paris, 1566), sig. k iv.

24 The significance of the royal arms of France is explored in detail in Jacques de Lamothe, *Le Blason des célestes et très chrétiennes armes de France* (Rouen, 1549).

25 Erasmus, *Education of a Christian Prince*, p. 187.

26 These same models recur throughout the century. Claude d'Albon's comment may be taken as typical: 'Ce qui a mis les Rois en telle veneration, a esté principalement les vertus et puissances divines qui ont esté veües en eux seuls, et non és autres hommes' (That which has put kings in such veneration has principally been the virtues and divine power which are exhibited in kings alone and not in other men); *De la majesté royale* (Lyons, 1575), f. 29^{v}.

27 See L. Mirot, *L'Hôtel et les collections du connétable de Montmorency* (Paris, 1920), pp. 78, 85, for the duke's art collections. Anne-Marie Le Coque examines the significance of the wall paintings at Ecouen in 'Les Peintures murales d'Ecouen', in *Le Colloque de Fontainebleau* (Paris, 1972), pp. 161–73.

28 Christophe Longueil, *De laudibus divi Ludovici atque Francorum* (Paris, 1510).

29 Anthony Blunt, *Art and Architecture in France, 1500–1700* (London 1953), pp. 15–16, and plate 13. There is an extended description of this monument in Jean Second's Elegy 17, bk 3, entitled 'De statuis et sepulchris in templo orbis S. Dionysii spectandis prope Lutetiam,' in *Oeuvres* (Paris, 1938), pp. 198–206.

30 In Garnier's *Hymne de la monarchie*, the comparisons with Augustus begin on p. 10.

31 See Belleforest, *L'Histoire*, p. 82; T. Sébillet, *Art poétique françoys* [1548] (Geneva, 1932), pp. 14–15.

32 See Budé, *De l'institution*, p. 46; and J. de Silly, *La Harangue de par la noblesse de toute la France, au roy Charles 9e*, (Paris, 1561), f. 6ᵛ. Courtesy books gave similar advice; see B. de Castiglione, *Il Cortegiano* [1528], trans. Thomas Hoby [1561] as *The Courtier* (London, 1959), p. 265: 'enflame him to them [virtues] with examples of manye famous captaines'.

33 Guillaume de la Perrière, *La Morosophie* (Lyons, 1553), p. 63.

34 J. de Sacrobosco, *Tractatus de sphaera*, trans. G. Desbordes as *La Sphère* (Paris, 1584), p. 14. For Henri II's library, see E. Quentin-Bauchart, *La Bibliothèque de Fontainebleau* (Paris, 1891).

35 The text of the Bibliothèque Nationale, Ms. fr. 2579, which provides a unique account of the 'momerie', is reprinted by Ph. A. Becker in 'La Vie littéraire à la cour de Louis XII', *Neuphilologus* 23 (1922): 138–39.

36 See Orontius Finé, *Protomathesis* (Paris, 1532) and Gabriel Symeoni, *Interpretation grecque, latine, toscane, et françoyse du monstre ou enigme d'Italie* (Lyons, 1555), plate opposite p. 41.

37 Some examples of the persistence of the King-Sun image are Louis Le Caron, *Les Dialogues* (Paris, 1556), f. 10ᵛ and f. 30; Pontus de Tyard, *L'Univers* (Lyons, 1557), p. 40; Belleforest, *L'Histoire*, p. 4; the anonymous *De l'authorité du roy* (Paris, 1587), p. 15; and Jean de Seville, *Brief Discours sur la bonne et ioyeuse reception faicte a la maiesté du roy . . .* (Rouen, 1588), sigs Aiiiᵛ–Aiiij:

> car il y a analogie et proportion de ce petit monde au grand monde, auquel nous voyons le Soleil prince des autres Planettes estre porté comme un grand Roy en son char magnifiquement attelé

because there is analogy and proportion between this tiny world and the large one in which we see the Sun, prince of the other planets, carried around like a great king in his magnificently drawn chariot.

38   Notable among critics is Pasquier, whose hostility is made clear in his correspondence. Referring to Catherine de' Medici, he wrote:

> Cette princesse, qui n'estimoit l'Eglise de S. Denis, ancien tombeau de nos Roys, assez capable pour recevoir ny le corps du Roy son mary, ny le sien, ny de Messieurs ses enfans, avoit fait travailler, par trente ans, au bastiment de trois chapelles hors l'église, pour leur servir de sepulchres; et fait dresser les pourtraitures en marbre, tant de son mary, que la sienne, avec une despense pareille à celle des Rois d'Aegypte, en leurs mausolées.

> This princess, who did not like the Church at St. Denis, which housed the tombs of our ancient kings, and did not consider it as appropriate for the bodies of her husband, herself, and her children, for thirty years had builders working on three chapels adjacent to the church, in which their sepulchres might be placed; she had made marble portraits of herself and her husband, spending as profusely as the kings of Egypt when they erected their tombs.

His opposition is here ironically expressed; the 1580s brought even more undisguised criticism; see Pasquier, *Lettres historiques*, pp. 387–88.

39   Claude de Seyssel, *Les Louenges du roy Louis XIIe de ce nom* (Paris, 1508), 'Le proheme'.

40   Jean Bouchet, *Les Triomphes de François Ier* (Poitiers, 1550), f. L^v.

41   Seyssel, *Les Louenges*, f. 1^v. In *Claudian: Poetry and Propaganda at the Court of Honorius* (Oxford, 1970), Alan Cameron provides a suggestive analysis of Claudian's work that emphasises the role of panegyric in imperial ceremonial.

42   The speech to Elizabeth is cited in E. W. Talbert, 'The Interpretation of Jonson's Courtly Spectacles', *PMLA* 60 (1945): 457, "In thies [panegyricae] were sett forth the commendations of Kings and Emperors, with the sweet sound whereof, as the ears of evil Princes were delighted by hearing their undeservid praises, so were good Princes by the pleasant remembrances of their knowen and true vertues made better, being put in mynde of their office and government'.

43   Seyssel, *Les Louenges*, p. 2.

44   For further details on the significance of the funeral service, see Ralph E. Giesey, *The French Funeral Ceremony* (Geneva, 1960), and E. H. Kantorowicz, *A Study in Mediaeval Political Theology* (Princeton, 1957).

45   Du Chastel, *Les Trepas, obseques, et enterrement de . . . François Ier* (Paris, 1547). Giesey, *French Funeral Ceremony*, relies heavily on Du Chastel's account. From the comments of Ronsard in his *Hymne de Henri IIe de ce nom*, it is clear

that the elaborate ceremonies organised for the funeral of François I greatly impressed contemporaries.

> Que les autres enfans prenoyent exemple à toy,
> Tant peut la charité; de rechef, tu l'honores,
> Comme un fils pitoyable, apres sa mort encores,
> Environnant son corps d'un tombeau somptueux,
> Où le docte cizeau, d'un art presomptueux,
> A le marbre animé de batailles gravées,
> Dedans ce Mausolée, enclos en mesme estuy,
> Tes deux freres esteints dorment avecques luy,
> Et ta mere à ses flancs, lesquels t'aiment et prisent,
> Et du Ciel où ils sont, tes guerres favorisent.
>
> (lines 210–20; P 2:247; L 8:15–16)

May other children follow your charitable and filial example; straightaway, we honour you, a sorrowing son, who immediately after your father's death covered his body with a splendid tomb, where ambitious skill and knowledgeable tools have engraved the marble and made it live with battle scenes; within the tomb, enclosed within the same lead, your two brothers sleep alongside him, and your mother lies beside him, they all love and value you, and from heaven, they favour your wars.

46 Jerome de la Rouvere, *Les Deux Sermons funebres et obseques et enterrement de feu roy treschrestien Henri 2e* (Paris, 1559); the first sermon was given in Notre Dame, the second at St. Denis. For another account of the funeral, see F. de Signac, *Le Trespas et ordre des obseques . . . Henri 2e* (Paris, 1559).

47 See Blunt, *Art and Architecture*, pp. 98–100 and plate 63; p. 87, n. 138.

48 Bibliothèque Nationale, Ms. fr. 306, dated 8 Feb. 1562; see J. Guiffrey, 'Nicolas Hoüel apothicaire parisien', *Mémoires de la Société de l'Histoire de Paris et de l'Ile de France* 25 (1898): 179–270.

49 See Pasquier's remarks in n. 38 above.

50 For the early history of medals used as propaganda, see N. Rondot, *Les Médailleurs et graveurs de monnaies, jetons, et médailles en France* (Paris, 1904). Henri's edicts relating to this matter can be consulted in *Les Ordonnances et edictz faictz par le roy Henri 2e* (Paris, 1557), ff. 159ᵛ–160.

51 On the immortalising power of medals, see Antoine Le Pois, *Discours sur les medalles et graveures antiques principalement Romaines* (Paris, 1579), pp. 13, 37.

52 Henri de Latour, *Catalogue des jetons de la Bibliothèque Nationale: Rois et reines de France* (Paris, 1897); plate 1, no. 10, shows this coin.

53 Claude Paradin, *Devises héroiques* (Lyons, 1557), pp. 20–21; these remarks are repeated verbatim by F. d'Amboise, *Devises royales* (Paris, 1621), pp. 18–19;

they also occur in P. Dinet, *Cinq Livres des hieroglyphes* (Paris, 1614), p. 559; and G. Ruscelli accorded his approval in *Le imprese illustri* (Venice, 1568), pp. 180–82.

54   Normally the crescent moon was shown in triple form to represent Henri II as ruler of France, England, and Scotland.

55   See Margaret M. McGowan, ed., *L'Entrée de Henri II, Rouen 1550* (Amsterdam, 1974).

56   Bibliothèque Nationale, Ms. fr. 25560, f. 79. The eagle was Charles V's device and *plus ultra* his motto.

57   Etienne Perlin, *Description des royaulmes d'Angleterre et d'Escosse* (Paris, 1558), p. 2.

58   For the use of medals in political propaganda, see W. McAllister Johnson, 'Numismatic Propaganda in Renaissance France', *Art Quarterly* 31 (1968): 123–53.

59   For the king's regard for religion, see Raoul Spifame, *Dicæarchiae Henrici regis, Christianissimi progymnasmata* (n.p. [1556]), f. 60, f. 185ᵛ. Earlier writing on Jean Duvet concerned itself little with these drawings; they are merely mentioned by E. Jullien de La Boullaye in his *Etude sur la vie et les oeuvres de Jean Duvet* (Paris, 1876). They are, however, studied by Colin Eisler, *The Master of the Unicorn: The Life and Work of Jean Duvet* (New York, 1979), catalogue nos 62, 63, 64.

60   See M. Jenkins, *The State Portrait: Its Origin and Evolution* (n.p., 1947).

61   Lucio Mauro records the presence of a portrait of François I alongside representations of Roman emperors, in *Le antichita de la città di Roma* (Venice, 1556), p. 136; the private collections of Catherine de' Medici and the duke of Montmorency boasted of many portraits of the French royal family. See Mirot, *L'Hôtel*, pp. 74, 112, 127, 156; and E. Bonnaffé, *Inventaire des meubles de Catherine de' Médicis* (Paris, 1874), nos 12, 176, 327, 612–55, 657–716.

62   The theme of imperialism is discussed by Frances A. Yates in *Astraea* (London, 1977); see also M. Volker-Hoffmann, 'Donec totum impleat orbem: Symbolisme impérial au temps de Henri II', *Bulletin de la Société de l'Art Français* (Paris, 1980), pp. 29–42.

63   G. P. Lomazzo, *Trattato dell'arte della pittura* [Milan, 1584], trans. Richard Haydocke as *A Tracte Containing the Artes of Curious Paintinge . . .* (Oxford, 1598), pp. 30–31; and in Jenkins, *State Portrait*, p. 44.

64   In recent years, scholars have made clear the political and artistic significance of royal entries, and the relevant bibliography is now quite large. See chapter 4 for a detailed discussion.

65 Georges Péré, *Le Sacre et le couronnement des rois de France* (Paris, 1921).

66 T. Godefroy, *Le Cérémonial françois* (Paris, 1649), notes in sig. ē iiij that in 1548 Henri set up a commission because of 'la nécessité de faire un recueil des rangs et seances entre les Princes' (the necessity of making an account of the ranks and precedence between princes).

67 Lodewick Lloyd, *The Triplicitie of Triumphs* (London, 1591), specialised in recording the detail of royal ceremonies, and his work conveniently brings together information from disparate sources. The two quotations in this paragraph are from the section entitled 'of the maner and forme of the inauguration and annointing of the kings of France at their coronations with al other ancient ceremonies and solemnities', ff. 1ᵛ–3.

68 Latour, *Catalogue des jetons*, plate 1, no. 14.

69 E. E. J. Bourciez, *Les Moeurs polies et la littérature de cour sous Henri II* (Paris, 1886), discusses Henri's court as an Olympus, pt 2, ch. 2. See also Sylvie Béguin, *L'Ecole de Fontainebleau* (Paris, 1960), and 'Remarques sur la chambre du Roi', in *Le Colloque de Fontainebleau* (Paris, 1972), pp. 199–230. See also the special issue of *Revue de l'Art* (1972) on the castle at Fontainebleau; and W. McAllister Johnson, 'Les Débuts de Primatice à Fontainebleau', *Revue de l'Art* (1969), pp. 9–18. In 1539, at Venice, P. A. Mattioli published his verse account of *Il magno palazzo del cardinale di Trento*, in which all the gods are to be found assembled in *Il Tempio*. Du Bellay developed the Olympus theme for *L'Enterprise du roy daulphin*; see his *Poésies* 2:443–50. Abbé P. Guilbert gives a detailed description of this ceiling in his *Description historique des château, bourg, et forêt de Fontainebleau*, 2 vols (Paris, 1731), 2:14–45.

70 Built for Gouffier, the king's master of the horse. A recent reconstruction of the decorations at Oiron has been issued by E. Rostain, D. Canard, and A. Labrousse, *Le Château de Oiron* (Paris, 1974).

71 M. de Saint-Gelais, *Oeuvres*, 3 vols, ed. P. Blanchemain (Paris, 1873), 1:26–27; this edition incorporates the annotations of the eighteenth-century antiquary Marepas.

72 There has been much discussion about the Tanlay fresco and the Montmorency dish. See *Revue Archéologique*, 1855–56, p. 321; C. H. Oulmont, 'La Fresque de la tour de la ligue au château de Tanlay', *Revue de l'Art Ancien et Moderne* 64 (1933): 183–84; F. Ed. Schneegans, 'A propos d'une note sur une fresque mythologique du XVIe siècle', *Humanisme et Renaissance* 2 (1935): 441–44; and M. G. Christol, 'La Fresque du château de Tanlay', *Bulletin de la Société de l'Histoire du Protestantisme Français* 101 (1951): 231–36.

73 Olivier de Magny, *Oeuvres poétiques* (Paris, 1557), ff. 68–70ᵛ. Bas-reliefs showing Catherine as Juno and Diana as Venus sculptured by Pilon or one of his school for the castle at Anet can be seen at the Musée de Cluny.

74 *Discours du grand et magnifique triumphe faict au mariage de . . . François . . . et . . . Marie d'Estrevart . . .* (Paris, 1558; London, 1818, f. B.); this account is anonymous. Jean Dorat developed the same olympic theme in his *Epithalamium* for the marriage of Henri de Navarre and Marguerite de Valois in 1572, freely imitated by Amadis Jamyn in his *Epitalame* (1572), in *Oeuvres* (Paris, 1575), ff. 22ᵛ–24ᵛ.

75 Claude Chappuys, *Le Discours de la court* (Paris, 1543), sig. E.

76 *Les Oeuvres de Virgile translatées de latin en françois* by Nicolas Cousteau (Paris, 1529), preamble on back of title page.

77 Virgil, *Les Georgiques*, ed. L. Larombière (Paris, 1882–85), 1 : 147; and *Les Georgiques* (Paris, 1519), sig. ã iiijᵛ.

78 Virgil, *Oeuvres*, preamble.

79   car le celeste Pan, Roy et Dieu des Bergers
    A lié noz Pasteurs avec les Estrangers
    D'une perpetuelle et divine concorde.

        (FRANÇOIS HABERT, *Eglogue pastorale* [Paris, 1559])

because celestial Pan, King and Lord of the shepherds, has bound our pastoral friends in a perpetual and divine concord with strangers.

Catherine de' Medici was very keen on decorating the gardens at Fontainebleau; and on the grounds of the palace, she had built a pavilion where she and her ladies could imagine they lived a life of shepherdesses; see L. de Laborde, *Les Comptes des bâtiments du roi, 1528–71*, 2 vols (Paris, 1887–80), 2 : 49–50, 96, 195.

80 See Ménager's excellent discussion of the *Discours* in *Ronsard*, pp. 187–276.

81 The records published by Laborde offer some idea of the works done for the festivals given at Fontainebleau (1563–64) before the court set out on its two-year tour of France (*Les Comptes* 2 : 102); see also the accounts given by Victor E. Graham and W. McAllister Johnson, *The Royal Tour of France by Charles IX and Catherine de' Medici, 1564–66* (Toronto, 1979).

82 Alice Hulubei describes the vigour of the pastoral tradition, *L'Eglogue en France au XVIe siècle, 1515–89* (Paris, 1938). The particular influence of Naugerius on Ronsard has been studied by P. Kuhn, 'Influence néo-latine dans les églogues de Ronsard', *Revue d'Histoire Littéraire de la France* 21 (1914): 311–25.

83 For the elm-vine topos, see P. Demetz, 'The Elm and the Vine: Notes Towards the History of a Marriage Topos', *PMLA* 73 (1958): 521–32. The pledges offered by the shepherds are considered in more detail in chapter 5.

84 Kuhn shows how Naugerius probably gave Ronsard the idea of introducing violence into the pastoral in this way ('Influence néo-latine', pp. 311–12).

85 Ronsard is building on the Roman (and principally Virgilian) development that linked the return of the golden age and Augustus in the earlier pastoral tradition; see Elizabeth Armstrong, *Ronsard and the Age of Gold* (Cambridge, 1968).

86 Throughout the sixteenth century authors claimed that the golden age had been restored; in 1551, for example, Béranger de la Tour d'Albenas wrote (referring to Henri II's recent victories): 'Depuis aussi que la France ha cest heur de l'avoir recouvert, par le moyen de son Cesar Auguste' (Since then, too, France has had the good fortune of recovering it, through the actions of its own Caesar Augustus; *Le Siècle d'or* [Lyons, 1551], p. 5). For the most systematic French account of the golden age, see Guillaume Michel, *Le Siècle doré* (Paris, 1521).

87 See T. G. Rosenmeyer, *The Green Cabinet* (Berkeley, 1962), especially pp. 63–88.

88 For an extended sixteenth-century discussion on generalising and particularising in poetry, see Hathaway, *Age of Criticism*, pp. 129–31.

89 See Filleul, *Les Théâtres de Gaillon* [Rouen, 1566], ed. Françoise Joukovsky (Geneva, 1971).

90 The sentiment was expanded by Michel de l'Hôpital in a letter to Jean Morel dated 1 Dec. 1552: 'Or, qu'y a-t-il de plus glorieux que d'être célébré par les vers d'un poète fameux' (What is more glorious than being celebrated in the verse of a famous poet); the letter was published by P. de Nolhac in the *Revue d'Histoire Littéraire*, 1899, pp. 351–56.

91 Du Bellay, *Deffence*, p. 210. In *Recherches de la France*, bk 7, Pasquier extends the idea to include the poet himself: 'C'est le propre d'un poète de se louer, même qu'il a diversifié cette espérance en tant de sortes, qu'il n'y a placard plus riche de ces oeuvres que cestui-ci' (It's the job of a poet to praise himself, even if he has spread this aspiration in many ways; there's no richer canvas than the works of this particular poet).

92 Henri Weber notes these resemblances in 'Structure des odes chez Ronsard', *Cahiers de l'Association des Etudes Françaises* 21 (1969): 99–118. For Du Bellay's use of these metaphors, see *Deffence*, pp. 198–99.

93 See Hathaway's detailed analysis, *Age of Criticism*, pp. 136–42.

94 E. A. Havelock discusses the Greek poets' concept of the preserving power of poetry in *Prefaces to Plato* (Oxford, 1963), ch. 6 ('Hesiod on Poetry').

95 Isidore Silver, 'Ronsard's Theory of Allegory: The Antimony Between Myth and

Truth', *Kentucky Review Quarterly* 18, no. 4 (1971): 363—407, gives a thorough examination of the ways poetry responded to the wonders of the world. His monumental volumes *The Intellectual Evolution of Ronsard* (St. Louis, 1969, 1973) set forth the background to the ideas we have been examining.

96   The poem has twenty-four sections, and the passage quoted occurs in the antistrophe of section 11; Zeus's granting of the request is placed exactly at the centre of the poem in the twelfth section. R. J. Clements traces the influence of the platonism in Ronsard's poem in 'Ronsard and Ficino on the Four Furies', *Romanic Review* 45 (1954): 161—69. Pontus de Tyard uses an expression similar to Ronsard's describing poetry as consisting of 'le labeur à tirer l'Ame embourbée hors de la fange terrestre' (the work of drawing out the Soul from its earthly mud); *Le Solitaire premier*, ed. Silvio F. Baridon (Geneva, 1950), p. 13.

97   Boccaccio, preface to *Genealogia Deorum*, bk 14 [composed ca. 1366; pub. Venice, 1472], in *Boccaccio on Poetry*, trans. Charles G. Osgood (Princeton, 1930), p. 24.

98   Tyard, *L'Univers*, p. 98. J. Peletier du Mans's earlier explanation is simpler: 'La Strophe était à l'exemple et imitation du droit tour ou mouvement du Ciel étoilé: et l'Antistrophe qui signifie retour ou reversion était à l'imitation du cours retrograde des Planettes' (The strophe matched the example of the right course and movement of the starry sky: and the antistrophe imitated the retrograde motion of the planets signifying as it does return and reversal; *L'Art poétique* [Lyons, 1555], p. 66). Blaise de Vigenère also gives a very precise account in his commentaries on Livy, *Les Décades de Tite Live* (Paris, 1583), col. 1293.

99   Du Bellay, *Deffence*, 'Chante-moy ces odes incongnus encor' de la Muse Françoyse . . .' p. 208.

100   Natale Conti, *Mythologie ou explication des fables* [Venice, 1568] (Paris, 1627), p. 52, cites a generally held view on the benefits and necessity of praise. A good example of what he has in mind is Callimachus's *Hymn to Zeus*. I quote from the eighteenth-century French translation (Paris, 1775, p. 12):

> O Jupiter, tu t'es réservé l'élite des mortels: ce ne sont ni les nochers, ni les guerriers, ni les poètes: tu laisses à des Dieux inférieurs le soin de les protéger; mais ce sont les Rois eux-mêmes, les Rois, qui tiennent sous leur main le laboureur, le guerrier, le matelot, tout enfin; car est-il rien qui n'obéisse à son Roi? Qu'à Vulcain donc soit consacré le forgeron, à Diane le chasseur, à Mars le soldat, à Phoebus le chanteur; à Jupiter appartiennent les Rois. Rien n'est plus saint que les Rois, aussi toi-même en as fait ton partage. Tu leur as confié la garde des villes; mais, du haut des citadelles, tu veilles sur ceux d'entre eux qui dirigent ou détournent les voies de la justice. Tu leur accordes à tous les richesses et l'opulence, mais avec inégalité: témoin mon Roi, qui l'emporte de si loin sur les autres. Il accomplit le soir les projets du matin; le soir les plus vastes, les moindres aussitôt qu'il les forme, tandis que pour remplir les leurs, il faut au reste des Rois une année, souvent plus: et combien de fois encore n'as-tu pas confondu leurs desseins et rompu leur effort.

Oh, Jupiter, you reserve to yourself the elite among mortals: neither seamen, warriors, nor poets, you leave to lesser gods the role of protecting them; but, it's kings, kings themselves, who have charge of labourer, warrior, sailor, everything indeed; because, is there anyone who doesn't obey his king? Let, therefore, the blacksmith be dedicated to Vulcan, the hunter to Diana, the soldier to Mars, the singer to Phoebus; kings belong to Jupiter. Nothing is more saintly than kings; you, too, have taken your part. You have given them the safety of towns; but from the top of citadels you watch over those who direct or divert the ways of justice. You give them riches and opulence, but unevenly; witness my king, who outshines all others. The same evening he completes projects made in the morning; by evening, the largest of them, the smallest as soon as they're conceived; whereas to achieve theirs, other kings require a year, and often more; and, how many times their plans are not realised and all their effort wasted.

101 Sébillet, *Art poétique*, p. 13. These attitudes were of very long standing; for instance, the troubadour poet Peire Vidal wrote: 'Conte de Poitiers, mon bon seigneur vous et moi, nous méritons d'être honorés par tous: vous, par vos actes glorieux, et moi, parceque je les conte si bien' (Count of Poitiers, my good lord, you and I deserve to be honoured by all: you, for your generous deeds, and myself because I tell them so well); cited by Istvan Frank, 'Du rôle des troubadours dans la formation de la poésie lyrique moderne', *Mélanges Roques* (Paris, 1950), p. 71.

102 Ronsard, *Abbrégé de l'art poétique françois* [1565], P 2:996; L 14:4. On the affinities of kings and poets, see also Du Bellay, *Deffence*, p. 241. Earlier, in 1540, Charles de Sainte-Marthe had expressed the advantage of praise: 'Louer aultruy, est une bonne eschange, / Car on a part, louant en la louange,' (Praising others is a good business, because in attributing praise one has a part of it); 'A Madame du Perrault', in *La Poesie françoise* (Lyons, 1540), p. 155.

103 P. de Bourdeille Seigneur de Brantôme, *Oeuvres*, 9 vols, ed. L. Lalanne (Paris 1864–82), 3:280, 288–89. Many writers drew the same parallel; for example, Guillaume Des Autelz, *Remonstrance au peuple françoys* (Paris, 1559), f. 2ᵛ; Du Bellay, *La Louange de la France au Roy Henri IIe*, in *Poésies* 1:139–95; Belleforest, *L'Histoire*, p. 82; and Guy le Fèvre de la Boderie, *Encyclie des secrets de l'eternité* (Paris, 1570), p. 25. On this theme L. Roubichon-Stretz, *La Vision de l'histoire dans l'oeuvre de la Pléiade* (Paris, 1973), should be consulted.

104 Pierre Paschal, *Henrici II galliarum regis elogius* (Paris, 1560), p. 12. It was Henri II who gave permission to J. Androuet Du Cerceau to publish his *Livre des Grotesques*; see Baron Henri de Geymüller, *Les Du Cerceau, leur vie et leur oeuvre d'après de nouvelles recherches* (Paris, 1887), pp. 335–36.

105 This building fervour is well documented by Maurice Roy in his two large volumes *Artistes et monuments de la Renaissance en France* (Paris, 1929); more recent research is presented by Sylvie Béguin (see works cited in n. 69), and in the catalogue *Colloque de Fontainebleau*. The earlier work of P. D. Roussel, *Histoire et description du château d'Anet* (Paris, 1875), is still instructive. See also Spifame, *Dicæarchiae*, edict 4.

106 Castiglione, *Courtier*, pp. 288–89. The book enjoyed extraordinary favour at the French court. Hoby's translation continues: 'as did duke Fredericke in this noble pallace, and now doeth Pope July in the temple of Saint Peter, and the way that goeth from the pallace to his house of pleasure Belvedere, and many other buildings, as also the old auncient Romanes did, whereof so many remnants are to be seene about Rome, Naples, Pozzolo, Baie, Civita Vecchia, Porto, and also out of Italy, and so many other places, which be a great witnesse of the prowesse of those divine courages. So did Alexander the great in like manner . . .'.

107 François de Saint Thomas, *La Vraye Forme de bien et heureusement regir* (Lyons, 1569), pp. 74–75; see also Brantôme, *Oeuvres* 3 : 122, 125, 280:

> Voylà quelle fut la court de ce grand roy, et son regne, qu'on pouvoit accomparer à l'empire de Caesar Auguste, qui fleurit si bien à Rome en toutes grandeurs, magnificences, esbattemens et plaisirs, apres avoir mis fin aux guerres civiles

> Such was the court of this great king and such his reign that one can compare it to that of Caesar Augustus who flourished so well in Rome with all kinds of pleasures, greatness, magnificences, and diversions after he had put an end to the civil wars.

108 Nicolas Hoüel, *L'Histoire de la royne d'Arthemise* [1562; Bibliothèque Nationale, Ms. fr. 306], f. 6ᵛ: 'Je ne parle point de l'architecture, de la poesie, peinture, musique, qu'il sçavoit plus que suffisamment' (Not to speak of architecture, poetry, painting, and music, which he knew more than adequately).

109 Comments of ambassadors Cavalli (1546) and Jean Michel (1561), in P. M. Smith, *The Anti-Courtier Trend in Sixteenth-Century French Literature* (Geneva, 1966), p. 98. Henri II appears to have used any means to enhance the splendour of his court, even to the appropriation of the *Bedford Hours*, into which he had inserted (at f. 15) his own device and that of his wife Catherine.

110 For a similar trend in Italy, see Gérard Labrot, *Le Palais Farnese de Caprarola* (Paris, 1970).

111 Spifame, *Dicæarchiae*, edict 8; Claude Binet, however, in *La Vie de Pierre de Ronsard*, ed. P. Laumonier (Paris, 1909), p. 9, argues that Henri II had much affection for the poet.

112 See Mirot, *L'Hôtel*, p. 71.

113 Jean Martin, 'Brève Exposition de quelques passages du premier livre des odes de Pierre de Ronsard', *Revue d'Histoire Littéraire de la France* 10 (1903): 267–73.

114 It is interesting to follow this view of poetry in Francesco Giorgio, *De harmonia mundi* [1545], translated as *L'Harmonie du monde* (Paris, 1579), where another of David's psalms develops thus:

> Yvres seront de la fecondité
> De ta maison et séjour habité

Et du torrent de delices et gloire
Leur donnera la liqueur doulce à boire.

(p. 266)

Drunk they will be from the abundance of thy house and their sojourn there, from the torrent of glorious delights that will give them sweet cordial to drink.

115 There are obviously many other olympic reflections in sixteenth-century poetry; for the most notable (other than Ronsard's), see Du Bellay, *Louange de la France et du Roy treschrestien Henri II*, in *Poésies* 1:139–45.

116 The preface to the first edition of the odes shows Ronsard's knowledge—see P 2:973; L 1:47. The rhetorical rules were evolved by Quintilian and Cicero; Ronsard's adherence to the thematic structures they suggest is thoroughly explored by Alex Gordon, *Ronsard et la rhétorique* (Geneva, 1970).

117 There are a good many precedents for this panegyric on France. Among them are Bouchet, *Epistres*, bk 2, no. 14, f. xvij; Jean d'Ivry, *Les Triomphes de France* (Paris, 1508), sig. g vij; Nicolas Bourbon, *Nugae* [Paris, 1533], in *Bagatelles*, ed. V. L. Saulnier (Paris, 1945), pp. 114–16; and Du Bellay's adaptation of Annibale Caro's *Venite all'ombra*, in *Louange de la France*, in *Poésies* 1:139–45.

II. Art and Poetry Parallels in Sixteenth · Century France

1 Rensselaer W. Lee, 'Ut pictura poesis: The Humanistic Theory of Painting', *Art Bulletin* 22 (1940): 197–269 (reprint, New York, 1967); E. H. Gombrich, *Symbolic Images: Studies in the Art of the Renaissance* (London, 1972); Jean H. Hagstrum, *The Sister Arts: The Tradition of Literary Pictorialism and English Poetry from Dryden to Gray* (Chicago, 1958); John R. Spencer, 'Ut rhetorica pictura: A Study in Quattrocento Theory of Painting', *Journal of the Warburg and Courtauld Institutes* 20 (1957): 26–44; Mario Praz, *Mnemoysne: The Parallel Between Literature and the Visual Arts* (New York, 1970); and, more recently, Lucy Gent, *Picture and Poetry, 1560–1620* (Leamington Spa, 1981).

2 Typical examples of ways of expressing the connections were: 'La poésie est comme la Pincture' (Poetry is like painting)—Barthelémy Aneau, *L'Imagination poétique* (Lyons, 1552), p. 4; or 'La poésie est une peinture parlante' (Poetry is a speaking picture)—G. de Saluste Du Bartas, *advertissement* to the 1584 edition of *La deuxieme sepmaine*, in *The Works*, 3 vols, ed. U. T. Holmes (Chapel Hill, N.C., 1935–40) 1:220.

3 Hagstrum, *The Sister Arts*, pp. 9–10.

4 On Ronsard and mannerism, see especially M. Raymond, *La Poésie française et le maniérisme* (London, 1971); and Richard Sayce, 'Ronsard and Mannerism', *L'Es-*

prit Créateur 4, no. 4 (1966): 234–47. (An important exception is the work of Terence Cave: see above, Introduction, n. 1.) The most recent biographical works are Jean Adhémar, 'Ronsard et l'Ecole de Fontainebleau', *Bibliothèque d'Humanisme et Renaissance* 2 (1958): 344–48; and D. Cuisiat, 'La Lyre crossée: Un Episode de la vie de Ronsard', *Bibliothèque d'Humanisme et Renaissance* 31 (1969): 467–80.

5   Praz, *Mnemoysne*; Helmut A. Hatzfeld, *Literature Through Art: A New Approach to French Literature* (New York, 1952); F. P. Pickering, *Literature and Art in the Middle Ages* (London, 1970).

6   I refer chiefly to Sylvie Béguin, *L'Ecole de Fontainebleau* (Paris, 1960); 'La Suite d'Arthémise', *L'Oeil* 38 (Feb. 1958): 32–39; 'Le Maître de Flore de l'Ecole de Fontainebleau', *Art de France* 1 (1961): 300–305; 'Remarques sur la chambre du roi', *Colloque de Fontainebleau*, pp. 199–230; and to Henri Zerner, *The School of Fontainebleau: Etchings and Engravings* (New York, 1969); Bruno Thomas, 'Les Armures de parade des Rois de France', *Colloque de Fontainebleau* pp. 57–67; the catalogues produced for the exhibition 'The School of Fontainebleau', in Ottawa in 1972; J. F. Hayward, *The Virtuoso Goldsmiths and the Triumph of Mannerism, 1540–1620* (London, 1976); and Y. Hackenbroch, 'Bijoux de l'Ecole de Fontainebleau', *Colloque de Fontainebleau*, pp. 71–74, and 'New Knowledge on Jewels and Designs After Etienne Delaune', *Connoisseur* 162 (1966): 82–89; I have not yet had an opportunity to see her book on Renaissance jewelry.

7   See Spencer, 'Ut rhetorica pictura'. Alberti began to compose his treatise in 1435. For a close parallel, see Cesare Ripa, who, over a century later, in the preface to his *Iconologie* (Paris, 1644), sig. ẽ i, noted 'quelque sorte de ressemblance entre l'Art du Peintre, et celuy de l'Orateur; puisqu'il arrive souvent, que l'un ne persuade pas moins bien par les yeux que l'autre par les paroles' (some sort of resemblance between the art of the painter and that of the orator; since it frequently happens that the one persuades no less well through the eyes than the other through words).

8   L'Hôpital, *Oeuvres* 2:73.

9   Cited by Gombrich, *Symbolic Images*, p. 144.

10   Blaise de Vigenère, *Images des deux Philostrates grecs* (Paris, 1578), p. 9.

11   Franciscus Junius, *The Painting of the Ancients* (London, 1638), p. 43; and he continues, 'in so much as we doe not love, our joy interrupted, byt we doe rather entertaine it with all possible care and studie'.

12   Dolce began writing *L'Aretino* in 1547 and published it in 1557; here I cite *L'Aretino*, trans. Mark Roskill (New York, 1968), p. 97; Tahureau, *Odes*, 2 vols, ed. P. Blanchemain (Paris, 1869), 1:66–67. There is abundant evidence on the

similarity of ancient and modern views on the natural; see, for example, Pliny's story about 'un tableau de raisins peints si au vif que les oiseaux y estoient trompez' (a painting of grapes so accurately rendered that the birds themselves mistook them), in *L'Histoire du monde*, 2 vols, trans. Antoine du Point (Lyons, 1566), 2:642.

13   Spencer, 'Ut rhetorica pictura', examines in detail these matters.

14   For a detailed discussion of the processes of textual elaboration, consult the work of Cave (cited above, Introduction, n. 1) and the analyses of G. Demerson, *La Mythologie dans l'oeuvre de la Pléiade* (Geneva, 1972).

15   Du Bellay, *Deffence*, pp. 86–87.

16   Halicarnassus, *Jugement on Lysis*, sec. 7, in *Opuscules rhétoriques*, 2 vols, ed. Germaine Aujac (Paris, 1978); also cited by Chamard in his edition of *La Deffence*, p. 86, n. 3. Quintilian, *Institutes*, 2 vols, trans. J. Selby Watson (London, 1909), 2:102; rendered in French as 'à exprimer trait par trait toute l'image des choses comme dans un tableau' (to express line by line the image of things as if in a painting)—*In de institutione oratoria libros XII* [1556] (Paris, 1718), p. 518.

17   For a discussion of Belleau, see pp. 74–76. For Ronsard's views, see P 2:1017; L 16:337.

18   Du Bellay, *Poésies* 1:148. Pindar's poem reads:

> Vous connaissez, je pense, la bravoure d'Ajax qui sur la fin de la nuit, se perça de son glaive meurtrier, et reste un opprobre pour les enfants des Hellènes. . . . Mais Homère l'a rendu fameux parmi les hommes; il a exalté tous ses exploits, la baguette du rhapsode en main, dans ses vers divins, pour les délices de la posterité. Car la voix des beaux poèmes va toujours retentissant; elle est immortelle. Par toute l'étendue de la terre fertile, par les mers rayonne toujours, inextinguable, la gloire des belles actions.
>
> (*Oeuvres*, 4 vols [Paris, 1923] 4:45–46)
>
> You know, I think, of the bravery of Ajax at the end of the night, who pierced his own body with the murderous sword, an opprobrious remains for the children of the Greeks. . . . But, Homer has made him famous among men; he exalted his deeds, the wand of the prophet in his hand, through his divine verse, to the delight of posterity. Since the voice of beautiful poems goes on sounding, it is immortal. Across the range of earth's fertile lands and across the seas shines forever inextinguishable the glory of noble deeds.

A Greek-Latin parallel text of Pindar's poems was issued in Lyons in 1598 under the title *Olympia, Pythia, Nemea, Isthmia*. There is no sixteenth-century French translation of Pindar.

19   P 2:1024; L 16:344.

20 Du Bellay, *Deffence*, p. 314. These sentiments were much expanded by later authors; for example, Daniel de l'Auge, *Deux Dialogues de l'invention poetique* (Paris, 1560) p. 32:

> Il [le poète] scaura non seulement faire exordes, proposes et donner commencement à parlemens, ains encores former raisons et argumens, extenuer, amplifier, mouvoir, reprendre, admonnestrer, jouer, excuser, confermer, confuter, sesiouir, se douloire, et tout ce qui est acquis pour exprimer les conceptions, les mouvemens, et les passions de l'esprit, et les qualitez convenantes à leurs choses et à leurs effects.

> He [the poet] should know not only how to make beginnings, propositions, and the start of speeches but also how to formulate reasons and arguments, attenuate, amplify, move, revise, admonish, play, excuse, confirm, argue, rejoice, lament, and all that is needed to express notions, movements, and passions of the mind, and the qualities appropriate to things and to their effects.

21 Quoted by Junius, *Painting of the Ancients*, p. 148, who might have been quoting directly from Sallust's *De bello Jugurtha* or from Dolce, *L'Aretino*, p. 113: 'Again, Sallust records that Quintus Fabius and Publius Scipio used to say that, when they looked at their ancestral images, they felt themselves on fire to show their worth'.

22 See, for example, Varchi, *Due Lezzioni* (Florence, 1549), in which are published various letters concerned with the comparative excellence of the arts; some of these are reprinted in Elizabeth G. Holt, *A Documentary History of Art*, 2 vols (New York, 1958), 2:15.

23 For an example of such concerns, consider P. de Sapet, *Les Enthousiasmes* (Paris, 1556), sig. ã viij: 'Nous avons depuis quelque temps la Poësie pareille ou plus pleine que celle des anciens en quelques endroits en nostre langue' (Recently, we have produced poetry similar to, or even with more substance than that of the ancients, in some parts of our language).

24 Anthony Blunt offers a fairly full discussion of these matters in *Artistic Theory in Italy, 1450–1600* (Oxford, 1962).

25 Preface to the reader, in the 1550 edition of the *Odes*. We know, furthermore, that Ronsard marked in his books those poems that Du Bellay had imitated.

26 P 2:973, 996; L 14:4.

27 Sapet, *Enthousiasmes*, sigs Dij and Eiv. Such conviction surfaced in the writings of even mediocre poets—see J. Bastier de la Peruse, *Les Oeuvres* (Paris, 1573), f. 57ᵛ.

> Plus qu'en Tableau ou en Cuivre
> L'Admiré peut faire vivre
> Ta soeur par ses beaux épcris.

More than in a painting or in bronze, the admired one can make your sister live on with his beautiful writings.

There is an amusing assumption of the superiority of the poet in the royal entry into Tours in 1565, in this comment on the triumphal arch at La Riche:

Il y avoit un arc lequel estoit avec plusieurs peintures exquises, mais comme tout homme de bon scavoir s'estimera heureux de louer les lettres mieulx que ne pouroit faire un ignorant peintre sa peinture, comme celuy lequel estant appellé pour tirer des tableaux demandoit s'il y falloit point de cypres à cause qu'il ne savoit que ceste peinture et chanson. Ainsi fut enrichy le lieu de ceste poësie tellement que d'un costé on lisoit ces vers,

> Je ne suis point ceste parque qui fille
> Sur mon fuseau le destin des humains,
> Mais bien la soye, honneur de ceste ville.

(*The Royal Tour of France by Charles IX and Catherine de' Medici, 1564–66,* ed. Victor E. Graham and W. McAllister Johnson [Toronto, 1979], p. 382).

There was an arch on which there were several exquisite paintings, but as every well-informed man would consider himself happy in being able to praise letters better than an ignorant painter can praise his painting, as he, when asked to draw some painting, asked whether a pine tree was needed since he only knew how to paint that with its motto. And so, the place of the poem was enriched with these lines, which could be read on the one side: I'm not that fate that spins on my shuttle the destiny of human beings, but silk, the only honour of this town.

28 Philibert de l'Orme, *Le Premier Livre d'architecture* (Paris, 1567), f. 1ᵛ. Consider the following passage from Louis Le Caron, *Les Dialogues* (Paris, 1566), f. 137ᵛ:

Pourtant le poëte inspiré des Muses, et haussant le vol de son meilleur esprit a congneu l'ordre, la convenance et l'harmonie de l'Univers, les mouvements, les accords et les dispositions non seulement des cieux ou globes, ainsi aussi des intelligences plus hautes et surnaturelles. Davantage cette sainte fureur l'a tant fait divin, qu'il a peu comprendre en une certaine raison de nombres et de mesures les proportions et consonances, aussi bien de tout l'Univers que de ses parties entre elles.

However, the poet inspired by the Muses, and lifting the flight of his best thought has known the order, rightness, and harmony of the universe; the movements, harmonies, and dispositions not only of the heavens or globes but also of the highest and supernatural intelligences. Moreover, that saintly inspiration has made him so divine that he has been able to comprehend, within a certain range of numbers and measures, the proportions and agreements of the whole universe as well as between all its parts.

29 Martin, *Architecture ou l'art de bien bastir* (Paris, 1547), sig. ã i; the work is dedicated to Henri II.

30 On this influence, see Karl Lehmann-Hartleben, 'The *Imagines* of the Elder Philostratus', *Art Bulletin* 23 (1941): 16–44.

31 For the literary sources used by Titian, see Edwin Panofsky, *Problems in Titian, Mostly Iconographic* (London, 1969); for their aesthetic considerations, consult David Rosand, 'Ut Pictor Poeta: Meaning in Titian's Poesie', *New Literary History* 3 (1971–72): 527–46.

32 Dolce writes to Alessandro Contarini about Titian's work as though each piece were a poem; see the opening sentence of his description of a painting, 'This poem on the subject of Adonis was carried out a short while back and sent by the divine Titian to the King of England . . .' (*L'Aretino*, p. 214).

33 For a general discussion of the state of criticism in the sixteenth century, see B. Hathaway, *The Age of Criticism: The Late Renaissance in Italy* (Ithaca, N.Y., 1962). On Giovio's views, see T. C. Price Zimmerman, 'P. Giovio and the Evolution of Renaissance Art Criticism', in *Cultural Aspects of the Italian Renaissance in Honor of P. O. Kristeller*, ed. Cecil Clough (Manchester, 1976), pp. 406–24; Sebastiano Serlio, *Tutte l'opere e d'architettura et prospetiva* (Venice, 1619), pp. 50, 66, 105, 107, 112, and passim; Dolce, *L'Aretino*, and Giorgio Vasari, *Vite de piu eccellenti pittori, scultori, et architetti*, 16 vols (Milan, 1810).

34 The judgement on Marot occurs in Des Autelz's *Réplique*, cited by Margaret Young, *Guillaume Des Autelz* (Geneva, 1961), p. 83; Vasari's comment on Rosso appears in *Vite* 9 : 260.

35 Dolce, *L'Aretino*, p. 90.

36 On Dolce and Castiglione, see Roskill's analysis in his edition of *L'Aretino*, pp. 21 ff. Citations from Du Bellay, *Oeuvres*, 2 : 167.

37 The relationships between the criteria of the court and those of poetry in Elizabethan England have been recently examined by Daniel Javitch in *Poetry and Courtliness in Renaissance England* (Princeton, 1978).

38 Vigenère, *Images*, pp. 12–13. This view is also stated by Du Bellay, *Deffence*, pp. 152–53, 266.

39 Serlio, *Tutte l'opere*, p. 92.

40 Svetlana Leontief Alpers discusses Vasari's views in 'Ekphrasis and Aesthetic Attitudes in Vasari's *Lives*', *Journal of the Warburg and Courtauld Institutes* 23 (1960): 190–215; Michael Baxandall, *Giotto and the Orators* (Oxford, 1971), should be consulted for Alberti and earlier writers.

41 P 2 : 973; L 1 : 47.

42 Terence Cave's work on the influence of Erasmus precludes the need to labour this point; see 'Copia and Cornucopia' and *The Cornucopian Text*.

43 Peletier du Mans, *L'Art poëtique* (Lyons, 1555), p. 80. Peletier is here expanding on two passages from Horace, who gave equal power of invention to painter and poet.

44 The same idea is developed by François Habert, who thus praises Des Essarts's rendering of the Amadis romances:

> Et comme un paintre enrichit sa paincture
> D'or, et d'azur, aussi par tes beaulx dicts
> Tu fais trouver à toute creature
> Cent foys plus beau le livre d'Amadis.
>
> (Cited by E. Bourciez, *Les moeurs*, p. 6)

> And, just as a painter enriches his work with gold and azure, also through your beautiful songs you make every being find the book of Amadis a hundred times more satisfying.

The same criterion is in force in Bertrand's comments on Desportes, *Les p:emières oeuvres* (Annecy, 1576), sig.**2: 'la plaisante facilité, la delectable varieté, la faconde abondance' (pleasing facility, delightful variety, rich abundance).

45 P 2:1021; L 16:340. Jean Plattard, 'Les Arts et les artistes de la Renaissance française jugés par les écrivains du temps', *Revue d'Histoire Littéraire de la France* 21 (1914):481–502, shows how this technical language infiltrated the work of other poets.

46 Dolce, *L'Aretino*, p. 129; cf. Alberti, *Della Pittura* [1435], trans. Cecil Grayson (London, 1972), p. 97, paragraph 54.

47 *L'Aretino*, p. 169; see also Lee's analysis of the impact of the *Gerusalemme Liberata* on early seventeenth-century painters, 'Ut pictura poesis', pp. 242ff.

48 The detailed programme is analysed by Gérard Labrot, *Le Palais Farnese de Caprarola* (Paris, 1970); Egon Verheyen offers another elaborate example in *The Palazzo del Te in Mantua* (Baltimore, 1977), where he examines the use made of the suggestions of Equicola; and Erika Langmuir, 'Niccolo dell'Abbate's *Aeneid* Frescoes for the *Gabinetto* of the Castle at Scandiano, near Modena', *Journal of the Warburg and Courtauld Institutes* 39 (1976):151–60, also discusses other cycles at Modena (1546) and Bologna (1548 and 1550).

49 François Eraud, "Peintures murales de la deuxième moitié du XVIe siècle découvertes au château de Villeneuve-Lembron (Puy-de-Dôme)', in *Colloque de Fontainebleau*, pp. 185-197; and Rostain, Canard, and Labrousse, *Le château d'Oiron*; and Petrarch's triumphs were used at the château de Lude. The intermediary for many of these sixteenth-century provincial châteaux appears to have been the engravings of Bernard Salomon.

50 According to Denise Gluck, "Les Entrées provinciales de Henri II', *L'Information d'Histoire de l'Art* 10 (1965):215–19.

51   An authoritative edition of the 1548 entry into Lyons is given by George Guigue, *La Magnificence de la superbe et triumphante entrée de la noble et antique cité de Lyon* (Lyons, 1928). V. L. Saulnier devotes a chapter of *Maurice Scève*, 2 vols (Paris, 1948), to an analysis of the entry; see 1 : 328–70.

52   Etienne Jodelle, *Oeuvres complètes*, 2 vols, ed. E. Balmas (Paris, 1965), 1 : 176. Jodelle's view of himself was perhaps not so exaggerated. Charles de la Mothe, for instance, admired his abilities:

> Il estoit grand architecte, docte en la peinture, et sculpture, et de tout il discouroit avec tel jugement, comme s'il eust esté accompli de toutes les cognoissances.
>
> > (Cited by Victor E. Graham and W. McAllister Johnson, eds,
> > *Le Recueil des inscriptions* [Paris, 1558] [Toronto, 1972], p. 6)

> He was a good architect, knowledgeable about painting and sculpture, and he talked about everything with such judgement as if he were accomplished in every kind of knowledge.

53   Jodelle also remarks (*Recueil*, p. 75), 'Je me fei quasi de tous mestiers, et assés heureusement' (I can do almost all trades, and quite pleasingly), and Pasquier commented, 'Estienne Jodelle qui pensoit rien ne luy estre impossible' (Estienne Jodelle who thought that nothing was impossible for him); *Recherches de la France*, 2 vols (Paris, 1723), 1 : 746.

54   Baptiste Pellerin engraved the *Figures et pourtraits des sept ages de l'homme*, a work commissioned by Nicolas le Camus and published in 1579, to which Ronsard contributed verses.

55   Jodelle, *Recueil*, pp. 74, 101.

56   There are two modern editions of this entry: the first by Frances A. Yates, *L'Entrée de Charles IX à Paris, 1571* (Amsterdam, 1974), the second by Graham and McAllister Johnson (Toronto, 1974). The latter includes all the detailed accounts and contracts made between the city and the artists; I cite from p. 297, where the minute instructions concerning this statue continue for another dozen lines.

57   Sig. D ij (Yates, *L'Entrée*, p. 14):

> Au costé d'icelle estoient deux petits pilliers ou termes: sur l'un desquelz s'eslevoit un sceptre, & à costé un oeil & une aureille: au pied duquel terme estoit une grue, un lievre, & un Daulphin, pour faire entendre que ceste Roine tresvertueuse a soustenu & supporté la France renversee & desreglee au plus fort de son mal: l'oeil significant comme aussi fait la Grue, le Lievre, et le Daulphin la vigilance & promptitude dont elle a usé en si grandes affaires: & l'aureille la facile audience qu'elle a presté sans iamais se facher d'importunité.

> On either side of this statue were two small pillars or *thermae*: on which was erected a sceptre, and to the side an eye and an ear; at the foot of the said pillar were a crane, a hare, and a dolphin, to let it be understood that this very virtuous queen has up-

held and supports a disordered France, full of upheaval at the worst of her ills; the eye (as also the crane, hare, and dolphin) signified the vigilance and the speed she employed in important affairs; the ear stood for the ready audience she offered without ever getting angry at being importuned.

58   Cited in *L'Entrée*, Graham and McAllister Johnson, pp. 276–77.

59   François Rose, *Hymne sur l'entrée du très excellent et très-chrestien, roy de France en sa fameuse ville de Paris* (Paris, 1571), sigs Biij–Biijᵛ.

60   *L'Entrée*, Graham and McAllister Johnson, p. 281.

61   For a discussion of the increasing imperial preoccupations of the French royal house, see Yates, *Astraea*.

62   It is noteworthy that twenty-four lines from Ronsard's epic poem and many of his other poems were printed by Bouquet in his official account.

63   The frieze and poem are discussed at some length by Yates in her introduction to *L'Entrée*.

64   Emblem books flooded the book market in the sixteenth and seventeenth centuries. Some idea of the number of such works can be gained by consulting Mario Praz, *Studies in Sixteenth- and Seventeenth-Century Imagery*, 2 vols (London, 1939, 1947).

65   *L'Amour de Cupido et de Psiché*, of which there were many versions in the sixteenth century; I cite from a modern facsimile edition, introd. Ruth Calder, (The Hague, 1970). See also L. Magne, *L'Oeuvre des peintres verriers français* (Paris, 1885), pp. 131–63; and Françoise Perrot, 'Les Vitraux du château d'Ecouen', *Colloque de Fontainebleau*, pp. 175–84.

66   See Edith A. Standen, 'The Tapestries of Diane de Poitiers', *Colloque de Fontainebleau*, pp. 87–98; and Françoise Bardon, *Diane de Poitiers et le mythe de Diane* (Paris, 1963).

67   Tyard, *Douze Fables de fleuves ou fontaines* (Paris, 1586), f. 15ᵛ.

68   Ibid., f. 15ᵛ. The sonnet reads as follows:

> Narcisse ayme sa soeur, sa chere seur iumelle
> Sa seur aussi pour luy brusle d'ardeur extreme
> L'un en l'autre se sent estre un second soymesme:
> Ce qu'elle veut pour luy, il veut aussi pour elle,
> De semblable beauté est ceste couple belle,
> Et semblable est le feu qui fait que l'un l'autre ayme,
> Mais la seur est premiere à qui la Parque blesme

Ferme les ieunes yeuz d'une nuit eternelle.
Narcisse en l'eau se void, y pensant voir sa seur:
Ce penser le repaist d'une vaine douceur,
Qui coulle en son coeur, luy amoindrit sa peine.
De luy son nom retient l'amoureuse fonteine,
Dans laquelle reçoit, quiconque aymant s'y mire,
Quelle douce allegeance à l'amoureux martire.

Narcissus loves his sister, his dear twin sister; she also burns with extreme ardour for him, each one feeling like another self; what she wants for him, he also wants for her; of equal beauty is this lovely couple, and equal is the fire that makes each one love; but the sister is the first for whom pale Fate closes young eyes in an eternal night. Narcissus sees himself in the water, thinking that he sees his sister: this thought feeds him with vain sweetness that enters his heart and diminishes his pain. From him, the loving fountain keeps the name and whoever gazes into its water receives from it sweet release from the martyrdom of love.

69 Hoüel, *Histoire de la Royne d'Arthemise* [1562] (Ms. fr. 306, Bibliothèque Nationale), f. 8; and he continues (f. 9), 'De laquelle [histoire] suivant les desseins mis par bon ordre, vous pourrez faire voir de riches tapisseries pour l'ornement de vos maisons des Tuileries' (From that [story], following the drawings in the right order, you can have made rich tapestries to decorate your Tuilleries palace).

70 Such scenes include, for example, the *Colossus at Rhodes*; see Sylvie Béguin's careful reconstruction, 'La Suite d'Arthémise', *L'Oeil*, 38 (Feb. 1958): 32–39.

71 Jacques Gohorry, *Livre de la conqueste de la toison d'or* (Paris, 1563).

72 The phenomenon is by no means confined to the pastoral form, however. Giovanni Rucellai uses Leonardo's *Leda* as a means of introducing Oreste to his sister in *Oreste* (act 4, lines 394–431). This use of ecphrasis in drama is discussed by John A. Bertolini, 'Leonardo's *Leda* in G. Rucellai's *Oreste*', *Renaissance Drama*, n.s. 7 (1976): 151–76.

73 Citation from Sannazaro, *Arcadia* [1504], trans. Ralph Nash (Detroit, 1966), pp. 29–30. The temple's entrance is depicted on pp. 42–44.

74 Rémy Belleau, *Oeuvres poétiques*, 2 vols, ed. Ch. Marty-Laveaux (Paris, 1878), 1:220; Jacques Yver, seigneur de Plaisance, was clearly inspired by Belleau in his description of the castle, its contents, and the activities of its inhabitants in *Le Printemps* (Paris, 1572).

75 Belleau, *Oeuvres* 1:182.

76 Doris Delacourcelle, *Le Sentiment de l'art dans 'La Bergerie' de Rémy Belleau* (Oxford, 1945) discusses the tapestries, pp. 40–51.

77 Belleau, *Oeuvres* 1:196.

78 Michel Jeanneret, 'Les Oeuvres d'art dans *La Bergerie* de Belleau', *Revue d'Histoire Littéraire de la France* 70 (1970): 1–13, was the first to notice the blurring effects of the poem and to point to the elevating power of the paintings described.

79 P 1:105; L 6:152–60.

80 *Discours à P. L'Escot, seigneur de Clany*, P 2:422–25; L 10:307. Marianna Jenkins shows the closeness of the French poet's connections with painters, and uses Ronsard's verse as a way of exploring sculptured imagery; see 'The Henri II Wing of the Louvre', *Journal of Medieval and Renaissance Studies* 7, pt 2 (1977): 289–307.

81 Isidore Silver reprints the Latin poem of Robert de la Haye (dated 1555) in *Ronsard and the Hellenic Renaissance in France* (Washington, D.C., 1961), p. 417; for arguments contesting any Ronsardian influence see W. McAllister Johnson, 'Ronsard et la renommée du Louvre', *Bibliothèque d'Humanisme et Renaissance* 30 (1968): 7–17.

82 See *A Jean Martin*, ode 15, P 1:425–27; L 1:131–35; and *Hymne de Henri II*, P 2:147; L 8:5–46.

83 Claude Binet, *La Vie de Pierre de Ronsard*, p. 45.

84 I discuss this passage at the beginning of chapter 5; L 18:470–79.

85 Giles Corrozet appealed to poets and artists alike to produce works adequate to express the profound sorrow felt on the occasion of the dauphin's death, *Triste Elegie ou déploration lamentant . . . Françoys de Valloys* (Paris, 1536), sigs Cii^v–Ciii.

86 Guillaume Du Choul, *Des bains et antiques excercitations grecques et romaines*, bound in with *Discours de la religion des Romains* (Lyons, 1556), p. 2, dedication to the king. For Brantôme's comments, see *Oeuvres* 3:125.

87 Details of Ronsard's travels with the court are provided by D. Cuisiat, 'La Lyre crossée'.

88 P 1:457–58; L 1:183–88; for the *Epistre à Charles* and sonnet to Aubert, mentioned earlier, see P 2:860; L 8:328–50 and 7:310–11.

89 Destruction of natural beauty is a Renaissance topos. The tones of objection are just as fervent in Cornelius Agrippa's reflection on contemporary building madness:

> Les rochers ont esté tranchés, les vallees comblées, les monts applanis, les grands escueils persés, donner passage à la mer au travers des montagnes, la terre fouillée

iusques au centre, les fleuves détornés, les mers assemblées l'une à l'autre, . . . par vaine ostentation.

(*Declamation sur l'incertitude, vanité et abus des sciences* [n.p., 1582], p. 114)

Rocks have been cut up, valleys filled in, mountains flattened, and great basins cut through to allow the sea to penetrate the mountains, the earth excavated right to its centre, rivers rerouted, seas joined one with the other . . . simply for vain show.

90 On Fantuzzi's and others' engravings see Henri Zerner, *The School of Fontainebleau*, and works cited in n. 6 above. Among paintings on these themes, one of Charles V's fleet and camp at Tunis is displayed at the Courtauld Institute in London; it is attributed to the school of Niccolo dell'Abbate. Hayward also points to at least two examples of gilt and enamelled cups and basins, the entire surfaces of which have been embossed and chased in low relief with scenes illustrating the Tunis campaign of Charles V; see *Virtuoso Goldsmiths*, plates 288, 288a, 596, 597.

91 *L'Ecole de Fontainebleau: Grand Palais, Paris, 1972–73* (Paris, 1972), no. 104. A further close parallel can be seen in the third eclogue (1559), in which Bellot's basket with its story of Mercury, Io, and Argus, seems an accurate representation of Ovid's myth engraved in the workshops of Jean de Tournes at Lyons.

92 Michel Dassonville, *Ronsard: Prince des poètes ou poète des princes, 1550–56* (Geneva, 1976), p. 69. It is certainly rare to find in Ronsard's love sonnets the explicit parallels developed by Olivier de Magny, for example, in *Voeu du portraict de sa Marguerite, faict apres le naturel, par le Comte d'Alsinois, in Gaiettez* (Paris, 1557), sig. Aiij.

93 Du Bellay had advocated the explicit use of examples from painting in *Deffence*, pp. 303–4; and Ronsard returned several times in his theoretical writings to painting parallels: in the *Art poétique*, he advises the poet to emulate Homer 'sur lequel tu tireras au vif les plus parfaicts lineamens de ton tableau' (from whose example you will draw from life the most perfect elements of your painting; P 2:1000; L 14:15). For suitable comparisons, Homer is again cited, in *Avertissement* (1587), as the example to follow, 'comme Homere, pescheurs, architectes, massons' (like Homer, with fishermen, architects, and masons; P 2:1023; L 16:347). And in a passage that insists on the need to be true to nature, the term *peinture* is the first Ronsard uses (P 2:1025; L 16:346–47).

94 Quotations in this paragraph from P 1:374, 521; L 1:79 and *Olympiques*, poem 3, 'Pour Théron d'Agrigente, vainqueur à la course des chars à l'occasion des Théoxénies', strophe 1.

95 The uplifting power of poetry is argued at length by Ronsard in the preface to the *Livre des meslanges au Roy Charles IX*, P 2:978–79.

96 P 1:556; L 2:148.

97 The lasting power of verse is a commonplace. For other examples, see Du Bellay, *Deffence*, 242–43, and Brantôme, *Oeuvres* 5:236, where he cites Ronsard:

Car, comme luy [Charles IX] dist Monsieur de Ronsard, les beaux pallais et bastimens sont subjectz à ruyne et ne durent que quelque Temps, voire les généreux actes et beaux faictz, mais les escritz durent eternellement.

Because as he [Charles IX] said to Ronsard, beautiful palaces and edifices are subject to ruin and only last a certain time, even so good deeds and wonderful feats, but writings last forever.

98 The following sonnet is a good example of excessive attention to contemporary artistic preoccupations.

J'avois l'esprit tout morne et tout pesant,
Quand je receu du lieu qui me tourmente
La pomme d'or comme moy jaunissante
Du mesme mal qui nous est si plaisant.

Les pomes sont de l'Amour le present:
Tu le scays bien, ô guerriere Atalante,
Et Cydipé qui encor se lamente
D'elle et d'Aconce et d'Amour si nuisant

Les pomes sont de l'amour le vray signe:
Heureux celuy qui de tel bien est digne,
Bien qui fait vivre heureusement les homes.

Venus a plein de pomes tout le sein
Ses deux enfans en ont pleine la main,
Et bref l'Amour n'est qu'un beau jeu de pomes.

(G, 315–16)

My mind was desolate and heavy when, from that place which continues to torment me, I received the golden apple, yellowing like myself from the same source of illness that charms us. Apples are the gift of Love; you know that well, oh warlike Atalanta, and Cydippe who still laments Acontius, the apple and the wounds of Love. Apples are the true sign of Love. Happy is he who is worthy of such a good, one which makes men live in contentment. The bosom of Venus is full of apples; her two children's hands are laden with them; in short, Love is no more than a game of apples.

The heavy, overreferential nature of the poem is set into particular relief when it is considered beside the anonymous engraving preserved in the Print Room of the Bibliothèque Nationale and reproduced by Henri Weber in his edition of the *Amours*, opposite p. 316. If we compare these two interpretations of the theme—the poem and the engraving—we see clearly that the artist has outpaced the poet. His scene is lively and exuberant, and it is infinitely varied, with each little cupid-body adopting a different pose. The poem falls flat with its insistent messages, affirmed and not suggested, like a lesson recited through duty rather than feeling.

99 Printed in full in Ronsard, *Oeuvres*, 2 vols (Paris, 1623), 1:1686; and in *Oeuvres complètes*, 7 vols, ed. Hugues Vaganay (Paris, 1924), 7:24–65.

III. Iconic Forms

1 Mazzoni, quoted by Hathaway, *Age of Criticism*, p. 122.

2 For an account of the vigorous preoccupation with time in the Renaissance, see Ricardo J. Quinones, *The Renaissance Discovery of Time* (Cambridge, Mass., 1972).

3 The bringing together of such decoration and an educative purpose was not uncommon in classical writing. A particularly striking and extended example can be found in Catullus; in poem 64 he says that the coverlet on the marriage bed of Peleus and Thetis 'portrays the virtues of heroes with wonderous art'.

4 Claudianus, *De raptu Proserpinae* (*Oeuvres complètes*, 2 vols [Paris, 1798]); the relevant descriptions begin at vol. 1, line 246, and vol. 2, line 36. In the Renaissance, readers avidly welcomed numerous editions of Claudian. The British Library has ten editions of Claudian's works published before the middle of the sixteenth century, and nine editions of *De raptu*; many are accompanied by detailed commentaries. Ronsard knew the work well, admired it, and in the *avertissement* of 1587 he remarks, 'Claudien est poëte en quelques endroits, comme au Ravissement de Proserpine' (In some places, Claudian is a good poet, as in the *Rape of Proserpine*; P 2:1020; L 16:339).

5 Ovid, *Ovide moralisé* (C. Legonais) [ca. 1328], ed. De Boer (Amsterdam, 1915) 5 vols, 2:5:1079—1555.

6 Vigenère, *Images*, p. 513; of the statue in Athens, he reports: 'il y avoit une statue de la Deesse de la main du très excellent ouvrier Phidias, toute d'or et d'ivoire, de la haulteur de 26 coudees, qui reviennent à 39 pieds' (there was a statue of the Goddess carved by the hand of Phidias, all in gold and ivory, about twenty-six measures high, that is, about thirty-nine feet).

7 Boccaccio, *Genealogia Deorum*, proem to bk 14, in *Boccaccio on Poetry*, p. 15. His words are: 'We are taught by the wise that from the past we may infer the future'.

8 See Alan Cameron's discussion in *Claudian: Poetry and Propaganda at the Court of Honorius* (Oxford, 1970), especially, pp. 269—71.

9 Ariosto reapplies these techniques of description and prophecy in *Orlando Furioso*; see canto 33, in which French military interventions in Italy are foretold in murals, and canto 46, in which Ercole d'Este's life and virtues are stitched into gorgeous pavilions.

10 P 1:546—53, 2:833—39, 2:125—42; L 2:133—48, 8:255—93, 8:72—84.

11 Neptune's power was also depicted on one of the mirrors in Belleau's *Bergerie*; Delacourcelle, *Sentiment de l'art*, p. 45. Among the enamelled works, H. Ton-

nochy and H. Read describe a large panel: '15 plaques of painted enamel subjects from the *Aeneid*, copied from Marcantonio's engraving after Raphael and known as the "Quos ego". The central panel represents Neptune in his chariot stilling the winds, painted in grisaille, with flesh tints and hue, with gilding'; *The Waddeston Bequest* (London, 1927), no. 21. See also Philippe Verdier, *The Walters Art Gallery: Catalogue of the Painted Enamels of the Renaissance* (Baltimore, 1967), nos 49 and 152. Further examples are discussed by M. Marcheix, 'Les Emaux à l'exposition de l'Ecole de Fontainebleau', *Bulletin de la Société Archéologique et Historique du Limousin* 100 (1973): 163–92. Others appear in the inventories drawn up on Germain Pilon's death, see Ern. Coyecque, 'Au domicile mortuaire de Germain Pilon, 10 fév. au 13 mars 1590', *Humanisme et Renaissance* 7 (1940): 45–101. The basin by Androuet Du Cerceau is shown by Hayward, *Virtuoso Goldsmiths*, plate 376.

12 Although, as we noted, there are distinct verbal reminiscences of Virgil in the poem, and although the principal idea comes from Ovid, neither of the two classical poets embroidered a cloak for Neptune. Ovid's version, of course, was kept alive throughout the medieval and Renaissance periods by editions, interpretations, and commentaries; and, especially in the sixteenth century, by the beautiful engraved editions of the *Metamorphoses*, such as that from Jean de Tournes (1557); sig. kk, for 'Céphale et Aurore'.

13 I. Besly, *Les Hymnes de Ronsard* (Paris, 1604), p. 30.

14 See, for example, F. de Colonna, *Hypnerotomachia Poliphili* (first edition 1499), Albert Marie Schmidt's facsimile version (Paris, 1963) of Jean Martin's French translation (1546), pp. 57–58; and *C'est l'ordre qui a esté tenu à la nouvelle et joyeuse entrée . . . Henri II* (Paris, 1549), sigs di^v–dii^v, where the scenes are displayed. The Argonauts were also the principal actors in Jodelle's celebrations in 1555, see *Recueil des inscriptions*; C. Valerius Flaccus mentions their royal origin and describes the mountains, river Eurota, and the father swan (*Argonautica* 1:429–30).

15 Brantôme waxed eloquent on the subject of the good memory and intelligence of this prince, *Oeuvres* 3:256–57.

16 A very detailed account, which recalls the energy and phenomenal activity of the duke of Guise, is offered by Bertrand de Salignac de la Mothe Fénelon, *Le Siege de Mets* (Paris, 1553). For a modern assessment see G. Zeller, *Le siège de Metz* (Nancy, 1943), which leans very heavily on Fénelon's account. For critical comment on the aesthetic qualities of Ronsard's *Harangue*, see Philip J. Ford, 'George Buchanan's Court Poetry and the Pléiade', *French Studies* 34 (1980): 137–52, especially p. 146.

17 Michelangelo had sculptured such a group, and it was copied many times by La Fréry and others; and L. Mauro records a beautiful example in the Belvedere, *Le antichita*, p. 118. That Alberti used Hercules and Antaeus as an example might also explain its popularity as a theme. For a general account of the popularity of

Hercules at this time, see M.-R. Jung, *Hercule dans la littérature française du XVIe siècle* (Geneva, 1966).

18 Junius, *Painting of the Ancients*, p. 152.

19 A. de Baïf, *Euvres en rime*, 3 vols (Paris, 1573), 2:38–40; see also, C. de Taillemont, *Discours des champs faez* (Paris, 1553), p. 3:

> Une damoiselle non moins pourveue de singuliere beauté, que de grande et hautaine maiesté, armée d'un riche et somptueux corps de cuirace, avec le bouclier en escharpe, au milieu duquel estoit la teste de Meduse aux cheveux serpentins attachée.

> A damsel no less gifted with singular beauty than with noble and impressive majesty, armed with a rich and sumptuous breastplate, with a shield held obliquely, to the middle of which was attached Medusa's head with her serpent locks.

20 Guilio Romano influenced art at Fontainebleau principally through his pupil Primaticcio; his 'sala dei giganti' in the Palazzo del Te had astonished everyone.

21 Edict cited by Spifame, *Dicæarchiae Henrici*, p. 68. On decorations at Fontainebleau, see Sylvie Béguin, 'Remarques sur la chambre du roi', *Colloque de Fontainebleau*, pp. 199–230. The transformations began to be effected by dell'Abbate in 1557; see Laborde's accounts, *Comptes des bâtiments* 2:195.

22 On Henri's armour, see James C. Mann, 'Henri II's Armour', *Connoisseur* 92 (1933): 414–17; and 'A Parade Armour of Henri II, King of France', *Country Life* 83 (1938): 603–5; and Charles Buttin, 'L'Armure de Henri II, Dauphin', *Aréthuse*, 1929, no. 25. Roy, *Artistes et monuments* 1:258–89, describes the work after Henri's death. On the display at Oiron, see Rostain, Canard, and Labrousse, *Le Château d'Oiron*: 'Icy sont les figures retraites au naturel des plus renommés chevaux du Roy Henry, 2e du nom, qui estoient en son Escuyerie à son advenement à la couronne' (Here [above the entrance to the ground-floor hall] the figures are drawn from nature, from the most famous of King Henri's horses, those that were in his stables at the time he came to the throne; p. 18).

23 According to the compendious Lomazzo, quoted by Jenkins, in *State Portrait*, p. 40.

24 Pierre Paschal, *Henrici II galliarum*, figure opposite p. 7. For a photograph of the suit, see A. Blum, *La Miniature française au XVe et au XVIe siècles* (Brussels, 1930), plate 7. C. Maumené and L. d'Harcourt, *Iconographie des rois de France* (Paris, 1928) no. 174, p. 145; no. 201, p. 154, shows an engraved armour bust of Henri II, from the workshop of Germain Pilon.

25 The French court was so proud of the tapestries that they were brought out to adorn every important festive occasion; they even travelled to Bayonne for the meeting between Spain and France in 1565. On the enamelled plaques and caskets, see Verdier, *The Walters Art Gallery*, nos 66, 67, 110, 111.

26 See Y. Hackenbroch, 'New Knowledge on Jewels'.

27 Hayward's research is our principal source; see *Virtuoso Goldsmiths*, pp. 322–23.

28 Delaune's design for the vizier is preserved at the Tower of London. For detailed discussion of Delaune's armour designs, see Bruno Thomas 'Die München Harnish vorzeichnungen des Etienne Delaune und die Emblem und die Schlangen Garnitur Henriche II von Frankreich', *Jahrbuch der Kunsthistorischen Sammlungen in Wein*, 56 (1960): 7–62; and 'Les Armures de parade des rois de France', *Colloque de Fontainebleau*, pp. 57–67.

29 In *Remonstrance d'un bon catholique françoys aux trois estats* (Blois, 1576), pp. 72–74, the scenes on Achilles' shield, forged by Vulcan, are used as exhortations for peace. Other shields belonging to Henri II show similar crowded battle scenes; for example, the oval shields in the Louvre and at Turin (Royal Armoury) depict the history of Jugurtha; see Thomas, 'Les Armures', p. 67.

30 Sir Guy Francis Laking, *A Record of European Armour and Arms Through Seven Centuries*, 5 vols, (London, 1920–22), 4:247 (fig. 1317), translates the Latin message thus:

> This very small rim includes the great (spirit of) ambition, which overturns Kingdoms, destroys Empires; / It raised from the midst (of others) the life and glory of the great Pompey, / It took away the Empire of Caesar, the mild clemency of Caesar is extolled to Heaven, / Which, however, was at length destructive to him. / The ring and severed neck of Pompey drew forth tears from him. / He had made manifest to this man how upright he would be. / The garment bespattered with blood in the Sacred Rites taught / that for him they would be such fateful foretellings of woe. If therefore you regard the power of ambition / You may see that there is no greater evil than the seeking for honours.

31 See Stephen V. Grançsay, 'The Armor of Henry II of France from the Louvre Museum: Royal Armorers, Antwerp or Paris', *Metropolitan Museum Bulletin* 10 (1952): 68–80.

32 For details of the astonishing richness of Delaune's extant designs, drawings, and engravings, see Thomas's two articles (cited in n. 28) and Hayward, *Virtuoso Goldsmiths* and 'Mannerist Goldsmith'.

33 An idea of the taste for pictorial representation of recent victories can be gained from L. Mirot's catalogue of Montmorency's art collections, *L'Hôtel et les collections*, and from Belleau's *Bergerie*, pp. 36–37:

> Le troisième tableau estoit tout guerrier, d'un costé c'estoient sieges et prises de ville, comme de Metz, de Calais, et de Theonville, c'estoient camps, assemblez et camps partis, escaramouches, saillies, embuches, entreprises, aproches, bateries, camisades, sappes, mines, sentinelles et escalades.

> The third picture was all warlike, on one side the sieges and victories over towns

such as Metz, Calais, and Thionville; there were camps, meetings and groups of soldiers, skirmishes, sorties, ambushes, feats of arms, preparations, fights, sudden assaults, caves, mines, soldiers, and escapades.

34 See the illustrations in Hayward, *Virtuoso Goldsmiths*: a monochrome plate (no. 710) of Charles IX's parade shield and a coloured plate (no. 24) of the enamelled gold morion.

35 For example, S. de Sainte Marthe, *Les Genealogies des très illustres et très puissans princes les Ducz de Lorraine* (Paris, 1549), sig. ã iᵛ:

> A tres bon droict la maison de Lorraine
> Porte ce vers [*Fecit potentiam in brachio suo*] pour sa devise
> . . . .
> Car son fort bras, puissance souveraine
> Deffend tousjours (peuple) noblesse esglise,
> Et n'a iamais sa force esté submise:
> Prouver le peint Iherusalem conquise
> Par le bon roy Godefroy de Boullogne
> Le Roi René.

> With good reason the house of Lorraine carries this device [May there be power in your arm] . . . because its strong arm, its sovereign power always defends people, nobles, and church; and never has its force been subdued: to prove it, is painted there Jerusalem conquered by the good king Godfrey of Bouillon, King René.

36 François de Belleforest, *Harangues militaires* (Paris, 1588), p. 1403.

37 The origin of the lyre is discussed by most sixteenth-century mythographers; see, for example, Giovanni Piero Valeriano (1477–1558?), *Les Hieroglyphiques* (Paris, 1615), pp. 636–38; Valeriano had, in his turn, relied on precise borrowings from Philostratus.

38 Du Bellay, *Deffence*, pp. 120–22. For the noble connotations of the lyre, see Isabelle Cazeaux, *French Music in the Fifteenth and Sixteenth Centuries* (Oxford, 1975), p. 219. Images of Apollo and Marsyas persist: on the frontispiece of the 1575 edition of the music for the verse of Ronsard, Desportes, and others, for example, appear their images: *Chansons de P. de Ronsard, Ph. Desportes et autres mises en musique par M. de la Grotte* (Paris, 1575), illustrated in John Grand-Carteret, *Les Titres illustrés et l'image au service de la musique* (Turin, 1904), p. 21.

39 See R. J. Clements, 'Ronsard and Ficino on the Four Furies', *Romanic Review* 45 (1954): 161–69, for a discussion of Ronsard's close dependence on Ficino. The four kinds of furies are clearly set out by Pontus de Tyard (*Solitaire premier*, p. 17):

> fureur poétique procedent du don des Muses; intelligence des mysteres et secrets des religions souz Bacchus; pour ravissement de prophetie, vaticination ou divination souz Apollon; pour la violence de l'amoureuse affection souz Amour et Venus.

poetic fury, arising from a gift of the Muses; understanding of the mysteries and secrets of religion, from Bacchus; inspiration and prophecy, divination, and the gift to foretell the future, from Apollo; the force of amorous affections, from Venus and Love.

40 The Muses appear at the end of *La Lyre*, described as having the power to 'surmonter les siecles et la mort' (overcome the centuries and death; line 428).

41 Terence Cave explores these extremes of feeling in 'Mythes de l'abondance'.

42 *A son lut* was withdrawn from his collected works by Ronsard in 1578.

43 Vigenère, *Images*, pp. 92, 92ᵛ, 97ᵛ, 99. The same development occurs in contemporary Italian poetic theory and practice; see, for example, Charlton's translation from Minturno's dedication to his *Arte Poetica*—H. B. Charlton, *Castelvetro's Theory of Poetry* (Manchester, 1913), pp. 145–46.

44 There, the reader could also see the contest of Apollo and Marsyas, see sig. q i, in *Metamorphose d'Ovide figurée*.

45 On tableware design, see Verdier, *Walters Art Gallery*, no. 169; and Madeleine Marcheix, 'Les Emaux'. Pilon's carving is listed by Coyecque, 'Au domicile mortuaire'.

46 Or le plaisir se prend par trois sortes, par l'esperance, par la fruition, et par la souvenance. D'avant que vous eussiez esté à la guerre, lorsque vous fustes designé pour estre lieutenant general du feu roy, vostre seigneur et frere, par l'esperance vous conceviez déjà la guerre, l'ordonnance des soudars, l'assiette du camp, le commandement des capitaines, canons, tabourines, estandars, et desjà vous jouyssiez du plaisir de la guerre par l'esperance imaginative. A la bataille de Moncontour vous jouissiez de ce plaisir par effait, et, après la bataille, racontant au feu roy vostre frere et à la royne vostre mere ce qui estoit passé, vous jouyssiez par la souvenance de vostre plaisir, mais la souvenance est la meilleure partie du plaisir, car l'esperance n'est que par imagination, la fruition est pronte et soudaine et la souvenance dure longuement.

(L 18:476)

There are three kinds of pleasure: through hope, fulfilment, or memory. Before you went to the war—when you were given the title of the lieutenant general of your late king, lord, and brother—through hope you already imagined the war, the order of the soldiers, the site of the camp, the authority of the captains, canons, tambourines, and standards, and already you enjoyed the pleasures of war through the imaginings granted by hope. At the battle of Montcontour, you enjoyed this pleasure in fact; and after the fighting, relating what had happened to your late king and to the queen your mother, you enjoyed your pleasure through the force of memory. But, memory is the best part of pleasure, since hope exists only in the imagination, fulfilment is prompt and sudden, and memory lasts for a very long time.

47 Ronsard, *Abbrégé de l'art poétique, 1565*, P 2:998; L 14:10. Relevant here, too, are the comments Ronsard makes in the next section of this work on the use of varied vocabulary and 'significant' words.

Tu te dois travailler estre copieux en vocables et trier les plus propres et signifians que tu pourras pour servir de ners et de force à tes carmes, qui reluyrent d'autant plus que les mots seront significatifs et choisis avec jugement. Tu n'oublieras les comparaisons, les descriptions des lieux; fleuves, forêts, montaignes, de la nuict, du lever du soleil, du midy, des vents, de la mer, des Dieux et Déesses, avecques leurs propres mestiers, habits, chars et chevaux, te façonnant en cecy à l'imitation d'Homere, que tu observeras comme un divin exemple, sur lequel tu tireras au vif les plus parfaicts lineamens de ton tableau.

(P 2 : 1000; L 14ᵉ: 15)

You must work to be rich in words and sort out those most appropriate and that signify the most, which you can use as the nerves and strength of your songs, which will shine all the more as the words signify and are chosen with judgement. Do not forget comparisons and descriptions of place; rivers, forests, mountains, night, sunrise, midday, winds, sea, gods and goddesses with their proper duties, habits, vehicles, and horses, shaping yourself in all this by imitating Homer, whom you will observe as a divine example on which you will draw, from life, the most perfect elements of your painting.

48 Both classical and contemporary poets recognised these advantages. For instance, Catullus interrupted his tale of the marriage of Peleus and Thetis with a dazzling description of the marriage-bed coverlet, while Ariosto delays the nuptials of Ruggiero and Bradamante in order to describe an embroidered pavilion whose decoration celebrated his patron Ercole d'Este (*Orlando Furioso*, canto 46).

IV. Triumphal Forms

1 Du Cerceau, *Des plus excellents bastiments de France* (Paris, 1576), p. 2.

2 Vitruvius, *De architectura*, trans. Jean Martin and annot. Jean Goujon as *Architecture ou art de bien bastir de Marc Vitruve* (Paris, 1547), sig. ã i.

3 Guillaume Michel, *Le siècle doré*, sig. Jviii ᵛ, 'De la magnificence, magnanimite et mansuetude des princes' (On the magnificence, magnanimity, and generosity of princes):

Pour embellir de noblesse l'essence
Parer la fault et de magnificence
Lampliffier (car cest vertu moult belle)
Tu doubs avoir sus cela congnoissance
Qu'il te convient sy tu as la vaillance
Faire bastir fondacion nouvelle
Palais royaulx fondez par sy hault zelle.

To embellish the essence of nobility, it must be decorated with magnificence; to amplify it (since it's a most beautiful virtue) you must have knowledge of it, and if you are brave, it belongs to you to establish new foundations and build royal palaces from deep zeal.

4   François de Saint Thomas, *La vraye forme*, p. 74.

5   See, for instance, *Le Tocsain contre les massacreurs en France* (Rheims, 1579), p. 24; writing of Catherine the anonymous author complained that she exerted herself 'tous les jours en depenses folles et superflues, comme entre autres en plusieurs nouveaux bastimens, dont un seul cousta 60 et 100.000 livres' (every day in useless and superfluous expense, among other things on several new buildings, a single one costing 160,000 *livres*). See also the milder criticism of Jean Baptiste de la Fosse, who comments that Charles IX enriched the Louvre more lavishly than any of his predecessors while 'le royaulme ne fut jamais en telle pauvreté à cause des guerres civiles' (the kingdom never was in such poverty as a result of civil wars); *Journal d'un curé ligueur de Paris*, ed. E. de Barthélemy (Paris, n.d.), p. 129.

6   Vitruvius, *Architecture*, p. 3.

7   There has been much scholarly work on Serlio, of which the most authoritative is William Bell Dinsmoor, 'The Literary Remains of Sebastiano Serlio', *Art Bulletin* 24 (1942): 55–154.

8   Guillaume Du Choul, *Discours de la religion des anciens romains* (Lyons, 1556), p. 38.

9   Jacques de Bie, *La France métallique* (Paris, 1636), plate 56, for example, shows the use of classical images of majesty and virtue as symbols of Henri II in 1552.

10 This is made clear in the *Registres et délibérations de la ville de Paris* (Paris, 1883), 3 : 172, and in the printed account of the entry, *C'est l'ordre qui a esté tenu à la nouvelle et joyeuse entrée . . .* (Paris, 1549).

11 The royal tapestry collection was very rich. It included hangings that depicted the months of the year, the seven ages of man, and stories from the life of King David and from other models of perfect kings, as well as tapestries and embroideries worked from the cartoons of Bosch, Van Orley, Giulio Romano, and Andrea del Sarto, and showing the world, paradise, and hell; the antiquity and origin of Rome; the story of Scipio; and Charity. Other items developed stories from Virgil's *Bucolics* and from the *Triumphs* of Petrarch. See Laborde, *Comptes* 1 : 205, and the details of the work, which continued to be done from the 1530s, given in the catalogue of the Amsterdam exhibition of 1955, *Le Triomphe du maniérisme européen* (Amsterdam, 1955), pp. 159–287. See also S. Schneebalg-Perelman, 'Richesses du garde-meuble parisien de François Ier', *Gazette des Beaux Arts* 78 (1971): 251–304; and E. Berkenhagen, *Die Französischen Zeichnungen der Kunstbibliothek Berlin* (Berlin, 1970).

12 Details of this series of frescoes can be found in Rostain, Canard, and Labrousse, *Le Château d'Oiron*.

13 Art historians are, however, bringing to light evidence of other examples of highly decorated Renaissance castles: see F. Eraud, 'Peintures murales'.

14 Nicolas Hoüel, *L'Histoire de la royne d'Arthemise* (Bibliothèque Nationale, Ms. fr. 306); the comments on political events and artistic successes—for instance, that *assemblées d'état* are good and necessary, and that the poetry of Ronsard and Du Bellay is excellent—are in bk 2, ff. 37–41.

15 A group of artists seems to have been involved in the designs. Of the fifty-nine drawings known to survive, attributions have been made to Niccolo and Giulio Camillo dell'Abbate and to Antoine Caron.

16 Hoüel, *Histoire*, f. 9; also cited by Jules Guiffrey, 'Nicolas Hoüel, apothicaire parisien', p. 195.

17 See Sylvie Béguin, 'La Suite d'Arthémise'.

18 The tapestry is reproduced by Pierre Quarre, 'Histoire d'Artémise—tapisserie', *La Revue du Louvre*, 1964, pp. 249–54.

19 See Béguin, 'La suite d'Arthémise', notes to fig. 1, which shows the mausoleum; and Guiffrey, 'Nicolas Hoüel', p. 205, no. 38, on the drawings in the Cabinet des Estampes.

20 Gilles Corrozet, *Les Antiquitez, histoires et singularitez de Paris, ville capitale du royaume de France* (Paris, 1550), ff. 162–162ᵛ.

21 P 2 : 1025–26; L 16 : 346–47. For contemporary English use of these themes, see Gordon Kipling, *The Triumph of Honour* (Leiden, 1977), especially chap. 4.

22 Jean Lemaire de Belges, *Le Temple d'Honneur et de Vertu* [composed 1504], ed. H. Hornik (Geneva: 1957), lines 1351–81. For similar use of names as symbols, see the account of Henri II's coronation, published by Godefroy, *Le Cérémonial françois* 1 : 303–8.

23 A good example of the influence of Petrarch's triumphs can be seen in the engravings of Nicoletta da Modena, recorded in Bartsch, *Illustrated Bartsch, Early Italian Masters*, ed. Mark Zucker (New York, 1980), pp. 112–17.

24 Du Bellay, *Deffence*, pp. 208–9; Du Bellay devotes an entire chapter (bk 2, chap. 5; pp. 233–46) to the discussion of the epic.

25 Du Bellay, *Poésies* 1 : 163–69.

26 Du Bellay, *Discours au roy sur la trefve de l'an 1555*, in *Poésies* 1 : 246–47.

27 For Ronsard's attention to the advice of rhetoricians, see Gordon, *Ronsard et la rhétorique*. The lives of Montmorency's wife, children, and brothers, their deeds

and genealogy are recorded in detail in the church at Montmorency and at Ecou-
en; see Magne, *L'oeuvre des peintres verriers*, pp. 91–112.

28 In this rather clumsy description, Ronsard is probably recalling the figure that was
prominent on one of the arches at the Lyons entry; see the Italian account, *La
Magnifica et triumphale intrata del christianiss. re di Francia Henrico secundo . . .*
(Lyons, 1548), sig. G1.

29 Odet's learning was legendary, and he would have been well equipped to appreciate Ronsard's references; see Brantôme, *Oeuvres* 3 : 302.

30 A representative list of works might include, A. Fulvius, *Illustrium imagines*
(Lyons, 1524); Dion Cassius, *Des faicts et gestes insignes des romains* (Paris,
1542); J. Huttichius, *Imperatorum et caesarum vitae cum imaginibus* (Paris,
1550); G. Symeoni, *L'Histoire d'Hérodien* (Lyons, 1554); F. Josephus, *Antiquatum Iudaicarum* (Lyons, 1556); D. Acciajuoli, *Les vies d'Hannibal et de Sci-
pion* (Paris, 1567); and Aemylius Probus, *Les vies des grands et vertueux et excellents capitaines* (Paris, 1568). Copies of Caesar's commentaries, the works of
Appian and Quintus Curtius, as well as the *Triumphs* of Petrarch crammed the
Royal Library; see H. Michelant, *Catalogue de la bibliothèque de François Ier*
(Paris, 1863); and E. Quentin-Bauchart, *Bibliothèque de Fontainebleau*.

31 Bertrand Jestaz analysed the export to France of marbles from Rome, and his researches suggest that the period of greatest activity was 1541–55; 'L'Exportation
des marbres de Rome 1535–1571', *Mélanges d'Archéologie et d'Histoire* (Ecole
française de Rome, Paris) 75, no. 2 (1963): 415–66.

32 The details of papal briefs and correspondence from the Florence archives can be
found in L. Romier, *Origines politiques des guerres de religion*, 2 vols (Paris,
1913–14), 1 : 47–48. On the tomb of Claude de Lorraine, Dominique Florentin
depicted the prince as a Roman emperor with triumphal chariot drawn by horses
and crowned with laurel; fragments of the tomb can be seen in the Louvre. Antoine Le Pois, *Discours sur les medalles*, sig. ẽi^v, takes his reader's knowledge of
the collecting craze for granted when he writes: 'je ne feray icy mention d'aucuns
seigneurs de nostre temps, qui les ont achettes à prix excessifs' (I won't mention
here some gentlemen of our times who have bought them at excessive prices).

33 Pierre Woeriot, *Pinax iconicus* (Lyons, 1554); this work is discussed by L. Jouve
in *Les Wiriot et les Briot, artistes lorrains* (Paris, 1891), p. 61.

34 Gilles Corrozet, *Les Antiquitez*, f. 200^v. On the decoration, see M. Roy, *Artistes
et monuments* 1 : 482. The grotto was probably inspired by that at the Palazzo del
Te, which was decorated with a frieze depicting a Roman triumph; see Frederick
Hartt, *Giulio Romano* (New Haven, 1958), p. 234.

35 See P. Biver, *Histoire du château de Meudon* (Paris, 1923), p. 30; Arnold van
Buchel includes a long description of the grotto at Meudon in *Description de
Paris*, ed. L. A. van Langeraad and A. Vidier (Paris, 1899), pp. 92–93.

36 Michel Bouterone, *Le Petit Olympe d'Issy* (Paris, 1609), p. 5.

> La grotte jadis consacrée
> Aux Muses de Henry Second
> . . . .
> C'estoit bien l'age d'or à l'heure
> Que ce Roy liberalement,
> Donnoit aux Muses pour demeure,
> Un si superbe bastiment.

> The grotto was at one time dedicated to the muses of Henry II . . . it was indeed the golden age at the hour when this king liberally gave such a superb building to the muses for their home.

37 Gabriel Symeoni, *Les Illustres Observations antiques* (Lyons, 1558); the passage cited is in the dedication.

38 Romier, *Origines politiques* 2:62. Another sign of this interest is that Charles Estienne, for example, always notes for his princely readers the towns with significant Roman remains; see *Les Voyages* (Paris, 1552), p. 177, for his comments on Arles.

39 Charles V's reliance on Caesar and Alexander is reported by Claude d'Espence, *Deux Notables traictez* (Paris, 1575), ff. 17–17ᵛ. For the story of Strozzi's translation, see Brantôme, *Oeuvres* 2:241.

40 Vasari, *The Lives of the Painters, Sculptors, and Architects*, 4 vols (London, 1927) 4:318. See P. A. Mattioli, *Il magno palazzo*, sig. Hiiiᵛ.

41 Tyrtaeus was available only in fragments, of which H. Estienne's edition, *Theocriti aliorumque poetarum idyllia* (Paris, 1549), was the first. A typical example, as translated by Leconte de Lisle, *Fragments de Tyrtée*, 2 vols (Paris, 1849), reads as follows:

> Mais il est beau celui qui marche d'un pied ferme, mordant ses lèvres de ses dents, couvrant de l'orbe de son large bouclier ses cuisses, sa poitrine, et ses épaules, brandissant de sa droite la lance solide, et agitant sa crinière terrible sur sa tête.
>
> (2:326)

> But it's wonderful to see the man who walks with confident tread, biting his lips with his teeth, with the broad globe of his shield covering his thighs, breast, and shoulders, brandishing a solid lance in his right hand, and shaking his terrible mane on his head.

42 Statius, *Silvae*, bk 4, chap. 6, 'The Hercules Statuette of Norius Vindex'. The stirring effect of such works is also described by Dolce, who refers to Sallust's statement that 'Quintus Fabius and Publius Scipio used to say that, when they looked at their ancestral images, they felt themselves on fire to show their worth' (*L'Aretino*, p. 113).

43 Philibert de l'Orme, *Le Premier Livre d'architecture* (Paris, 1567–68), p. 202.

44 See Jean Guillaume, 'La Gallerie d'Oiron', *Colloque de Fontainebleau*, pp. 145–60.

45 L. Dimier, *Le Primatice, peintre, sculpteur, et architecte des rois de France* (Paris, 1900), p. 59; and E. Bourges, 'Les Satyres de la galerie Henri II, retrouvés à Rome', *Annales de la Société Historique du Gâtinois* (1892), pp. 1–17; and Serlio, *Tutte l'opere*, bk 8, chap. 40, p. 96. Much work was needed on the copies before they could be cast—see Laborde, *Comptes* 1 : 191–94, 199–202.

46 Du Choul, *Discours de la religion*, p. 40.

47 Symeoni, *La Description de la Limague d'Auvergne en forme de dialogue* (Lyons, 1561), pp. 78–82.

48 I have consulted the seventeenth-century collection engraved from Agostino Veneziano's work, *Recueil de vases* (Paris, 1680); see nos 72, 73, 109, 110.

49 Neither volume of Enea Vico's *Discorsi sopra le medaglie de gli antichi* (Venice, 1555, 1558) is illustrated, but the following of Vico's works are: *Ex libris XXIII commentariorum in vetera imperatorum romanorum numismata liber primus* (Venice, 1560); *Le imagini delle donne auguste* (Venice, 1557); *Augustarum imagines aeris formus expressae; vitae quoque earundem* (Venice, 1558); *Omnium Caesarum verissimae imagines ex livia antiquis numismata desumptae* (Venice, 1553, 1554). See also Antonio Zantani, *Le imagini con tutti i riversi* (Venice, 1548).

50 J. P. Hayward, 'The Mannerist Goldsmith: France and the School of Fontainebleau', *Connoisseur* 153 (1963): 11–15; *Virtuoso Goldsmiths*, no. 254; and R. H. H. Cust, *The Life of B. Cellini*, 2 vols (London, 1927), 1 : opposite p. 84 for the illustration of Cellini's work. A further example of the interest in triumphs are the triumphs of Caesar that decorate the borders of Simon Vostre's *Heures à l'usage de Châlons-sur-Marne* (n.p., 1514).

51 F. Roland, 'A. La Fréry, 1512–77', *Mémoires de la Société de l'Emulation du Doubs* (1910), pp. 320–78. Composite collections of La Fréry's engravings—*Speculum Romanae Magnificentiae*, 1519–75—can be found in major libraries and print rooms. For the latest bibliographical information on this very complex subject, see L. R. McGuinness and H. Mitchell, *Catalogue of the Earl of Crawford's 'Speculum Romanae Magnificentiae' Now in the Avery Architectural Library* (New York, 1976).

52 Etienne Du Pérac, *I vestigi dell'antichità di Roma raccolta et ritratti in perspectiva . . .* (Paris, 1575); dedication dated 1574.

53 J. Androuet Du Cerceau, who first published his *Arcs de triomphe* in 1549, con-

tinued to promote this interest into the 1560s with his *Arcs et monuments antiques d'Italie et de France*; see Geymüller's bibliographical discussion, *Les Du Cerceau*, pp. 302–4. Guilbert refers to the 'salle des douze Césars' (the room of the twelve Caesars) at Fontainebleau, before the changes effected by Louis XIII, *Description historique* 1:152.

54   For examples of hat jewels, see A. G. Somers Cocks, *Princely Magnificence: Court Jewels of the Renaissance, 1500–1630* (London, 1980), catalogue no. 69. On coins or images of the twelve Caesars, see P. A. Mattioli, *Il magno palazzo*, sig. Liii–Mi; Verheyen, *Palazzo del Te*, p. 33; H. Delaborde, *Marc-Antoine Raimondi* (Paris, 1887), pp. 216ff.; and Mirot, *L'Hôtel*, p. 82: 'table d'attente d'ébène ornée de 12 médailles de bronze des douze Césars' (an ebony side table decorated with twelve bronze medals of the twelve Caesars).

55   Calendar of State Papers, Foreign, 2 Oct. 1561, Letter of Queen Elizabeth I to Throckmorton, in Paris.

56   The first manuscript is in the British Library (Harleian 6205), while the second and third are in Paris, at the Arsenal and Bibliothèque Nationale, respectively. Godefroy also illustrated the beautiful *Triomphes de Pétrarque* in the Bibliothèque de l'Arsenal. Jeannette M. A. Beer, *A Medieval Caesar* (Geneva, 1976), traces his popularity up to the Renaissance, noting that Caesar was the 'ideal prince of the middle ages', p. 90.

57   Vasari, *Lives* 3:52–53.

58   See W. Weisbach, *Trionfi* (Berlin, 1919); and Giovanni Carandente, *I trionfi nel primo Rinascimento* (n.p., 1963).

59   Colonna, *Hypnerotomachia Poliphili* (Venice, 1499), ff. 55ᵛ, 60; Tory, *Champfleury* (Paris, 1529), ff. 29ᵛ–30.

60   Sannazaro's *Arcadia* was translated by Jean Martin in 1544. One of the prizes for wrestling was 'un beau vase d'Erable enrichy de plusieurs peintures, faictes de la main d'André Mantegna' (a beautiful maple vase enriched with several paintings made by the hand of Andrea Mantegna), f. 86. See also Pomponius Gauricus, *De sculptura* [1504], ed. A. Chastel and R. Klein (Geneva, 1969), pp. 100, 194–96.

61   Vasari, *Lives* 3:271. On the engravings of Nicolas Hogenberg and Robert Péril, see *Les Fêtes de la Renaissance*, vol. 2, ed. J. Jacquot (Paris, 1960), p. 425; and Andrew Martindale, *The Triumph of Caesar by Andrea Mantegna* (London, 1979). For Mantegna's own engravings see Bartsch, *The Illustrated Bartsch* 25:42–48.

62   The description is by Jacopo Probo d'Atri (ca. 1517) in a correspondence discovered by Roberto Weiss and published in 'The Castle of Gaillon in 1509–10', *Jour-*

nal of the Warburg and Courtauld Institutes, 1953, pp. 1–13; the quotation is from p. 7.

63   Du Bellay, *Deffence*, p. 338.

64   Jean Goujon, annotations to Vitruvius, *Architecture*, trans. Martin, sig. Diii.

65   De Vigenère, *Images*, p. 12.

66   Account of the entry, *La Magnificence de la superbe et triumphante entrée de la noble et antique cité de Lyon* (Lyons, 1549), p. 12.

67   Ibid., sig. ii ᵛ.

68   Account of the entry, *C'est l'ordre . . .* , sig. G3 ᵛ.

69   John Stewart, *De adventu Henrici . . . valesii . . . in metropolian* (Paris, 1549), pp. 10–11. Later, around 1571, after the triumph of the official entry into Paris that Ronsard and Dorat orchestrated, Charles IX took part in chivalric exercises where knights fought for the honour of a place on the Temple of Glory, which (as Jamyn ingeniously relates) could only be built in modern times:

> Si les anciens n'ont basti pour la Gloire
> Un temple sainct comme pour la Victoire
> Ou la Vertu: c'est qu'ils n'avoyent trouvé
> Devant ce Roy par armes esprouvé,
> Un qui fust digne estre au milieu de temple.
>
> (*Oeuvres* [Paris, 1575], f. 57 ᵛ)

If the ancients did not build for Glory a sacred temple like those for Victory and Virtue, it's that they did not find before this king, proven in arms, one who was worthy of being placed at the centre of the temple.

70   There are four sources for the Rouen entry: *C'est la deduction du somptueux ordre, plaisantz spectacles et magnifiques theatres dresses . . . a la sacree maiesté . . . Henry second* (Chez Robert le Hoy, Robert et Jehan dictz Du Gord, Rouen 1551); Robert Masselin, *L'Entrée du Roy nostre sire . . .* (Paris, 1550); *L'Entrée du très magnanime . . . Roy de France Henry . . .* , manuscript preserved at Rouen; *Les poutres et figures du somptueux ordre . . .* (Jean Dugort, Rouen, 1557). I discuss and analyse these in my introduction to the facsimile edition of the first of the sources listed; see McGowan, *L'Entrée de Henri II, Rouen 1550* (Amsterdam, 1974).

71   See McGowan, introduction to *L'Entrée de Henri II*.

72   Jean Du Tillet's account of his processions of devotion and executions, in *Les Faits memorables advenus depuis Pharamond . . .* (Lyons, 1557), p. 344, can be taken as typical:

Le quatriesme jour de Juillet [1549] le Roy meu de devotion, fit celebrer à Paris une procession solennelle ou led. Seigneur et la Royne assisterent, accompagnez des Princes et Princesses, Cardinaux, Prelas, gentilhommes de son hostel, et de tous les estatz de ladite ville portant chacun un Cierge blanc à la main, avec les chasses et saints Reliquaires, affin de prier Dieu qu'il luy plaist extirper les heresies et fausses doctrines qui regnent et pullulent en la Chrestienté. Le dit iour furent par feu executez à mort plusieurs sacramentaires, et mal sentans de la sainte foy catholique.

The fourth day of July [1549] the king, moved by devotion, had celebrated in Paris a solemn procession. He was present with his queen, accompanied by princes and princesses, cardinals, prelates, and gentlemen of his household, and with all the guilds in the town, each one carrying a white candle in his hand, with monstrance and holy relics, in order to pray to God that it please him to uproot the heresies and false doctrines that invade and multiply throughout Christianity. The said day were executed by fire several Protestants in bad odour with the holy Catholic faith.

73 Ibid., p. 359 [15 May 1550].

74 Parallel examples may be found in Du Choul, *Discours de la religion*, pp. 204–5.

75 See Jean Ehrmann, 'La Belle Cheminée du château de Fontainebleau', *Colloque de Fontainebleau*, pp. 117–24; B. Tonnochy and H. Read, *Waddeston Bequest*, no. 28; and Jacques de Bie, *La France métallique*, plate 59.

76 Montaigne does, very occasionally, refer to individual works of art, such as the sepulchre of a praetor on the road to Ostia, or the statues in the Belvedere gardens; *Journal de voyage*, ed. M. Rat (Paris, 1955), pp. 118, 131–32.

77 Etienne Pasquier, *Lettres familières*, ed. D. Thickett (Geneva, 1974), bk 7, p. 91.

78 The Rouen manuscript is not consistent with the printed account; the former shows white unicorns, while the latter depicts white steeds; see McGowan, *L'Entrée de Henri II*.

79 Lines 109–10; P 1:430–32; L 1:67–73.

80 P 2:122–25; L 8:246–54.

v. *La Belle Forme*

1 The bibliography on this subject is extensive; see Ruth Kelso, *Doctrine for the Lady of the Renaissance* (Evanston, Ill., 1956); and a more recent study, in Elizabeth Cropper, 'On Beautiful Women, Parmigianino, Petrarchismo, and the Vernacular Style', *Art Bulletin* 58 (1976): 374–94. There was, of course, a contrary trend to all this praise, examined by P. M. Smith in *The Anti-Courtier Trend*; one of its most eloquent exponents was Jacques Tahureau (*Dialogues* [Paris, 1565], pp. 17–18) who, in another mood, was happy to extol the lady.

2 'De la Joie et de la Tristesse', L 18:470–79.

3 Corneille's work was praised as early as 1537; see Eustorg de Beaulieu, *Rondeau à la louange d'un painctre de Flandres*, in *Des divers rapportz* (Lyons, 1537), f. xxxij.

> Pour bien tirer un personnage au vif
> Ung Painctre dict Cornylle, est aloue
> Et de plusieurs estime et loue
> N'avoir en France aulcung comparatif.
> Car veu son oeuvre, on dict de cueur hastif
> Cest tel, cest telle, O lhomme bien doue
> Pour bien tirer.
> Bref, ce qu'il painct monstre ung Incarnatif
> Quon diroit Chair, dont il est advoue
> Navoir en peu puis le temps de Noe
> Non Apelles, iadis superlatif
> Pour bien tirer.

> For drawing a person from life, a painter like Corneille is to be praised, esteemed, and held in high opinion as having no one comparable to him in France. Because, seeing his work, one immediately exclaims, it's him, it's her. O, man well gifted in drawing. In short, what he paints shows a redlike flesh, which few have managed since the time of Noah—not even Apelles, once so superlative in drawing.

4 Ronsard's views are especially consonant with Vasari's descriptions of graceful women; see chapter 2, pp. 59–60; Alpers, 'Ekphrasis', p. 205; and Blunt, *Artistic Theory in Italy*, p. 93.

5 Brantôme's account (*Oeuvres* 7:343) is corroborated by Daniel Heinsius; the relevant part of the latter's journal is cited by P. de Nolhac, 'Jean Second et Corneille de Lyon', *Mélanges offerts à Paul Laumonier* (Paris, 1935), pp. 109–12.

6 See Cropper's important article, 'On Beautiful Women'. Another contemporary beauty, much praised, was Paule de Vignier; see Gabriel de Minut, *De la beauté, avec la Paule-graphie* (Lyons, 1587), pp. 209–30. Among the works referring to Zeuxis, see Alberti, *Della pittura*, p. 15; Dolce, *L'Aretino*, p. 131; and Ficino *La Diffinition et perfection d'amour* (Paris, 1542), f. 58.

7 Junius, *Painting of the Ancients*, p. 6, where he refers both to Michelangelo and Sir Philip Sidney.

8 Agnolo Firenzuola, *Dialogo delle bellezze delle donne* (Florence, 1548); I quote from the French translation of 1578, f. 11. Among the many other such examples, see Cardan, *Subtilitez* (Paris, 1556), p. 275; and Louis le Roy's translation of Plato's *Symposium*, *Le Sympose* (Paris, 1558), f. 108. See also Kelso's extensive catalogue of discourses on ideal proportions for the human form, in *Doctrine for the Lady*.

9 Brantôme, *Oeuvres* 7:183, 'M. du Cua et moy lisions une fois un petit livre en italien, qui s'intitule de la Beauté fait en dialogue par le signeur Angelo Firenzolle, florentin' (Once M. du Cua and I read together a little book in Italian, called *On Beauty*, in dialogue form by Angelo Firenzuola, a Florentine). Innocenzio Ringhieri, *Cento givochi liberali* (Bologna, 1551).

10 Obsessive concern with detail was, of course, familiar to French audiences from the *Blasons du corps féminin*, in which individual parts of the body were isolated and individually promoted. For example, see Albert-Marie Schmidt's anthology, *Poètes du XVIe siècle* (Paris, 1953), pp. 293–364.

11 See André M. J. Festugière, *La Philosophie de l'amour de Marsile Ficin et son influence sur la littérature française au XVIe siècle* (Paris, 1941).

12 Firenzuola, *Dialogo*, f. 8ᵛ. Spenser, *The Works* (London, 1940) pp. 596–99, lines 90–91.

13 Quotations in this paragraph cited from Junius, *Painting of the Ancients*, p. 266; Charles Turrin, *Les Oeuvres poétiques* (Paris, 1572), sig. * iijᵛ; and Brantôme, *Oeuvres* 7:230. Portraits of Brantôme's ladies are included in Henri Bouchot's *Les Femmes de Brantôme* (Paris, 1890). For details on attitudes towards nudity, see Kenneth Clark, *The Nude* (London, 1956).

14 Boccaccio, *Teseida* 12:53–63.

> crin . . . lunghie assai. . . . La fronte sua era ampia e spaziosa . . . due ciglie . . . nerissime e sottil . . . naso . . . affilatetto; le guance . . . dilicate e graziose, bianche e vermiglie . . . la bocca piccioletta, tutta ridente . . . dente suoi . . . bianche perle . . . la gola candida . . . il collo e lungo e ben sedente sovra gli omeri candidie ritondi . . . el petto poi un pochetto eminente . . . lunghe le mani . . . e il pié piccolin.

15 Dolce, *L'Aretino*, p. 131; Sannazaro, *Arcadia* [1504], trans. Jean Martin (Paris, 1544), p. 21; for Armida, see Tasso, *Gerusalemme Liberata* 4:23–32. Contemporary French examples abound; for instance, in Guillaume Belliard, *Le Premier Livre des poèmes* (Paris, 1578), ff. 90–112ᵛ. C. de Taillemont gives a detailed account of *la belle dame* in *La Tricarite* (Lyons, 1556), pp. 43–70.

16 A parallel treatment is made in sonnet 183; G, 116. Ronsard's ideal women became famous so rapidly that they too are cited as standard by later writers; see Mario Equicola, *Les Six Livres de la nature d'amour*, trans. Gabriel Chapuis (Paris, 1584), sig. ã iiᵛ.

17 G, 158–68; this elegy to Janet influenced Belleau's description of his beautiful woman in *La Bergerie*. Other examples of references to painters in Ronsard's love poems include his appeal to Denisot to paint that perfection of womanly beauty that constitutes 'le patron desrobé sur les dieux' (the pattern stolen from the gods; sonnet 132; G, 83—see also sonnet 9; G, 9). In a later sonnet, composed for Hélène de Surgères, 'Madame se levoit un beau matin d'Esté' (Madame arose one

beautiful summer morning; sonnet 108; G, 417), he compares her beauties to those sculptured by Praxiteles and Phidias. In sonnet 210, 'Telle qu'elle est, dedans ma souvenance' (Such as she is in my memory; G, 131–32), the mental portrait of his mistress outdoes any painted version. R. A. Sayce's interesting article 'Ronsard and Mannerism' is limited to an attempt to draw precise parallels between the poem and Clouet's *Bain de Diane* (Rouen).

18   Compare his comment in the elegy to Marie:

> Ceus qui liront les vers que j'ay chantez pour vous
> D'un stile varié entre l'aigre et le dous,
> Selon les passions que vous m'avez données
> Vous tiendront pour déesse.

(lines 8–12; G, 290)

> Those who will read the verses I have sung for you, in a varied bittersweet style, according to the feelings you have aroused in me, will hold you for a goddess.

19   On the portrait of Catherine as Juno, see P. D. Roussel, *Histoire*, p. 45. On Reymond's enamelled cup, see Bardon, *Diane de Poitiers*, p. 84. The portrait of Mary Stuart and François II is discussed by Roger Trinquet, 'Le Bain de Diane du Musée de Rouen', *Gazette des Beaux Arts* 71 (1968): 1–16; and the depiction of Flora, by H. Bouchet, *Exposition des primitifs français au Palais du Louvre et à la Bibliothèque Nationale* (Paris, 1904), no. 202.

20   For a more detailed analysis of this poem, see my discussion in *French Literature and Its Background*, vol. 1, ed. J. Cruickshank, (Oxford, 1968), chap. 8.

21   Montaigne, *Essais*, ed. Albert Thibaudet (Paris, 1950), bk 3, chap. 5, p. 949.

22   Ripa, *Iconologie*, chap. 20 ('Beauté celeste'), p. 29.

23   Cardinal de Lorraine's letter is printed in *Lettres, instructions et mémoires de Marie Stuart, Reine d'Ecosse*, ed. Alexandre Labanoff, 7 vols (London, 1844), 1:9.

24   Jean Capello's comment cited by N. Tommaseo, *Les Relations des ambassadeurs vénitiens sur les affaires de France, au XVIe siècle*, 2 vols (Paris, 1838), 1:373.

25   For Ronsard's several poems to Mary, see P 2:290–303. These poems are well known and have been much discussed; however, by being placed in the double context of artistic and social conventions, they are further illuminated. Marcel Raymond writes most suggestively about these poems in *La Poésie française et le maniérisme* (London, 1971).

26   *Discours du grand et magnifique triumphe faict au mariage de . . . François . . . et . . . Marie d'Estrevart . . .* [Paris, 1558], ed. William Bentham (London, 1818), p. 13.

27 Renaud de Beaulne, *Oraison funèbre de la très chrestienne, très illustre, et très constante Marie Royne d'Escosse* (Paris, 1588), pp. 40–41.

28 In the elegy beginning 'L'Huillier, si nous perdons ceste belle Princesse, / Qui en un corps mortel resemble une déesse' (L'Huillier, if we lose this princess, who in her mortal form resembles a goddess), see especially lines 59–60: 'Celle que desroba le Boeuf Sidonien, / Que le Cygne trompa, pres d'elle ne sont rien' (The one who stole the Sidonian bull, who was tricked by the swan, beside her are as nothing); P 2:299–301; L 12:189–99.

29 M. Marcheix, 'Les Emaux', p. 183; Lucile M. Golson, 'Landscape Prints and Landscapists of the School of Fontainebleau, c. 1543–c. 1570', *Gazette des Beaux Arts* 71 (1969): 95–110; le père Dan, *Le Trésor des merveilles de la maison royale de Fontainebleau*, (Paris, 1642), p. 94. Léonard Limosin's son designed a plate with the rape of Europa at its centre; it is now in the Herzog-Anton Ulrich Museum (Brunswick, West Germany); see the catalogue *Le Triomphe du maniérisme européen* (Amsterdam, 1955), no. 478. The work of Achilles Tatius was translated into Latin in 1544, into Italian in 1551, into English in 1597, and into French in 1635. For parallel inspiration in Titian's work, see especially D. Rosand, 'Ut pictor poeta'; and evidence accumulated by Hayward, *Virtuoso Goldsmiths*, no. 242.

30 See David Summers's long and important discussion, 'Maniera and Movement: The Figura Serpentinata', *Art Quarterly* 35 (1972): 269–301. Leonardo was very preoccupied with the Leda figure and always came back to it, as Summers discusses; see the copies made by Cornelis Bos, *A Study of the Origins of the Netherland Grotesque* (Stockholm, 1965).

31 Dan, *Le Trésor de Fontainebleau*, pp. 94–132, describes the painting in the *cabinet*. Writing from Venice (16 April 1542) Aretino says:

> L'una de le due imagine è Leda, ma in modo morbida di carne, vaga di membra e svelta di persona, e talmente dolce, piana e suave d'attitudine, e con tanta grazia ignuda da tutte le parti de lo ignudo, che non si può mirar senza invidiare il cigno, che ne gode con affetto tanto simile al vero che pare, mentre stende il collo per basciarla, che le voglia essalare in bocca lo spirito de la sua divinità.
>
> (*Lettere sull'arte* [Milan, 1957], no. 456)

> One of the two paintings was a Leda, the flesh painted in a soft style, beautiful and sweet of limb and person, the attitude so sweet, full, and suave, and so much grace in the whole stretch of her nakedness, one can't see her without envying the swan who enjoys feelings that so match the real sight while it stretches its neck to kiss her and it wants to breathe into her mouth the spirit of its own divinity.

32 See the collections of Catherine de' Medici and of Germain Pilon, described by Coyecque, 'Au domicile mortuaire', p. 56.

33 Cust, *Life of Cellini* 2:449–97.

34 Hayward, *Virtuoso Goldsmiths*, plate 87; C. Delange, *Monographie de l'oeuvre de Bernard Palissy* (Paris, 1862); and M. Armand-Durand, *Le Livre de la bijouterie de R. Boyvin d'Angers* (Paris, 1876).

35 Maurice Scève, *Délie*, ed. E. Parturier (Paris, 1916), woodcut printed in front of no. 366. The use made by Scève of the theme is discussed by Dorothy Coleman in *An Illustrated Love "Canzoniere": The Délie of Maurice Scève* (Geneva, 1981), pp. 68–69; Coleman makes very clear the integral part played by the woodcuts in the reading of the *Délie*. These, in turn, inspired many decorative elements in noble homes; see François Eraud, 'Peintures murales dans la deuxième moitié du XVIe siècle', *Colloque de Fontainebleau*, pp. 185–97.

36 *La Défloration* was written before 1546 and, according to Isidore Silver, was probably inspired by the marriage of Cassandra Salviati to Jean Peigné, seigneur du Pré; see Silver, *Ronsard and the Hellenic Renaissance*, p. 225.

37 I quote from J. M. Edmund's translation (lines 37–62) of Moschus's text, in *The Greek Bucolic Poets* (London, 1916), pp. 430–31. Baïf provides a fairly literal translation in his *Second Livre des poèmes*, published in Paris in 1573, but conceived in about 1550, as he tells us.

38 Hayward, *Virtuoso Goldsmiths*, passim. An inventory of the jewels and tableware of the house of Lorraine—Bibliothèque Nationale, Ms. fr. 22441, ff. 49ʳ–54ʳ—gives some idea of the richness of the material used and of the extravagance of the jewels.

39 Hayward, *Virtuoso Goldsmiths*, plates 60, 76; see also C. Eisler, 'Etienne Delaune et les graveurs de son entourage', *L'Oeil* 44 (1965): 10–13; and Henri Zerner, *School of Fontainebleau*.

40 Martin's translation of Sannazaro's *Arcadia* reads:

> En son milieu est taillé le rouge Priapus embrassant une Nymphe bien serré, et la veult baiser maugré qu'elle en ayt dont elle enflambée de cholere, tourne le visaige en derriere, et faict tous ses effortz de s'en developper, luy esgratignant le nez de sa main gauche, et de la droicte arrachant sa rude barbe.
>
> (ff. 23–23ᵛ)

In its middle was hewn the red Priapus holding a nymph in tight embrace, wishing to kiss her despite the fact that she is evidently enflamed with anger, turning her head back while he strives to envelop her, and she scratches his nose with her left hand and pulls at his shaggy beard with her right.

Theocritus's description of the cup (*Idyll* 1) is thus given in the 1688 translation (*Les Idylles*, p. 7):

> Au dedans est gravée une jeune Beauté
> Effort divin de l'art, dont l'oeil est enchanté;
> Sa grace est augmentée encor par sa parure,
> Près d'elle deux Amans à longue Chevelure,

Semblent luy reprocher tour à tour ses dédains;
Mais la Belle insensible à leurs reproches vains,
Tantost paroist sur l'autre arrester son caprice,
Pour eux, brûlans d'amour, et les yeux enflamez,
Ils s'empressent en vain, d'un feu lent consumez,
Aux yeux un peu plus loin s'offre un rocher aride,
Avec un vieux pescheur, qui d'une ardeur avide
Traîne un vaste filet; et prest à le jetter,
On diroit qu'il s'efforce; il semble s'agiter.
Ses forces à pescher paroissent rassemblées;
Car tout autour du cou ses veines sont enflées;
Et quoique dejà vieux, et les cheveux tout blancs,
Il a mesme vigueur que dans ses plus beaux ans.
Près de ce vieux pescheur, avec art cizelé
On voit de raisins murs une vigne accablée,
Que garde un jeune enfant vers une haie assis.

Within is engraved a young beauty, a sublime effort of art whose eye is enchanted. Her grace is enhanced further by her dress. Close to her, two long-haired lovers seem to reproach her for her disdain, in turn; but the beauty, impervious to their vain reproaches now seems to let her fancy stray to the other. For them, enflamed with love, with burning eyes, they vainly strive and are consumed by a slow fire. A little further away, an arid rock presents itself to one's gaze, and an old fisherman with thirsty eagerness trails his vast nets; about to throw them forth, he seems to strain and become suddenly agitated. All his effort seems concentrated on his fishing because around his neck the veins swell; and although he is old and his hair is all white, he has the same strength as in his prime. Beside the old fisherman, chiselled skilfully, can be seen ripe grapes weighing down the vine, looked after by a young child, sitting by a hedge.

There were many sixteenth-century adaptations of this theme, for example, see Jean Godard, *La Fontaine de Gentilly* (Paris, 1595).

41 Du Bellay, *Deffence*, pp. 35–36; see also Castor's discussion of invention, in *Pléiade Poetics*, especially pp. 63–67.

42 In the *Hypnerotomachia*, the picture that confronted Poliphile on the building erected at the fountain where he first met the five nymphs, and where he saw a sculptured sleeping nymph 'mère de toutes choses' (mother of all things), was the object of the lustful attention of three satyrs. Guy de Tervarent traces the recurrent theme of the nymph and satyr to Macrobius's *Saturnales*, where they were evident signs of *voluptas*; see his *Les Enigmes de l'art savant*, 3 vols (Brussels, n.d.), 3 : chap. 5.

43 Belleau, *Bergerie*, pp. 278–79. Michel Jeanneret comments on the sophistication of this mirror and other art works in Belleau's *Bergerie*, in 'Les Oeuvres d'art dans *La Bergerie* de Belleau', *Revue d'Histoire Littéraire de la France* 70 (1970): 1–13.

44 See J. Bereau, *Les Eglogues* (Paris, 1565), sigs D4–Ei ᵛ, for Perot's 'beau vase enrichi de figures maintes' (beautiful vase enriched with many figures) and Jacquet's

plat, which carried scenes of the rape of Europa. From the visual arts, many examples can be cited; the catalogue *L'Ecole de Fontainebleau: Grand Palais, Paris 1972–73* (Paris, 1972), shows Delaune's frontispiece (plate 75) and Fantuzzi's cartouche (plate 316).

45   For this dating see James Hutton, *The Greek Anthology* (Ithaca, N.Y., 1946), pp. 123, 334, 339.

46   Belleau's translations of Anacreon are printed in his *Oeuvres poétiques*, 2 vols (Paris, 1578), 1:ff. 12–25ᵛ.

47   There are ten epigrams praising the naked Venus of Cnidus; for changes in her depiction, see Paul Vitry, 'Etude sur les épigrammes de l'anthologie palatine qui contiennent la description d'une oeuvre d'art', *Revue Archéologique* 24 (1894): 315–64. Kenneth Clark explores these changes in *The Nude*, pp. 26–27, 67–161.

48   I quote from Belleau's translation, *Oeuvres* 1:f. 16ᵛ; many English translations gave only very incomplete versions of the poems.

49   Letter to Alessandro Contarini, translated by Roskill, *L'Aretino*, pp. 213–17.

50   Philibert de l'Orme, *Premier Livre d'architecture*, pp. 124–25. Montaigne praises the statues as the best he saw in Italy, *Journal*, pp. 130–32, while Lucio Mauro, in his guidebook *Le antichità*, conscientiously lists important finds: a bronze Apollo, p. 16; statues in the Belvedere gardens, pp. 112–121; an Amazon woman thought by Michelangelo to be the most beautiful thing in Rome and of which a copy was made for François I, p. 122; a naked Leda, p. 132; a naked Bacchus, p. 142; Danae, naked, p. 145; the three Graces, p. 147; a naked Venus coming from the baths, p. 158; a naked Venus, born from the foam of the sea, p. 212; and Jove in the form of a bull, carrying Europa, p. 242.

51   Roy, *Artistes et monuments* 1:306.

52   See also Coyecque, 'Au domicile mortuaire', p. 53, on two paintings in Pilon's collection: 'Femme au bain, tableau sur toile, huile, enchâssure dorée, 4 écus', and 'Deux Femmes au bain [de même]'.

53   See Georges Wildenstein, *Le Goût pour la peinture dans la bourgeoisie parisienne entre 1550 et 1610* (Paris, 1962); Jacques Thirion, 'Rosso et les arts décoratifs', *Revue de l'Art*, 1971, pts 11–14, pp. 32–47; and J. Plattard, 'Bibliothèque et collection de tableaux d'un chanoine de Poitiers en 1581', *Revue du XVIe Siècle*, 1920, pp. 253–55.

54   Brantôme, *Oeuvres* 9:50.

55   Regarding Venus and Adonis, Caro also advises concentration on the two principal figures only. Cited by E. H. Gombrich, *Heritage of Apelles*, p. 125. When-

ever painters want to render beautiful women they always come to Venus, asserts Aristaenetus (Cyre Foucault, sire de la Coudrière) *Les épistres amoureuses* (Rouen, 1597).

56   Vigenère, *Images*, p. 12.

57   Cited from I. Silver's edition of the 1587 version of the *Oeuvres* (Paris, 1966), 1:121.

58   'Soit que son or . . .' is sonnet 90 in *Amours* (1552—53); G, 56. 'Ecumiere Vénus . . .' appears in the ninth poem in *Bocage* (*Amours*, 1554); G, 148.

59   Poems in which Ronsard compares the hair of his mistress to that of Venus are numerous; see, for example, *Sonets pour Hélène* 2:32; G, 436.

60   Pierre Boton's description of Venus in *La Camille* (Paris, 1573), ff. 7ᵛ—8, seems to have been much influenced by this poem as well as by the conventional description: 'Elle estoit de stature assez haute: elle avoit les cheveux qui tiroient sur la couleur de l'or, qui flottaient au sommet de la teste iusques sur le talon arrangez et entortillez' (She was rather tall; her hair, the colour of gold, flowed curling and well-groomed from the top of her head to her heels).

61   The motif of the shell seems originally to have come from Lucian (*Dialogues* 15:300), though it can be found in Roman poets and in Roman art; see Marion Lawrence, 'The *Birth of Venus* in Roman Art' in *Essays in the History of Art Presented to Rudolf Wittkower*, ed. Douglas Fraser, Howard Hibbard, and Milton J. Lewine (Phaidon, 1967), pp. 10—16. Although Venus was depicted with a shell on various sarcophagi, we do not know whether these were known to Ronsard.

62   The final version of the poem shows Ronsard also trying to move further away from convention; the traditional blond hair becomes brown ('brunement' substituted for 'jaunement').

63   That Ronsard was particularly moved by hair blowing in the breeze can be seen from the number of times he returned to this image. See, for example, *Les Amours*, 1552—53, poem 139 (G, 87):

> Quel or ondé en tresses s'allongeant
> Frapoit ce jour sa gorge nouvelette,
> Et sus son col, ainsi qu'une ondelette
> Flotte aux zephyrs, au vent alloit nageant?
>
> (lines 5—8)

What wavy gold stretching down in curls today touched her youthful throat, and above her neck like a tiny stream floats on the air and blows in the breeze?

64   The inspiration may go back to Giovanni Bellini's *Lady at Her Toilet*; an example of the diffusion of interest can be seen in G. Francesco Penni's drawing of the *Toilet of Venus* (after Raphael) in P. Pouncey and J. A. Gere, *Italian Drawings in*

the Department of Prints and Drawings in the British Museum (London, 1962), no. 69. See also three paintings in Montmorency's collection; Mirot, *L'Hôtel*, p. 74: 'Adonis et Venus, enchassé, d'un bois d'or; Vénus couchée; Diane' (Adonis and Venus set in wood and painted in gold; a sleeping Venus; Diana); and the drawings of the School of Salviati and attributed to René Boyvin, given by Hayward, *Virtuoso Goldsmiths*, nos 80, 99.

65 A sight evoked by Ronsard again in *Continuation des amours* (1555), poem 66 (G, 211):

> Sa teste en ce beau mois, sans plus, estoit couverte
> D'un riche escofion ouvré de soie verte,
> Où les Graces venoient à l'envy se nicher,
> Et dedans ses cheveux choysissoient leur demeure.
>
> (lines 9–12)

In this lovely month, only her head was covered with a rich cloth worked in green silk, where the graces vied to find a place, and chose to inhabit her hair.

The poem is imitated by Philippe Desportes in *Premières Oeuvres*, f. 143:

> Qu'il vienne voir apres, l'or de vos tresses blondes,
> Soit quand vous les laissez flotter, comme des ondes,
> A l'abandon du vent, qui s'empestre au dedans,
> Des filés blons-dorez de vos cheveux pendans;
> Soit quand vous les tenez sur le chef amassées,
> Les ayant par devant mignonnement troussées:
> Ou qu'avec un bonnet vous nous representez
> D'Hylas ou d'Adonis les celestes beautez.
> Qu'il vienne voir ce front, large tableau d'ivoire
> Plaine, claire et polie.

Let him then come to see the gold of your hair when it floats like waves in the wind, when it stirs the white-gold ringlets of your hanging locks; or when you have delightfully put them up; or, when bonnetted, you offer us the celestial beauty of Hylas or Adonis; let him come to see this brow, a broad painting in ivory, polished and clear.

66 Belleau's commentary appears in Ronsard's *Oeuvres* (1587), 2:66–67.

67 In addition to pictorial examples, a powerful literary tradition stands behind the kinds of fusion that Ronsard attempts in this poem; for an early sixteenth-century example, see Jean le Blond, 'Description d'une feuillée', in *Le Printemps* (Paris, 1536), ff. 30ᵛ–32; also, Jacques Bereau's description of Amarante, *Eglogues*, sigs G4ᵛ–Hiʳ.

68 The same double perspective is achieved in *Le Voyage de Tours* (G, 279–88); see also my discussion in chapter 6.

69 Other examples of this fusion of female beauty and flowers include poem 62 of the *Amours*:

Dedans des Prez je vis une Dryade,
Qui comme fleur s'assisoyt par les fleurs.

(G, 40)

In the fields, I spied a dryad who, like a flower, sat among flowers.

And also poem 107 (G, 67), which begins:

Je vy ma Nymphe entre cent damoyselles,
Comme un Croyssant par les menuz flambeaulx,
Et de ses yeulx plus que les astres beaulx
Faire obscurcir la beaulté des plus belles.
Dedans son sein les graces immortelles,
La Gaillardize, et les freres jumeaux,
Alloyent vollant comme petitz oyseaux
Parmy le verd des branches plus nouvelles.
Le ciel ravy, que son chant esmouvoyt,
Roses, et liz, et girlandes pleuvoyt
Tout au rond d'elle au meillieu de la place

I see my nymph among a hundred damsels, like a crescent amid tiny sparks, and from the stars of her eyes, she darkens the beauty of the most lovely. In her breast, immortal graces, happiness, and the twin brothers flit about like tiny birds in the new green of the trees. The sky is ravished, which her song so moves that roses, lilies, and bouquets shower down upon her in the centre of all.

70 R. Ritter, *Le Château de Pau, étude historique et archéologique* (Paris, 1919), p. 226.

VI. Dancing Forms

1 *Chant pastoral à très illustre et vertueuse Princesse, Marguerite de France, Duchesse de Savoie,* P 1:966–73; L 9:174–92.

2 *L'Amour amoureux,* P 1:351–53; L 17:174–78.

3 Jean Capello, cited by Abel Desjardins, *Négociations diplomatiques de la France avec la Toscane,* 6 vols (Paris, 1859–86), 1:423.

4 Brantôme, *Oeuvres* 8:23–24.

5 Brantôme, *Oeuvres* 8:34:

Lorsqu'elle parut ainsi parée en ses Tuileries, je dis à M. de Ronsard, qui estoit près de moy: 'Dites le vray, Monsieur, ne vous semble-t-il pas voir ceste belle reyne en tel appareil comme la belle aurore quand elle vient à naistre avant le jour avec sa belle face blanche, et entourée de sa vermeille et incarnate couleur? Car leur face et leur accoutrement ont beaucoup de sympathie et ressemblance'. M. de Ronsard me l'advoua; et sur cette comparaison qu'il trouva fort belle, il fit un beau sonnet qu'il me donna.

When she appeared thus decorated in her Tuileries I said to M. de Ronsard, who was close to me, 'Tell me the truth, sir, don't you think that this beautiful queen in such an equipage is like the lovely dawn when she is born before the day, when her beautiful white face is edged in warm red colour? The face and its accoutrement are alike and in sympathy with each other'. M. de Ronsard admitted that he found the comparison to be a good one, and he made a beautiful sonnet that he gave to me.

He cites another instance, this time at Blois, when Marguerite's beauty was also seen to remarkable advantage:

> Je la vis parestre en la procession si belle que rien au monde de plus beau n'est sceu se faire voir; car, oultre la beauté de son visage et de sa belle taille de corps, elle estoit très superbement et richement parée et vestue: son beau image blanc, qui ressembloit un ciel en sa plus grande et blanche sérenite, estoit orné par la teste de si grande quantité de grosses perles et riches pierreries, et surtout de diamans brillans mis en forme d'estoilles, qu'on eust dict que le naturel du visage et l'artifice des estoilles en pierreries confondoient avec le ciel, quand il est bien estoillé pour en tirer la forme.

(*Oeuvres* 8 : 36)

I saw her appear in the procession, so beautiful that nothing in the world was lovelier to see because, in addition to the beauty of her face and the wonder of her form, she was superbly and richly apparelled and dressed; her white image, which seemed like the sky in its most beautifully white sereneness, was decorated at her head with such a great quantity of huge pearls and rich stones, especially of rich diamonds in the shape of stars, that one would have said that the natural aspect of her face and the artifice of her stars of precious stones were indistinguishable from the sky when it is so star-filled that it casts its own form.

6   I. D. McFarlane rightly views *movement* as one of the most powerful among Ronsard's intuitions; 'Aspects of Ronsard's Poetic Vision', in *Ronsard the Poet*, ed. Cave, pp. 30–34.

7   Veneziano, *Recueil*, no. 1, 'sic Romae antiqui sculptores ex aere et marmore faciebunt', such is the artist's gloss on his engraving (dated 1530) of an ancient Roman vase. The saltcellar is no. 243 in Hayward, *Virtuoso Goldsmiths*.

8   From a letter by Dolce to Alessandro Contarini, *L'Aretino*, trans. Roskill, pp. 213–17.

9   See Pierre Du Colombier, *Jean Goujon* (Paris, 1949), plate 6.

10   See Per Bjurström, *Drawings in Swedish Public Collections* (Stockholm, 1976), no. 52.

11   Among many examples, see Ronsard, *Second Livre*, ode 10 (P 1 : 445; L 1 : 207),

> Fay venir Janne, qu'elle apporte
> Son luth pour dire une chanson:
> Nous ballerons tous trois au soir.

(lines 3–5)

Let Jane come forth, and let her bring her lute to sing a song; we'll all three dance into the evening.

Or see Jean Godard's song of the faun, *La Fontaine de Gentilly*, pp. 15−17.

12 P. Bembo, *Les Azolains*, trans. Jean Martin (Paris, 1545), p. 92:

> Ou si elle danse en quelque compagnie, luy veoir accommoder ses gestes au temps et aux cadences se tenant droicte sur sa personne et en compartissant ses pas, presenter une maieste digne de toute reverence. Ou quand vient a se tourner, le faire de tant bonne grace, que son maintien remplit de souverain plaisir tous ceulx qui assistent au bal: lequel finy, si elle poursuyt une gaillarde, passepied, ou autre courante, il pourra veoir ses mouvemens frapper en la veue des hommes comme un Soleil qui ne faict que passer.

> Or if she dances in company, one sees her adjust her gestures to the tempo and the beat; holding herself straight, accommodating her steps, she presents a vision of majesty full of respect. And when you need to turn, she does it with such good grace, and her bearing fills all those at the ball with remarkable pleasure; when the dance is finished, if she continues with a galliard, a passepied or another courante, you can see her movements strike the sight of men like a sun that just passes by.

13 The first lines cited are from the sonnet that begins 'Le doux sommeil qui toute chose appaise' (Sweet sleep that appeases everything); lines 7−8; G, 315). The second quotation is the opening quatrain of *Amours* (1552−53), poem 164; G, 105.

14 On the power and theory of dancing, the following works should be consulted: McGowan, *L'Art du ballet de cour en France* (Paris, 1963); Yates, *French Academies* and *The Valois Tapestries*; and Jacquot, *Les Fêtes de la Renaissance*.

15 P 1:954−66; L 9:75−100. Ronsard also contributed to the marriage celebrations in Lorraine at Bar-le-Duc in 1564, as did Belleau; *Bergerie* 1:283−93.

16 P 2:862−66; L 9:131−41. See also the dance of the graces around the nuptial couch of the duc de Joyeuse, *Epithalame de Monseigneur de Joyeuse, Admiral de France* (P 2:7−9; L 18:116−20).

17 See the engraving with banquet and dancing scenes in the poems of Jan van der Noot, *Divers Oeuvres poétiques* (Antwerp, 1580), p. 41, plate 12; he modelled this work closely upon Ronsard's bacchic dances in *L'Hymne de l'Automne* (P 2:248, lines 382−86; L 12:63).

18 Jamyn, *Elégie à Callirée*, in *Oeuvres*, ff. 122^v−123^v. The rest of the poem explores the passionate effects of experiencing this type of dancing, which was often described as 'wanton' and 'wayward', even by Toinot Arbeau; see *Orchésographie* [Lengres, 1588], trans. Mary S. Evans (New York, 1948), p. 87. Arbeau also gives the details of the figures and steps of the dance (pp. 119−23). An impression of *la volta* can be gained from the anonymous sixteenth-century painting in the museum in Rennes (which is now thought to depict Elizabeth I and Leicester

dancing). Charles IX enjoyed *la volta* danced before him on the square at Bri-
gnoles, 26 October 1563; see Graham and McAllister Johnson, *Royal Tour*, p. 93.

19 The painting now in the Louvre is reproduced by Blum, *Miniature française*, plate
24; for another example, see Yates, *The Valois Tapestries*, plate 24.

20 Brantôme, *Oeuvres* 8:29–30; Brantôme muddles a little the various poems Ronsard dedicated to Marguerite, but the reference is quite clear:

> Vous voyez dans cette elégie une très belle et riche description des beautez de cette
> accomplie princesse, soubs le nom et le corps de la belle charite Pasithee. La lecture
> n'en peut que fort plaire à tout le monde.
>
> *(Oeuvres 8:30)*

> You see in this elegy a beautiful and rich description of the charms of this accom-
> plished princess beneath the name and the form of the lovely grace, Pasithea. Its
> reading can only most wonderfully please everybody.

He returns to Marguerite's abilities to say:

> J'ay veu assez souvent la mener dancer *la pavanne d'Hespaigne* . . . les yeux de toute
> la salle ne se pouvoyent saouller, ny assez se ravir par une si agreable veue; car les
> passages estoient si bien dansez; les pas si sagement conduitz, et les arrestz faicts de
> si belle sorte qu'on ne savoit que plus admirer . . . *le vazzemeno d'Italie* . . . en y
> faisant de fort beaux, gentils et graves passages, que nul autre ou prince ou autre y
> pouvoit approcher, ny dame, car la majesté n'y estoit point espargnée; . . . au retour
> du roy de Poullongne . . . elle dansa ce bransle, devant forces estrangiers de Savoie,
> de Piedmont, d'Italie et autres, qui dirent n'avoir rien veu de si beau que ceste reyne,
> si belle et grave, danser si belle et grave danse.
>
> *(Oeuvres 8:73)*

> I've often seen her dance the Spanish pavane . . . all the eyes in the room could not
> drink in enough of her nor be sufficiently ravished by such a lovely sight; the move-
> ments were so well performed, the steps so wisely performed, and the stops so well
> done that it's not possible to admire them more. . . . The Italian dance . . . here,
> there were many impressive, solemn, and serious figures where no one, prince nor
> commoner, could equal her excellence, nor any lady for she did not spare her dig-
> nity. . . . On the return of the prince from Poland . . . she danced the branle, before
> many strangers from Savoy, Piedmont, Italy, and other countries, all of whom said
> that they had never seen anything as beautiful as the serious and beautiful queen
> who danced such lovely and solemn ballet.

The popularity of these and other dances is attested by the researches of Daniel
Heartz, who has collected an impressive bibliography of the editions of music for
dancing published by the enterprising d'Attaingnant; in *Pierre d'Attaignant*
(Berkeley, 1969).

21 This description was much appreciated by Ronsard's contemporaries, and much
copied; see, for example, Pierre Le Loyer, *Les Oeuvres et meslanges poétiques*
(Paris, 1579), poem 46, f. 17ᵛ:

> Dieux que ie fu ravi de desirs soucieux
> Le jour que ie la vey meslee en une dance,

Là où meinte jeunesse allant à la cadance,
Contr'imitoit le tour de la sphere des cieux.

My God, I was so overcome by preoccupying thoughts the day I saw her taking part in a dance, when so many young ones went out to perform imitating the motion of the heavenly spheres.

22 For an analysis of all the events at this meeting and for the history of court festivals during the lifetime of Catherine de' Medici, see Yates, *The Valois Tapestries*; and Graham and McAllister Johnson, *Royal Tour*.

23 Marguerite de Valois, *Mémoires* (Paris, 1628), pp. 9–10.

24 Simon Goulart, *Memoires de l'estat de France sous Charles IX*, 3 vols (Middelburg, 1578), 1 : 263–69.

25 For Brantôme's account, see *Oeuvres* 5 : 59–60; for Jean Dorat's account, see *Magnificentissimi spectaculi* (Paris, 1573)—the engraved figure is appended to the British Library's copy of the text.

26 Ronsard and Baïf made significant contributions to these entertainments, and were paid 2,000 crowns each; see Yates, *French Academies*, pp. 236–74, and my own introduction to a facsimile edition of *Le Balet comique* (Binghamton, N.Y., 1982).

27 Balthazar de Beaujoyeulx, *Balet comique de la reyne* (Paris, 1582), ff. 22^v, 55^v–56.

28 On Ronsard's knowledge of music, see Daniel Heartz, 'The Chanson in the Humanist Era', in *Current Thought in Musicology*, ed. John W. Grubbs (Austin, Tex., 1976), pp. 193–230. For the text of the preface to the *Meslanges* dedicated to Charles IX, see P 2 : 321–30, 978–81. The moral dimensions of musical effects are mentioned everywhere at this period, with remarkable care and detail by Tyard in *Solitaire premier* and *Solitaire second*; see also Henrich Glareau's handbook *Dodecachordon* (Basle, 1547).

29 P 2:979. The same sentiments can be found in the *Lettres patentes* issued by Charles IX for the Académie de poésie et de musique; see Henri Weber, *La Création poétique au XVIe siècle en France*, 2 vols (Paris, 1955), 1 : 58. For a thorough discussion of Plutarch and of Greek thought about music, François Lasserre, *Plutarque: De la musique: Sur l'éducation musicale dans la Grèce antique* (Lausanne, 1954), should be consulted.

30 See Yates, *French Academies*, pp. 77–94; and D. P. Walker, *Studies in Musical Science in the Late Renaissance* (London, 1978).

31 Beaujoyeulx, *Balet comique*, sig. ẽ iij^v.

32 Vigenère, *Images*, ff. 289–290^r, refers directly to Plutarch:

Que la poësie et par conséquent l'oraison mesuree, a une grande convenance et af-
finité avec le bal et l'art de danser; le tout a cause des cadences qui doibvent estre
observees en l'une et en l'autre; sans lesquelles il n'y a langage qui ne soit comme un
corps sans ame.

How great an accord and affinity have poetry, and thus measured oratory, with the
ball and the art of dancing, because cadences must be observed in both, without
which any language is like a body without a soul.

Amyot's translation of the relevant passage reads

Là où entre le bal et la poësie toutes choses sont communes, et participent en tout
l'une de l'autre, toutes deux representans une mesme chose, mesmement és chansons
à danser, qui s'appellent Hyparchemes, où la représentation se fait plus efficacement
de l'une par les gestes et mimes; et de l'autre par les paroles.

(PLUTARCH, Oeuvres morales 2:248)

There, where the dance and poetry have everything in common and share everything
together, both representing the same thing, even in dance songs called *hyparchemes*,
where representation is best done by gestures and mime.

Sir Thomas Elyot wrote many pages on the importance of dancing in *The Boke
Named the Gouvernour* [1531], ed. H. Herbert and S. Croft, 2 vols (London,
1883), 1:218–69.

33 As we noted in chapter 1, Pontus de Tyard similarly explained the Greek lyric
poets' use of chanting and structure in their odes.

34 Works referred to in this paragraph are: Ronsard, P 2:979; and Julius Caesar
Scaliger, *Poetices libri septem* (Lyons, 1561), bk 1, chap. 9, pp. 16–17.

35 Works cited are: Agrippa, *Declamation*, p. 89 (Latin edition published in Paris,
1531); Le Caron, 'Le démon d'Amour', *Poesies* (Paris, 1554), f. 29^v; and Jean
Dorat, *Epithalame ou chant nuptial sur le mariage de tres-illustres Prince et Princesse Henri de Lorraine duc de Guyse et Catarine de Cleves Contesse d'Eu* [Paris,
1570] in *Oeuvres poétiques*, ed. Ch. Marty-Laveaux (Paris, 1875), pp. 53–60.

36 Sir John Davies, *Orchestra* (London, 1596), stanza 96. See also stanza 17:

> Dancing (bright Lady) then began to be,
> When the first seedes whereof the World did Spring,
> The Fire, Ayre, Earth and Water did agree,
> By Love's persuasion, Nature's mighty King,
> To leave their first disordered combatting;
> And in a daunce such measure to observe,
> As all the world their motion should preserve.

Sarah Thesiger details the role of the dance as a paradigm of natural order in 'The
Orchestra of Sir John Davies and the Image of the Dance', *Journal of the Warburg
and Courtauld Institutes* 36 (1973): 277–304. See also Elyot, *Boke Named the
Gouvenour*, p. 218.

37 These phrases occur frequently in Ronsard's poems; for example, in *Hymne du ciel* (P 2:191; L 8:143) he writes eloquently and with great fervour on the subject; see also *Hymne des estoilles* (P 2:199; L 17:37), and *Hymne des astres* (P 2:846; L 8:151); for the dance movements of the elements and the seasons, see *Hymne du Printemps* (P 2:231; L 12:29) and *Hymne de l'Automne* (P 2:246; L 12:48).

38 Béranger, *Choréide, autrement, louenge du bal* (Lyons, 1556), p. 8; see also Davies, *Orchestra*, stanza 77.

39 Arcangelo Tuccaro, *Trois Dialogues de l'exercice de sauter et voltiger en l'air* (Paris, 1599), p. 36; for further details see McGowan, *Art du ballet*, pp. 20–22.

40 See Lucian of Samosate, *Oeuvres*, trans. Filbert Bretin (Paris, 1582), pp. 365–70. In the sixteenth century the *De saltatione* was thought to be a work of Lucian; see also Hoüel, *L'Histoire de la royne d'Arthemise*, ff. 25–32 on the scholarly art of the dancer.

41 See the dedicatory poems in the *Balet comique*, sigs ē i and ē iᵛ. Beaujoyeulx himself insists that his work is 'à la mode des anciens Grecs' (in the style of the ancient Greeks; p. 1).

42 Béranger, *Choréide*, p. 6; Claude François Menestrier, *Des ballets anciens et modernes* (Paris, 1682), p. 41. Elyot also stressed the moral qualities of dance, *Boke Named the Gouvenour*, p. 238.

43 See Godefroy, *Cérémonial françois* 2:3, 'premierement, marchoient les sept Planettes, vestues selon l'habit que les poëtes leur ont baillé' (first, the seven planets walked along clothed in the costume poets have given them). The ballet drawings of the planets that Bjurström found at Stockholm might have been intended for such a performance; see *Drawings*, nos 51, 57.

44 See P. Moreau, 'Ronsard et la danse des astres', *Mélanges d'histoire littéraire offerts à Raymond Lebègue* (Paris, 1969), pp. 75–82.

45 *A Apollon Pythien*, in *Hymnes homériques* II, trans. Louis Dimier (Paris, 1937), p. 7.

46 Ronsard, *Hymne de l'Hiver* (P 2:258; L 12:84):

> Apollon fist venir les Muses en la dance;
> La belle Calliope alloit à la cadance
> Sur toutes la premiere, et dessus le troupeau
> Paroissoit comme un pin sur le haut d'un coupeau.

> Apollo made the Muses come to dance; lovely Calliope first took up the steps and, above the troupe, appeared like a pine on the summit of a hill.

47 *Discours à Pierre Lescot*, P 2 : 422–25; L 10 : 300–307. For a parallel circumstance in English, see Edmund Spenser, *The Faerie Queene*, bk 6, canto 10. Recently Philip Ford has explored the complex web of sources used by Ronsard to transmit his views on poetic inspiration, in 'Ronsard and the Theme of Inspiration', in *The Equilibrium of Wit*, ed. Peter Bayley and Dorothy G. Coleman (Lexington, Ky., 1982), pp. 57–69.

48 Ronsard, *Discours à Odet de Colligny, Cardinal de Chastillon*, line 157 (P 2 : 426–30; L 10 : 5–15). Philippe Desportes was much impressed by these sentiments and he copied them in a *chanson, Les Premières Oeuvres* (Paris, 1573), ff. 63–64:

> Que de plaisir de voir la lune brune,
> Quand le soleil a faict place à la lune,
> Au fond des bois les Nymphes s'assembler,
> Monstrer au vent leur gorge descouverte,
> Danser, sauter, se donner cette verte,
> Et sous leurs pas tout l'herbage trembler,
> Leur bal fini, ie dresse en haut la veüe
> Pour voir le teint de la lune cornuë.

What a pleasure to see the darkened light when the sun makes way for the moon, when in the depths of the forest, nymphs assemble to bare their breasts to the wind, to jump, dance, and to make the grass shake beneath their feet; once their dance is finished, I look up and glimpse the shape of the crescent moon.

49 Du Bellay, *A Pierre Ronsard*, in *Poesies* 2 : 119–21.

50 *The Works of Hesiod, Callimachus, and Theognis*, trans. J. Banks (London, 1914), p. 1.

51 Vigenère, *Commentaire sur les décades de Tite Live* (Paris, 1583), col. 1293. Vigenère's detailed paralleling closely resembles Pontus de Tyard's discussion (see chapter 1). Vigenère continues:

> La strophe à sçavoir qui alloit de la main droicte vers la main gauche, representant le mouvement de l'univers de l'Orient à l'Occident; l'antistrophe au rebours qui retournoit de la gauche à la droicte, le mouvement particulier des corps celestes; et l'epode quelques pas en avant et autant en arriere, le flux et reflux de la mer; Et la pause finablement qui intervenoit entre les coupplets, le repos et l'immobilité de la terre.

> The strophe, that is to say, the movement from right to left, represents the movement of the universe from east to west; on the contrary, the antistrophe went from left to right, the particular movement of the heavenly spheres; and the epode, with its four steps frontwards and backwards, shows the ebb and flow of the sea; and the final pause that comes before the couplets, represents the repose and immobility of the earth.

52 Sylvia Pressouyre explores the sacred influences that connect the birth of Venus

and the dance of the dryads: 'Les Fresques de la galerie François Ier après restauration', *Bulletin de la Société Nationale des Antiquaires de France*, March 1970, pp. 123—37.

53 Concerning archival research on this motif, see Yves M. Metman, 'Un graveur inconnu de l'Ecole de Fontainebleau: Pierre Millan', *Bibliothèque d'Humanisme et Renaissance* 1 (1940): 202—14. The Renaissance *secrétaire* is described by Thirion, 'Rosso et les arts décoratifs'.

54 Ronsard, sixth ode, *A Mes Dames, filles du Roy Henri IIe*; P 1:495—98; L 8:75—80.

55 Ronsard, *Discours I, en forme d'elégie*, lines 127, 129—30; P 2:14—25; L 12: 256—77.

Conclusion

1 Du Bellay, *Deffence* p. 155, 'Finablement, j'estimeroy l'Art pouvoir exprimer la vive energie de la Nature, si vous pouviez rendre cete fabrique renouvelée semblable à l'antique' (Finally, I'll esteem Art capable of expressing the living energy of nature, if you can make this renewed building similar to the ancient ones).

2 Letter by Dolce to Contarini, *L'Aretino*, p. 217; see Golson, 'Landscape Prints', on sixteenth-century taste for landscapes.

3 See Junius, *Painting of the Ancients*, pp. 300—304, where he provides several examples of *enargia* (lively representation).

4 Cited by Roy, *Artistes et monuments* 1:482.

5 Belleforest, *Cosmographie*, p. 278, col. 1.

6 *Discours du grand et magnifique triumphe faict au mariage de . . . François . . .* (Paris, 1558), sig. c i; *Recueil des choses notables faites à Bayonne à l'entrevue de Charles IX . . .* (Paris, 1566), f. 54ᵛ.

7 Letter by Aretino to Messer Titian, *Letters*, trans. George Bull (London, 1970), no. 94; also cited by F. Saxl, *A Heritage of Images* (London, 1970), pp. 82—83.

8 Agrippa, *Declamation*, pp. 102—3.

9 For a discussion of the concepts of representation, description, and imitation, see Castor, *Pléiade Poetics*, pp. 178—79.

10 Ably demonstrated by G. Gadoffre, *Du Bellay et le sacré* (Paris, 1978), and by Coleman, *The Chaste Muse*.

11 Belleforest, *Cosmographie*, p. 323, col. 1.

12 Bruce R. Leslie, *Ronsard's Successful Epic Venture: The Epyllion* (Lexington, Ky., 1979).

13 Montaigne, *Essais*, pp. 268–69.

14 Nicolas Caussin, cited by Marc Fumaroli, *L'Age de l'éloquence* (Geneva, 1980), p. 293.

15 Antoine de Laval, 'Des Peintures convenables aux basiliques et Palais du Roy, et mesmes à sa Gallerie du Louvre', p. 4, in *Desseins et professions* (Paris, 1605).

Bibliography

This select bibliography is divided into three principal sections: manuscript sources, classical and Renaissance printed texts, and modern studies. Accounts of the French royal entries in the sixteenth century are grouped at the beginning of the second section; catalogues of museum exhibitions, at the beginning of the third.

Manuscript Sources

Bibliothèque Nationale

Ms. fr. 306. N. Hoüel, *L'Histoire de la royne d'Arthemise* (1562).

Ms. fr. 2585. *Plusieurs discours tenuz devant le feu roy* [16th century].

Ms. fr. 13429. *Commentaires de la guerre gallique* (1519).

Ms. fr. 22441. *Inventaire des joyaux de la maison de Lorraine.*

Ms. fr. 25560. Collection of poems, many written against Ronsard.

Ms. fr. 25561. Copies of many poetic works written for French festivals.

Ms. ital. 799. *Le Feste e trionfi fatti dalla seren. signoria de Venetia nella felice venuta di Henrico III* [1574].

British Library

Harleian 6205. *Les Commentaires de la guerre gallique* (1520).

Add. 18.850. *The Bedford Hours* (with French royal arms).

Add. 25.710. *Horae Beatae Virginis* (with portraits of François II and of Mary, Queen of Scots).

Early Printed Books

Royal Entries

Lyons, 1548: *La Magnificence de la superbe et triumphante entrée de la noble et antique cité de Lyon.* Lyons, 1549. Edited by G. Guigue. Lyons, 1928.

La Magnifica et triumphale intrata del christianiss. re di Francia Henrico secundo. . . . Lyons, 1548. Edited by G. Guigue. Lyons, 1928.

Paris, 1549: *C'est l'ordre qui a esté tenu à la nouvelle et joyeuse entrée que le Roy tres chrestien Henry deuxiesme de ce nom a faicte en sa bonne ville et cité de Paris . . . le seziesme jour de juin 1549.* Paris, 1549.

Rouen, 1550: *C'est la deduction du somptueux ordre, plaisantz spectacles et magnifiques theatres dresses . . . a la sacree maiesté . . . Henry second. . . .* Rouen, 1551. Edited by M. McGowan. Amsterdam, 1974.

Paris, 1571: *Bref et sommaire recueil de ce qui a esté faict et de l'ordre tenü à la joyeuse. . . . Entree de . . . Charles IX. . . .* Paris, 1572. Edited by F. Yates. Amsterdam, 1974. Edited by V. E. Graham and W. A. McAllister Johnson. Toronto, 1974.

Agrippa, H. C. *Declamation sur l'incertitude, vanité et abus des sciences.* N.p., 1582.

Alberti, L. *Della pittura* [1435]. Translated by C. Grayson. London, 1972.

Albon, C. d'. *De la majesté royalle.* Lyons, 1575.

Alciat, A. *Emblemes.* Lyons, 1549.

Amboise, F. d'. *Devises royales.* Paris, 1621.

L'Amour de Cupido et de Psiché. Introduction by R. Calder. The Hague, 1970.

Aneau, B. *L'Imagination poétique.* Lyons, 1552.

Apollonius Rhodius. *Argonautica.* N.p., 1541.

Arbeau, T. *Orchésographie.* Lengres, 1588. Translated by Mary S. Evans. New York, 1948.

Aretino, P. *Lettere sull'arte.* Edited by F. Pertile, C. Cordie, L. Camesasca. Milan, 1957.

———. *Letters.* Translated by G. Bull. London, 1970.

Ariosto, L. *Orlando Furioso.* Lyons, 1550.

Aristotle. *Works.* Edited by Robert Maynard Hutchins. 2 vols. Chicago, 1952.

Auge, D. de l'. *Deux Dialogues de l'invention poetique.* Paris, 1560.

Aurigny, G. d'. *La Genealogie des dieux poétiques.* Poitiers, 1545.

Bacon, Sir F. *The Works of Francis Bacon.* Edited by J. Spedding. 14 vols. London, 1860.

Baïf, A. de. *Euvres en rime.* 3 vols. Paris, 1573.

Beaujoyeulx, B. de. *Balet comique de la reyne.* Paris, 1582.

Beaulieu, E. de. *Des divers rapportz.* Lyons, 1537.

Beaulne, R. de (arch. de Bourges). *Oraison funèbre de la très chrestienne, très illustre, et très constante Marie Royne d'Escosse.* Paris, 1588.

Belleau, R. *La Bergerie.* Paris, 1572.

———. *Les Amours et nouveaux eschanges des pierres precieuses.* Paris, 1576.

———. *Les Oeuvres poétiques.* 2 vols. Paris, 1578.

Belleforest, F. de. *L'Histoire des neuf roys Charles de France.* Paris, 1568.

———. *La Cosmographie.* Paris, 1575.

———. *Harangues militaires.* Paris, 1588.

Belliard, G. *Le Premier Livre des poèmes.* Paris, 1578.

Bembo, P. *Les Azolains.* Translated by J. Martin. Paris, 1545.

Béranger de la Tour d'Albenas. *Le Siècle d'or.* Lyons, 1551.

———. *Choréide, autrement, louenge du bal.* Lyons, 1556.

———. *L'Amie des amies.* Lyons, 1558.

Bereau, J. *Les Eglogues et aultres oeuvres poétiques.* Poitiers, 1565.

Besly, I. *Les Hymnes de Ronsard.* Paris, 1604.

Bie, J. de. *La France métallique*. Paris, 1636.

Binet, C. *La Vie de Pierre de Ronsard*. Edited by P. Laumonier. Paris, 1909.

Boccaccio. *Boccaccio on Poetry*. Edited by C. G. Osgood. Princeton, 1930.

Boton, P. *La Camille*. Paris, 1573.

Bouchet, J. *Le Chappellet des princes*. Paris, 1517.

————. *Epistres morales et familieres du Traverseur*. Poitiers, 1545.

————. *Les Genealogies . . . des roys de France* . Paris, 1545.

————. *Les Triomphes de François Ier*. Poitiers, 1550.

Bourbon, N. *L'Epithalamion*. Paris, 1549.

————. *Nugae*. Paris, 1533. French edition *Bagatelles* by V. L. Saulnier. Paris, 1945.

Bouterone, M. *Le Petit Olympe d'Issy*. Paris, 1609.

Brantôme, P. de Bourdeille Seigneur de. *Oeuvres*. 9 vols. Edited by L. Lalanne. Paris, 1864–82.

Breche de Tours, J. *Premier Livre de l'honneste exercise du prince*. Paris, 1544.

Budé, G. *De l'institution du prince* [Paris, 1547]. Facsimile edition. Farnborough, 1966.

Callimachus. *Hymni*. Paris, 1546.

Cardan, J. *Subtilitez*. Paris, 1556.

Castiglione, B. de. *Il Cortegiano*. Venice, 1528. French translation, *Le Courtisan*. Lyons, 1538. English translation by Thomas Hoby [London, 1561]. London, 1959.

Catherine de' Medici. *Lettres*. 5 vols. Edited by M. le Cte. Hector de la Ferrière. Paris, 1885.

Cermenate, J. P. de. *Discours de la droite administration des royaumes et republiques*. Lyons, 1561.

Chappuys, C. *Le Discours de la court*. Paris, 1543.

Chasseneux, B. de. *Catalogus gloriae mundi*. Lyons, 1546.

Chrestien, F. *Panegyrique de Labirus Pacatus prononcé à Rome devant l'Empereur Theodose*. Paris, 1578.

Claudian, C. *Poetae celeberrimi opera*. Lyons, 1551.

————. *Oeuvres complètes*. 2 vols. Paris, 1798.

Colonna, F. de. *Hypnerotomachia Poliphili*. Venice, 1499. Translated by J. Martin. Paris, 1545.

Conti, N. *Mythologie ou explication des fables*, [Venice, 1568]. Paris, 1627.

Corbin, J. *La Royne Marguerite, où sont descrittes la grandeur de ceste grande princesse, sa beauté, ses vertus*. Paris, 1605.

Corrozet, G. *Triste Elegie ou déploration lamentant le trespas de feu et treshault et puissant prince Françoys de Valloys*. Paris, 1536.

————. *Les Antiquitez, histoires et singularitez de Paris, ville capitale du royaume de France*. Paris, 1550, 1577.

Dan, P. *Le Trésor des merveilles de la maison royale de Fontainebleau*. Paris, 1642.

Davies, Sir J. *Orchestra*. London, 1596.

Denisot, N. *Cantiques du premier advenement de Jesu-Christ*. Paris, 1553.

Des Autelz, G. *Replique aux furieuses defenses de L. Meigret.* Lyons, 1551.
———. *Amoureux repos.* Lyons, 1553.
———. *Remonstrance au peuple françoys envers la majesté du roy.* Paris, 1559.
Desportes, P. *Les Premières Oeuvres.* Paris, 1573. Annecy, 1576.
Dion Cassius. *Des faicts et gestes insignes des romains.* Paris, 1542.
Dionysius of Halicarnassus. *Opuscules rhétoriques.* 2 vols. Edited by G. Aujac. Paris, 1978.
Discours du grand et magnifique triumphe faict au mariage de . . . François . . . et Marie d'Estrevart. . . . Paris, 1558. Edited by W. Bentham. London, 1818.
Dolce, L. *L'Aretino.* Translated by M. Roskill. New York, 1968.
Dorat, J. *Triomphalis odae.* Paris, 1558. Edited by G. Demerson. Clermont-Ferrand, 1979.
———. *Paenes sive hymni in triplicem victoriam.* Paris, 1569.
———. *Magnificentissimi spectaculi in Henrici regis Poloniae gratulationem descriptio.* Paris, 1573.
———. *Oeuvres.* Paris, 1575.
———. *Oeuvres poétiques.* Edited by Ch. Marty-Laveaux. Paris, 1875.
Du Bartas, G. de Saluste. *La Sepmaine, ou creation du monde.* Paris, 1578.
———. *Oeuvres.* Paris, 1611. Edited by U. T. Holmes. 3 vols. Chapel Hill, N.C., 1935–40.
Du Bellay, J. *La Deffence et illustration de la langue françoyse.* Paris, 1549. Edited by H. Chamard. Paris, 1904.
———. *Poésies françaises et latines.* 2 vols. Edited by E. Courbet. Paris, 1918.
Du Cerceau, J. Androuet. *Des plus excellents bastiments de France.* Paris, 1576.
Du Chastel. *Les Trespas, obseques, et enterrement de tres-hault, tres-puissant, et tres-magnanime François Ier.* Paris, 1547.
Du Choul, G. *Discours de la religion des anciens romains.* Lyons, 1556.
Du Haillan, B. *L'Histoire de France.* Paris, 1576.
Du Pérac, E. *I vestigi dell'antichita di Roma raccolta et ritratti in perspectiva con ogni diligentia da Stephano Du Perac.* Paris, 1575.
Du Tillet, J. *Les Faits memorables advenus depuis Pharamond . . . jusques à l'an 1557.* Lyons, 1557.
———. *Recueil des rois de France.* Paris, 1580.

Elyot, Sir T. *The Boke Named the Gouvernour.* London, 1531. 2 vols. Edited by H. Herbert and S. Croft. London, 1883.
Equicola, M. *Les Six Livres de la nature de l'amour.* Translated by Gabriel Chapuis. Paris, 1584.
Erasmus, D. *The Education of a Christian Prince.* Translated and edited by L. K. Born. New York, 1936.
———. *The Correspondence.* Edited by R. A. B. Mynors and D. F. S. Thompson. Vol. 2. Toronto, 1975.
Espence, C. d'. *Deux Notables traictez.* Paris, 1575.
———. *Institution du prince.* Paris, 1575.
Estienne, C. *Les Voyages.* Paris, 1552.
Estienne, H., ed. *Theocriti aliorumque poetarum Idyllia.* Paris, 1549.

Ficino, M. *La Diffinition et perfection d'amour.* Paris, 1542.

Filleul, N. *Les Théâtres de Gaillon*. Rouen, 1566. Edited by F. Joukovsky. Geneva, 1971.

Finé, O. *Protomathesis*. Paris, 1532.

Firenzuola, A. *Dialogo delle bellezze delle donne*. Florence, 1548. French edition, Paris, 1578.

La Fleur de la vraye poesie françoyse. Paris [1540].

Foucault, C. (sire de la Coudrière). *Les Épistres amoureuses*. Rouen, 1597.

Fulvius, A. *Illustrium imagines*. Lyons, 1524.

Garnier, R. *Hymne de la monarchie*. Paris, 1567.

Gauricus, P. *De sculptura* [1504]. Edited by A. Chastel and R. Klein. Geneva, 1969.

Giorgio, F. *De harmonia mundi*. Venice, 1545. French translation, Paris, 1579.

Glareau, H. *Dodecachordon*. Basle, 1547.

Godard, J. *La Fontaine de Gentilly*. Paris, 1595.

Godefroy, T. *Le Cérémonial françois*. Paris, 1649.

Gohorry, J. *Livre de la conqueste de la toison d'or*. Paris, 1563.

Goulart, S. *Memoires de l'estat de France sous Charles IX*. 3 vols. Middelburg, 1578.

Guazzo, S. *Dialoghi piacevoli*. Venice, 1586.

Gueroult, G. *Epitome de la corographie d'Europe*. Lyons, 1553.

————. *Hymnes du temps et de ses parties*. Lyons, 1560.

Guilbert, P. *Description historique des château, bourg, et forêt de Fontainebleau*. 2 vols. Paris, 1731.

Habert, F. *Eglogue pastorale sur l'union nuptiale*. Paris, 1559.

Henri II. *Les Ordonnances et edictz faictz par le roy Henri 2e*. Paris, 1557.

Hesiod. *Le Premier Livre, intitulé les oeuvres, et les ioürs*. Translated by R. Le Blanc. Lyons, 1547.

Hesteau, C. *Oeuvres poétiques*. Paris, 1578.

Homer. *Les XXIIII Livres de l'Iliade; avec le premier et second de l'Odysée*. Translated by P. Salel, A. Jamyn, and J. Peletier. Paris, 1580.

Huttichius, J. *Imperatorum et caesarum vitae cum imaginibus*. Lyons, 1550.

Ivry, J. d'. *Les Triomphes de France*. Paris, 1508.

Jamyn, A. *Oeuvres*. Paris, 1575.

Jodelle, E. *Recueil des inscriptions, figures devises et masquarades*. Paris, 1558. Edited by V. E. Graham and W. A. Johnson. Toronto, 1972.

————. *Oeuvres complètes*. 2 vols. Edited by E. Balmas. Paris, 1965.

Josephus, F. *Antiquatum Iudaicarum*. Lyons, 1556.

Jouan, A. *Recueil et discours du voyage du roy Charles IX*. Paris, 1566.

Junius, F. *The Painting of the Ancients*. London, 1638.

La Madeleine, J. de. *Discours de l'estat et office d'un roy, prince, et monarque*. Paris, 1575.

Lamothe, J. de. *Le Blason des célestes et très chrétiennes armes de France*. Rouen, 1549.

La Perrière, G. de. *La Morosophie*. Lyons, 1553.

La Peruse, J. Bastier de. *Les Oeuvres*. Paris, 1573.

La Porte, M. de. *Les Epithètes*. Lyons, 1593.

La Rouvere, J. de. *Les Deux Sermons funèbres et obseques et enterrement du feu roy treschrestien Henri 2e*. Paris, 1559.

Laval, A. de. *Desseins et professions nobles et publiques*. Paris, 1605.

Laval, P. de. *Rimes*. Paris, 1576. Edited by G. Hermann. Périgueux, 1901.

Le Blond, J. *Le Printemps*. Paris, 1536.

Le Caron, L. *Poesies*. Paris, 1554.

———. *Les Dialogues*. Paris, 1556.

———. *Panegyrique ou oraison de louange au roy Charles IX*. Paris, 1566.

Le Fèvre de la Boderie, G. *Encyclie des secrets de l'eternité*. Paris, 1570.

Le Frère de Laval. *L'Histoire de France sous les rois Henri et François II, Charles IX, et Henri III*. Paris, 1581.

Le Loyer, P. *Les Oeuvres et meslanges poétiques*. Paris, 1579.

Lemaire de Belges, J. *Oeuvres*. Louvain, 1882–85.

———. *Le Temple d'Honneur et de Vertu*. Edited by H. Hornik. Geneva, 1957.

Le Pois, A. *Discours sur les medalles et gravures antiques principalement romaines*. Paris, 1579.

L'Hôpital, M. de. *Oeuvres complètes*. 5 vols. Edited by P. J. S. Duféy. Paris, 1824–26.

Lloyd, L. *The Triplicitie of Triumphs*. London, 1591.

Lomazzo, G. P. *Trattato dell'arte della pittura*. Milan, 1584.

Longueil, C. *De laudibus divi Ludovici atque Francorum*. Paris, 1510.

Magny, O. de. *Les Amours*. Paris, 1553.

———. *Gaiettez*. Paris, 1557.

———. *Oeuvres poétiques*. Paris, 1557.

Malvyn, G. de. *Gallia gemens*. Paris, 1563.

Marguerite de Valois. *Mémoires*. Paris, 1628.

Mattioli, P. A. *Il magno palazzo del cardinale di Trento*. Venice, 1539.

Mauro, L. *Le antichità de la città di Roma*. Venice, 1556.

Menestrier, C. F. *Des ballets anciens et modernes*. Paris, 1682.

Michel, G. *Le Siècle doré*. Paris, 1521.

Minut, G. de. *De la beauté, avec la Paule-graphie*. Lyons, 1587.

Montaigne, M. de. *Essais*. Edited by A. Thibaudet. Paris, 1950.

———. *Journal de Voyage*. Edited by M. Rat. Paris, 1955.

Moschus. Edited and translated by J. M. Edmunds. In *The Greek Bucolic Poets*. London, 1916.

Nifo, A. *De pulchro et amore* [Rome, 1531]. Lyons, 1549.

Ovid. *Ovide moralisé* (Claude Legonais) [ca. 1328]. 5 vols. Edited by De Boer. Amsterdam, 1915.

————. *La Metamorphose d'Ovide figurée*. Lyons, 1557.
————. *Les Quinze Livres*. Translated by F. Habert, Paris, 1573.

Paradin, C. *Devises héroiques*. Lyons, 1557.
Paschal, P. *Henrici II galliarum regis elogius*. Paris, 1560.
Pasquier, E. *Recherches de la France*. 2 vols. Paris, 1723.
————. *Choix de Lettres*. Edited by D. Thickett, Geneva, 1956.
————. *Lettres historiques*. Edited by D. Thickett. Geneva, 1966.
————. *Lettres familières*. Edited by D. Thickett. Geneva, 1974.
Peletier du Mans, J. *L'Art poëtique*. Lyons, 1555.
Pellerin, B. *Les Figures et portraicts des sept ages de l'homme*. Paris, 1595.
Perlin, E. *Description des royaulmes d'Angleterre et d'Escosse*. Paris, 1558.
Philibert de l'Orme. *Le Premier Livre d'architecture*. Paris, 1567–68.
Pindar. *Olympia, Pythia, Nemea, Isthmia*. Lyons, 1598. French edition 4 vols.
  Paris 1922–23.
Plato. *The Dialogues*, 5 vols. Edited by B. Jowett. Oxford, 1867.
————. French translation of *The Symposium*, L. Le Roy, *Le Sympose*. Paris,
  1558.
Plutarch. *Oeuvres morales*. Translated by J. Amyot. 2 vols. Paris, 1572.

Quintilian. *In de institutione oratoria libros XII*. Paris, 1556. French translation,
  Paris, 1718.
————. *Institutes*. 2 vols. Translated by J. Selby Watson. London, 1909.

*Recueil des choses notables faictes à Bayonne à l'entrevue de Charles IX avec la
  royne catholique sa soeur*. Paris, 1566.
Registres et délibérations de la ville de Paris. Vol. 3. Paris, 1883.
Remonstrance d'un bon catholique françoys aux trois estats. Blois, 1576.
Ringhieri, I. *Cento givochi liberali*. Bologna, 1551.
Ripa, C. *Iconologie* [1581]. Paris, 1644.
Romei, A. *The Courtiers Academie*. Translated by J. Kepers. London, 1598.
Ronsard, P. de. *Oeuvres complètes*. Edited by P. Laumonier (completed by I. Silver
  and R. Lebègue). 20 vols. Paris, 1914–75.
————. *Oeuvres complètes*. Edited by G. Cohen. 2 vols. Paris, 1950.
————. *Les Amours*. Edited by H. Weber and C. Weber. Paris, 1963.
Rose, F. *Hymne sur l'entrée du très-excellent et très-chrestien, roy de France en sa
  fameuse ville de Paris*. Paris, 1571.
Ruscelli, G. *Le imprese illustri*. Venice, 1568.

Sacrobosco, J. de. *Tractatus de sphaera* [ca. 1220]. Translated by G. Desbordes.
  Paris, 1584.
Sainte-Marthe, C. de. *La Poesie françoise*. Lyons, 1540.
Sainte-Marthe, S. de. *Les Genealogies des très illustres et très puissans princes les
  Ducz de Lorraine*. Paris, 1549.
Saint-Gelais, M. de. *Oeuvres*. 3 vols. Edited by P. Blanchemain. Paris, 1873.
Saint Thomas, F. de. *La Vraye Forme de bien et heureusement regir*. Lyons, 1569.

Sannazaro, J. *Arcadia*. Naples, 1504. Translated by J. Martin. Paris, 1544. English rendering by Ralph Nash. Detroit, 1966.

Sapet, P. de. *Les Enthousiasmes*. Paris, 1556.

Savigny, C. de. *Tableaux accomplis de tous les arts libéraux*. Paris, 1587.

Scaliger, J. C. *Poetices libri septem*. Lyons, 1561.

Scève, M. *Délie*. Lyons, 1544. Edited by I. D. McFarlane. Cambridge, 1966.

Sébillet, T. *Art poétique françoys*. Paris, 1548. Geneva, 1932.

Second, J. *Oeuvres*. Paris, 1938.

Serlio, S. *Des antiquitez*. Paris, 1550.

————. *Livre extraordinaire de architecture*. Lyons, 1551.

————. *Tutte l'opere et d'architecture*. Venice, 1619.

Seville, J. de. *Brief Discours sur la bonne et joyeuse reception faicte à la maieste du roy par ses tresfidelles et obëissants sujects de la ville de Rouen*. Rouen, 1588.

Seyssel, C. de. *Les Louenges du roy Louis XIIe de ce nom*. Paris, 1508.

————. *Le Grant monarchie de France*. Paris, 1519.

Sidney, Sir P. *An Apology for Poetry*. Edited by G. Smith. Oxford, 1959.

Signac, F. de. *Le Trespas et ordre des obseques de . . . Henri 2e*. Paris, 1559.

Silly, J. de. *La Harangue de par la noblesse de toute la France, au roy Charles 9e*. Paris, 1561.

Spifame, R. *Dicæarchiae Henrici regis, Christianissimi progymnasmata*. N.p. [1556].

Statius, P. P. *Silvae*. Lyons, 1559. Translated by J. H. Mosley. 2 vols. London, 1928.

Symeoni, G. *L'Histoire d'Hérodien*. Lyons, 1554.

————. *Interpretation grecque, latine, toscane, et françoyse du monstre ou enigme d'Italie*. Lyons, 1555.

————. *Les Illustres Observations antiques*. Lyons, 1558.

————. *La Description de la Limague d'Auvergne en forme de dialogue*. Lyons, 1561.

Tahureau, J. *Les Dialogues*. Paris, 1565.

————. *Odes*. Edited by P. Blanchemain. 2 vols. Paris, 1869.

————. *Poesies*. Edited by P. Blanchemain. Paris, 1870.

Taillemont, C. de. *Discours des champs faez*. Paris, 1553.

————. *La Tricarite*. Lyons, 1556.

Tatius, A. *Les Amours de Clytophon et de Leucippe*. Paris, 1635.

Theocritus. *Les Idylles*. Paris, 1688.

Le Tocsain contre les massacreurs en France. Rheims, 1577. Rheims, 1579.

Tory, G. *Champfleury*. Paris, 1529.

Traité de l'authorité des Rois. Paris, 1561.

Tuccaro, A. *Trois Dialogues de l'exercice de sauter et voltiger en l'air*. Paris, 1599.

Turrin, C. *Les Oeuvres poetiques*. Paris, 1572.

Tyard, Pontus de. *Le Solitaire second, ou prose de la musique*. Lyons, 1555.

————. *L'Univers*. Lyons, 1557.

————. *Douze Fables de fleuves ou de fontaines*. Paris, 1586.

————. *Le Solitaire premier ou dialogue de la fureur poetique.* Edited by F. S. Baridon. Geneva, 1950.

Tyrtaeus. *Works.* In *Theocriti aliorumque poetarum idyllia.* Edited by H. Estienne. Paris, 1549.

Valeriano, G. *Commentaires hiéroglyphiques.* Paris, 1576.

Valerius Flaccus, C. *Argonauticon.* Paris, 1532.

Van Buchel, A. *Description de Paris.* Edited by L. A. van Langeraad and A. Vidier. Paris, 1899.

Van der Noot, J. *Divers Oeuvres poétiques.* Antwerp, 1580.

Varchi, B. *Due Lezzioni.* Florence, 1549.

Vasari, G. *Vite de piu' eccellenti pittori, scultori, et architetti.* 16 vols. Milan, 1810.

————. *The Lives of the Painters, Sculptors, and Architects.* 4 vols. London, 1927.

Veneziano, A. *Recueil de vases.* Paris, 1680.

Vico, E. *Omnium Caesarum verissimae imagines ex livia antiquis numismata desumptae.* Venice, 1553, 1554.

————. *Discorsi sopra le medaglie de gli antichi.* Venice, 1555, 1558.

————. *Le imagini delle donne auguste.* Venice, 1557.

————. *Augustarum imagines aereis formus expressae; vitae quoque earundem.* Venice, 1558.

————. *Romanorum numismata liber primis.* Venice, 1560.

Vigenère, B. de. *Les Images des deux Philostrates grecs.* Paris, 1578.

————. *Commentaire sur les décades de Tite Live.* Paris, 1583.

————. *Les Commentaires de Jules Cesar.* Paris, 1589.

Virgil. *Les Oeuvres.* Translated by N. Cousteau. Paris, 1529.

————. *Les Georgiques.* Paris, 1519.

Vitruvius. *Architecture ou l'art de bien bastir.* Translated by J. Martin. Paris, 1547.

Vostre, S. *Heures à l'usage de Châlons-sur-Marne.* N.p., 1514.

Woeriot, P. *Pinax iconicus.* Lyons, 1554.

Yver, J. *Le Printemps.* Paris, 1572.

Zantani, A. *Le imagini con tutti i riversi.* Venice, 1548.

Modern Studies

Catalogues of Exhibitions

Le Triomphe du maniérisme européen. Amsterdam, 1955.

The School of Fontainebleau. Fort Worth Art Center, 1965.

Le Colloque de Fontainebleau. Paris, 1972.

L'Ecole de Fontainebleau: Grand Palais, Paris, 1972–73. Paris, 1972.

Princely Magnificence, Court Jewels of the Renaissance, 1500–1630. Victoria and Albert Museum, 1980.

Adhémar, J. 'French Sixteenth-Century Genre Paintings'. *Journal of the Warburg and Courtauld Institutes* 8 (1945): 191–95.
———. 'Ronsard et l'Ecole de Fontainebleau'. *Bibliothèque d'Humanisme et Renaissance* 2 (1958): 344–48.
Alpers, S. L. 'Ekphrasis and Aesthetic Attitudes in Vasari's *Lives*'. *Journal of the Warburg and Courtauld Institutes* 23 (1960): 190–215.
Armand-Durand, M. *Le Livre de la bijouterie de R. Boyvin d'Angers.* Paris, 1876.
Armstrong, E. *Ronsard and the Age of Gold.* Cambridge, 1968.
Aronson, N. *Les Idées politiques de Rabelais.* Paris, 1973.

Bardon, F. *Diane de Poitiers et le mythe de Diane.* Paris, 1963.
Bartlett-Giametti, A. *The Earthly Paradise and the Renaissance Epic.* Princeton, 1966.
Bartsch. *The Illustrated Bartsch, Early Italian Masters.* Edited by M. Zucker. New York, 1980.
Becker, Ph. A. 'La Vie littéraire à la cour de Louis XII'. *Neuphilologus* 23 (1922): 138–39.
Beer, J. M. A. *A Medieval Caesar.* Geneva, 1976.
Béguin, S. 'La Suite d'Arthémise'. *L'Oeil* 38 (Feb. 1958): 32–39.
———. *L'Ecole de Fontainebleau.* Paris, 1960.
———. 'Le Maître de Flore de l'Ecole de Fontainebleau'. *Art de France* 1 (1961): 300–305.
———. 'Remarques sur la chambre du roi'. In *Le Colloque de Fontainebleau.* Paris, 1972. Pp. 199–230.
Bell, D. M. *L'Idéal éthique de la royauté en France au Moyen Age.* Geneva, 1962.
Berkenhagen, E. *Die Französischen Zeichnungen der Kunstbibliothek Berlin.* Berlin, 1970.
———. 'Entre Jean Goujon et Philibert de l'Orme'. *Berliner Museen* 1 (1971): 9–23.
Bertolini, J. A. 'Leonardo's *Leda* in G. Rucellai's *Oreste*'. *Renaissance Drama,* n.s., 7 (1976): 151–76.
Biver, P. *Histoire du château de Meudon.* Paris, 1923.
Bjurström, P. *Drawings in the Swedish Public Collections.* Stockholm, 1976.
Bloch, M. *Les Rois thaumaturges.* Strasbourg, 1924.
Blunt, A. *Art and Architecture in France, 1500–1700.* London, 1953.
———. *Artistic Theory in Italy, 1450–1600.* Oxford, 1962.
Bonnaffé, E. *Inventaire des meubles de Catherine de' Médicis.* Paris, 1874.
Born, L. K. 'The Perfect Prince, According to the Latin Panegyrists'. *American Journal of Philology* 55 (1934): 20–35.
Bouchet, H. *Exposition des primitifs français au Palais du Louvre et à la Bibliothèque Nationale.* Paris, 1904.
Bouchot, H. *Les Femmes de Brantôme.* Paris, 1890.
———. *Les Clouet et Corneille de Lyon.* Paris, 1892.

Bourciez, E. E. J. *Les Moeurs polies et la littérature de cour sous Henri II*. Paris, 1886.

Bourdéry, L., and E. Lachenaud. *L'Oeuvre des peintres émailleurs de Limoges*. Paris, 1897.

Brun, R. *Le Livre illustré au XVIe siècle*. Paris, 1930.

Burgess, T. C. *Epideictic Literature*. Chicago, 1962.

Buttin, C. 'L'Armure de Henri II, dauphin'. *Aréthuse*, 1929, no. 25.

Cahen, E. *Callimaque et son oeuvre poétique*. Bibliothèque des Ecoles françaises d'Athènes et de Rome. Fasc. 134.

Cameron, A. *Claudian: Poetry and Propaganda at the Court of Honorius*. Oxford, 1970.

Carandente, G. *I trionfi nel primo Rinascimento*. N.p., 1963.

Carroll, E. A. 'Some Drawings by Rosso'. *Burlington Magazine* 103 (1961): 446–54.

———. 'Rosso in France'. In *Le Colloque de Fontainebleau*. Paris, 1972. Pp. 17–28.

Castor, G. *Pléiade Poetics*. Cambridge, 1968.

———. 'Imitation in Ronsard: O de Nepenthe . . .' *Modern Language Review* 63 (1968): 332–39.

———. 'The Theme of Illusion in Ronsard's *Sonets pour Hélène*'. *Forum for Modern Language Studies* 7 (1971): 361–73.

Cave, T. 'Ronsard's Bacchic Poetry: From the *Bacchanales* to the *Hymne de l'Automne*'. *L'Esprit Créateur* 10 (1970): 104–16.

———. 'The Triumph of Bacchus and Its Interpretation in the French Renaissance'. In *Humanism in France*. Edited by A. Levi. Manchester, 1970.

———. 'Ronsard as Apollo: Myth, Poetry, and Experience in a Renaissance Sonnet Cycle'. *Yale French Studies* 47 (1972): 76–90.

———. 'Mythes de l'abondance et de la privation chez Ronsard'. *Cahiers de l'Association Internationale des Etudes Françaises* 25 (1973): 247–60.

———. 'Ronsard's Mythological Universe'. In *Ronsard the Poet*. Edited by T. Cave. London, 1973.

———. 'Copia and Cornucopia'. In *French Renaissance Studies*. Edited by P. Sharratt. Edinburgh, 1976.

———. *The Cornucopian Text*. Oxford, 1979.

Cave, T., ed. *Ronsard the Poet*. London, 1973.

Cazeaux, I. *French Music in the Fifteenth and Sixteenth Centuries*. Oxford, 1975.

Charlton, H. B. *Castelvetro's Theory of Poetry*. Manchester, 1913.

Chirol, G. *Un Premier Foyer de la Renaissance en France, le château de Gaillon*. Paris, 1955.

Christol, M. G. 'La Fresque du château de Tanlay'. *Bulletin de la Société de l'Histoire du Protestantisme Français* 101 (1951): 231–36.

Clark, J. E. *The Fortunes of a Classical Genre in Sixteenth-Century France*. The Hague, 1975.

Clark, K. *The Nude*. London, 1956.

Clements, R. J. 'Ronsard and Ficino on the Four Furies'. *Romanic Review* 45 (1954): 161–69.

————. *Picta Poesis, Literary and Humanistic Theory in Renaissance Emblem Books*. Rome, 1960.

Cloulas, I. *Un Portrait de Catherine de Médicis*. Paris, 1979.

Coleman, D. *The Gallo-Roman Muse*. Cambridge, 1979.

————. *The Chaste Muse: A Study of Joachim du Bellay's Poetry*. Leiden, 1980.

Coyecque, E. 'Au domicile mortuaire de German Pilon, 10 fév. au 13 mars 1950'. *Humanisme et Renaissance* 7 (1940): 45–101.

Cropper, E. 'On Beautiful Women, Parmigianino, Petrarchismo, and the Vernacular Style'. *Art Bulletin* 58 (1976): 374–94.

Cruickshank, J. *French Literature and Its Background*. Vol. 1. Oxford, 1968.

Cust, R. H. H. *The Life of B. Cellini*. 2 vols. London, 1927.

Dassonville, M. *Ronsard: Prince des poètes ou poète des princes, 1550–56*. Geneva, 1976.

Delaborde, H. *Marc-Antoine Raimondi*. Paris, 1887.

Delacourcelle, D. *Le Sentiment de l'art dans 'La Bergerie' de Rémy Belleau*. Oxford, 1945.

Delange, C. *Monographie de l'oeuvre de Bernard Palissy*. Paris, 1862.

Demerson, G. 'Trois Poètes français, traducteurs d'un idylle de Moschus'. In *Mélanges d'histoire littéraire offerts à Raymond Lebègue*. Paris, 1969.

————. *La Mythologie dans l'oeuvre de la Pléiade*. Geneva, 1972.

Demetz, O. 'The Elm and the Vine: Notes Towards the History of a Marriage Topos'. *PMLA* 73 (1958): 521–32.

Desjardins, A. *Négociations diplomatiques de la France avec la Toscane*. 6 vols. Paris, 1859–86.

Dickinson, G. *Du Bellay in Rome*. Leiden, 1960.

Dimier, L. *Le Primatice, peintre, sculpteur, et architecte des rois de France*. Paris, 1900.

————. *Histoire de la peinture du portrait*. Paris and Brussels, 1924.

————. *Le Château de Fontainebleau*. Paris, 1930.

Dinsmoor, W. B. 'The Literary Remains of Sebastiano Serlio'. *Art Bulletin* 24 (1942): 55–154.

Du Colombier, P. *Jean Goujon*. Paris, 1949.

Du Molin, M. *Le Château d'Oiron*. Paris, 1931.

Ehrmann, J. *Antoine Caron*. Geneva and Lille, 1955.

————. 'La Belle Cheminée du château de Fontainebleau'. In *Le Colloque de Fontainebleau*. Paris, 1972. Pp. 117–24.

Eisler, C. 'Etienne Delaune et les graveurs de son entourage'. *L'Oeil* 44 (1965): 10–13.

————. *The Master of the Unicorn: The Life and Work of Jean Duvet*. New York, 1979.

Eraud, F. 'Essais sur les peintures décoratives de Tanlay'. *Bulletin de la Société d'Archéologie et d'Histoire du Tonnerois* 23 (1970): 79–87.

————. 'Peintures murales dans la deuxième moitié du XVIe siècle découvertes au château de Villeneuve-Lembron (Puy-de-Dôme)'. *Le Colloque de Fontainebleau*. Paris, 1972.

Festugière, A. M. J. *La Philosophie de l'amour de Marsile Ficin et son influence sur la littérature française au XVIe siècle*. Paris, 1941.

Ford, P. J. 'George Buchanan's Court Poetry and the Pléiade'. *French Studies* 34 (1980): 137–52.

Fumaroli, M. *L'Age de l'éloquence*. Geneva, 1980.

Gadoffre, G. *Ronsard par lui-même*. Paris, 1960.

———. *Du Bellay et le sacré*. Paris, 1978.

Gallatier, ed. *Panégyristes latins*. 2 vols. Paris, 1949.

Gallet, A. 'Les Peintures murales du château d'Ecouen'. *Réunion de la Société des Beaux Arts des Départements*, 1882, pp. 89–95.

Garrison, J. D. *Dryden and the Tradition of Panegyric*. Berkeley, 1975.

Gent, L. *Picture and Poetry, 1560–1620*. Leamington Spa, 1981.

Geymüller, Baron H. de. *Les Du Cerceau, leur vie et leur oeuvre d'après de nouvelles recherches*. Paris, 1887.

Giesey, R. E. *The French Funeral Ceremony*. Geneva, 1960.

Glauser, A. *Le Poème symbole*. Paris, 1967.

Gluck, D. 'Les Entrées provinciales de Henri II'. *L'Information d'Histoire de l'art* 10 (1965): 215–19.

Golson, L. M. 'L. Penni, a Pupil of Raphael at the Court of Fontainebleau'. *Gazette des Beaux Arts* 51 (1957): 17–36.

———. 'Landscape Prints and Landscapists of the School of Fontainebleau, c. 1543–c. 1570'. *Gazette des Beaux Arts* 71 (1969): 95–110.

Gombrich, E. H. *The Heritage of Apelles: Studies in the Art of the Renaissance*. Oxford, 1978.

———. *Symbolic Images: Studies in the Art of the Renaissance*. London, 1972.

Gordon, A. *Ronsard et la rhétorique*. Geneva, 1970.

Graham, V. E., and W. McAllister Johnson. *The Royal Tour of France by Charles IX and Catherine de' Medici, 1564–66*. Toronto, 1979.

Grançsay, S. V. 'The Armor of Henry II of France from the Louvre Museum: Royal Armorers, Antwerp or Paris'. *Metropolitan Museum Bulletin* 10 (1952): 68–80.

Grand-Carteret, J. *Les Titres illustrés et l'image au service de la musique*. Turin, 1904.

Guiffrey, J. 'Nicolas Hoüel apothicaire parisien'. *Mémoires de la Société de l'Histoire de Paris et de l'Ile de France* 25 (1898): 179–270.

———. *Les Dessins de l'histoire des rois de France*. Paris, 1920.

Guillaume, J. 'La Galerie d'Oiron'. In *Le Colloque de Fontainebleau*. Paris, 1972.

———. 'Oiron: Fontainebleau poitevin'. *Monuments Historiques* 101 (1979): 77–96.

Hackenbroch, Y. 'New Knowledge on Jewels and Designs After Etienne Delaune'. *Connoisseur* 162 (1966): 82–89.

———. 'Bijoux de l'Ecole de Fontainebleau'. In *Le Colloque de Fontainebleau*. Paris, 1972.

Hagstrum, J. H. *The Sister Arts: The Tradition of Literary Pictorialism and English Poetry from Dryden to Gray*. Chicago, 1958.

Hardison, O. B. *The Enduring Monument*. Chapel Hill, N.C., 1962.

Hartt, F. *Guilio Romano*. New Haven, 1958.

Hathaway, B. *The Age of Criticism: The Late Renaissance in Italy*. Ithaca, N.Y., 1962.

Hatzfeld, H. A. *Literature Through Art: A New Approach to French Literature*. Oxford, 1952.

Havelock, E. A. *Prefaces to Plato*. Oxford, 1963.

Hayward, J. F. 'The Mannerist Goldsmith: France and the School of Fontainebleau'. *Connoisseur* 153 (1963): 11–15.

———. *The Virtuoso Goldsmiths and the Triumph of Mannerism, 1540–1620*. New York, 1976.

Heartz, D. *Pierre d'Attaignant*. Berkeley, 1969.

———. 'Voix de Ville: Between Humanist Ideals and Musical Realities'. In *Words and Music: The Scholar's View*. Edited by L. Berman. Cambridge, Mass., 1972.

Herbet, F. *Les Graveurs de l'Ecole de Fontainebleau*. Paris, 1897.

Holt, E. G. *A Documentary History of Art*. 2 vols. New York, 1958.

Hulubei, A. *L'Eglogue en France au XVIe siècle, 1515–89*. Paris, 1938.

Hutton, J. *The Greek Anthology*. Ithaca, N.Y., 1946.

Jacquot, J., ed. *Les Fêtes de la Renaissance*. 3 vols. Paris, 1956, 1960, 1975.

Javitch, D. *Poetry and Courtliness in Renaissance England*. Princeton, 1978.

Jeanneret, M. 'Les Oeuvres d'art dans *La Bergerie* de Belleau'. *Revue d'Histoire Littéraire de la France* 70 (1970): 1–13.

Jenkins, M. *The State Portrait: Its Origin and Evolution*. N.p., 1947.

———. 'The Henri II Wing of the Louvre'. *Journal of Medieval and Renaissance Studies* 7 (1977): 289–307.

Jestaz, B. 'L'Exportation des marbres de Rome 1535–1571'. *Mélanges d'Archéologie et d'Histoire*, (Ecole française de Rome, Paris) 75 (1963): 415–66.

Jeudwine, W. R. *Art and Style in Printed Books*. London, 1979.

Joukovsky, F. *La Gloire à la Renaissance*. Geneva, 1969.

Jouve, L. *Les Wiriot et les Briot, artistes lorrains*. Paris, 1891.

Jung, M.-R. *Hercule dans la littérature française au XVIe siècle*. Geneva, 1966.

Kantorowicz, E. H. *The King's Two Bodies*. Berkeley, 1957.

Kelso, R. *Doctrine for the Lady of the Renaissance*. Champaign, Ill., 1956.

Kipling, G. *The Triumph of Honour*. Leiden, 1977.

Kuhn, P. 'Influence néo-latine dans les églogues de Ronsard'. *Revue d'Histoire Littéraire de la France* 21 (1914): 311–25.

Laborde, L. de. *Les Comptes des bâtiments du roi, 1528–71*. 2 vols. Paris, 1887–80.

La Boullaye, E. J. de. *Etude sur la vie et les oeuvres de Jean Duvet*. Paris, 1876.

Labrot, G. *Le Palais Farnese de Caprarola*. Paris, 1970.

Lafeuille, G. *Cinq Hymnes de Ronsard*. Geneva, 1973.

Laking, G. F. *A Record of European Armour and Arms Through Seven Centuries*. 5 vols. London 1920–22.

Langmuir, E. 'Niccolo dell'Abbate's *Aeneid* Frescoes for the *Gabinetto* of the Castle at Scandiano, near Modena'. *Journal of the Warburg and Courtauld Institutes* 39 (1976): 151–60.

Lasserre, F. *Plutarque: De la musique: Sur l'éducation musicale dans la Grèce antique.* Lausanne, 1954.

Latour, H. de. *Catalogue des jetons de la Bibliothèque Nationale: Rois et reines de France.* Paris, 1897.

Laumonier, P. *Ronsard poète lyrique.* Paris, 1932.

Lavedan, P. *L. Limosin et les émailleurs français.* Paris, 1913.

Lawrence, M. 'The Birth of Venus in Roman Art'. In *Essays in the History of Art Presented to Rudolf Wittkower.* Edited by D. Fraser, H. Hibbard, and M. T. Lewine. London, 1967.

Lebègue, R. 'Ronsard, ou comment se comporter avec des souverains critiquables'. In *Culture et pouvoir au temps de l'humanisme et de la Renaissance.* Geneva, 1978.

Le Coque, A.-M. 'Les Peintures murales d'Ecouen'. In *Le Colloque de Fontainebleau.* Paris, 1972.

Lee, R. W. 'Ut pictura poesis: The Humanistic Theory of Painting'. *Art Bulletin* 22 (1940): 197–269; rpt. New York, 1967.

Lehmann-Hartleben, K. 'The *Imagines* of the Elder Philostratus'. *Art Bulletin* 23 (1941): 16–44.

Leslie, B. R. *Ronsard's Successful Epic Venture: The Epyllion.* Lexington, Ky., 1979.

McAllister Johnson, W. 'Primaticcio Revisited'. *Art Quarterly* 29 (1966): 245–68.

———. 'Numismatic Propaganda in Renaissance France'. *Art Quarterly* 31 (1968): 123–53.

———. 'Ronsard et la renommée du Louvre'. *Bibliothèque d'Humanisme et Renaissance* 30 (1968): 7–17.

———. 'Les Débuts de Primatice à Fontainebleau'. *Revue de l'Art*, 1969, pts 1–6, pp. 9–18.

———. 'Prolegomena to the Images ou Tableaux de Platte Peinture'. *Gazette des Beaux Arts* 73 (1969): 277–304.

McFarlane, I. D. 'Aspects of Ronsard's Poetic Vision'. In *Ronsard the Poet.* Edited by T. Cave. London, 1973.

McGowan, M. M. *L'Art du ballet de cour en France.* Paris, 1963.

———. *L'Entrée de Henri II, Rouen 1550.* Amsterdam, 1974.

McGuinness, L. R., and H. Mitchell. *Catalogue of the Earl of Crawford's 'Speculum Romanae Magnificentiae' Now in the Avery Architectural Library.* New York, 1976.

Magne, L. *L'Oeuvre des peintres verriers français.* Paris, 1885.

Mann, J. 'Henri II's Armour.' *Connoisseur* 92 (1933): 414–17.

———. 'A Parade Armour of Henri II, King of France'. *Country Life* 83 (1938): 603–5.

Marcel, P. *J. Martin.* Paris, 1927.

Marcheix, M. 'Les Émaux à l'exposition de l'Ecole de Fontainebleau'. *Bulletin de la Société Archéologique et Historique du Limousin* 100 (1973): 163–92.

Margolin, J. C. 'L'Hymne de l'or et son ambiguïté'. *Bibliothèque d'Humanisme et Renaissance* 28 (1966): 271–93.

Martindale, A. *The Triumph of Caesar by Andrea Mantegna*. London, 1979.

Maumené, C., and L. d'Harcourt. *Iconographie des rois de France*. Paris, 1928.

Mazerolle, F. *Les Médailleurs français*. Paris, 1902.

Ménager, D. *Ronsard: Le Roi, le poète, et les hommes*. Geneva, 1979.

Metman, Y. M. 'Un Graveur inconnu de l'Ecole de Fontainebleau: Pierre Millan'. *Bibliothèque d'Humanisme et Renaissance* 1 (1940): 202–14.

Michelant, H. *Catalogue de la bibliothèque de François Ier*. Paris, 1863.

Mirot, L. *L'Hôtel et les collections du connétable de Montmorency*. Paris, 1920.

Monnier, G., and W. McAllister Johnson. 'Caron antiquaire: A propos de quelques dessins du Louvre'. *Revue de l'Art*, 1971, pts 11–14, pp. 23–30.

Morcay, R., and A. Muller. *La Renaissance*. Paris, 1960.

Moreau, P. 'Ronsard et la danse des astres'. In *Mélanges d'histoire littéraire offerts à Raymond Lebègue*. Paris, 1969.

Morrison, M. 'Ronsard and Catullus'. *Bibliothèque d'Humanisme et Renaissance* 18 (1956): 240–74.

———. 'Catullus and the Poetry of the Renaissance'. *Bibliothèque d'Humanisme et Renaissance* 25 (1963): 25–56.

———. 'Ronsard and Desportes'. *Bibliothèque d'Humanisme et Renaissance* 28 (1966): 294–322.

Nolhac, P. de. *Ronsard et l'humanisme*. Paris, 1921.

———. 'Jean Second et Corneille de Lyon'. *Mélanges Laumonier*. Paris, 1935.

Osgood, C. G. *Boccaccio on Poetry*. Princeton, 1930.

Oulmont, C. H. 'La Fresque de la tour de la ligue au château de Tanlay'. *Revue de l'Art Ancien et Moderne* 64 (1933): 183–84.

Panofsky, E. 'The Iconography of the Galerie François Ier at Fontainebleau'. *Gazette des Beaux Arts* 52 (1958): 113–90.

———. *Studies in Iconography*. London, 1967.

———. *Problems in Titian, Mostly Iconographic*. London, 1969.

Parent, A. *Les Métiers du livre à Paris au seizième siècle*. Geneva, 1974.

Patterson, A. 'Ecphrasis in Garcilaso's Egloga Tercera'. *Modern Language Review* 72 (1977): 73–92.

Péré, G. *Le Sacre et le couronnement des rois de France*. Paris, 1921.

Perrot, F. 'Les Vitraux du château d'Ecouen'. In *Le Colloque de Fontainebleau*. Paris, 1972.

———. 'Vitraux héraldiques venant du château d'Ecouen'. *La Revue du Louvre*, 1973, pp. 77–82.

Pickering, F. P. *Literature and Art in the Middle Ages*. London, 1970.

Plattard, J. 'Les Arts et les artistes de la Renaissance française jugés par les écrivains du temps'. *Revue d'Histoire Littéraire de la France* 21 (1914): 481–502.

———. 'Bibliothèque et collection de tableaux d'un chanoine de Poitiers en 1581'. *Revue du XVIe Siècle* 7 (1920): 253–55.

Pouncey, P., and J. A. Gere. *Italian Drawings in the Department of Prints and Drawings in the British Museum*. London, 1962.

Praz, M. *Studies in Sixteenth- and Seventeenth-Century Imagery*. 2 vols. London, 1939, 1947.

———. *Mnemoysne: The Parallel Between Literature and the Visual Arts*. New York, 1970.

Pressouyre, S. 'Le Château de Tarascon'. In *Congrès Archéologique de France*. Avignon, 1963.

———. 'Les Fresques de la galerie François Ier après restauration'. *Bulletin de la Société Nationale des Antiquaires de France*, March 1970, pp. 123–37.

Price Zimmermann, T. C. 'P. Giovio and the Evolution of Renaissance Art Criticism'. *Cultural Aspects of the Italian Renaissance in Honor of P. O. Kristeller*. Edited by C. Clough. Manchester, 1976.

Quarre, P. 'Histoire d'Artémise—tapisserie'. *La Revue du Louvre*, 1964, pp. 249–54.

Quentin-Bauchart, E. *La Bibliothèque de Fontainebleau*. Paris, 1891.

Quinones, R. J. *The Renaissance Discovery of Time*. Cambridge, Mass., 1972.

Raymond, M. *L'Influence de Ronsard sur la poésie française, 1550–85*. 2 vols. Paris, 1927.

———. *La Poésie française et le maniérisme*. London, 1971.

Ritter, R. *Le Château de Pau, étude historique et archéologique*. Paris, 1919.

Roland, F. 'A. La Fréry, 1512–77'. *Mémoires de la Société d'Emulation du Doubs*. (1910): 320–78.

Romier, L. *Origines politiques des guerres de religion*. 2 vols. Paris, 1913–14.

Rondot, N. *Les Médailleurs et graveurs de monnaies, jetons, et médailles en France*. Paris, 1904.

Rosand, D. 'Ut pictor poeta: Meaning in Titian's Poesie'. *New Literary History* 3 (1971–72): 527–46.

Rosenmeyer, T. G. *The Green Cabinet*. Berkeley, 1962.

Rostain, E., D. Canard, and A. Labrousse. *Le Château d'Oiron*. Paris, 1974.

Roubichon-Stretz, L. *La Vision de l'histoire dans l'oeuvre de la Pléiade*. Paris, 1973.

Roussel, P. D. *Histoire et description du château d'Anet*. Paris, 1875.

Roy, M. *Artistes et monuments de la Renaissance en France*. 2 vols. Paris, 1929.

Saulnier, V. L. *Maurice Scève*. 2 vols. Paris, 1948.

Saxl, F. *A Heritage of Images*. London, 1970.

Sayce, R. A. 'Ronsard and Mannerism'. *L'Esprit Créateur* 4, no. 4 (1966): 234–47.

Schneebalg-Perelman, S. 'Richesses du garde-meuble parisien de François Ier'. *Gazette des Beaux Arts* 78 (1971): 251–304.

Schneegans, F. Ed. 'A propos d'une note sur une fresque mythologique du XVIe siècle'. *Humanisme et Renaissance* 2 (1935): 441–44.

Schutz, H. *Vernacular Books in Parisian Private Libraries of the Sixteenth Century According to Notorial Inventories*. Chapel Hill, N.C., 1955.

Silver, I. *The Pindaric Odes of Ronsard*. Paris, 1937.

———. *Ronsard and the Hellenic Renaissance in France*. Washington, D.C., 1961.

———. *The Intellectual Evolution of Ronsard*. St. Louis, 1969, 1973.

———. 'Ronsard's Theory of Allegory: The Antimony Between Myth and Truth'. *Kentucky Review Quarterly* 18 (4) (1971): 363–407.

———. *Ronsard and the Hellenic Renaissance in France*. Geneva, 1981.

Smith, M. C. 'Ronsard and Queen Elizabeth I'. *Bibliothèque d'Humanisme et Renaissance* 29 (1967): 93–119.

Smith, P. M. *The Anti-Courtier Trend in Sixteenth-Century French Literature*. Geneva, 1966.

Somers Cocks, A. G. *Princely Magnificence: Court Jewels of the Renaissance, 1500–1630*. London, 1980.

Spencer, J. R. 'Ut rhetorica pictura: A Study in Quattrocento Theory of Painting'. *Journal of the Warburg and Courtauld Institutes* 20 (1957): 26–44.

Standen, E. A. 'The Tapestries of Diane de Poitiers'. In *Le Colloque de Fontaine-bleau*. Paris, 1972.

Stone, D. *Ronsard's Sonnet Cycles: A Study in Tone and Vision*. New Haven, 1966.

Summers, D. 'Maniera and Movement: The Figura Serpentinata'. *Art Quarterly* 35 (1972): 269–301.

Summers, J. 'Contropposto: Style and Meaning in Renaissance Art'. *Art Bulletin* 59 (1977): 335–61.

Talbert, E. W. 'The Interpretation of Jonson's Courtly Spectacles'. *PMLA* 60 (1945): 454–73.

Tervarent, G. de. *Les Enigmes de l'art savant*. 3 vols. Brussels, n.d.

Thirion, J. 'Rosso et les arts décoratifs'. *Revue de l'Art*, 1971, pts 11–14, pp. 32–47.

Thomas, B. 'Die München Harnisch Vorzeichnungen des Etienne Delaune und die Emblem und die Schlangen Garnitur Heinrichs II von Frankreich'. *Jahrbuch des Kunsthistorischen Sammlungen in Wien* 56 (1960): 7–62.

———. 'Les Armures de parade des rois de France'. In *Le Colloque de Fontainebleau*. Paris, 1972.

Tommasseo, N. *Les Relations des ambassadeurs vénitiens sur les affaires de France au XVIe*. 2 vols. Paris, 1838.

Tonnochy, H., and H. Read. *The Waddeston Bequest*. London, 1927.

Trinquet, R. 'Le Bain de Diane du Musée de Rouen'. *Gazette des Beaux Arts* 71 (1968): 1–16.

Verdier, P. *The Walters Art Gallery: Catalogue of the Painted Enamels of the Renaissance*. Baltimore, 1967.

Verheyen, E. *The Palazzo del Te in Mantua*. Baltimore, 1977.

Vitry, P. 'Etude sur les épigrammes de l'anthologie palatine qui contiennent la description d'une oeuvre d'art'. *Revue Archéologique* 24 (1894): 315–64.

Volker-Hoffmann, M. 'Donec totum impleat orbem: Symbolisme impérial au temps de Henri II'. *Bulletin de la Société d'Art Français*, 1980, pp. 29–42.

Walker, D. P. *The Ancient Theology*. London, 1972.

———. *Studies in Musical Science in the Late Renaissance*. London, 1978.

Weber, H. *La Création poétique au XVIe siècle*. 2 vols. Paris, 1955.

———. 'Structure des odes chez Ronsard'. *Cahiers de l'Association des Etudes Françaises* 21 (1969): 99–118.

Weisbach, W. *Trionfi*. Berlin, 1919.

Wildenstein, G. 'La Collection des tableaux d'un admirateur de Ronsard'. *Gazette des Beaux Arts* 52 (1958): 5–8.

———. *Le Goût pour la peinture dans la bourgeoisie parisienne entre 1550 et 1610*. Paris, 1962.

Wilson, D. *Ronsard, Poet of Nature*. Manchester, 1961.

———. *Descriptive Poetry in France from Blason to Baroque*. Manchester, 1967.

Yates, F. A. *French Academies in the Sixteenth Century*. London, 1947.

———. *The Valois Tapestries*. London, 1959.

———. *Astraea*. London, 1977.

Young, M. *Guillaume Des Autelz*. Geneva, 1961.

Zeller, G. *Le Siège de Metz*. Nancy, 1943.

Zerner, H. *The School of Fontainebleau: Etchings and Engravings*. New York, 1969.

Index

Académie de Poésie et de Musique, 230, 306n.29

Académie du Palais, 77, 118, 160, 207, 283n.46

Academies. *See* Académie du Palais; Académie de Poésie et de Musique

Achilles, 84, 85, 90, 91, 92, 94, 100, 103, 105, 125, 132, 281n.29

Achilles Tatius, 182, 296n.29

Admetus, 114

Adonis, 85, 193, 196, 201, 215, 243, 270n.32, 299n.55, 301nn.64, 65

Aeneas, 91, 93, 94, 95, 96, 105

Aesthetic judgment, 2, 58–59, 77

Agamemnon, 105

Age, 156

Aglionby, Mr (orator), 22

Agrippa, Cornelius, 231, 246, 247, 275–76n.89

Aigipans, 235

Aigueneau, island of, 226

Ajax, 267n.18

Alberti, Leon-Battista, 53, 57, 60, 63, 124, 127, 279n.17

Albon, Claude d', 254n.26

Alciati, Andrea, 68

Alcina, 165, 166

Alexander, 11, 19, 105, 135, 147, 216, 288n.39

Allegory, 219, 230, 261–62n.95

Allegory in painting, 205

Amadis de Gaule (hero in romances), 271n.44

Amadis de Gaule, 223

Amarantha, 166

Amathonte, 240

Amazons, 94

Amboise, Georges d', 142

Amphion, 117

Amplification, 163. *See also* Copia

Amyot, Jacques, 209, 306–7n.32

Anacreon, 193

Analogy, 11, 19, 247. *See also* Interart analogies

Andromeda, 86

Aneau, Barthélémy, 64, 68

Anet, palace of, 44, 70, 72, 79, 174, 194, 259n.73

Anjou, province of, 136

Antaeus, 104, 111, 279n.17

Antea, 161

Antiquities, 7, 137, 138, 148, 194, 245, 287n.31. *See also* Roman remains

Antony, 173

Apelles, 81, 193, 197, 293n.3

Aphrodite, 193, 197. *See also* Venus

Apollo, 33, 74, 85, 95, 114, 115, 116, 118, 150, 156, 157, 233, 234, 236, 241, 282nn.38, 39, 299n.50. *See also* Phoebus; Sun

Apollonius of Rhodes, 93

Apostles, Acts of the, 23

Apostrophe, 170

Appian, 141, 145, 287n.30

Arachne, 93

Arbeau, Toinot, 304n.18

Arcadia, 35, 36, 38, 74. *See also* Eden; Elysian Fields

Aretino, Pietro, 184, 245, 246, 296n.31

Argo (ship), 135

Argonauts, 84, 124, 279n.14

Argus, 68, 74, 104, 276n.91

Ariadne, 174

Ariosto, Lodovico, 68, 165, 166, 246, 278n.9, 284n.48

Aristaenetus. *See* Foucault

Aristotle, 12–13, 21, 40, 122

Armida, 166

Arms and armour, 2, 7, 29, 43, 52, 85, 89, 93, 97, 102–14, 121, 247, 280n.22, 281nn.28, 30

Art, applied, 2, 23, 24, 52, 61, 74, 85, 89, 97, 98, 118, 132, 135, 137, 138, 139, 141, 147, 151, 157, 174, 182, 184, 189, 190, 191, 192, 202, 207, 215, 216, 276n.10, 278–9n.11, 280n.25

Art collecting, 17, 43, 44, 81, 105, 107, 117, 133, 139, 147, 184, 194, 245, 255n.27, 258n.61, 281n.33, 285n.11, 287n.31, 296n.32, 297n.38, 301n.64

Arthemise (queen), 23, 72, 73, 126, 127, 129

Artifice, 5, 59, 94, 134, 191, 232, 244, 245

Artist: creative powers of, 1, 6; idealising skill of, 30

Ascanius, 95

Ascra, 102

Astraea (Goddess of Justice), 154, 155

Athenians, 94

Athens, 94

Attigny (town), 133

Aubert, Guillaume, 80

Augsburg, 108

Augustus, 95, 197, 261n.85. *See also* Caesar Augustus; Rome: Roman emperors

Aurora, 100, 171, 186, 302n.5, 303n.5

Austria, 108

Avesnes (town), 133

Avignon (town), 133

Bacchantes, 193

Bacchus, 79, 114, 115, 116, 148, 149, 150, 156, 193, 282–83n.39, 299n.50

Bacon, Sir Francis, 12, 37

Baïf, Jean Antoine de, 66, 105, 193, 213, 230

Balet Comique de la reine, 227, 230, 233. *See also* Beaujoyeulx

Ballet des Polonais, 228

Bastier de la Peruse, Jean, 268–69n.27

Bathyllus, 193

Battus, 74

Baudelaire, Charles, 248

Bayonne, festivals at, 226, 227, 245, 280n.25

Beatrizet, Nicholas, 43

Beaujoyeulx, Balthazar de, 227, 228, 229, 230, 232, 233

Beauty: as aesthetic norm, 159; ironically portrayed, 171; a moving form, 209–18; moving power of, 163, 164, 168, 199, 201, 223, 233, 248; praise of, 198; rape of, 181, 190, 191; sensuous power of, 181, 189, 198, 204, 207; sixteenth-century views of, 160–74; as source of virtue, 164; standard of, 165, 168; transformation of, 193; transforming power of, 168, 179, 181

Béchot, Marc, 24, 29, 53

Belacueil, 219

Belgius, 124

Bellange, Jacques de, 208, 209

Belleau, Rémy, 55, 66, 74–76, 118, 192, 193, 203, 274n.74, 281n.33, his *Bergerie*, 118

Belleforest, François de, 112, 113, 134, 245, 248

Bellini, Giovanni, 300n.64

Belot, Jean, 115

Belvedere gardens, 137, 194, 292n.76, 299n.50

Bembo, Pietro, 219, 304n.12

Béreau, Jacques, 192, 298n.44

Berlin, Kunstbibliothek, 108

Bertrand, 271n.44

Bethune (town), 133

Bie, Jacques de, 285n.9

Binet, Claude, 77

Bjurström, Per, 308n.43

Blois, festivities at, 20, 303n.5

Boccaccio, Giovanni, 41, 95, 165, 168, 294n.14

Boethius, 230

Boiardo, Matteo Maria (count), 35

Bonhomme, Guillaume de, 68

Bontemps, Pierre, 77

Borgia, Cesare, 141

Bosch, Hieronimo, 285n.11

Boton, Pierre, 300n.60

Botticelli, 196, 198, 201

Bouchet, Jean, 14, 21

Boulogne (town), 130, 133, 145

Bouquet, Simon, 65–68

Bourges, archbishop of, 180

Bourgueil (village), 214, 215

Bourguignons, their dance, 226

Boyvin, René, 72, 190, 301n.64

Branle (dance), 223, 226, 305n.20

Brantôme, Pierre de Bourdeilles, seigneur

de, 135, 161, 164, 165, 194, 210, 212, 223, 227, 264n.107, 277n.97, 288n.39, 294n.9, 302n.5, 303n.5, 305n.20

Brennus, 124

Bretons, their dance, 226

Bronzino, Il (Angelo Allori), 194

Broughton Castle (Oxfordshire), 238

Budé, Guillaume, 13, 14, 15, 19, 22, 31, 48, 49, 50, 139, 253n.16, *De l'institution*, 13, 14, 15

Burgmaier, Hans, 141

Burgundy, duke of, 31

Cadmus, 68

Caesar (title of emperors of Rome), 151, 281n.30, 287n.30, 290n.50. *See also* Augustus; Caesar Augustus; Germanicus Caesar; Julius Caesar; Tiberius Caesar; Caesars (The Twelve)

Caesar, triumphs of, 289n.50

Caesar Augustus, 18, 42, 95, 122, 138, 261n.86, 264n.107

Caesars (The Twelve), 139, 144, 145, 151, 290n.53

Calais (town), 64, 75, 130, 281–82n.33

Callimachus, 262n.100

Calliope (muse of poetry), 40

Cameos, 138

Capello, Jean (Venetian ambassador), 176, 210

Caprarola, palace of, 63

Cardan, Jérome, 57

Carle, Lancelot de, 133

Carnavalet, seigneur de, 121

Caro, Annibale, 63, 196, 299n.55

Caron, Antoine, 72, 73, 103, 127, 150, 160, 286n.15

Carthage, 94

Cassandra (Ronsard's mistress), 4, 166, 168, 170, 175, 184, 204, 206; portrait of, 167

Castiglione, Balthazar de, 44, 59, 161, 255n.32, 264n.106

Castor, 97, 100

Castor, Grahame, 298n.41, 310n.9

Catherine de' Medici (queen of France), 13, 35, 36–37, 39, 44, 45, 65–66, 72, 107, 122, 126, 127, 155, 159, 161, 174, 226, 236, 245, 253–54n.16, 258n.61, 259n.73, 260n.79, 272n.56, 273n.57, 274n.69, 285n.5, 295n.19, 306n.22; as

Astraea, 155; portrait of, 162

Cato, 109

Catullus, 278n.3, 284n.48

Caussin, Nicolas, 249

Celebration, 1, 5, 7, 12, 23, 35, 37, 39–42, 46, 62, 116, 121, 125, 129, 130, 131, 133, 144, 147, 158, 203, 204, 206, 213, 219, 234, 236, 238, 240, 248, 261n.90. *See also* Exaltation; Praise

Cellini, Benvenuto, 138, 184, 189

Centaurs, 92, 94, 107, 197

Cephalus, 100

Ceres, 29

Chambord, palace of, 44, 78, 79

Chantilly, palace of, 29, 107, 140

Chaos, 92

Chappuys, Claude, 33

Chareih-Cintrat, castle at, 63

Charité, 2–3, 59. *See also* Grace

Charites, 116. *See also* Graces

Charity, 285n.11

Charles V (king of Spain and Holy Roman Emperor), 17, 81, 103–14, 135, 276n.90, 288n.39; his device, 25, 67, 103, 104, 113

Charles IX (king of France), 36, 37, 38, 72, 91, 111, 123, 138, 222, 230, 231, 253n.16, 277n.97, 282n.34, 285n.5, 291n.69, 305n.18, 306n.29; his device, 67; his entry into Paris (1571), 65–68, 216

Charles de Lorraine (duke), 219. *See also* Lorraine, house of

Chasseneux, Barthélemy de, 57, 80

Chastillon (Odet de Coligny) cardinal de, 97, 101, 131, 132; his learning, 287n.29. *See also* Coligny, Gaspard de; Coligny, François de

Chastity, 71

Chimay (town), 133

Chiron, 85

Choreographers, superiority of, 233

Church Militant, 24, 145

Cicero, 59, 122, 134

Circe, 228

Classical influences, 6, 7, 17, 18, 22, 51, 52, 58, 63, 64, 66, 72, 87, 92–97, 103, 105, 114, 118, 121, 122, 123, 124, 126, 129, 131, 133, 134, 136, 141, 144, 185, 192, 193, 198, 215, 243, 278n.3

Classical parallels, 139, 141, 145, 148

Classical Triumphs, 126, 135, 142, 144, 147, 151

Claude de France (daughter of Henri II), 75, 219

Claudian, 22, 90, 92, 95–96, 256n.41, 278n.4

Clements, R. J., 282n.39

Cleopatra, 173

Cloaks, 89, 90, 93

Clouet, François, 28, 29, 56, 76, 159, 172, 173, 178, 194, 195, 211, 294n.17

Clouet, Jean, 28

Coins, 24, 30, 31, 108, 121, 257n.52

Colchos, 240

Coleman, Dorothy, 6

Coligny, François de, 102, 132

Coligny, Gaspard de, 102, 132

Collaboration between poets and painters, 51–88

Colonna, Francesco, 141, 184, 298n.42

Columns, 123, 124, 126, 127, 129, 130, 131, 132, 134, 137, 144, 145, 147

Competitiveness, 5, 6, 54, 57, 58, 88. See also Rivalry

Connoisseurship, 5, 35, 37, 57, 91, 118, 133, 190, 196, 206

Constantine (emperor of Rome): his triumphal arch, 137. See also Triumphal arches

Contarini, Alessandro, 270n.32

Context, social and political, 1, 5, 6, 7, 50, 68, 90, 247

Conti, Natale, 262n.100

Copernicus, 20

Copia, 60. See also Amplification; Variety

Corneille de Lyon, 28. See also La Haye, Corneille de

Cornelia (wife of Pompey), 109

Coronation of French kings, 14, 30–31, 32, 48, 129, 130, 156, 259n.67, 286n.22

Correspondences between heaven and earth, 19–20, 42, 230, 231, 232, 255–56n.37, 269n.28

Corrozet, Gilles, 128

Cosmos, 19, 92, 117, 230, 232, 255–56n.37

Courante (dance), 304n.12

Court, Jean de, 118

Court ball, 218, 221, 222, 223, 253n.16

Court ballet, 218, 219, 224, 225, 226–41

Courteys, Pierre, 98, 118

Court festivities, 63, 75, 151, 216, 219, 220, 221, 226, 227, 234, 247, 260n.79, 280n.25, 306n.22

Courtier, 3, 7, 33, 48, 59, 88, 124, 143, 163, 264n.106; his handbooks, 20, 41, 59, 255n.32; his taste, 124. See also French court

Courts: European, 1, 7; ideal, 32–39, 47. See also French court

Cousin, Jean, 124, 182

Cupid, 69–70, 83, 108, 115, 171, 184, 190, 194, 196, 202, 220, 221, 224. See also Eros; Love

Cyclops, 81–82, 93, 150

Cypris, 197. See also Venus

Cyprus, 198, 203

Danae, 182, 299n.50

Dancing, 7, 76, 114, 149, 209–41; as destroyer of discord, 307n.36; divine effects of, 224, 229–30, 233, 244; incantatory power of, 232; as mode of Elevation, 218–26, 233, 236; moving power of, 224, 234, 236, 304n.12, 304n.18; of the Muses, 234–41; nature of, 224, 227, 228, 229, 233, 304n.18; as poetic inspiration, 234–41; as a sign of Beauty, 218; source of Harmony, 231; transforming power of, 220, 223, 224, 229, 230

Danvillers (town), 133

Dauphin, 33. See also François II (king of France)

David (king), 35, 46, 264–65n.114

Davies, Sir John, 231, 232, 307n.36

Decoration, 2, 44, 47, 54–55, 61, 62, 63, 74, 78–79, 89, 90, 93, 96, 100, 101, 102–12, 115, 117, 118, 119, 124, 126, 128, 130, 132, 139, 157, 159, 165, 175, 192, 246, 247, 248, 278n.3, 278n.9, 284n.3; as aesthetic norm, 114

Decorum as aesthetic norm, 58, 59, 60, 61, 84, 184

Delaune, Etienne, 24, 25, 53, 71, 107, 108, 109, 110, 111, 118, 189, 192, 281n.32, 299n.44

Delbene, Alphonse, 76

Dell'Abbate, Camillo, 65, 68, 72, 286n.15

Dell'Abbate, Niccolo, 65, 68, 72, 105, 118, 134, 244, 276n.90, 286n.15

Della Casa, Niccolo, 106, 107
Del Sarto, Andrea, 285 n.11
Demosthenes, 134
Denisot, Nicolas, 76, 294 n.17
Denys of Halicarnassus, 55
Deruet, Claude, 160
Des Autelz, Guillaume, 2–3, 59
Desbordes, Guillaume, 19
Des Essars, le sieur, 223, 271 n.44
Desportes, Philippe, 271 n.44, 301 n.65
Devices, 20, 24, 67, 104
Diana, 33, 70, 71, 194, 195, 225, 262–63 n.100, 301 n.64; at Ephesos, 129; temple of, 126
Diane de Poitiers (duchesse de Valentinois, mistress of Henri II), 32, 44, 71, 72, 174
Dido, 94
Dijon Museum, 127
Dinant (town), 133
Diodorus, 72
Dis, 95
Discord, 156, 231
Display, 5, 6, 9, 15, 23, 59, 85, 89, 103, 104, 105, 108, 113, 114, 121, 123, 124, 128, 131, 139, 141, 147, 159, 190, 194, 206, 226, 276 n.89
Divine beauty, 168, 180, 223, 224, 229
Divine love, 163
Divine right of kings, 19, 254 n.26
Dolce, Lodovico, 54, 58, 59, 60, 63, 166, 193, 215, 243, 270 n.32, 288 n.41
Dorat, Jean, 15, 65, 66, 67, 227, 228, 231, 260 n.74, 291 n.69; *Paenes*, 15
Dryads, 229, 237, 238, 239, 240, 310 n.52
Du Bellay, Jean (cardinal), 194
Du Bellay, Joachim, 4, 39, 42, 54, 55, 56, 57, 59, 129, 130, 131, 136, 143, 192, 235, 236, 248, 253 n.16, 263 n.102, 276 n.93; *Discours au Roy*, 55; *La Deffence*, 54, 115, 129, 243, 253 n.16; *Les Regrets*, 234–35; *L'Olive*, 4
Du Cerceau, Androuet J., 98, 122, 126, 189, 192, 263 n.104
Du Chastel, 23
Du Choul, Guillaume, 64, 78–79, 123, 136, 137
Du Jardin, François, 107
Du Maine (count), 104
Du Pérac, Etienne, 138, 139
Du Perron, Jacques (cardinal), 88
Durazzo, battle of, 109

Dürer, Albrecht, 142
Du Thier, Jehan, 80
Du Tillet, Jean, 291–92 n.72
Duvet, Jean, 26–27, 28

Ecouen, castle of, 17, 107, 132, 255 n.27, 287 n.27
Ecphrasis, 274 n.72
Eden, 38
Edonides, 149, 150
Effigies, 23, 88
Elements, 156
Elizabeth (queen of Spain, daughter of Henri II), 35, 226
Elizabeth I (queen of England), 22, 39, 139, 159, 256 n.41, 304 n.18
Elizabeth of Austria (wife of Charles IX, king of France), 123
Eloquence, 18, 96
Elyot, Sir Thomas, 307 n.32
Elysian Fields, 33, 227
Emblem books, 68
Embroidered cloaks, 95–96, 97–106, 118
Embroidery, 102, 118
Emilia, 165, 169
Enargia, 55
Encomia, 1, 105
Endymion, 74
England, 25, 37, 130, 215
Engravings, 2, 25, 68, 98, 111, 137–39, 141, 142, 167, 182, 190, 192, 194, 238, 239, 271 n.49, 289 n.51
Envy, 166
Ephesos, 129
Epigrams, 197, 198
Epitaphs, 1, 126
Epithalamia, 1
Equestrian portrait at Fontainebleau, 147
Equestrian statue of Marcus Aurelius, 137, 138
Equité, 129
Erasmus, 11, 12, 13, 17, 22, 31, 50, 60, 253 n.16, 270 n.42; *Institutio*, 11, 13
Eria, 240
Eros, 193. *See also* Cupid; Love
Espence, Claude d', 288 n.39
Esperance, 129
Estampes (or Etamps), Anne de Pisseleu, duchess of, 105
Este, Ercole d' (duke of Ferrara), 35, 246, 278 n.9, 284 n.48

Estienne, Charles, 288n.38
Estienne, Henri, 4, 288n.41
Eternity, 144, 156, 157
Europa, 181, 182, 184, 185, 296n.29, 299n.50; rape of, 299n.44
Europe, 130, 141, 156, 238, 247
European courts, 159. *See also* Courts; French court
Eva Prima Pandora (painting by Jean Cousin), 182
Evocation, 169, 174–81, 206, 234
Exaltation, 11, 129, 267n.18
Exemplary, 9, 105, 133

Fables, 3, 11, 55, 93, 246, 273nn.67, 68
Fairies, 235, 237, 240
Faith, 144
Fame, 27, 29, 144, 146, 147, 151, 152, 155
Fantuzzi, Antonio, 81, 190, 192, 299n.44
Farnese: palace of, 63
Fates, 157
Feats of arms, 7, 46, 73, 103, 105, 112, 114, 121, 124, 125, 129, 132, 133, 135, 136, 139, 144, 145, 147, 151, 155, 219, 253–54n.16, 279n.16, 282n.33, 291n.69
Festivals (Italian), 141. *See also* Court festivals
Ficino, Marsilio, 163, 164, 165
Filleul, Nicolas, 39
Finé, Orontius, 20
Firenzuola, Agnolo, 161, 164, 294n.9
Flattery, 10, 11, 22
Fleur-de-lis, 27
Flora, 147, 174, 182, 183, 213, 295n.19
Florence, 141
Florence, duke of, 133
Florentin, Dominique, 287n.32
Foix, Paul de (French ambassador in Rome), 148
Folly, 194
Fontainebleau, palace of, 35, 43, 62, 63, 78, 83–84, 96, 103, 105, 110, 118, 135, 179, 184, 260n.79, 280n.20, 290n.53; ballroom at, 44, 62, 98, 118, 233; *cabinet des peintures*, 184; equestrian portrait at, 147; Galerie François Ier, 79, 85, 182, 194, 195, 196, 198, 199, 238, 239, 246, 249–50; Galerie

d'Ulysse, 32; *Salle des bains*, 182, 184; School of, 200, 201, 299n.44
Fontaine des Innocents, 182, 183, 216, 217
Fortune, 113
Foucault, Cyre (sire de la Coudrière), 300n.55
Francine (Jean Antoine de Baïf's mistress), 213
François I (king of France), 13, 14, 17, 18, 20, 21, 23, 28, 32, 35, 77, 83, 85, 107, 122, 128, 141, 142, 145, 147, 184, 187, 189, 194, 246, 249, 250, 257n.45, 258n.61, 299n.50; his device, 20; as Julius Caesar, 139–40; as Roman emperor, 139, 258n.61
François II (king of France), 174, 233, 295n.19; as Dauphin, 151, 155, 233
Frankness of expression, 4
French court, 3–4, 5, 13, 14–15, 33, 35, 36, 48, 57, 58, 64, 68, 72, 90, 107, 160, 174, 233, 264n.107, 292n.72; factions at the, 10; as Olympus, 9, 32; as theatre, 14–15, 30–31, 48; its habits, 5, 6, 44, 57, 59, 62, 163, 220, 221, 233, 253n.16; its tastes, 72, 85, 105, 109, 118, 124, 127, 128, 130, 133, 135, 142, 151, 166, 190, 192, 194, 204, 281n.33. *See also* Valois court
French kings, 9, 10, 13, 14, 16–17; appropriation of classical models, 18; ignorance of, 10; image of, 22–31; official portraits of, 107; as representatives of God, 19, 30–31
Frescoes, 33, 47, 61, 62, 63, 85, 95, 124, 125, 132, 137, 157, 194, 238, 239, 246, 247, 259n.72, 285n.11
Funeral ceremonies, 22–23

Gaillon, castle at, 142; festivities at, 39
Gallia (Gaul), 65
Galliard (dance), 304n.12
Gambres, Baptiste de, 107
Gambres, Caesar de, 107
Garnier, Robert, 19, 66, 255n.30
Germanicus Caesar, 138
Germany, 29, 108
Giants, 47, 82, 94. *See also* Titans
Giorgio, Francesco, 264n.114
"Giovanni" (unidentified artist), 18

Giovio, Paolo, 58

God, 10, 14, 19, 27, 30, 58, 112, 117, 139, 154, 164, 173, 292n.72, 306n.21

Godefroy (calligrapher), 139, 140

Godefroy, Denis, 286n.22

Godefroy de Bouillon, 104, 112, 282n.35

Gods, 5, 39, 41, 42, 44, 47, 55–56, 58, 92, 93, 94, 95, 105, 114, 115, 116, 129, 133, 136, 141, 150, 154, 157, 174, 175, 185, 220, 233, 234, 237, 238, 249–50. See also Olympus

Gohorry, Jacques, 72

Golden Age, 37, 38, 145, 154, 155, 261nn.85, 86

Gombrich, Sir Ernst, 51

Good fortune, 147, 151

Good government, 48

Gorgon, 104, 105, 111

Gouffier, Guillaume (master of the horse), 107, 124, 259n.70

Goujon, Jean, 124, 143, 182, 183, 216, 217

Grace as aesthetic norm, 2–3, 58, 59, 60, 75, 137, 159, 160, 161, 184, 193, 210, 215, 222, 226, 233, 304n.12. See also Charité

Graces, 114, 171, 174, 194, 203, 240, 299n.50, 304n.16

Granacci, Francesco, 141

Greek anthology, 72, 171, 193, 197, 198

Greek chorus, 231

Greek writers: imitation of, 3, 40, 41, 57, 59, 66, 72; influence of, 193, 198, 203, 204, 206, 215, 233, 240, 243, 261n.94

Guise: family of, 75; Charles de (cardinal of Lorraine), 79; François de (duke), 75, 103–14, 279n.16. See also Charles de Lorraine

Habert, François, 35, 260n.79, 271n.44

Haemus, 102

Hagstrum, Jean H., 51, 52

Halicarnassus: city of, 126; mausoleum at, 127

Hampton Court, triumphs at, 142

Harmony in the state, 19–20, 25, 37, 38, 48, 68, 92

Hatzfeld, Helmut A., 52

Heavenly spheres, movement of, 41, 42, 93, 117, 156, 230, 231, 232, 233, 238, 306n.21, 309n.51

Hector, 94, 112, 125, 145, 147

Helen of Troy, 175

Hélène (Ronsard's mistress), 4

Hélène de Surgères, 166, 229, 294–95n.17

Helicon, 241

Henri II (king of France), 13, 19, 20, 23, 24–25, 26, 27, 30–31, 32–33, 37, 42, 43, 44, 45, 47, 48–50, 53, 63, 64, 68, 71, 75, 77, 81, 82–83, 90, 108, 109, 110, 111, 112, 113, 120, 122, 124, 127, 128, 131, 135, 137, 141, 143, 151, 174, 209, 210, 219, 221, 253–54n.16, 256n.38, 259n.66, 261n.86, 263n.104, 281n.29, 285n.9, 286n.22, 292n.72; as art collector, 105; his covered cup, 138; his device, 24, 25, 27, 71, 107, 124, 129, 145, 147, 152, 258n.54, 264n.109; his entry into Lyons, 144; his entry into Paris (1549), 83, 124, 144; his entry into Rouen, 144, 146, 152, 153, 154–55, 155; his love of architecture, 43, 44; portrait of, 43, 106, 107, 129; victories of, 123, 129, 130

Henri III (king of France), 10, 77, 160, 227, 283n.46, 305n.20; his court, 221

Henri de Guise, 36

Henri de Navarre (the future Henri IV, king of France), 36

Henry VIII (king of England), 17

Hephaestus, 186

Heraldry, 17. See also Devices

Hercules, 84, 91, 92, 93, 104, 105, 107, 111, 112, 124, 135, 145, 147, 279–80n.17, 288n.41

Heroes and heroic vision, 6, 7, 12, 38, 84, 111, 124, 127, 133, 135, 136, 137, 145, 147, 148, 151, 157, 159, 247, 248

Hesdin (town), 133

Hesiod, 7, 40, 91, 92, 93, 102, 105, 204, 237, 238

Hillard, Nicolas, 159

History versus poetry, 12, 55–56, 62

Holy Spirit, 27, 31

Homer, 5, 57, 72, 89, 90, 91, 92, 105, 118, 129, 175, 276n.93, 284n.47

Homeric hymns, 234

Honour, 129, 144

Horace, 45, 234, 271n.43

Hoüel, Nicolas, 23, 44, 72, 73, 126, 127, 274n.69

Hydra, 145
Hymns, 1, 41, 46, 148, 157, 203, 234, 252 n.3
Hyperbole, 145, 192, 225, 236, 252 n.3

Iconic status, 114
Iconic tradition, 102
Icons, 89, 96
Ideal courts, 35–39
Ideal forms, 5, 6, 7, 89–120; as consolation, 7; as stimuli, 9, 22
Idealisation as artistic and poetic norm, 9, 62
Idealising techniques, 1, 12, 30. See also Analogy; Fables; Images; Ideal courts; Ideal types; Mythology
Ideal types, 12–13, 17, 18, 32, 35
Ignorance, 26, 198, 199
Illustrated texts, 68–69, 136, 139, 141, 151, 273 n.64, 297 n.35. See also Devices; Emblem books
Illustration, 54
Images, general, 3, 24, 61, 88, 103, 124, 129, 135, 137, 141, 147, 154, 209; in motion, 209; power of, 53–55, 73; of princes, 10, 19, 24
Imagination, 247, 248
Imitation, 3, 51, 52, 54, 247, 248, 310 n.9
Imperialism, 67, 107, 121, 122, 123, 127, 135, 138, 143, 147, 258 n.62, 273 n.61, 274 n.69
Imperium, 15
Inscriptions, 126
Interart analogies, 6, 50, 51
Invention, 247, 248, 298 n.41
Io, 276 n.91
Ireland, 130
Isocrates, 11
Italian writers, influence of, 3, 7, 13, 74, 165, 192, 283 n.43, 294 n.9
Italy, 29, 37, 40, 95, 133

Jallier, Noël, 32, 63, 124, 125, 137
Jamyn, Amadis, 65, 220, 291 n.69
Janus, 150
Jason, 93
Jerusalem, 129, 282 n.35
Jestaz, Bertrand, 287 n.31
Jewelry, 2, 7, 11, 51, 85, 98, 102, 107, 138, 139, 184, 201, 207, 247

Jodelle, Etienne, 64–65, 66, 272 nn.52, 53, 279 n.14
Joinville, castle at, 74–75
Joyeuse, Anne de (duke), 227, 304 n.16
Jugurtha, 281 n.29
Julia (Pompey's daughter), 108
Julius III (pope), 133
Julius Caesar, 109, 110, 135, 138, 139, 141, 145, 147, 197; triumph of, 110, 141, 142, 147
Junius, Franciscus, 53, 56, 89, 104, 268 n.21
Juno, 33, 47, 61, 74, 81, 85, 171, 174, 295 n.19
Jupiter, 9, 19, 32, 33, 47, 49, 71, 78, 81–82, 92, 115, 123, 175, 182, 184, 185, 186, 262–63 n.100, 299 n.50; his temple on the Capitol, 123. See also Zeus
Justice, 15, 16–17, 18, 23, 30–31, 35, 38, 48, 109, 117, 129, 154

Kerquefinen, Claude de, 4
Kings, 42; divine right of, 254 n.26; as God's lieutenants, 17; symbols of, 16–17. See also Devices
Kings and poets, affinities of, 42, 263 n.102

La Calandria (1548), 118
Lacedaemonians, 123
Lactantius, 164
La Fosse, Jean Baptiste de, 285 n.5
La Four, Béranger, 233
La Fréry, Antoine, 138, 139, 279 n.17, 289 n.51
La Haye, Corneille de, 77, 160, 161, 162, 293 n.3. See also Corneille de Lyon
La Haye, Robert de, 76
Laking, Sir Francis, 281 n.30
La Mothe, Charles de, 272 n.52
La Mothe Fénelon, Bertrand de Salignac, 279 n.16
Lapithae, 92, 94, 107
La Planche, François de, 127
La Rouvere, Jerome de, 23
Lasserre, François, 306 n.29
Latin writers, imitation of, 3, 57, 72, 243
La Tour d'Albenas, Béranger de, 232, 261 n.86
L'Auge, Daniel de, 268 n.20

Laval, Antoine de, 249, 250
La Volta (dance), 220, 222, 226, 304−5 n.18
Learning, 2−3, 57, 63, 68, 97, 105, 127, 135, 137, 139, 142, 144, 145, 203, 206, 231, 233, 243, 244, 264 n.108, 268 n.20, 271 n.45, 287 nn.3, 29, 308 n.40
Lebethra, 102
Le Caron, Louis, 58, 231, 269 n.28
Leda, 184, 186, 187, 196, 274 n.72, 296 n.31, 299 n.50
Lee, Rensselaer W., 51
Leicester, Robert Sidney, earl of, 304 n.18
Le Loyer, Pierre, 305−6 n.21
Lemaire de Belges, Jean, 68, 128, 129
Leonardo da Vinci, 13, 57, 142, 184, 274 n.72
Leonidas, 197, 198
Le Pois, Antoine, 287 n.32
Lescot, Pierre, 65, 76
L'Hôpital, Michel de, 15, 50, 261 n.90
Limosin, Léonard, 32, 33, 132, 181, 201, 202, 296 n.29
Livy, 20
Lloyd, Lodewick, 259 n.67
Loire (river), 213
Lomazzo, Giovanni, 30
Longueil, Christophe de, 18
Lorenzo the Magnificent, 141. See also Medici
Lorraine: court of, 76; Charles de (cardinal), 79, 86, 102, 105, 133, 134, 135, 176, 245; house of, 75, 103, 112, 134, 282 n.35, 297 n.38. See also Guise
Lorraine, Charles de (duke), 75, 219; Claude de, 287 n.32
Louis XII (king of France), 18, 20, 21, 22, 139
Louis XIV (king of France), 20
Louise de Vaudemont (queen of France, wife of Henri III), 229
Louvain, University of, 11
Louvre: museum, 281 n.29, 287 n.32; palace of, 33, 44, 76, 109, 212, 221, 249, 285 n.5; Salle de Bourbon, 228
Love, 114, 116, 144, 163, 166, 282−83 n.39. See also Cupid
Lucian, 300 n.61
Lucian of Samosate, 233, 308 n.40

Lucius Piso (Caesar's father-in-law), 139
Lucretius, 203
Lucrezia Borgia, 246
Luigini, Federigo, 161
Lyons: royal entry into, 68, 118, 143, 272 n.51, 287 n.28; town of, 64, 68, 134, 161, 276 n.91
Lyre, 234, 282 n.37; as icon, 114−19
Lysias, 11

Maecenas, 131
Magnanimity, 12, 13−14, 19, 104, 122, 144, 230, 285 n.3
Magnificence of princes, 9, 11, 12−13, 17, 30, 44, 47, 98, 121−28, 130−31, 136, 159, 245, 275−76 n.89, 277 n.97, 284 n.3, 285 n.5
Magny, Olivier de, 33, 259 n.73
Maître de Flore, 183, 205
Maître L. D., 182
Majesty, 6, 15, 17, 23, 24, 26, 30, 31, 47, 48, 49, 67, 98, 99, 131, 133, 285 n.9. See also Imperium
Mannerist, 52, 265 n.4
Mantegna, Andrea, 142, 143, 145, 238, 290 n.60; his classical style, 142, 143
Marcus Aurelius, 29, 137
Marguerite de Navarre, 156
Marguerite de Savoie, 156, 209, 210, 212
Marguerite de Valois, 38, 210, 212, 216, 221, 222, 223, 226, 227, 246, 302−3 n.5, 305 n.20; her gifts, 223; portrait of, 211
Marie (Ronsard's mistress), 4, 170, 171, 172, 295 n.18
Marion (Ronsard's mistress), 213, 214
Marot, Clément, 2−3, 53, 59
Mars, 19, 25, 33, 47, 83, 84, 92, 132, 156, 174, 194, 196, 249−50, 262−63 n.100
Marsyas, 114, 115, 282 n.38
Martin, Jean, 44, 46, 58, 77, 124, 290 n.60, 297 n.40, 304 n.12
Mary, Queen of Scots, 33, 174, 176, 177, 179, 180, 181, 233, 245, 295 n.25; portrait of, 178; wedding of, 180, 233
Mascarades, 75, 219
Massacre of Saint Bartholomew, 227
Mauléon (protonotary), 86
Mauregard, Jean de, 72

Mauro, Lauro, 299n.50
Mausolus, 23, 126
Maximilian (emperor of Rome), 141
Mazzoni, 90
Meander (river), 224
Measured music, 230
Medals, 24, 30, 52, 108, 121, 123, 132, 133, 134, 136, 137, 138, 147, 257nn.50, 51, 258n.58
Medici, Ippolito de', 117. *See also* Catherine de' Medici; Lorenzo the Magnificent
Ménager, Daniel, 5
Menestrier, Claude François, 233
Mercenaries, 37
Mercury, 19, 33, 47, 69, 74, 114, 150, 276n.91
Metamorphosis, 114, 182, 185, 193, 206, 220, 223, 229
Metz, siege of, 75, 103, 118, 279n.16, 281–82n.33
Meudon, 79, 134, 244, 245, 287nn.34, 35, 288n.36
Mezières (town), 133
Michel, Guillaume, 122, 284n.3
Michelangelo, 23, 52, 56, 57, 143, 161, 184, 187, 196, 279n.17, 299n.50
Mignon, Jean, 194, 196
Military triumphs, 122
Millan, Pierre, 238, 239
Minerva, 25, 33, 47, 66, 68, 74, 91, 93, 94, 114, 115, 150
Modena, Niccolo da, 28
Molinet, Jean, 129
Monceaux, palace of, 126
Montaigne, Michel de, 2, 148, 176, 194, 249, 292n.76, 299n.50
Montmédy (town), 133
Montmorency, Anne de (duke and constable of France), 17, 32, 44, 69, 132, 255n.27, 258n.61, 286–87n.27, 301n.64; as collector, 107; his palace, 139
Moon, 19, 24, 25, 27, 117, 236, 309n.48
Morçay, Raoul, 10
Morel, Jean, 261n.90
Moschus, 185
Moses, 17
Muret, Marc-Antoine, 193, 197, 198
Musée de l'Armée, 107
Muses, 78, 79, 87, 102, 115, 116, 117, 132, 145, 176, 177, 233, 235, 244, 269n.28, 282–83n.39; dance of, 234–41
Music, therapeutic effects of, 230, 306n.28
Mute poetry, 51–88, 209, 246
Mythology, 9, 28, 41, 54, 55, 58, 72, 75, 94, 102, 114, 116, 150, 174, 175, 184, 185, 187, 202, 250, 252n.3

Naiads, 214, 219, 229
Napeans, 235
Narcissus, 72, 175, 273–74n.68
Narrative insets, 6, 39, 74, 118, 119
Narrative set-pieces, 90, 93, 94, 95, 96, 97, 100
Natural as aesthetic norm, 58, 60, 134, 243, 245, 267n.12
Nature, 5, 51, 54, 76, 79, 92, 114, 151, 156, 157, 164, 165, 167, 171, 172, 206, 213, 243, 244, 310n.1
Naugerius, 260n.82, 261n.84
Naumachia, 105
Navarre, king of (the future Henri IV, king of France), 221
Navières, Charles de, 65, 66
Nemea, 135
Neoplatonism, 41, 53, 114–15, 164, 282n.39
Neptune, 47, 97, 98, 99, 100, 114, 132, 278–79n.11, 279n.12
Nicquée, 223
Nifo, Agostino, 161
Nonnos, 68
Nymphs, 108, 144, 147, 182, 183, 190, 191, 194, 216, 217, 221, 225, 226, 235, 236, 237, 238, 297n.41, 298n.42, 309n.48

Obelisks, 126, 127
Odes, 1, 41, 42, 129, 130, 131, 148, 155, 157, 204, 209, 231, 234, 236, 238, 240
Oiron, castle at, 32, 63, 107, 124, 125, 127, 135, 137, 259n.70, 280n.22
Olympus, 9, 19, 32, 33, 34, 47, 49, 86, 93, 219, 234, 259n.69, 260n.74, 262n.99, 265n.115
Orations, 1, 23, 88, 103, 107, 112, 113, 180
Oreades, 235
Originality as aesthetic criterion, 197
Orpheus, 145, 157, 230

Ovid, 58, 63, 68–69, 72, 92, 93, 118, 181, 182, 184, 276n.91, 279n.12

Painted insets, 103. *See also* Narrative insets
Painter as orator, 266n.7
Paintings, 11, 17, 32, 33, 61, 62, 72, 85, 102, 107, 126, 133, 150, 184, 187, 194, 197, 201, 221, 243, 245, 255n.27; as poem, 193, 265n.1, 270n.32; power of, 78, 160; superiority of, 57, 58; taste for, 74
Palazzo del Te, 139, 287n.34
Pallas, 47, 65, 79. *See also* Minerva
Pan, 235, 260n.79
Pandora, 204
Panegyric, 1, 11, 22, 33, 35, 42, 43, 50, 95, 165, 166, 169, 253n.15, 256nn.41, 42, 265n.117
Pantheon (Rome), 137
Paradin, Claude, 24
Paradise, 32, 33, 37, 38. *See also* Arcadia; Eden; Elysian Fields
Paradox, 8, 12
Paris: city of, 63, 64, 66, 74, 82–83, 108, 124, 128, 134, 249, 292n.72; royal entry into (1549), 83, 124, 144; royal entry into (1571), 65–68, 75, 144, 216, 262n.56, 272n.57, 291n.69
Parmigianino, 161
Parnassus, 66, 233, 240
Paschal, Pierre, 43, 55–56, 107, 263n.104
Pas de Suze, 133
Pasithea, 221, 222, 246, 305n.20
Pasquier, Estienne, 4, 10, 39, 148, 261n.91, 272n.53
Passe-pied (dance), 304n.12
Passions, the arousing of, 2–3, 12, 40–41, 47, 52, 56, 60, 77, 115, 163, 249
Pastoral tradition, 33, 35, 36, 38, 39, 73, 74, 75, 190, 260n.82, 261n.85, 274n.72, 301n.67
Patroclus, 124
Patronage, 2, 5, 17, 51, 57, 58, 62, 65, 86, 89, 90, 101, 102, 115, 128, 132, 133, 141, 181, 190, 196, 197, 243, 244, 247
Pau, castle at, 207
Pausanias, 72
Pavane (dance), 223, 306n.20
Peace, 130, 150, 154
Pelerin, Baptiste, 64

Peletier du Mans, Jacques, 60–61, 262n.98, 271n.43
Peleus, 97, 278n.3, 284n.48
Penelope, 174
Penni, Francesco, 300n.64
Penni, Luca, 118
Perfect princes, 9–50
Péricaud, 98
Periphrasis, 55, 61
Perseus, 86, 93, 105
Peruzzi, 142
Petrarch, 1, 129, 141, 271n.49, 285n.11, 286n.22, 287n.30
Phidias, 86, 91, 94, 194, 278n.6, 295n.17
Philibert de l'Orme, 43, 44, 58, 80, 136, 137, 194
Philip II (king of Spain), 35, 58
Philip of Burgundy (archduke), 11
Philopaemen, 104
Philostratus, 3, 58, 117
Phoebus, 33, 262–63n.100. *See also* Apollo; Sun
Phrixus the Minyan, 93
Phrygian pillars, 151, 243, 244
Pickering, F. P., 52
Pierre II (duke of Bourbon), 129
Pilon, Germain, 23, 65, 68, 77, 118, 259n.73
Pindar, 39–40, 45, 46, 56, 60, 66, 86, 131, 231, 234, 267n.18, 276n.94
Planets, 19–20, 33, 117, 232, 233, 255–56n.37, 262n.98, 308n.43
Plato, 13, 21, 115, 248
Platonism, 262n.96. *See also* Neoplatonism
Pléiade, poets of the, 66
Pliny, 11, 13, 22, 92, 127
Plutarch, 72, 92, 141, 145, 209, 230, 306nn.29, 32, 307n.32
Pluto, 80
Poem as painting, 193, 265n.1
Poetic enthusiasm, 38, 40, 50, 56, 58
Poetic fury, 236–37
Poetic idealising, 166
Poetic inspiration, 269n.98, 309n.47
Poetry: affinities with dancing, 307n.32; moving power of, 7, 12, 55, 78, 114, 115, 116, 119, 133, 149, 156, 235, 248–49, 262n.18, 268n.20, 276n.95; music of, 155, 157, 158, 169, 170, 179, 202, 206, 210, 212, 215; as painting, 267n.16; status of, 115, 131, 158; su-

Poetry: affinities (*continued*)
periority of, 57, 58, 80, 87, 88, 240,
268n.22, 269n.27, 277n.97; transferring power of, 237; transforming power
of, 214, 215
Poets: creative powers of, 1, 6, 55, 119,
128, 157; as discoverers, 93; as painters,
130, 150, 172, 173, 174, 177, 179, 184,
186, 187, 192, 193, 202, 204, 207,
210, 246, 271n.44, 276n.92, 277n.98,
284n.47, 294n.17; as philosophers, 92;
as priests, 130; as prophets, 58, 115,
116, 117, 154, 157, 278n.9; status of,
42, 115, 235, 237, 238, 241; as transformers, 246
Poets and kings, affinities of, 42, 263n.102
Poitou, dances of, 226
Poliphile, 298n.42. *See also* Colonna, F.
Polish ambassadors, 221, 227
Poliziano, Angelo, 63
Pollux, 97, 100
Pompey, 108, 109, 110, 281n.30
Pont, Marquis de, 76
Portraits, 13, 28, 30, 102, 138, 160, 167,
172, 173, 174, 177, 178, 179, 193, 201,
202, 210, 212, 216, 258n.61
Power, 156, 159
Praise: aesthetic consequences of, 2, 5–6,
39, 105, 118, 128; distrust of, 1; as elevation, 159; as exhortation to virtue, 11,
12, 22, 23, 38, 42, 56–57, 123, 124,
129, 131, 135, 145, 249, 252n.3,
256n.41, 263n.101; the necessity of, 5,
10, 11–22, 42, 128, 262n.99; oblique
approach to, 174; in poetry, 1, 5; of
princes, 11–12, 21–22, 47–50; Renaissance preoccupation with, 1–3, 10, 20,
62; transposition of, 186. *See also*
Celebration; Encomia; Epitaphs; Epithalamia; Exaltation; Hymns; Odes; Orations; Panegyric
Praxiteles, 66, 194, 295n.17
Praz, Mario, 51, 52
Pressouyre, Sylvia, 309–10n.52
Priam, King, 94
Priapus, 297n.40
Primaticcio, Francesco, 35, 44, 62, 134,
216, 244, 280n.20
Princely magnificence, 122, 131, 139, 144,
189. *See also* Magnificence
Princes: mirrors of, 13, 21; obsession

with art, 79, 86, 121–28, 131, 135,
263n.104. *See also* Paintings, taste for
Princes in the Renaissance, 6. *See also* Per-
fect princes
Processions, 9, 23, 92, 155, 212, 291–
92n.72, 303n.5
Propaganda, 9, 30, 44, 53, 67, 68, 141,
147, 257n.50, 258n.58
Proportion as aesthetic norm, 60, 75, 137,
144, 159, 160, 165, 231
Proserpine, 92, 95
Protestants, 23, 24, 27, 29, 112, 122,
292n.72
Provence, dances of, 226
Prudence, 129
Psalms, 46, 264n.114
Psyche, 69–70
Publius Scipio, 268n.21, 288n.41
Pyramids, 126
Pyrrhic, 144
Python, 171

Quintilian, 55, 59, 267n.16
Quintus Curtius, 287n.30
Quintus Fabius, 288n.41

Raimondi, Marc-Antoine, 98, 99, 139,
238, 279n.11
Raison, 129
Raphael, 32, 63, 99, 137, 142, 279n.11,
300n.64
Redon, Pierre, 91, 111
Religion, 26, 129, 145, 146, 147, 258n.59
René, King, 104, 282n.35
Rennes, 304n.18
Reymond, Pierre, 147, 182
Reymond, René, 98
Rheims (town), 30, 31
Rhesus, 94
Rhetoric, devices of, 1, 54. *See also*
Eloquence
Rhodes, 126
Rhône (river), 132
Ridolphi (cardinal), 133
Rijksmuseum, 238
Ringhieri, Innocenzio, 163
Ripa, Cesare, 176, 266n.7
Rivalry, 17, 51, 64, 76–88, 109, 127, 128,
130, 131, 132, 155, 156, 157, 166, 172,
173, 174, 182, 184, 187, 188, 190, 191,
192, 194, 196, 202, 204, 215, 233,

240, 247, 269 n.27, 275 nn.80, 81, 277 n.98. *See also* Competitiveness; Connoisseurship

Robertello, 253 n.12

Rodemark (town), 133

Romano, Giulio, 105, 137, 142, 280 n.20, 285 n.11

Rome, 7, 23, 29, 95–96, 124, 133–43, 157, 194, 264 n.107, 285 n.11, 299 n.50; Roman customs, 107, 131, 134, 136, 144, 145, 147; Roman emperors, 18, 24, 30, 33, 79, 85, 107, 123, 134, 136, 137, 138, 139, 140, 141, 258 n.61, 287 n.32; Roman remains, 135, 147, 194, 288 n.38; Roman temple, 130; Roman triumph, 142, 287 n.34

Romances, medieval, 105, 133

Roman de la Rose, 219

Ronsard, Pierre de, 5, 6, 7, 8, 20, 22, 35–39, 40–41, 42, 44, 45–46, 47–50, 52, 55, 60, 61, 76, 97, 98, 100, 102, 104, 114, 115, 116, 118, 130, 131, 132, 133, 158, 160, 167, 168, 169, 179, 180, 181, 184, 185, 186, 187, 190, 191, 193, 197, 198, 199, 201, 205, 206, 209, 210, 212, 213, 218, 219, 223, 225, 226, 227, 229, 230, 231, 232, 233, 238, 240, 244, 276 n.93, 277 n.97, 291 n.69, 302 n.5; as Apollo, 47; compared to Homer, 5; his embroidered cloaks, 97–106; as festival organiser, 65–68; his heroic vision, 5–6, 7; his ideal of beauty, 160; influence of, 5, 301 n.65, 304 n.16, 305 n.21, 309 n.48; influence of the court on, 4; the king's poet, 5 (*see also* Kings and poets, affinities of); knowledge of art, 76–78; knowledge of music, 230; modes of idealisation, 165, 166; as painter, 55–56, 61, 62–63, 99, 156; his popularity, 5, 55, 66; portrait of, 167; spirit of rivalry, 76–88 (*see also* Competitiveness; Connoisseurship; Rivalry); style, economy of, 175, 185, 213; style, ornateness of, 2--3, 53, 55, 56, 61, 62, 103, 105, 114, 118, 119, 128, 131, 133, 148–58, 192, 248; superiority of as poet, 3, 5, 56, 57, 62, 76, 87, 207, 220; triumphant forms of, 148–58

Ronsard, Pierre de, works of: *Abbrégé poétique*, 57–58, 119, 247–48; *Les Amours*, 4, 166–67, 167–74, 175,

192–204, 224, 302 n.69; *A son lict*, 83; *A son Lut*, 78, 117; *Les Avaricieux qui bastissent* . . . , 80; *Avertissement aux oeuvres* (1587), 102–3; *Bergerie*, 35–39, 74, 190–91; *Bocage* (1560), 39; *Chant de Liesse*, 219; *La Charite*, 221–23, 224, 225, 246; *La défloration de Lède*, 184–90; *Discours à Pierre Lescot*, 235; *Eclogue V*, 191–92; *Epistre à Charles*, 80; *La Franciade*, 68, 124, 248; *La Harangue . . . duc de Guise* (1553), 103–14; *Hymne de l'Automne*, 236–37, 243–44; *Hymne de Calays et Zethés* (1556), 97, 101; *Hymne de l'Esté*, 148–50; *Hymne de l'Eternité*, 156; *Hymne de France*, 79; *Hymne de Henri II*, 33, 44, 47, 156, 256–57 n.45; *Hymne de l'Hiver*, 85, 234, 308 n.46; *Hymnes*, general, 10, 44; *Institution à Charles IX*, 85; *La Lyre* (1569), 114–19, 230; *Meslanges* (1560), 230; *Ode à la Fontaine Belerie* (1553), 204–7; *Ode à Henri II*, 155; *Ode à Joachim du Bellay*, 40–41; *Ode à Michel de l'Hospital*, 40, 78, 116, 248; *Ode à Monseigneur le Dauphin* (1555), 151–58; *Odes*, general, 44, 45; *Peintures d'un voyage*, 81–83, 84; *Le Ravissement de Céphale*, 97; *Le Temple des Messeigneurs*, 97–101, 131–33, 155; *Le Voyage de Tours*, 212–15, 223

Rose, François, 66

Rosso, Giovanni Battista, 35, 59, 62, 83–84, 118, 187, 188, 189

Rouen: city of, 25, 145; royal entry into (1550), 118, 120, 144, 146, 151, 152, 153, 154

Roville, Guillaume de, 68

Royal entries, 9, 25, 30, 63–64, 65–68, 68, 123, 127, 143–48, 151, 157, 216, 258 n.64, 269 n.27, 272 nn.51, 56, 57, 291 n.69

Ruins, 136, 143, 148

Sacrobosco, Jean de, 19

Saint-Gelais, Mellin de, 32

Saint Germain, Palace of, 31, 44, 139

Sainte-Marthe, Charles de, 263 n.102

Sainte-Marthe, Scévole de, 282 n.35

Saint-Maur, palace of, 126

Saint Michel, Order of, 27, 107

Saint Thomas, François de, 122
Sallust, 56, 268 n.21, 288 n.41
Salomon, Bernard, 64, 271 n.49
Salviati, 189, 301 n.64
Sannazaro, Jacopo, 36, 74, 142, 166, 192, 290 n.60, 297 n.40
San Sebastiano, palace at, 142
Sapet, Pierre de, 58, 268 nn.23,27
Sarcophagi, 136, 137, 215, 300 n.61
Saturn, 19, 155, 156, 204
Satyrs, 108, 148, 189, 190, 191, 193, 226, 235, 298 n.42
Savoy, 209
Scaliger, Julius Caesar, 231
Scève, Maurice, 64, 68, 184
Scipio, triumphs of, 107, 285 n.11
Scotland, 25
Sculpture, superiority of, 57, 58, 126
Seasons, 75, 148–51, 231
Sébillet, Thomas, 42, 124
Second, Jean, 255 n.29
Sensuality, 207
Serlio, Sebastiano, 44, 58, 60, 77, 123, 127, 136, 137, 142, 143, 285 n.7
Seville, Jean de, 255 n.37
Sextus, 234
Seyssel, Claude de, 21, 22
Shields, 89, 90, 91, 92, 93, 94, 95, 104, 105, 109, 110, 111, 281 n.29, 282 n.34
Sidney, Sir Philip, 59, 253 n.16
Silenus, 149, 150
Simplicity as aesthetic criterion, 209, 210
Sirens, 226
Sister arts, 51, 52
Social dances, 226, 227, 305 n.20
Solomon, King, 14, 17, 19, 129
Spain, 37
Spanish court, 226
Spanish writers, imitation of, 3
Sparta, 122
Speaking dance, 209
Speaking pictures, 51–88, 90, 93, 209, 246
Spencer, John R., 51
Spenser, Edmund, 164
Spoils of war, 145, 147, 151, 152
Sprezzatura, 59
Stained glass, 17, 69, 132
Statius, 135, 288 n.41
Statues, 7, 23, 88, 133, 134, 135, 136,

147, 245, 272 n.57, 278 n.6, 299 n.50
Status symbols, 115
Stewart, John, 144
Stilicho, 96
Stockholm (Tessin Collection), 216–18, 308 n.43
Strada, Jacques de, 137
Strozzi, Philip, 135, 288 n.39
Style: conceptions of, 2, 54–55; lowly, 2–3, 53, 59, 74; ornateness of, 2–3, 53, 55, 56, 61
Suetonius, 141, 145
Summers, David, 296 n.30
Sun, 92, 117, 130, 156, 186, 255–56 n.37, 304 n.12, 309 n.48; evocation of the, 38; as image of kingship, 19, 20, 37. See also Apollo; Phoebus
Sun-King, 255 n.37
Sylvans, 149
Symeoni, Gabriel, 20, 134, 137
Symmetry, 159
Syracuse, 185

Tableware, 2, 98
Tahureau, Jacques, 54
Tanlay, castle at, 33, 47, 132, 174, 259 n.70
Tapestries, 17, 23, 52, 61, 62, 69, 71, 72, 73, 75, 76, 85, 95, 107, 118, 124, 126, 127, 128, 220, 226, 280 n.25, 285 n.11
Tarquinius Priscus, 123
Tarquinius Superbus, 123
Tasso, Torquato, 166
Telin, Guillaume, 35
Temples, 102, 121, 123, 126, 128–33, 136, 291 n.69
Tessin Collection, 216–18
Thalestis, 216
Themis, 47, 100
Theocritus, 35, 192, 196, 297–98 n.40
Theseus, 174
Thetis, 97, 278 n.3, 284 n.48
Thieron (Olympic victor), 86
Thionville (town), 75, 281–82 n.33
Thiry, Léonard, 72
Tiberius Caesar, 138
Time, 194
Titans, 94, 105, 107
Titian, 58, 63, 142, 193, 215, 243, 245, 246, 270 n.32, 296 n.29
Tory, Geoffrey, 141

Tournes, Jean de, 68, 276 n.91
Tours (town), 269 n.27
Tragedy, 12
Trajan, 123, 137, 138
Trento, cardinal of: his palace, 135, 139
Trissino, Giovanni-Giorgio, 253 n.12
Tritons, 226
Triumphs, 7, 30, 126; triumphal arches, 6,
    88, 121, 124, 137, 138, 144, 145, 147,
    150, 269 n.27, 287 n.28; triumphal cars,
    9, 23, 29, 98, 120, 121, 123, 127, 130,
    141, 144, 145, 147, 148, 150, 151; tri-
    umphal forms, 121–58; triumphs of
    Caesar, 141, 142, 145, 147, 289 n.50;
    triumph of Christian soldiers, 104
Troilus, 94
Trojan origins of France, 67–68
Trojan War, 124
Trophies, 123, 127, 138, 145, 152, 153
Troy, 94, 98, 100, 114
Tuccaro, Arcangelo, 232
Tuileries, palace of, 126, 137, 212,
    274 n.69, 302–3 n.5
Turin, Royal Armoury at, 281 n.29
Turks, 81
Turrin, Charles, 164
Tyard, Pontus de, 41, 72, 262 n.96,
    273 nn.67, 68, 282 n.39, 309 n.51
Tyrtaeus, 135, 288 n.41

Ulysses, 174, 250
Urban II (pope), 104, 112
Urbino, duke of, 184

Valenciennes (town), 133
Valeriano, Piero, 117
Valerius Maximus, 129
Valois, court of, 5, 46, 105, 174, 218, 220
Valois, François de, 85
Valois Tapestries, 220, 221, 226
Van de Noot, Jan, 304 n.17
Van Orley, 285 n.11
Varchi, Benedetto, 253 n.12, 268 n.22
Variety as aesthetic norm, 58, 60, 102,
    115, 118, 126, 172, 194, 271 n.44
Vasari, Giorgio, 58, 60, 135, 160, 184,
    196
Vaucelles, Treaty of, 25
Veneziano, Agostino, 137, 139, 215
Venice, 139, 245, 246

Venus, 19, 29, 61, 69–70, 74, 83, 85, 114,
    116, 174, 176, 192–203, 210, 215,
    221, 249–50, 259 n.73, 278 n.6,
    282–83 n.39, 299 nn.47, 50, 55,
    300 nn.60, 64, 309–10 n.52. See also
    Aphrodite; Cypris; Cythérée
Venus of Apelles, 197
Vesta, 147
Vice, 25–26, 38
Vico, Enea, 110, 137, 138, 139
Victory, 109, 111, 123, 129, 130, 144,
    155
Vidal, Peire, 263 n.101
Vigenère, Blaise de, 3, 4, 5, 53, 60, 94,
    117, 143, 197, 238, 306–7 n.32,
    309 n.51
Villeneuve-Lembron, castle at, 63
Villeroy, Nicolas de Neufville, seigneur de
    (secretary of state), 105
Vincennes, palace at, 44
Virgil, 33, 34, 36, 61, 63, 90, 91, 94, 95,
    98, 103, 105, 118, 129, 176, 279 n.12,
    285 n.11
Virgin Mary, 145, 156
Virtue, 129, 132, 159, 285 n.9
Virtuosity as aesthetic norm, 88, 97, 181,
    190, 207
Vitruvius, 44, 58, 60, 77, 122, 127, 143
Vitry, Paul, 197, 299 n.47
Volterra, Daniele de, 23
Voluptas, 149, 203
Vossius, Isaac, 57
Vostre, Simon, 289 n.50
Vulcan, 47, 81, 89, 92, 93, 95, 148, 150,
    156, 185, 243, 244, 262–63 n.100,
    281 n.29

Wallace Collection, 111
War, 10, 15, 16–17, 18, 19, 28, 29, 35,
    37, 38, 55–56, 76, 86, 92, 94, 95, 96,
    105, 112, 114, 121, 122, 126, 130, 132,
    133, 135, 138
Warwick, festivities at, 22
Wisdom, 27, 65–66
Woeriot, Pierre, 134, 190
Woman, idealisation of, 160

Yates, Frances A., 258 n.62
Youth, 149, 156

Yvers, Jacques (seigneur de Plaisance),
274n.74
Yvoir-sur-Meuse (town), 133

Zeus, 40. *See also* Jupiter
Zeuxis, 161, 197
Zodiac, 20
Zuccaro, Federico, 63

Designer: Marilyn Perry
Compositor: G & S Typesetters, Inc.
Printer: Malloy Lithographing, Inc.
Binder: Malloy Lithographing, Inc.
Text: 11/13 Sabon
Display: Sabon